Taking Sides: Clashing Views on Controversial Economic Issues

Edited, Selected, and with Introductions by
THOMAS R. SWARTZ
FRANK J. BONELLO
Notre Dame University

The Dushkin Publishing Group, Inc.
Guilford, Connecticut

"The man who pleads his case first seems to be in the right; then his opponent comes and puts him to the test."

STAFF

Jeremy Brenner	Series Editor
Brenda Filley	Production Manager
Charles Vitelli	Designer
Libra VonOgden	Typesetting Coordinator

Taking Sides: Clashing Views on Controversial **Economic** Issues

Where there is much desire to learn, there of necessity will be much arguing . . .

John Milton

Library of Congress Catalogue Card Number: 81-69170

Manufactured in the United States of America

First Edition, Second Printing

PREFACE

Each member of our society is affected by the economic policies adopted by our Government. Whether or not we understand the intricicies of economic theories, we must deal with their impact.

In a democracy such as ours, one way to deal with the effects of economic policy is to vote for or against political candidates on the basis of their economic convictions. In order to do this wisely, it is necessary to understand both the economic issues facing us, and the conflicting opinions concerning these issues. That is the purpose of this volume. Presented here are fifteen of the most critical and divisive economic issues. The outcome of the debates over these issues will have an impact on everyone living in America today. The taxes you pay, the mortgage rate you pay, the level of Government protection you can expect; all of these are, in part, determined by economists operating on the basis of certain assumptions and certain convictions. After you have studied the issues in this volume, you will have a greater understanding of the nature of economics itself. You will also be able to relate the headlines and news stories you read to coherent schools of economic thought.

As you read this book and find yourself in agreement or disagreement with the opinions presented, turn to the "Contributors" pages at the back. There, you will discover who the people are, making the decisions and pronouncements which so vitally concern your life. Make a mental note of these people. You can be sure that as time goes on, you will be hearing more from them.

In the course of preparing this manuscript, we encountered one major problem: choosing among the stimulating, provocative essays that are our favorites and the favorites of our friends and colleagues across several countries. These friends and colleagues have sent us many excellent suggestions which have markedly enhanced the quality of this book. We hope that as you read this book you too will be reminded of an essay that should be included in a future edition of this book. If that is the case, please drop us a note. We are happy with this problem and look forward to facing it in the future.

Those who were kind enough to share their favorites with us include: Charles Craypo, Mark Fitzgerald, C.S.C., Michael Francis, Kenneth Jameson, Roger Skurski, Charles Wilber and DeVon Yoho. Those who were our graduate assistants and did much of the leg-work include: Jeff Ankrom, Andy Kozak, Alice Lou, and Basil Merenda. Those who kept us moving and out of deep water include our two editorial advisors at the Dushkin Publishing Group: Jeremy Brenner and Ian Nielsen. And that one person who had to read that terrible handwriting, our typist, Teri Chapleski.

CONTENTS

PART II: MACROECONOMIC ISSUES

PART III: INTERNATIONAL ISSUES

Meany argues that the environment for international trade has changed
dramatically and the U.S. needs a new trade policy which stresses its own
self-interest. The Council of Economic Advisors believes that the benefits of
free trade are many and that the free trade policy of U.S. should be continued.

Sayers states that not only are multinational corporations a positive factor in the
economic development of poorer countries but they are a critical factor if
these countries are to develop. Muller believes that not only are the MNCs
a negative factor but their presence in these poorer countries insures that the
rich will get richer and the poor get poorer.

INTRODUCTION: ECONOMICS AND ECONOMISTS: THE BASIS FOR CONTROVERSY

Thomas R. Swartz
Frank J. Bonello

"I think that Capitalism, wisely managed, can probably be more efficient for attaining economic ends than any alternative system yet in sight, but that in itself it is in many ways extremely objectionable."
Lord John Maynard Keynes
THE END OF LAISSEZ-FAIRE (1926)

Although fifty years have passed since Lord Keynes penned these lines, many economists still struggle with the basic dilemma he outlined. The paradox rests in the fact that a free market system is extremely efficient. It is purported to produce more at a lower cost than any other economic system. But in the process of producing this wide array of low cost goods and services, problems are generated. These problems—most notably a lack of economic equity and economic stability—cause problems for some economists. Others choose to ignore or minimize these issues. These problems form the foundation for this book.

If the problems raised and analyzed in this book were merely the product of intellectual gymnastics undertaken by "egg-headed" economists, then we could sit back and enjoy these confrontations as theoretical exercises. Unfortunately, we are not afforded that luxury. The essays contained in this book touch each and every one of us in tangible ways. They are real-world issues. Some focus upon the current state of the U.S. economy and examine the underlying causes, effects, and cures for inflation, unemployment, and recession. Another set of issues deals with "microeconomic" topics.
We refer to these issues as "micro" problems not because they are small problems, but because they deal with small economic units such as households, firms or individual industries. The final set of issues concerns some international aspects of economic activity. This area has grown in significance as the volume of international transactions has grown and as society has come to realize the importance of international interdependence.

ECONOMICS AND ECONOMISTS: THE BASIS FOR CONTROVERSY

For each of the fifteen issues considered in this book, we have isolated those areas which historically have generated the most controversy among economists. In a few cases, this controversy represents a confrontation between extreme positions. Here, the views of the "free market economist" are contrasted with the views of the "radical reformist economist." In other cases, the conflicts are not as extreme. Rather they represent conflicts between one extreme and economists of more moderate persuasions. Finally, we could not ignore the conflicts which occur among economists who, on other issues, generally agree. Economists, even economists who identify strongly with a given philosophical perspective, rarely agree on all issues. Thus, these otherwise like-thinking economists sometimes differ on specific topics.

The underlying reason for this apparent conflict and disagreement among economists, can be explained, at least in part, in terms of Lord Keynes' 1926 remark. How various economists will react to the strengths and weaknesses found in an economic system will depend upon how they view the importance of efficiency, equity and stability. These are central terms, and we will define them in detail in the following pages. For now the important point is that some economists may view efficiency as overriding. In other cases, the same economists may be willing to sacrifice the efficiency generated by the market in order to insure increased economic equity and/or increased economic stability. Determining when efficiency should be given a high priority and when efficiency should give way to other considerations occupies a large portion of the professional economist's time.

Given this discussion of conflict, controversy, and diversity, it might appear that economists rarely, if ever, agree on any economic issue. We would be most misleading if we left the reader with this impression. Economists rarely challenge the internal logic of the theoretical models which have been developed and articulated by their colleagues. Rather, they will challenge either the validity of the assumptions used in these models or the value of the ends these models seek to achieve. For example, it is most difficult to discredit the internal logic of the microeconomic models employed by the "free market economist." These models are most elegant and their logical development is most persuasive. However, these models are challenged. The challenges typically focus upon such issues as the assumption of functioning, competitive, markets and the desirability of perpetuating the existing distribution of income. In this case, those who support and those who challenge the operation of the market agree on a large number of issues. But they disagree most assuredly on a few issues which have dramatic implications.

This same phenomenon of agreeing more often than disagreeing is also true in the area of economic policy. In this area, where the public is most acutely aware of differences among economists, these differences are not generally over the kinds of changes that will be brought about by a particular policy. Again, the differences more typically concern issues such as the timing of the change, the specific characteristics of the policy and the size of the resulting effect or effects.

As an example, consider the tax cut debate which occurred during 1980. Most economists of both liberal and conservative philosophies agreed that tax cuts were necessary, both to offset the inflation-induced Federal tax increases and in order to maintain the momentum of the business cycle recovery. The necessity of tax cuts was so apparent that specific tax cut planks were included in the 1980 political platforms of both the Democratic and Republican parties. The former stated:

> We commit ourselves to targeted tax reductions designed to stimulate production and combat recession as soon as it appears that tax reductions will not have a disproportionately inflationary effect. We must avoid untargeted tax cuts which would increase inflation. Any tax reduction must, if it is to help solve pressing economic problems, follow certain principles:
> —The inflationary impact must be minimized;
> —Reductions provided to individuals must be weighted to help low and middle income individuals and families, to improve consumer purchasing power, and to enhance a growing economy while maintaining and strengthening the overall progressive nature of the tax code;
> —Productivity, investment, capital formation, as well as incentives, must be encouraged, particularly in distressed areas and industries.
> —The effect on our economy must be one which encourages job formation and business growth.

The Republican platform was no less explicit:

> . . . the Republican Party supports across-the-board reductions in personal income tax rates, phased in over three years, which will reduce tax rates from the range of 14 to 70 percent to a range of from 10 to 50 percent.

These statements not only document the argument on the need for tax cuts but also reflect the practical differences regarding the specific character of the tax cuts. For example, the Democratic position supported tax cuts which must be directed to specific groups while the Republican proposal was for across-the-board, or sweeping tax cuts. Moreover, the nature of the tax cut proposed by the Republicans was such that upper income groups would benefit more from a reduction of tax rates from a range of 14 to 70 percent to a range of 10 to 50 percent.

Another area of practical difference between the two groups supporting the tax reduction policy centered on the size of the reductions and, of course, the size of subsequent effects. The conservative Republicans supported much larger tax cuts than the liberal Democrats. But even on a tax cut of a given size there was disagreement. From their perspective, the Republicans believed that their proposals would have a major impact on savings, investment,

3

productivity, and employment with no undesirable effects on the rate of inflation. In arguing for their proposals, the Democrats criticized the Republican program: it would do little to bring improvement to those persons, families, and areas that needed help; do little to improve productivity; and it would lead to a dramatic increase in the rate of inflation.

ECONOMISTS: WHAT DO THEY REPRESENT?

Newspaper, magazine and T.V. commentators all use handy labels to describe certain members of the economics profession. What do the headlines mean when they refer to the "Chicago School," the "Keynesians," the Antitrusters," or the "Radical Economists"? What do these individuals stand for? Since we too use our own labels throughout this book, we feel obliged to identify the principle groups or camps in our profession. Let us warn you that this can be a most misleading venture. Some economists, perhaps most economists, defy classification. They float from one camp to another selecting a gem of wisdom here and another there. Many are practical men and women who believe that no one camp has all the answers to all the economic problems confronting society. As a consequence, they may be ardent supporters of a given policy recommendation of one philosophic group but vocal critics of other recommendations emanating from the same philosophic group.

Recognizing this limitation, four major groups of economists can be identified. These groups are differentiated on the basis of several criteria: (i)how they view efficiency relative to equity and stability; (ii)what significance they attach to imperfectly competitive market structures; and (iii)how they view the evolution of an economic society. Before describing the views of the four groups on these criteria, it is essential to understand the meaning of certain terms to be used in this description.

Efficiency, equity and stability represent goals for an economic system. Efficiency reflects the fact that the economy produces those goods and services which people want and that it does so without wasting scarce resources. Equity in an economic sense has several dimensions. It means that income and wealth are distributed according to an accepted principle of fairness; that those who are unable to care for themselves receive adequate care; and that mainstream economic activity is open to all persons. Stability is viewed as the absence of sharp ups and downs in business activity, in prices, and in unemployment. In other words, stability is marked by steady increases in output, little inflation, and low unemployment.

When the term market structures is used, it refers to the number of buyers and sellers in the market and the amount of control they can exercise over price. At one extreme is a perfectly competitive market where there are so many buyers and sellers that no one has any ability to influence market price. One seller or buyer obviously would have great control over price. This extreme market structure, which we call pure monopoly, and other market structures which result in some control over price are grouped under the broad label of imperfectly competitive markets. That is, imperfect competition is a situation where the number of market participants is limited and as a consequence the participants have the ability to influence price. With these terms in mind, we can begin to examine the various schools of economic thought.

Free Market Economists

One of the most visible groups of economists and perhaps the easiest group to identify and classify is the "free market economists." These economists believe that the market, operating freely without interferences from government or labor unions, will generate the greatest amount of *well being* for the greatest number of people.

Economic efficiency is one of the priorities for free-market economists. In their well developed models, "consumer sovereignty"—consumer demand for goods and services—guides the system by directly influencing market prices. The distribution of economic resources which is caused by these market prices results not only in the production of an array of goods and services which are demanded by consumers, but this production is undertaken in the most cost-effective fashion. The free market economists claim that at any point, some individuals must earn incomes which are substantially greater than other individuals. They contend that these higher incomes are a reward for greater efficiency or productivity and that this reward-induced efficiency will result in rapid economic growth which will benefit all persons in the society. They might also admit that a system driven by these freely operating markets will be subject to occasional bouts of instability (slow growth, inflation, and unemployment). However, they maintain that government action to eliminate or reduce this periodic instability will only make matters worse. Consequently, government, according to the free market economist, should play a minor role in the economic affairs of society.

Although the models of free market economists are dependent upon functioning, competitive markets, the lack of these competitive markets in the real world does not seriously jeopardize their position. First, they assert that the imperfect competition found in the real world allows a firm to produce at an efficient level and these savings in turn provide for even greater efficiency since costs per unit of output are lower. Second, they suggest that the benefits associated with the free operation of markets are so great compared to government intervention that even a "second best solution" of imperfectly competitive markets still yields benefits far in excess of government intervention.

Lastly, the free market economists clearly view the market as the highest form of economic evolution. The efficiency of the system, the simplicity of the system, the power of the system, and above all, the personal freedoms inherent in the system demonstrate its superiority.

These advocates of the free market have been given various labels over time. The oldest and most persistent label is "classical economist." This is because the classical economists of the 18th century, particularly Adam Smith, were the first to point out the virtures of the market. Smith captured the essence of the system with the following words:

> "Every individual endeavors to employ his capital so that its produce may be of greatest value. He generally neither intends to promote the public interest nor knows how much he is promoting it. He intends only his own security, only his own gain. And he is in this led by an invisible hand to promote an end which was no part of his intention. By pursuing his own interest he frequently promotes that of society more effectively than when he really intends to promote it."

Adam Smith
THE WEALTH OF NATIONS, 1776

Since free market economists, and those who echo their views, resist most forms of government intervention, they are also sometimes referred to as "conservatives" or "libertarians." These labels are as much political labels as they are economic characterizations. It must be recalled that the classical economists of the 18th century, not only embraced the political philosophy of laissez-faire (roughly translated to: leave it—the economy—alone), but developed a set of economic theories which were totally consistent with this political theory. These "political-economists" were, as a result, called libertarians because they espoused political and economic policies which maximized personal freedoms or liberties. The 19th century libertarians are not to be confused with 20th century liberals. Modern-day Liberals, as we shall explain shortly in more detail, are often willing to sacrifice some freedoms in the marketplace, in order to insure the attainment of other objectives.

Still other labels which are sometimes attached to the free-market economists are; "monetarists," "Chicago School Economists" or "Friedmanites." Here the reference is to the modern day practitioners of the free market economics. Most notable among this group is the Nobel Laureate, Milton Friedman, formerly of the University of Chicago. He and others argue that the government's attempts to promote economic stability through the manipulation of the money supply actually causes more instability than would have occurred if the government had not intervened. As a consequence, this group of scholars advocates that the money supply should be allowed to grow at a reasonable, steady rate.

Before turning our attention to the other major camps of economists, we should note that the free market economists have been very successful in influencing the development of economics. Indeed, most major introductory economic text books present major portions of the basic theoretical concepts of the free market economist. It is because of this influence in many areas of both microeconomics and macroeconomics over long periods of time, that so many labels are used to describe them, so much is written about them and so much is written by these conservative economists. In the fifteen issues which are considered in this book, the free market position is represented in a substantial number.

Liberal Economists

Probably the single largest group of economists in the U.S. in one way or another can be classified as "liberal economists." Liberal in this instance refers to their willingness to intervene in the free operation of the market. These economists share with the free market economists a great respect for the market. However, the liberal economist does not believe that the explicit and implicit costs of a freely operating market should or can be ignored. Rather, the liberal maintains that the costs of an uncontrolled marketplace are often borne by those in society who are least capable of bearing them: the poor, the elderly, the infirm. Additionally, liberal economists maintain that the freely operating market sometimes results in economic instability and the resultant bouts of inflation, unemployment and slow growth. Thus, although liberal economists believe that economic efficiency is highly desirable, they find the attainment of economic efficiency at any cost to be unacceptable and perhaps even "extremely objectionable."

Consider for a moment the differences between free market economists and liberal economists at the microeconomic level. Liberal economists take exception to the free market on two grounds. First, these economists find a basic problem with fairness in the marketplace. Since the market is driven by the forces of consumer spending, there are those who through no fault of their own (they may be aged, young, infirm, physically or mentally handicapped) may not have the where-with-all to participate in the economic system. Others, however, perhaps because they are extremely lucky or because they have inherited wealth, may have not only the ability to participate in the system, but they may have the ability to direct the course of that system. Second, the unfettered marketplace does not and cannot handle spill-over effects or what are known as "externalities." These are the third party effects which may occur as a result of an economic act. Will a firm willingly compensate its neighbors for the pollutants it pours into the nearby lake? Will a truck driver willingly drive at 55 MPH and in the process reduce the highway accident rate? Liberal economists think not. These economists are therefore willing to have the government intervene in these and other, similar cases.

The liberal economists' role in macroeconomics is more readily apparent to the layman. Ever since the failure of free market economics during the Great Depression of the 1930s, Keynesianism (still another label for liberal economics) has become widely known. Lord John Maynard Keynes' 1935 book entitled THE GENERAL THEORY OF EMPLOYMENT, INTEREST AND MONEY, laid the basic groundwork for this school of thought. Keynes argued that the history of freely operating market economies was marked by periods of recurring recessions, sometimes very deep recessions which we call depressions. He maintained that government intervention through its fiscal policy—government tax and spending power—could eliminate, or at least soften these sharp reductions in economic activity and as a result move the economy along a more stable growth path. Thus for the Keynesians, or liberal economists, one of the "extremely objectionable" aspects of a free market economy is its inherent instability. Their call for active government participation is in sharp contrast to the policies of the monetarists or free market economists who argue that economic stability (growth, employment and prices) can be achieved by merely stabilizing the money supply.

Liberal economists are also far more concerned about the existence of imperfections in the marketplace than are their free market counterparts. They reject the notion that imperfect competition is an acceptable substitute for competitive markets. These economists may agree that the imperfectly competitive firms can achieve some savings because of their large size and efficiency, but they assert that since there is little or no competition the firms are not forced to pass these cost savings on to consumers. Thus liberal economists, who in some circles are labeled "antitrusters," are willing to intervene in the market in two ways. In some cases they are prepared to allow some monopolies, such as public utilities, to exist, but they contend that these monopolies must be regulated by government. In other cases they maintain that there is no justification for monopolies and they are prepared to invoke the powers of antitrust legislation to break up existing monopolies and/or prevent the formation of new monopolies.

Unlike the free market economist, the liberal economist does not believe that the free marketplace is the highest form of economic evolution. By definition, the liberal economist asserts that the highest form of economic evolution is a "mixed economy"—an economy where market forces are tempered by government intervention. These economists do not advocate extensive government planning and/or government ownership of productive resources. But, they are not always willing to allow the market to operate on its own. They maintain that the immense power of the marketplace can be controlled with government intervention and the benefits generated by the unfettered market can be equitably distributed throughout society.

We can conclude this section by making a hazardous guess. It would appear that during the 1940s, 1950s, 1960s, and up to the middle 1970s, liberal economics dominated economic policy in the U.S. In the late 1970s, there was a reemergence of free market economics, which for nearly 40 years had played an important but clearly secondary role. In the early 1980s, free market economics will dominate public policy decisions, but policymakers employing these classical models will encounter some stubborn economic problems. This will cause the pendulum to swing once again. The resting point of the pendulum may be liberal economics but it might also swing past this point and stop in the domain of "institutional economics" or "radical reformist economics." These two schools of thought are the subject of the next sections.

Institutional Economists

One of the most difficult groups of economists to classify and, as a consequence, one of the most misunderstood groups of economists is the "institutionalists." The difficulty in understanding and classifying this school of economists stems from the fact that institutional economics has no single body of theories. Institutional economists are vocal critics of traditional economics—the economics espoused by free market economists and liberal economists. They maintain that the models which are constructed by these economists may explain how economic actors would behave *if* these actors behaved in a rational, self-interested manner and *if* they lived in a competitive world. However, they assert that consumers, business firms, and other economic actors do not always act in a rational, self-interested fashion. They also see the world in which we live as a dual-economy world. One part of that world is competitive. Another part of that world is dominated by a few firms which have the power to set prices. The institutional economists, as a consequence, find traditional economics to be an eloquent theory that does not conform to reality. Unfortunately, to date, institutional economists have not developed their own set of integrated economic propositions or laws which they can offer as a substitute for traditional economics.

This does not mean however, that the institutionalists have nothing to offer. In their attempts to make economics conform to the reality it claims to explain and predict, institutional economists have shed light on many diverse topics. For example, some members of this school of thought have concentrated their efforts on the structure of corporations, particularly the multinational corporations, as economic institutions. These economists, sometimes referred to as structuralists, examine the economic planning these large economic units undertake; the impact they have on the system; their influence on inflation, unemployment, income distribution and efficiency; and the role they play in international affairs. Other institutional economists take a broader perspective. Since they generally believe that large corporate entities engage in massive economic planning that affects the whole of society, some institutional economists analyze alternative forms of regional and national economic planning which can be undertaken by the government. The basic point is that institutional economists work in many, seemingly unrelated areas. Since they have no integrated theory to tie all these pieces together, and since many of their ideas such as utility regulation, antitrust action, price controls, etc., have been accepted as public policy, it is at times difficult to keep in mind that the early work of Thorstein Veblen on financial capitalism, the more recent work of John Kenneth Galbraith on industrial structure, and many economists in between are all part of the institutional school of economics.

On the basis of our first criterion, institutional economists differ dramatically from free market economists and liberal economists. By rejecting the assumptions of rationality and self-interest, they maintain that whatever you set as your highest priority—be it efficiency, equity, or stabilization—you cannot achieve it by using the abstract models of the market economists. Indeed, their analysis indicates that the market as it exists in its concentrated form today leads to inefficiency, inequity and inherent instability.

The second and third criteria further distinguish the institutional economists from the other schools of economics. For the institutionalist, economics is in a constant state of evolution. (The importance of evolution for the institutional economists is best underscored by noting that this school is also referred to as evolutionary economics.) At one time, perhaps when Adam Smith and his fellow classical economists were formulating their basic models, the economy could be legitimately characterized as competitive. At that moment, free market economics reflected reality and therefore could explain and predict that reality. At this time, functional competition does not exist and a new body of theorems and concepts must be developed to explain and predict this reality. At some future date, still another set of economic institutions will exist and still another body of theorems and concepts will be needed. Consequently, the institutional economist does indeed attach a great importance to the existence of imperfect competition and to the process of economic evolution. The institutionalist knows that new theories must be developed to explain today's reality of imperfect competition, and they know that the economy is always in a constant state of evolution. What they don't know with certainty is which direction future evolution will take our current reality.

To confuse the issue further, there is yet another group within the structuralist-institutionalist camp. These economists call themselves the post-Keynesians. They are post-Keynesians because they believe that they are closer to the spirit of Keynes than is the interpretation of Keynes which is used to support the liberal economists' position. As some authors have suggested, the key aspect of Keynes' work as far as the post-Keynesians are concerned is his assertion that "expectations of the future are not necessarily certain." On a more practical level, post-Keynesians believe, among other things, that the productivity of the economic system is not significantly affected by changes in income distribution, that the system can still be efficient without competitive markets, that conventional fiscal policies cannot control inflation and, that "incomes policies" are the means to an effective and equitable answer to the inflationary dilemma. (This listing is drawn from Alfred S. Eichner's "Introduction" in A GUIDE TO POST-KEYNESIAN ECONOMICS White Plains: M.E. Sharpe, Inc., 1978.)

Radical Reformist Economists

As we move further and further away from the economics of the free market, we encounter the "radical reformist economists" or the "left." These economists, who actually spring from several theoretical foundations, share a belief that the market and the capitalist system no matter how well disciplined is fatally flawed and doomed to eventual failure. Out of the ashes of this system which is guided by the "invisible hand" of self-interest will rise the "visible hand" of public interest. That is, the fundamental institutions of private ownership will slowly fade and be replaced by government ownership of productive resources.

This does not mean that all private ownership will cease to exist at some distinct moment. Rather most radical reformists maintain that it is the ownership of the 1000 largest firms which cause the basic problems for the "capitalist economy." It is the operation of these highly concentrated economic entities for the benefit of a few which cause the basic problems and it is the private ownership of these 1000 firms which must eventually fade away. As a result not all property must be owned collectively. Only the most radical of the left would go that far.

As was the case with our other three broad clusters of economists, there is much diversity within this fourth cluster of economists. One group of economists within this cluster contains the radical, political economists who often focus upon microeconomic issues. They are concerned with issues such as the abuses which may result from "administered prices"—prices which can be administered or set by a firm because of the firm's monopoly influence in the marketplace. Another identifiable subgroup is the "Marxists." Their lineage can be traced to the 19th century philosopher-economist Karl Marx. Ironically Marx himself shares his economic roots with the free market economists. Before writing his most impressive work, the three volumes of DAS KAPITAL, Marx studied the work of the classical economists and incorporated a basic tenent of those works—David Ricardo's "surplus value"—into his own work. But unlike free market economics, which Marx prophesied would fall of its own weight, Marx laid the foundation for "Socialism." Socialism, where some form of public ownership of the means of production is substituted for private ownership, is far more prevalent throughout the world than is Capitalism. Thus, we in North America cannot afford to ignore this group of economists.

Note that Socialism may take many forms. It varies from the Democratic Socialism of Great Britain to the Eastern European Socialism—Communism—of the Soviet Union. The one common characteristic is public ownership of the means of production. However, the extent of this public ownership varies dramatically from one socialistic country to another.

Although it may be difficult to classify the different subgroups of radical reformist economists, we can differentiate them from the other broad classifications of economists on the basis of our three criteria. In terms of the first criterion—the relative importance of economic efficiency, equity and stabilization—they are clearly set apart from their non-radical counterparts. Not only do they set a much higher value on equity and stability when compared to the free market economists, (a posture they share with the liberal and institutional economists) but they have developed a set of economic models that attempts to insure the attainment of equity and stability. The radical reformist economists assert that not only is the economic efficiency which is supposed to exist in a market economy an illusion, but the market system is fundamentally flawed. These flaws, which result in unacceptable inequities and recurring bouts of economic instability, will eventually lead to the market's demise.

The Radicals are concerned by the existence of imperfect competition. For them the current reality is an immense concentration of economic power which is a far cry from Adam Smith's world of competitive markets. Today, in their view, the market economy operates to benefit a few at the expense of the masses. Firms with monopoly power control the economy. They administer prices. They are the invisible hand that guides the economy to their benefit.

So strong is their aversion to the market economy that they predict its demise as we know it. Indeed, if we look to the Marxist camp, they see Capitalism as one step, a necessary step, in the evolution of economic systems. Capitalism is needed to raise the economy out of the chaos of a fuedal society. But after capital has been accumulated and a modern economy is developed, the basic inequities and instabilities will bring the market economy to its knees and Socialism will emerge. Socialism itself is not the end of the evolutionary process. Socialism will eventually give way to Communism—where government is non-existent and everyone will work "according to their ability" and receive "according to their need."

Of course, not all radical reformist economists are Marxist. However, most radicals do share a desire for some form of socialism. Unlike their Marxist colleagues, most do not see socialism as evolving automatically, and they certainly do not see Communism emerging at the end of an evolutionary process. Rather these economists see a need to explicitly encourage the development of some form of socialism for North America. The socialism which results is then considered to be the likely end of the evolutionary process.

Before we turn to the next section, we must warn you again to interpret these labels with extreme care. Our categories are not hard and fast. There is much "grayness" around the edges and little that is "black and white" in these classifications. This does not mean, however, that there is no value to these classifications. It is important to understand the philosophical background of the individual authors. This background does indeed color or shade their work. This is best demonstrated by examining several of the issues included in this volume.

However, before discussing a few of the issues, it is useful to repeat several of the themes developed in the preceding section. First, there is much disagreement among economists and others on economic problems. There is, however, rhyme and reason to this disagreement. In large measure the disagreement stems from various ideologies or basic philosophies which these individuals may espouse. Indeed, the differences which exist between economists and groups of economists can be most sharply defined in terms of their respective views of efficiency, equity, and stability; on the relative merits of imperfect competition; and on the place of the current economy in the evolutionary process peculiar to economic systems.

Second, the identification of causes, effects, and cures for economic problems must be undertaken at the practical level. At this level, sharp distinctions tend to disappear, and actions may be recommended by certain individuals which seem inconsistent with their ideology. Here the economist must sacrifice "ideological purity" for practical solutions. The science of economics must deal with real-world problems or it loses its meaning for most people.

The Issues

It is not difficult to identify major problems in the American economy. Each month the news media discuss in detail the newly released figures which reveal the success or failure of policies designed to reduce inflation and unemployment. As we noted, for example, the 1980 political platforms were very concerned with economic issues. In addition to the issue of tax cuts, the Democratic and Republican platforms outline general principles as well as specific actions that should be undertaken to spur productivity, to stem the rising tide of automobile imports, to solve our energy predicament, and to make the American economy dynamic and vital. Each day it seems that some businessman, some labor leader, some consumer advocate, or some public official releases a new proposal that will remedy pollution, improve the quality and the safety of products or the workplace, restore health to the social security system, or halt and reverse the decay of our cities. Thus the difficulty in developing this book was not in identifying real and important economic problems or in locating alternative views on those problems. Rather, the difficulty was one of selecting only fifteen issues from what, at times, appears to be an endless list of both problems and views on those problems.

We have resolved this difficulty by attempting to provide a broad coverage of the conflicts which society faces. We have provided this generality in three different ways. First, the fifteen issues represent six macroeconomic, seven microeconomic, and two international issues. Second, within these sets of issues, the range of topics is broad. For example, within the macroeconomic set there are issues which represent basic disagreements among economists on specific policy topics, such as the wage and price control question, as well as disagreements that can be characterized as basic philosophical conflicts such as the desirability of economic growth. The third dimension concerns the ideologies of the views which are presented. The list of authors includes well regarded academic economists, politicians, businessmen, and labor leaders. These individuals represent the far right, the far left and many positions in between. Although ideology is sometimes tempered by practical considerations, the basic ideological positions remain apparent.

A summary of several of the issues may serve to indicate the extent of this generality. This discussion will also demonstrate the interplay that exists between basic philosophy and practical considerations in arriving at a real-world solution or position on an economic problem.

One of the macroeconomic issues is: "Can wage and price controls help solve our inflation problem?" This is a recurrent issue in national policy affairs, since most inflationary periods usually result in a demand for wage and price controls from some quarter. The current inflation is no exception. Normally, this issue finds conservative economists lining up against wage and price controls. The reason for their position is straightforward, given their belief in the efficiency of a capitalist market economy. Put simply, the conservatives maintain that the imposition of wage and price controls would destroy the basic functioning mechanism in the economy and therefore, destroy the efficient operation of the system. Liberals, on the other hand, are less enamored of efficiency and more concerned with equity. As a consequence they are willing to experiment with wage and price controls during inflationary periods because they believe that the controls will tend to preserve some of the equity which might be eroded if inflation were to proceed unchecked. The two readings selected for this issue reflect these two different points of view.

This is not to say that institutionalists and radical reformers have no position on this issue. The institutionalists would also support wage and price controls, not so much because of equity considerations but because of their belief that in current capitalist society, prices and wages are not effective as allocative mechanisms. The radical reformers would argue that wage and price controls can't do any good in redressing instability and inequity. They contend that instability is systemic and that the controls must benefit those in power or they would not be established. In this case, some radical reformers and conservatives would agree. Both groups would oppose wage and price controls but for very different reasons.

Having said this, it is important to recognize that the last experiment with wage and price controls in the U.S. occurred during the 1971-74 period. Ironically, the administration which imposed the controls was a Republican-conservative administration. Again, even though the basic philosophy of the Republican party would lead one to believe that they would always oppose wage and price controls, there were practical considerations which at that point led them to undertake this dramatic step.

"Should the Federal Government deregulate American business?" is one of the seven microeconomic issues. Again we can associate a position on this issue with each of the four basic economic philosophies. Clearly conservatives would strongly oppose government regulation. In support of their position they would cite the self-regulating nature of a free market capitalist system. No rational individual would buy products of inferior quality or products which are unsafe if alternatives were available at competitive prices. No rational individual would work for a firm that maintained an unsafe job site unless that individual found that job to be to his or her economic advantage. On the question of pollution or other so-called externalities, regulation, the conservatives might suggest, should be undertaken, but only if the benefits of regulation clearly are greater than the costs of the regulation.

Liberals of course, are much more tolerant, indeed supportive, of government regulation. In part, this follows from their emphasis on equity, but also because they may have a different measurement of both the costs and the benefits of regulations. Liberals generally estimate the costs lower and the benefits higher than their conservative colleagues. The institutionalists would also support the notion of regulation. Their support of regulation follows from their view that the structures and institutions of free market capitalism have changed in such a way that safe and high quality products and safe job sites, are no longer assured. In the absense of perfect competition, regulation of industry is in order. It is necessary, to prevent abuses by both buyers and sellers.

The radical reformists believe that most current regulation, to the extent that it exists, benefits the power structure; that regulation by definition serves the regulated. They attack the basic notion of cost-benefit analysis as a method of determining the appropriate amount of regulation. After all, they ask, how can one measure the worth or the benefits of saving a single life by making a job site safer?

In the selections addressing this issue, the emphasis is on the usefulness of cost-benefit analysis as a technique for determining the proper level of government regulation. One selection suggests that the use of cost-benefit analysis implies that government regulation is excessive. The other selection attacks the very heart of the cost-benefit procedure, laying bare all the implicit assumptions which such procedures make. In this sense the selection can be viewed as an argument between the conservative position and the radical reformist position.

As was the case with wage and price controls, we should mention an apparent paradox with respect to regulation policy. The above discussion implies that liberals should be more supportive of regulation than conservatives. However, deregulation or decontrol was a basic policy stance of the Carter administration. The Democratic Congress passed and the Democratic-executive branch signed into law, legislation which deregulated the airline industry, the trucking industry, and financial intermediaries. Again, practical considerations rather than basic philosophies often determine specific policy actions. Reality and philosophical considerations make strange bedfellows.

One of the two international issues concerns the actions of transnational or multinational corporations: "Do multinationals benefit less developed countries?" On this issue the clash is between conservative and institutional representatives. The conservative or pro-multinational position argues that these international corporations benefit the peoples of the world much as domestic corporations operate to benefit the residents of one nation. Immense efficiency is generated on this large global scale: the economies of less developed countries are stimulated toward economic progress, world output is expanded, and as a result, there is no loss of jobs in this country. They point to the development of transnationals as a "logical next step", as business firms repeatedly demonstrate that they are the mechanisms for the efficient production of goods and services. The institutionalists are less positive in their assessment of transnationals. They argue that in establishing foreign manufacturing sites, firms are really attempting to utilize cheap labor sources and circumvent the power of domestic labor unions. Through manipulation of transfer prices—prices which one branch of a company charges another branch of the same company—profits can be relocated so as to minimize the total taxes paid by the firm. The institutionalists also argue that the development and growth of these transnational companies is the business response to a new world situation, to an interdependent global economy, to tax laws, and to the growing power of both government and labor.

This debate could also be joined by liberals and radical reformists. The liberals, as usual, position themselves between the conservatives and institutionalists. They recognize that the transnationals may be beneficial both to their "mother" countries and to the less developed countries in which they undertake new operations. But in order to insure a proper flow of benefits to both countries, there must be an appropriate regulatory environment. In this way the potential abuses that might occur through transfer pricing may be avoided. The radical reformists would view the development of transnational corporations as another logical extension of domestic exploitation. Corporations extend themselves internationally because domestic constraints on their operations become too binding and by doing so they are able to restore profits.

As for appropriate policies regarding transnationals, the liberals and the institutionalists are in agreement: there must be appropriate regulation to eliminate potential abuses. The conservatives would disagree, and argue that the system itself provides sufficient checks and balances without the need for government regulation. The radical reformist maintains that real regulation of transnationals is needed. That is, public ownership and control of these corporations provides the only practical answer to the long run problems created by these large economic entities.

At the practical level we again find a compromise of the ideological positions. Conservatives do not demand that these firms be left totally alone and liberals agree that the transnationals should be given sufficient freedom so as to achieve some efficiencies that may arise from a global perspective on the organization of production.

Summary

It is clear that there is no shortage of economic problems. These problems demand solutions. At the same time there is no shortage of proposed solutions. In fact, the problem is often one of over-supply. The fifteen issues included in this volume will acquaint you, or more accurately, reacquaint you, with some of these problems. And, of course, there are at least two proposed solutions for each of the problems. Here we hope to provide new insights regarding the alternatives available and the differences and similarities of these alternative remedies.

If this introduction has served its purposes, you will be able to identify common elements in the proposed solutions to the different problems. For example, you will be able to identify the reliance on the free forces of the market advocated by free market economists as the remedy for several economic ills. This introduction should also help you understand why there are at least two proposed solutions for every economic problem; each group of economists tends to interpret a problem from its own philosophical position and to advance a solution which is grounded in that same philosophical framework.

Our intention, of course, is not to connect persons to one philosophic position or another. We hope instead to help discussion and promote understanding. To do this, people must see not only a proposed solution, they must also be aware of the roots of that solution. With greater understanding, meaningful progress in addressing economic problems can be achieved.

ISSUE 1

DO BUSINESSES HAVE ANY MORAL RESPONSIBILITY BEYOND MAKING PROFITS?

YES: Robert Almeder, from "The Ethics of Profits: Reflections on Corporate Responsibility," *Business and Society* (Winter, 1980).
NO: Milton Friedman, from "The Social Responsibility of Business is to Increase Its Profits," *New York Times Magazine* (September 13, 1970).

ISSUE SUMMARY

YES: Philosopher Almeder maintains that if capitalism is to survive, it must act in socially responsible ways that go beyond profit making.

NO: Free Market Economist Milton Friedman replies that the sole responsibility of business is to increase its profits.

Every economic society, whether it is a traditional society of Central Africa, a centrally planned Eastern European society or the fabulously wealthy capitalist society of North America, must address the basic economic problem of resource allocation. These societies must determine *what* goods and services they can and will produce, *how* these goods and services will be produced, and *for whom* these goods and services will be produced.

Scarcity necessitates the *what, how* and *for whom* questions. Even if a given society were indescribably rich, it would still confront the problem of scarcity. In this case, it would confront "relative scarcity." It might have all the resources it needs to produce all the goods and services it would *ever* want, but it can't produce all these things simultaneously. Thus it must set priorities and produce first those goods and services with the highest priority and postpone the production of those goods and services with lower priorities. If time is of the essence, *how* should these goods and services be produced? And since this society can't produce all it wants in an instant of time, *for whom* should the first bundle of goods and services be produced?

Few, if any, economic societies will be indescribably rich. On the other hand, we can cite many examples of economic societies which face grinding deprivation on a daily basis. In these cases and in all the cases between poverty and great affluence, the *what, how* and *for whom* questions are immediately apparent. Somehow these questions must be answered.

In some societies, such as the Amish communities of North America, answers to these questions are found in tradition. Sons and daughters follow in their parents' footsteps. Younger generations produce *what* older generations produced before them. The methods of production—the horse drawn plow, the hand held scythe, the use of natural fertilizers—remain unchanged, thus the *how* question is answered just as the *for whom* question is answered—by following historic patterns. In other societies, for example, self-sustaining religious communities, a different pattern of responses to these questions is elicited. In these communities the "elder" of the community determines *what* will be produced, *how* it will be produced and *for whom* it will be produced. If there is a well defined hierarchical system, we could liken this to one of the command economies of Eastern Europe.

Although elements of tradition and command are found in the industrialized societies of Western Europe, North America and Japan, profits provide the basic answers to the three questions of resource allocation in these countries. In these economic societies, *what* will be produced is determined by what will yield the greatest profit. Consumers, in their search for maximum satisfaction will bid for those goods and services which they want most. This consumer action drives the price of these goods and services upward, and in turn these higher prices increase producers' profits. The higher profits attract new firms into the industry and encourage existing firms to increase their output. Thus, profits are the mechanism which insures that consumers get *what* they want. In a like manner, the profit-seeking behavior of business firms determines *how* the goods and services that consumers want will be produced. Since firms attempt to maximize their profits, they select those means of production which are economically most efficient. Lastly, the *for whom* question is also linked to profits. Wherever there is a shortage of goods and services, profits will be high. In the producers' attempts to increase their output they must attract factors of production (land, labor and capital) away from other economic activities. This bidding increases factor prices or factor incomes and insures that these factors will be able to buy goods and services in the open marketplace.

Both Almeder and Friedman recognize the merits of a profit-driven economic system. They also do not quarrel over the importance of profits. But they do part ways over whether or not business firms have obligations beyond making profits. Almeder contends that businesses must act according to higher moral principals, to prevent damage done in the name of profits. Friedman holds that the *only* responsibility of business is to make profits. He argues that anyone who maintains otherwise is "preaching pure and unadulterated socialism."

YES

Robert Almeder

THE ETHICS OF PROFIT: REFLECTIONS ON CORPORATE RESPONSIBILITY

I. Introduction

International Telephone and Telegraph Corporation is alleged to have contributed large sums of money to 'destabilize' the duly elected government of Chile; General Motors Corporation and Firestone Tire and Rubber Corporation are both alleged to have knowingly and willingly marketed products which, owing to defective design, had been reliably predicted to kill a certain percentage of users. Finally, it is frequently said that numerous advertising companies happily accept and earnestly solicit accounts to advertise cigarettes, knowing full well that as a direct result of their advertising activities a certain number of people will die considerably prematurely and painfully. We need not concern ourselves with whether or not these charges are true; for our concern here is with what might count as a justification for such corporate behavior when it occurs. What is interesting is that sometimes, although not very frequently, corporate executives will admit to such behavior informally and then proceed proximately to justify that behavior in the name of their responsibility to the shareholders or owners to make as much profit as is legally possible. Thereafter, less proximately and more generally, they will proceed to urge the more general utilitarian point that the increase in profit engendered by such corporate behavior begets such an unquestionable

From, "The Ethics of Profits: Reflections on Corporate Responsibility", *Business and Society.* Vols. 19-2 and 20-1. Reprinted by permission.

overall good for society that the behavior in question is morally acceptable if not quite praiseworthy. More specifically, the justification in question can, and usually does, take two forms.

The first and most common form of justification consists in urging that, as long as one's corporate behavior is not illegal, the behavior will be morally acceptable because the sole purpose for being in business is to make a profit; and the rule of the marketplace are somewhat different from those in other places and must be followed if one is to satisfy the responsibility to the shareholder. Moreover, proponents of this view hasten to add that, as Adam Smith has claimed, the greatest good for society is achieved not by corporations seeking to act morally, or with a sense of social responsibility in their pursuit of profit, but rather by each corporation seeking to maximize its own profit, unregulated in that endeavor except by the laws of supply and demand along with whatever other laws are inherent in the competition process. Smith's view, that there is an invisible hand, as it were, directing an economy governed solely by the profit motive to the greatest good for society, is still the dominant motivation and justification for those who would have an economy unregulated by any moral concern which would, or could, tend to decrease profits in order to attain some alleged social or moral good. Milton Friedman, for example, has frequently asserted that the sole moral responsibility of business is to make as much profit as is legally possible. By that he means to suggest that attempts to regulate or restrain the pursuit of profit to effect what some people believe to be socially desirable ends are in fact *subversive* of the common good, since the greatest good for the greatest number is

achieved by an economy maximally competitive and unregulated by moral rules in its pursuit of profit. So, under this view, the greatest good for society is achieved by corporations acting legally but with no regard for what may be morally desirable. This begets the paradox that, *in business,* it is only by acting without regard for morality that the greatest good for society can be achieved. This is a fairly conscious commitment to the view that while one's personal life may well need to be governed by moral considerations, it is a necessity that, in the pursuit of profit; one's corporate behavior be unregulated by any moral concern other than that of making as much money as is legally possible; for, curiously enough, it is only in this way that society achieves the greatest good. So viewed, it is not difficult to see how a corporate executive could consistently adopt rigorous standards of morality in his or her personal life and yet feel quite comfortable in abandoning those standards in the pursuit of corporate profit. Mr. Carr, for example, likens the conduct of business to playing poker. As Carr would have it, moral busybodies, who insist on corporations behaving morally might just as well censure a good bluffer in poker for being deceitful. Society, lacking a perspective such as Friedman's and Carr's, is only too willing to view such behavior as strongly hypocritical and fostered by an unwholesome avarice.

A second way of justifying, or defending, corporate practices which may appear quite morally questionable is to argue that even if corporations were to take seriously the idea of limiting profits because of a desire to be moral or more responsible to social needs, they then would be involved in the unwholesome business of selecting and implementing

21

moral values which may not be shared by a large number of people. Besides, there is the overwhelming question of whether or not there can be any non-questionable moral values or non-controversial list of social priorities for corporations to adopt. After all, if ethical relativism is true, or if ethical nihilism is true (and philosophers can be counted upon to argue for both positions), then it would be fairly silly of corporations to limit profits for what may be quite a dubious reason, namely, being moral, when there are no clear grounds for doing so. In short, business corporations could argue (as Friedman has done) that corporate actions in behalf of society's interest would require of corporations an ability to clearly determine and rank in non-controversial ways the major needs of society, and it does not appear that this can be successfully done.

Perhaps another, and easier, way of formulating this second argument is to hold that, since philosophers generally fail to agree on what are the proper moral rules (if any) as well as on whether or not we should be moral, it would be imprudent to sacrifice a clear profit for a dubious or controversial moral gain. That would appear to be an abandonment of a clear responsibility for one that is unclear or questionable.

If there are any other basic modes of justification for the sort of corporate behavior noted at the outset, I cannot imagine what they might be. So, let us examine these two modes of justification. In doing this, I hope to show that neither argument is sound and, moreover, that corporate behavior of the sort in question is clearly immoral. In the end, we can reflect upon what effective means can be taken to prevent such behavior and what is philosophically implied by corporate willingness to act in such ways.

II.

Essentially, the first argument is that the greatest good for the greatest number will be, and can only be, achieved by corporations acting legally, but unregulated by any moral concern, in the pursuit of profit. As noted above, the evidence for this argument rests on a fairly classical and unquestioning acceptance of Adam Smith's view that society achieves a greater good when each person is allowed to pursue his/her own selfish ends than when each person's pursuit of his own selfish ends is regulated in some way or other by moral rules or concern. I know of no evidence ever offered by Smith for this latter claim although it seems clear that those who adopt it generally do so out of respect for the perceived good that has emerged for various modern societies as a direct result of the free enterprise system and its ability to raise the overall standard of living of all those under it. At any rate, there is nothing inevitable about the greatest good occurring under an unregulated economy. Indeed, we have good inductive evidence from the age of the Robber Barons that unless the profit motive is regulated in various ways (by statute or otherwise) great social evil can occur because of the natural tendency of the system to place ever increasing sums of money in ever decreasing numbers of hands. And if all this is so, then so much the worse for all philosophical attempts to justify what would appear to be morally questionable corporate behavior on the grounds that corporate behavior, unregulated by moral concern, is productive of the greatest good for the greatest number. Moreover, a rule-utilitarian would not be very hard-pressed to show the many unsavory implications to society as a whole if it were to take seriously a rule to the effect that, provided only that one acts legally, it is morally permissable to do whatever one wants to do to achieve a profit. Some of those implications we shall discuss below before drawing a conclusion.

The second argument cited above asserts that even if we were to grant, for the sake of argument, that corporations have social responsibilities beyond that of making as much money as legally possible for the shareholders, there would be no non-controversial way for corporations to discover just what these responsibilities are in the order of their importance. Since even philosophers can be expected to disagree on what one's moral responsibilities are, if any, it would seem irresponsible to limit profits to satisfy dubious moral responsibilities. But there are a few things wrong with this line of reasoning.

For one thing, it unduly exaggerates our potential for moral disagreement. Admittedly, there might well be important disagreements among corporations (just as there could be among philosophers) as to a priority ranking of major social needs; but that does not mean that most of us could not, or would not, agree that certain things ought not be done in the name of profit even when there is no law prohibiting such acts. There will always be a few who would do anything for profit; but that is hardly a good argument in favor of their having the moral right to do so. Rather, it is a good argument that they refuse to be moral. In sum, it is hard to see how this second argument favoring corporate moral nihilism is any better than the general argument for ethical nihilism based on the variability of ethical judgments or practices. Apart from the fact that it tacitly presupposes that morality is a matter of what we all in fact would, or

should, agree to, the argument is maximally counterintuitive (as I shall show) by way of suggesting that we cannot generally agree that corporations have certain clear social responsibilities to avoid certain practices. Accordingly, I would now like to argue that a certain kind of corporate behavior is quite immoral (although it may not be illegal) and that all corporations willing to act in this way do a disservice to humanity and themselves. The basic point I wish to make is that, Friedman notwithstanding, it is not difficult to show that there are some things that corporations ought not do in the pursuit of profit; even if there were no laws against such acts. But it is quite difficult to convince corporations, like persons, that they ought to be moral. I would like to probe the source of this difficulty in fairly general terms, concluding with a recommendation.

III.

Without entering into the reasons for the belief, I assume we all believe that it is wrong to kill an innocent human being for the sole reason that doing so would be financially more rewarding for the killer than if he were to earn his livelihood in some other way. Nor, I assume, would our moral feelings in this matter change depending upon the amount of money involved. Killing an innocent baby for fifteen million dollars would not seem to be any less objectionable than killing it for twenty cents. It is possible, however, that some self-professing utilitarian might be tempted to argue that the killing of an innocent baby for fifteen million dollars would not be objectionable if the money were to be given to the poor; for under these circumstances, greater good would be achieved by the killing of the innocent baby. But, I submit, if anybody were to argue this, his argument would be quite deficient because he will not have established what he needs to establish in order to make the argument sound. What is needed is a clearly convincing argument that raising the standard of living of an indefinite number of poor people by the killing of an innocent person is a greater good for all those affected by the act than if the standard of living were not raised by the killing of an innocent person. This is necessary because part of what we mean by having a basic right to life is that a person's life cannot be taken from him or her without a good reason. And if our utilitarian cannot convincingly justify his claim that a greater good is served by killing an innocent person to raise the standard of living for a large number of poor people, then it is hard to see how he can have the valid reason he needs to deprive an innocent person of his or her life. Now, it seems clear that there will be anything but unanimity in the moral community on the question of whether there is a greater good achieved in raising the standard of living by killing an innocent baby than in leaving the standard of living alone and not killing an innocent baby. Moreover, even if everybody were to agree that the greater good is achieved by the killing of the innocent baby, how could that be shown to be true? How does one compare the moral value of raising the standard of living by the taking of that life? Indeed, the more one thinks about it, the harder it is to see just what would count as objective evidence for the claim that the greater good is achieved by the killing of an innocent baby. Accordingly, I can see nothing that would serve to justify the utilitarian who might be tempted to argue that if the sum is large enough, and if the sum were to be used for raising the standard of living for an indefinite number of poor people, then it would be morally acceptable to kill an innocent person for money.

These reflections should not be taken to imply, however, that no utilitarian argument could justify the killing of an innocent person for money. After all, if the sum were large enough to save the lives of a large number of people who would surely die if the innocent baby were not killed, then I think one would as a rule be justified in killing the innocent baby for the sum in question. But this is obviously quite different from any attempt to justify the killing of an innocent person in order to raise the standard of living for an indefinite number of poor people. It makes sense to kill one innocent person in order to save, say, twenty innocent persons; but it makes no sense at all to kill one innocent person to raise the standard of living of an indefinite number of people. And this is because in the latter case, but not in the former, a comparison is sought as between things that are incomparable.

Assuming all this, it is remarkable and somewhat perplexing that certain corporations should seek to defend practices that are *in fact* instances of killing innocent persons for profit. Take, for example, the corporate practice of dumping known carcinogens into rivers. On Friedman's view, we should not regulate or prevent such companies from dumping their effluents into the environment. Rather we should, if we like, tax the company after the effluents are in the water and then have the tax money used to clear up the environment. For Friedman, and others, the fact that so many people will die as a result of this practice seems to be just part of the cost of doing business and making a profit. If there is any difference between such corporate practices and murdering innocent human beings for money, it is hard to see what it is. There are a host of other corporate activities which amount to deliberate killing of innocent persons for money. Such practices number among them: contributing funds to 'destabilize' a foreign government, advertising cigarettes, knowingly marketing children's clothing containing a known cancer-causing agent, and refusing to recall (for fear of financial loss) goods known to be defective enough to directly maim or kill a certain percentage of their users. On this latter item, we are all familiar, for example, with convincingly documented charges that certain prominent automobile and tire manufacturers have knowingly marketed equipment with defects which increased the likelihood of death of the users. Yet, they have refused to recall these products because the cost of recalling or repairing them would have a greater adverse impact on profit than if the products were not recalled and the company paid the projected number of suits predicted to be filed successfully. Of course, if the projected cost of the suits were to outweigh the cost of recall or repair, then the product would be recalled and repaired, but not otherwise. In cases of this sort the companies involved may admit to having certain marketing problems or design problems, and they may even admit to having made a mistake; but they do not view themselves as immoral or as murderers for keeping their product in the marketplace when they know people are dying because of it— people who would not die if the defect were corrected.

In all of this, the point is not whether in fact these practices have occurred in the past, or occur even now; for there can be no doubt that such practices have occurred and do occur. Rather, the point is that when companies as a matter of policy act in such ways, they must either not know what they do is murder (i.e., unjustifiable killing of innocent persons), or knowing that it is murder, seek to justify it in terms of profit. My argument is that it is difficult to see how any corporate manager could fail to see that these policies amount to murder for money, although there may be no civil statutes against such corporate behavior. If so, then where such policies exist, we can only assume that they are designed and implemented by corporate managers who either see nothing wrong with murder for money (which is implausible) or recognize that what they do is wrong, but simply refuse to act morally because it is financially rewarding to act immorally.

Of course, it is possible that some corporate executives do not recognize such acts as murder. They may, after all, view murder as a legal concept involving one person or persons deliberately killing another person or persons and prosecutable only under existing civil statute. If so, it is somewhat understandable how corporate executives might fail, at least psychologically, to see such corporate policies as murder rather than as, say, calculated risks. Still, for all that, the logic of the situation seems clear enough.

IV. Conclusion.

In addition to the fact that the only two plausible arguments favoring the Friedman doctrine are unsatisfactory, a strong case can be made for the claim that corporations *do* have a clear and noncontroversial moral responsibility not to design or implement, for reasons of profit, policies which they know, or have good reason to believe, will kill or otherwise seriously injure innocent persons affected by those policies. And we have said nothing about wage discrimination, sexism, discrimination in hiring, price fixing, price gouging, questionable but not unlawful competition, or other similar practices some will think businesses should avoid by virtue of responsibility to society. My main concern has been to show that since we all agree that murder for money is generally wrong, and since there is no discernible difference between that and certain corporate policies which are not in fact illegal, then these corporate practices are clearly immoral (that is, they ought not to be done) and incapable of being morally justified by appeal to the Friedman doctrine since that doctrine does not admit of adequate evidential support. In itself, it is sad that this argument needs to be made and, if it weren't for what appears to be a fairly strong commitment within the business community to the Friedman doctrine in the name of the unquestionable success of the free enterprise system, the argument would not need to be stated. Moreover, the fact that such practices do exist because they are designed and implemented by corporate managers who, for all intents and purposes, appear to be upright members of the moral community, only heightens the need for effective social deterrence. Naturally, any company willing to put human lives into the profit and loss column is not likely to respond to moral censure. This, I submit, implies that perhaps the most effective way to deal with the problem consists in structuring legislation such that principle corporate managers who knowingly concur in practices of the sort listed above can effectively be tried, at their own expense, for murder, rather than cen-

sured and fined a sum to be paid out of corporate profits. This may seem somewhat extreme or unrealistic. However, it seems more unrealistic to think that aggressively competitive corporations will respond to what is morally necessary if failure to do so could be very or even minimally profitable. In short, unless fairly strong and appropriate steps are taken to prevent such practices, society will continue to reinforce a mode of behavior which is destructive because it is maximally disrespectful of human life. It is also reinforcing a value system which so emphasizes monetary gain as a standard of human success that murder for profit would be a corporate policy if the penalty for being caught at it were not too dear.

In the long run, of course, corporate and individual willingness to do what is clearly immoral for the sake of monetary gain is a patent commitment to a certain view about the nature of human happiness and success, a view which will need to be placed in the balance with Aristotle's reasoned argument and reflections to the effect that money and all that it brings is a means to an end, and not the sort of end in itself that will justify acting immorally to attain it. What that beautiful end is and why being moral allows us to achieve it, may well be the most rewarding and profitable subject a human being can think about. Properly understood and placed in perspective, Aristotle's view on the nature and attainment of human happiness could go a long way toward alleviating the temptation to kill for money.

In the meantime, any ardent supporter of the capitalistic system will naturally want to see the system thrive and flourish; and this it cannot do if it invites and demands government regulation in the name of the public interest. A strong ideological commitment to what I have here described as the Friedman doctrine is counterproductive and not in anyone's long-range interest, since it is most likely to beget more and more regulatory laws. The only way to avoid such encroaching regulation is to find ways to move the business community into the long-term view of what is in its interest, and effect ways of determining and responding to social needs before society moves to regulate business to that end. This, of course, is to ask business to regulate its own modes of competition in ways that may seem very difficult. Indeed, if what I have been suggesting is correct, the only kind of capitalism that is likely to survive indefinitely is a humane one; and a humane one is one that is at least as socially responsible as society needs. By the same token, contrary to what is sometimes felt in the business community, the Friedman doctrine, ardently adopted for the dubious reasons generally given, will most likely undermine capitalism and motivate an economic socialism by assuring an erosive regulatory climate in a society that expects the business community to be socially responsible in ways that go beyond just making legal profits.

In sum, being socially responsible in ways that go beyond legal profit-making is by no means a dubious luxury for the capitalist in today's world. It is a necessity if capitalism is to survive at all; and, presumably, we shall all profit exceedingly with the survival of a vibrant capitalism. If anything, then, rigid adherence to the Friedman doctrine is not only philosophically unjustified, and unjustifiable, it is also unprofitable in the long run, and therefore, downright subversive of the common good in the long run. Unfortunately, taking the long run view is difficult for everyone; and that, of course, is

for the obvious reason that for each of us, tomorrow may not come. But living for today only, does not seem to make much sense either if that deprives us of any reasonable and happy tomorrow. Living for the future may not be the healthiest thing to do; but do it we must, if we have good reason to think that we will have a future. The trick is to provide for the future without living in it, and that just requires being moral.

Epilogue

After this article was written, an Indiana superior court judge refused to dismiss a homicide indictment against the Ford Motor Company. The company was indicted on charges of reckless homicide stemming from a 1978 accident involving a 1973 Pinto in which three girls died when the car burst into flames after being slammed in the rear. This is the first case in which Ford, or any other automobile manufacturer, has been charged with a criminal offense.

The indictment went forward because the state of Indiana adopted in 1977 a criminal code provision permitting corporations to be charged with criminal acts. At the moment, twenty-two other states allow as much.

The judge, in refusing to set aside the indictment, agreed with the prosecutor's argument that the charge was based not on the Pinto's design fault, but rather on the fact that Ford had permitted the car "to remain on Indiana highways knowing full well its defects."

This is an interesting example of social regulation which could have been avoided if corporate managers had not followed so ardently the Friedman doctrine. If society continues to regulate the business community, the emerging socialism (and all that it implies) can only be viewed as a direct effect of the business community's refusal to act morally because of its unquestioning adoption of the Friedman doctrine.

● ● ●

NO
Milton Friedman

THE SOCIAL RESPONSIBILITY OF BUSINESS IS TO INCREASE ITS PROFITS

When I hear businessmen speak eloquently about the "social responsibilities of business in a free-enterprise system," I am reminded of the wonderful line about the Frenchman who discovered at the age of 70 that he had been speaking prose all his life. The businessmen believe that they are defending free enterprise when they declaim that business is not concerned "merely" with profit but also with promoting desirable "social ends; that business has a social conscience" and takes seriously its responsibilities for providing employment, eliminating discrimination, avoiding pollution and whatever else may be the catchwords of the contemporary crop of reformers. In fact they are—or would be if they or anyone else took them seriously—preaching pure and unadulterated socialism. Businessmen who talk this way are unwitting puppets of the intellectual forces that have been undermining the basis of a free society these past decades.

The discussions of the "social responsibilities of business" are notable for their analytical looseness and lack of rigor. What does it mean to say that "business" has responsibilities? Only people can have responsibilities. A corporation is an artificial person and in this sense may have artificial responsibilities, but "business" as a whole cannot be said to have responsibilities, even in this vague sense. The first step toward clarity in examining the doctrine of the social responsibility of business is to ask precisely what it implies for whom.

Presumably, the individuals who are to be responsible are businessmen, which means individual proprietors or corporate executives. Most of the discussion of social responsibility is directed at corporations, so in what follows I shall mostly neglect the individual proprietor and speak of corporate executives.

In a free-enterprise, private-property system, a corporate executive is an employee of the owners of the business. He has direct responsibility to his employers. That responsibility is to conduct the business in accordance with

From, "The Social Responsibility of Business is to Increase its Profits", *New York Times Magazine*. September 13, 1970. ©1970 by The New York Times. Reprinted by permission.

their desires, which generally will be to make as much money as possible while conforming to the basic rules of the society, both those embodied in law and those embodied in ethical custom. Of course, in some cases his employers may have a different objective. A group of persons might establish a corporation for an eleemosynary purpose—for example, a hospital or a school. The manager of such a corporation will not have money profit as his objective but the rendering of certain services.

In either case, the key point is that, in his capacity as a corporate executive, the manager is the agent of the individuals who own the corporation or establish the eleemosynary institution, and his primary responsibility is to them.

Needless to say, this does not mean that it is easy to judge how well he is performing his task. But at least the criterion of performance is straightforward, and the persons among whom a voluntary contractual arrangement exists are clearly defined.

Of course, the corporate executive is also a person in his own right. As a person, he may have many other responsibilities that he recognizes or assumes voluntarily—to his family, his conscience, his feelings of charity, his church, his clubs, his city, his country. He may feel impelled by these responsibilities to devote part of his income to causes he regards as worthy, to refuse to work for particular corporations, even to leave his job, for example, to join his country's armed forces. If we wish, we may refer to some of these responsibilities as "social responsibilities." But in these respects he is acting as a principal, not an agent; he is spending his own money or time or energy, not the money of his employers or the time or energy he has contracted to

devote to their purposes. If these are "social responsibilities," they are the social responsibilities of individuals, not of business.

What does it mean to say that the corporate executive has a "social responsibility" in his capacity as businessman? If this statement is not pure rhetoric, it must mean that he is to act in some way that is not in the interest of his employers. For example, that he is to refrain from increasing the price of the product in order to contribute to the social objective of preventing inflation, even though a price increase would be in the best interests of the corporation. Or that he is to make expenditures on reducing pollution beyond the amount that is in the best interests of the corporation or that is required by law in order to contribute to the social objective of improving the environment. Or that, at the expense of corporate profits, he is to hire "hard-core" unemployed instead of better-qualified available workmen to contribute to the social objective of reducing poverty.

In each of these cases, the corporate executive would be spending someone else's money for a general social interest. Insofar as his actions in accord with his "social responsibility" reduce returns to stockholders, he is spending their money. Insofar as his actions raise the price to customers, he is spending the customers' money. Insofar as his actions lower the wages of some employes, he is spending their money.

The stockholders or the customers or the employes could separately spend their own money on the particular action if they wished to do so. The executive is exercising a distinct "social responsibility," rather than serving as an agent of the stockholders or the customers or the employes, only if he spends the money in a different way than they would have spent it.

But if he does this, he is in effect imposing taxes, on the one hand, and deciding how the tax proceeds shall be spent, on the other.

This process raises political questions on two levels: principle and consequences. On the level of political principle, the imposition of taxes and the expenditure of tax proceeds are governmental functions. We have established elaborate constitutional, parliamentary and judicial provisions to control these functions, to assure that taxes are imposed so far as possible in accordance with the preferences and desires of the public—after all, "taxation without representation" was one of the battle cries of the American Revolution. We have a system of checks and balances to separate the legislative function of imposing taxes and enacting expenditures from the executive function of collecting taxes and administering expenditure programs and from the judicial function of mediating disputes and interpreting the law.

Here the businessman—self-selected or appointed directly or indirectly by stockholders—is to be simultaneously legislator, executive and jurist. He is to decide whom to tax by how much and for what purpose, and he is to spend the proceeds—all this guided only by general exhortations from on high to restrain inflation, improve the environment, fight poverty and so on and on.

The whole justification for permitting the corporate executive to be selected by the stockholders is that the executive is an agent serving the interests of his principal. This justification disappears when the corporate executive imposes taxes and spends the proceeds for "social" pur-

poses. He becomes in effect a public employe, a civil servant, even though he remains in name an employe of a private enterprise. On grounds of political principle, it is intolerable that such civil servants—insofar as their actions in the name of social responsibility are real and not just window-dressing—should be selected as they are now. If they are to be civil servants, then they must be selected through a political process. If they are to impose taxes and make expenditures to foster "social" objectives, then political machinery must be set up to guide the assessment of taxes and to determine through a political process the objectives to be served.

This is the basic reason why the doctrine of "social responsibility" involves the acceptance of the socialist view that political mechanisms, not market mechanisms, are the appropriate way to determine the allocation of scarce resources to alternative uses.

On the grounds of consequences, can the corporate executive in fact discharge his alleged "social responsibilities"? On the one hand, suppose he could get away with spending the stockholders' or customers' or employes' money. How is he to know how to spend it? He is told that he must contribute to fighting inflation. How is he to know what action of his will contribute to that end? He is presumably an expert in running his company—in producing a product or selling it or financing it. But nothing about his selection makes him an expert on inflation. Will his holding down the price of his product reduce inflationary pressure? Or, by leaving more spending power in the hands of his customers, simply divert it elsewhere? Or, by forcing him to produce less because of the lower price, will it simply contribute to shortages? Even if he could

31

DO BUSINESSES HAVE MORAL RESPONSIBILITIES?

answer these questions, how much cost is he justified in imposing on his stockholders, customers and employes for this social purpose? What is the appropriate share and what is the appropriate share of others?

And, whether he wants to or not, can he get away with spending his stockholders', customers' or employes' money? Will not the stockholders fire him? (Either the present ones or those who take over when his actions in the name of social responsibility have reduced the corporation's profits and the price of its stock.) His customers and his employes can desert him for other producers and employers less scrupulous in exercising their social responsibilities.

This facet of "social responsibility" doctrine is brought into sharp relief when the doctrine is used to justify wage restraint by trade unions. The conflict of interest is naked and clear when union officials are asked to subordinate the interest of their members to some more general social purpose. If the union officials try to enforce wage restraint, the consequence is likely to be wildcat strikes, rank-and-file revolts and the emergence of strong competitors for their jobs. We thus have the ironic phenomenon that union leaders—at least in the U.S.—have objected to Government interference with the market far more consistently and courageously than have business leaders.

The difficulty of exercising "social responsibility" illustrates, of course, the great virtue of private competitive enterprise—it forces people to be responsible for their own actions and makes it difficult for them to "exploit" other people for either selfish or unselfish purposes. They can do good—but only at their own expense.

Many a reader who has followed the argument this far may be tempted to remonstrate that it is all well and good to speak of government's having the responsibility to impose taxes and determine expenditures for such "social" purposes as controlling pollution or training the hard-core unemployed, but that the problems are too urgent to wait on the slow course of political processes, that the exercise of social responsibility by businessmen is a quicker and surer way to solve pressing current problems.

Aside from the question of fact—I share Adam Smith's skepticism about the benefits that can be expected from "those who affected to trade for the public good"—this argument must be rejected on grounds of principle. What it amounts to is an assertion that those who favor the taxes and expenditures in question have failed to persuade a majority of their fellow citizens to be of like mind and that they are seeking to attain by undemocratic procedures what they cannot attain by democratic procedures. In a free society, it is hard for "good" people to do "good," but that is a small price to pay for making it hard for "evil" people to do "evil," especially since one man's good is another's evil.

I have, for simplicity, concentrated on the special case of the corporate executive, except only for the brief digression on trade unions. But precisely the same argument applies to the newer phenomenon of calling upon stockholders to require corporations to exercise social responsibility (the recent G.M. crusade, for example). In most of these cases, what is in effect involved is some stockholders trying to get other stockholders (or customers or employes) to contribute against their will to "social" causes favored by the activists. Insofar as they succeed, they are

again imposing taxes and spending the proceeds.

The situation of the individual proprietor is somewhat different. If he acts to reduce the returns of his enterprise in order to exercise his "social responsibility," he is spending his own money, not someone else's. If he wishes to spend his money on such purposes, that is his right, and I cannot see that there is any objection to his doing so. In the process, he, too, may impose costs on employes and customers. However, because he is far less likely than a large corporation or union to have monopolistic power, any such side effects will tend to be minor.

Of course, in practice the doctrine of social responsibility is frequently a cloak for actions that are justified on other grounds rather than a reason for those actions.

To illustrate, it may well be in the long-run interest of a corporation that is a major employer in a small community to devote resources to providing amenities to that community or to improving its government. That may make it easier to attract desirable employes, it may reduce the wage bill or lessen losses from pilferage and sabotage or have other worthwhile effects. Or it may be that, given the laws about the deductibility of corporate charitable contributions, the stockholders can contribute more to charities they favor by having the corporation make the gift than by doing it themselves, since they can in that way contribute an amount that would otherwise have been paid as corporate taxes.

In each of these—and many similar—cases, there is a strong temptation to rationalize these actions as an exercise of "social responsibility." In the present climate of opinion, with its widespread aversion to "capitalism," "profits," the

"soulless corporation" and so on, this is one way for a corporation to generate goodwill as a by-product of expenditures that are entirely justified in its own self-interest.

It would be inconsistent of me to call on corporate executives to refrain from this hypocritical window-dressing because it harms the foundations of a free society. That would be to call on them to exercise a "social responsibility"! If our institutions, and the attitudes of the public make it in their self-interest to cloak their actions in this way, I cannot summon much indignation to denounce them. At the same time, I can express admiration for those individual proprietors or owners of closely held corporations or stockholders of more broadly held corporations who disdain such tactics as approaching fraud.

Whether blameworthy or not, the use of the cloak of social responsibility, and the nonsense spoken in its name by influential and prestigious businessmen, does clearly harm the foundations of a free society. I have been impressed time and again by the schizophrenic character of many businessmen. They are capable of being extremely far-sighted and clear-headed in matters that are internal to their businesses. They are incredibly short-sighted and muddle-headed in matters that are outside their businesses but affect the possible survival of business in general. This short-sightedness is strikingly exemplified in the calls from many businessmen for wage and price guidelines or controls or incomes policies. There is nothing that could do more in a brief period to destroy a market system and replace it by a centrally controlled system than effective governmental control of prices and wages.

The short-sightedness is also exemplified in speeches by businessmen on social responsibility. This may gain them kudos in the short run. But it helps to strengthen the already too prevalent view that the pursuit of profits is wicked and immoral and must be curbed and controlled by external forces. Once this view is adopted, the external forces that curb the market will not be the social consciences, however highly developed, of the pontificating executives; it will be the iron fist of Government bureaucrats. Here, as with price and wage controls, businessmen seem to me to reveal a suicidal impulse.

The political principle that underlies the market mechanism is unanimity. In an ideal free market resting on private property, no individual can coerce any other, all cooperation is voluntary, all parties to such cooperation benefit or they need not participate. There are no "social" values, no "social" responsibilities in any sense other than the shared values and responsibilities of individuals. Society is a collection of individuals and of the various groups they voluntarily form.

The political principle that underlies the political mechanism is conformity. The individual must serve a more general social interest—whether that be determined by a church or a dictator or a majority. The individual may have a vote and a say in what is to be done, but if he is overruled, he must conform. It is appropriate for some to require others to contribute to a general social purpose whether they wish to or not.

Unfortunately, unanimity is not always feasible. There are some respects in which conformity appears unavoidable, so I do not see how one can avoid the use of the political mechanism altogether.

But the doctrine of "social responsibility" taken seriously would extend the scope of the political mechanism to every human activity. It does not differ in philosophy from the most explicitly collectivist doctrine. It differs only by professing to believe that collectivist ends can be attained without collectivist means. That is why, in my book "Capitalism and Freedom," I have called it a "fundamentally subversive doctrine" in a free society, and have said that in such a society, "there is one and only one social responsibility of business—to use its resources and engage in activities designed to increase its profits so long as it stays within the rules of the game, which is to say, engages in open and free competition without deception or fraud."

• • •

POSTSCRIPT

DO BUSINESSES HAVE ANY MORAL RESPONSIBILITY BEYOND MAKING PROFITS?

Philosopher Almeder argues that some corporate behavior is immoral and defense of this immoral behavior imposes great costs on society. More precisely, Almeder likens corporate acts such as cigarette advertising, marketing automobiles which cannot sustain moderate rear-end collisions, the contribution of funds to destabilize foreign governments, etc., to unjustifiably murdering innocent children for profit. He goes on to argue that although these acts are not illegal and indeed they may improve profits for business firms, society must not condone this behavior. Instead, society through federal and state legislation must continue to impose regulations upon businesses until businesses begin to regulate themselves.

Economist Friedman dismisses Almeder's arguments on the grounds that Almeder does not understand the role of the corporate executive in modern society. These executives are responsible to the corporate owners, who expect these executives to do all in their power to earn the owners a maximum return on their investment. If the corporate executive takes an action which he or she feels is "socially responsible" and this reduces the owners return on their investment, he or she has spent the owners money. This, Friedman maintains, violates the very foundation of our political-economic system: individual freedom. No individual should be deprived of his property without his permission. If the corporate executives wish to take socially responsible actions they should use their own money. They shouldn't impose a tax on the owners which would limit the social action they might wish to engage in.

Perhaps no one topic is more fundamental to microeconomics than the issue of profits. As a consequence, many pages have been written in defense of profits such as Milton and Rose Friedman's FREE TO CHOOSE: A PERSONAL STATEMENT (Harcourt, Brace and Jovanovich, 1980), Ben Rogge's CAN CAPITALISM SURVIVE? (Liberty Fund, 1979) and Frank H. Knight's classical book RISK, UNCERTAINTY, AND PROFITS (Kelley Press, 1921). This does not mean to imply that few criticize the classical economic perspective. In recent years a number of new books which are highly critical of the Freidman-Rogge-Knight position have appeared on the market. Included among those new books are James Robertson's PROFIT OR PEOPLE? THE NEW SOCIAL ROLE OF MONEY (Merrimack Book Service, 1978), Sam Aaronovitch's POLITICAL ECONOMY OF CAPITALISM (Beekman Publisher's 1977) and Sherman Howard's RADICAL POLITICAL ECONOMY: CAPITALISM AND SOCIALISM FROM A MARXIST HUMANIST PERSPECTIVE (Basic Book, 1972).

ISSUE 2

IS THE DECLINE IN U.S. PRODUCTIVITY THE RESULT OF A FAILURE OF MANAGEMENT?

YES: Robert H. Hayes and William J. Abernathy, from "Managing Our Way to Economic Decline" *Harvard Business Review* (July-August, 1980).
NO: John W. Kendrick, from "Curriculum for Economics 1981: Productivity and Economic Growth" *The AEI Economist* (November, 1980).

ISSUE SUMMARY

YES: Business professors Hayes and Abernathy contend that modern management practices are the real cause of the current malaise found in the U.S. Business community.
NO: Economics professor Kendrick alleges that misguided government regulations, taxes and expenditure programs have resulted in declining American productivity.

The U.S. economy has a long and impressive history of rising living standards which are a result, in large part, of the rising labor productivity that has characterized our economy. That is, the American economy has been characterized by rising output per man-hour worked. For example, since 1890, the U.S. has experienced an annual increase of 2 percent per year in real output per man-hour worked. The accumulated increase after ninety years has resulted in our becoming one of the wealthiest countries on the face of the earth.

What has caused this "golden goose" to lay larger and larger eggs each year? Numerous factors are involved. Most obvious is the willingness of our firms to engage in research and development, put in place new machines and technology, take advantage of any potential economies of scale (size efficiencies) and subject its operations to the rigors of market competition which rewards efficiency and penalizes inefficiency. In addition, a unit of labor is of a much higher quality than it was in years gone by. We are healthier, better educated, better trained for our jobs, in short, we are better equipped to participate in the production process. The public sector has also done its part. We have excellent communications and transportation systems, we have a stable political system, and our basic institutions have developed along lines which encourage productivity improvements. Lastly, our Judeo-Christian traditions have fostered the work ethic. Given all of these factors and the abundance of national resources which are at our disposal, there is little wonder that we have made such significant strides in improving our economic position.

Unfortunately, our long experience with productivity improvements was brought to an abrupt halt in the 1970s. In 1973, and again in 1978, productivity sagged markedly. Conservative economists immediately attributed the decline in productivity to unnecessary government intervention and declining worker initiatives. They maintained that high taxes and the existence of a growing body of government regulations reduced business incentives to invest and innovate. They went on to assert that welfare programs and minimum wage legislation reduced labor's willingness to work in the first instance and excluded some workers in the second instance.

Liberal economists, by and large, found the same set of sources for our current malaise. They contend that general economic conditions are the cause of the 1973 and 1978 reversals in productivity gains. In particular, some cite the energy shortage sparked by OPEC in 1973, the inflation that has plagued the country for the past 15 years, and the shifts in the composition of the workforce as more women enter the workplace. These factors coupled with the concerns of the conservative economists, explain declining productivity for the liberal economist.

Perhaps no one selection from the extensive literature on productivity is more representative of the mainline conservative-liberal position than our reading from the *AEI Economist*. Professor Kendrick details the basic concerns of the conservative-liberal camp and outlines the policies that should be pursued in the Halls of Congress.

Professors Hayes and Abernathy engage in a frontal attack on this conventional wisdom. They assert that the responsibility for sagging productivity must be laid at the feet of management. This, of course, is nothing short of heresy for the conservative-liberal camp.

YES

Robert H. Hayes
and William J. Abernathy

MANAGING OUR WAY TO
ECONOMIC DECLINE

During the past several years American business has experienced a marked deterioration of competitive vigor and a growing unease about its overall economic well-being. This decline in both health and confidence has been attributed by economists and business leaders to such factors as the rapacity of OPEC, deficiencies in government tax and monetary policies, and the proliferation of regulation. We find these explanations inadequate.

They do not explain, for example, why the rate of productivity growth in America has declined both absolutely and relative to that in Europe and Japan. Nor do they explain why in many high-technology as well as mature industries America has lost its leadership position. Although a host of readily named forces—government regulation, inflation, monetary policy, tax laws, labor costs and constraints, fear of a capital shortage, the price of imported oil—have taken their toll on American business, pressures of this sort affect the economic climate abroad just as they do here.

A German executive, for example, will not be convinced by these explanations. Germany imports 95% of its oil (we import 50%), its government's share of gross domestic product is about 37% (ours is about 30%), and workers must be consulted on most major decisions. Yet Germany's rate of productivity growth has actually increased since 1970 and recently rose to more than four times ours. In France the situation is similar, yet today that country's productivity growth in manufacturing (despite current crises in steel and textiles) more than triples ours. No modern industrial nation is immune to the problems and pressures besetting U.S. business. Why then do we find a disportionate loss of competitive vigor by U.S. companies?

Our experience suggests that, to an unprecedented degree, success in most industries today requires an organizational commitment to compete in the marketplace on technological grounds—that is, to compete over the long run by offering superior products. Yet, guided by what they took to be the newest and best principles of management, American managers have increasingly directed their attention elsewhere. These new principles, despite their sophistication and widespread usefulness, encourage a preference for (1)analytic detachment rather than the insight that comes from "hands on" experience and (2)short-term cost reduction rather than long-term development of technological competitiveness. It is this new managerial gospel, we feel, that has played a major role in undermining the vigor of American industry.

American management, especially in the two decades after World War II, was universally admired for its strikingly effective performance. But times change. An approach shaped and refined during stable decades may be ill suited to a world characterized by rapid and unpredictable change, scarce energy, global competition for markets, and a constant need for innovation. This is the world of the 1980s and, probably, the rest of this century.

The time is long overdue for earnest, objective self-analysis. What exactly have American managers been doing wrong? What are the critical weaknesses in the ways that they have managed the technological performance of their companies? What is the matter with the long-unquestioned assumptions on which they have based their managerial policies and practices?

A Failure of Management

In the past, American managers earned worldwide respect for their carefully planned yet highly aggressive action across three different time frames:

- *Short term*—using existing assets as efficiently as possible.
- *Medium term*—replacing labor and other scarce resources with capital equipment.
- *Long term*—developing new products and processes that open new markets or restructure old ones.

The first of these time frames demanded toughness, determination, and close attention to detail; the second, capital and the willingness to take sizable financial risks; the third, imagination and a certain amount of technological daring.

Our managers still earn generally high marks for their skill in improving short-term efficiency, but their counterparts in Europe and Japan have started to question America's entrepreneurial imagination and willingness to make risky long-term competitive investments. As one such observer remarked to us: "The U.S. companies in my industry act like banks. All they are interested in is return on investment and getting their money back. Sometimes they act as though they are more interested in buying other companies than they are in selling products to customers."

In fact, this curt diagnosis represents a growing body of opinion that openly charges American managers with competitive myopia: "Somehow or other, American business is losing confidence in itself and especially confidence in its future. Instead of meeting the challenge of the changing world, American business today is making small, short-term adjustments by cutting costs and by turning to the government for temporary relief. . . .Success in trade is the result of patient and meticulous preparations, with a long period of market preparation before the rewards are available. . . .To undertake such commitments is hardly in the interest of a manager who is concerned with his or her next quarterly earnings reports.

More troubling still, American managers themselves often admit the charge with, at most, a rhetorical shrug of their shoulders. In established businesses, notes one senior vice president of research: "We understand how to market, we know the technology, and production problems are not extreme. Why risk money on new businesses when good, profitable low-risk opportunities are on every side?" Says another: "It's much more difficult to come up with a synthetic meat product than a lemon-lime cake mix. But you work on the lemon-lime cake mix because you know exactly what that return is going to be. A synthetic steak is going to take a lot longer, require a much bigger investment, and the risk of failure will be greater."

These managers are not alone; they speak for many. Why, they ask, should they invest dollars that are hard to earn back when it is so easy—and so much less risky—to make money in other ways? Why ignore a ready-made situation in cake mixes for the deferred and far less certain prospects in synthetic steaks? Why shoulder the competitive risks of making better, more innovative products?

In our judgment, the assumptions underlying these questions are prime evidence of a broad managerial failure—a failure of both vision and leadership—that over time has eroded both the inclination and the capacity of U.S. companies to innovate. . .

This conclusion is painful but must be faced. Responsibility for this competitive listlessness belongs not just to a set of external conditions but also to the attitudes, preoccupations, and practices of American managers. By their preference for servicing existing markets rather than creating new ones and by their devotion to short-term returns and "management by the numbers," many of them have effectively forsworn long-term technological superiority as a competitive weapon. In consequence, they have abdicated their strategic responsibilities.

The New Management Orthodoxy

We refuse to believe that this managerial failure is the result of a sudden psychological shift among American managers toward a "super-safe, no risk" mind set. No profound sea change in the character of thousands of individuals could have occurred in so organized a fashion or have produced so consistent a pattern of behavior. Instead we believe that during the past two decades American managers have increasingly relied on principles which prize analytical detachment and methodological elegance over insight, based on experience, into the subtleties and complexities of strategic decisions. As a result, maximum short-term financial returns have become the overriding criteria for many companies.

For purposes of discussion, we may divide this *new* management orthodoxy into three general categories: financial control, corporate portfolio management, and market-driven behavior.

Financial Control

As more companies decentralize their organizational structures, they tend to fix on profit centers as the primary unit of managerial responsibility. This development necessitates, in turn, greater dependence on short-term financial measurements like return on investment (ROI) for evaluating the performance of individual managers and management groups. Increasing the structural distance between those entrusted with exploiting actual competitive opportunities and those who must judge the quality of their work virtually guarantees reliance on objectivity quantifiable short-term criteria.

Although innovation, the lifeblood of any vital enterprise, is best encouraged by an environment that does not unduly penalize failure, the predictable result of relying too heavily on short-term financial measures—a sort of managerial remote control—is an environment in which no one feels he or she can afford a failure or even a momentary dip in the bottom line.

Corporate Portfolio Management

This preoccupation with control draws support from modern theories of financial portfolio management. Originally developed to help balance the overall risk and return of stock and bond portfolios, these principles have been applied increasingly to the creation and management of corporate portfolios—that is, a cluster of companies and product lines assembled through various modes of diversification under a single corporate umbrella. When applied by a remote group of dispassionate experts primarily concerned with finance and control and lacking hands-on experience, the analytic formulas of portfolio theory push managers even further toward an extreme of caution in allocating resources.

"Especially in large organizations," reports one manager, "we are observing an increase in management behavior which I would regard as excessively cautious, even passive; certainly overanalytical; and, in general, characterized by a studied unwillingness to assume responsibility and even reasonable risk."

Market-Driven Behavior

In the past 20 years, American companies have perhaps learned too well a lesson they had long been inclined to ignore: businesses should be customer oriented rather than product oriented. Henry Ford's famous dictum that the public could have any color automobile it wished as long as the color was black has since given way to its philosophical opposite: "We have got to stop marketing makeable products and learn to make marketable products."

At last, however, the dangers of too much reliance on this philosophy are becoming apparent. As two Canadian researchers have put it: "Inventors, scientists, engineers, and academics, in the normal pursuit of scientific knowledge, gave the world in recent times the laser, xerography, instant photography, and the transistor. In contrast, worshippers of the marketing concept have bestowed upon mankind such products as new-fangled potato chips, feminine hygiene deodorant, and the pet rock. . . ."

The argument that no new product ought to be introduced without managers undertaking a market analysis is common sense. But the argument that consumer analyses and formal market surveys should dominate other considerations when allocating resources to product development is untenable. It may be useful to remember that the initial market estimate for computers in 1945 projected total worldwide sales of only ten units. Similarly, even the most carefully researched analysis of consumer preferences for gas-guzzling cars in an era of gasoline abundance offers little useful guidance to today's automobile manufacturers in making wise product investment decisions. Customers may know what

41

their needs are, but they often define those needs in terms of existing products, processes, markets, and prices.

Deferring to a market-driven strategy without paying attention to its limitations is, quite possibly, opting for customer satisfaction and lower risk in the short run at the expense of superior products in the future. Satisfied customers are critically important, of course, but not if the strategy for creating them is responsible as well for unnecessary product proliferation, inflated costs, unfocused diversification, and a lagging commitment to new technology and new capital equipment.

Three Managerial Decisions

These are serious charges to make. But the unpleasant fact of the matter is that, however useful these new principles may have been initially, if carried too far they are bad for U.S. business. Consider, for example, their effect on three major kinds of choices regularly faced by corporate managers: the decision between imitative and innovative product design, the decision to integrate backward, and the decision to invest in process development.

Imitative vs. Innovative Product Design

A market-driven strategy requires new product ideas to flow from detailed market analysis or, at least, to be extensively tested for consumer reaction before actual introduction. It is no secret that these requirements add significant delays and costs to the introduction of new products. It is less well known that they also predispose managers toward developing products for existing markets and toward product designs of an imitative rather than an innovative nature. There is in-

creasing evidence that market-driven strategies tend, over time, to dampen the general level of innovation in new product decisions.

Confronted with the choice between innovation and imitation, managers typically ask whether the marketplace shows any consistent preference for innovative products. If so, the additional funding they require may be economically justified; if not, those funds can more properly go to advertising, promoting, or reducing the prices of less-advanced products. Though the temptation to allocate resources so as to strengthen performance in existing products and markets is often irresistible, recent studies by J. Hugh Davidson and others confirm the strong market attractiveness of innovative products.

Nonetheless, managers having to decide between innovative and imitative product design face a difficult series of marketing-related trade-offs.

By its very nature, innovative design is, as Joseph Schumpeter observed a long time ago, initially destructive of capital— whether in the form of labor skills, management systems, technological processes, or capital equipment. It tends to make obsolete existing investments in both marketing and manufacturing organizations. For the managers concerned it represents the choice of uncertainty (about economic returns, timing, etc.) over relative predictability, exchanging the reasonable expectation of current income against the promise of high future value. It is the choice of the gambler, the person willing to risk much to gain even more.

Conditioned by a market-driven strategy and held closely to account by a "results now" ROI-oriented control system, American managers have increasingly refused to take the chance on innovative product/market development. As one of them confesses: "In the last year, on the basis of high capital risk, I turned down new products at a rate at least twice what I did a year ago. But in every case I tell my people to go back and bring me some new product ideas." In truth, they have learned caution so well that many are in danger of forgetting that market-driven, follow-the-leader companies usually end up following the rest of the pack as well.

Backward Integration

Sometimes the problem for managers is not their reluctance to take action and make investments but that, when they do so, their action has the unintended result of reinforcing the status quo. In deciding to integrate backward because of apparent short-term rewards, managers often restrict their ability to strike out in innovative directions in the future.

Consider, for example, the case of a manufacturer who purchases a major component from an outside company. Static analysis of production economies may very well show that backward integration offers rather substantial cost benefits. Eliminating certain purchasing and marketing functions, centralizing overhead, pooling R&D efforts and resources, coordinating design and production of both product and component, reducing uncertainty over design changes, allowing for the use of more specialized equipment and labor skills— in all these ways and more, backward integration holds out to management the promise of significant short-term increases in ROI.

These efficiencies may be achieved by companies with commoditylike products.

In such industries as ferrous and nonferrous metals or petroleum, backward integration toward raw materials and supplies tends to have a strong, positive effect on profits. However, the situation is markedly different for companies in more technological active industries. Where there is considerable exposure to rapid technological advances, the promised value of backward integration becomes problematic. It may provide a quick, short-term boost to ROI figures in the next annual report, but it may also paralyze the long-term ability of a company to keep on top of technological change.

The real competitive threats to technologically active companies arise less from changes in ultimate consumer preference than from abrupt shifts in component technologies, raw materials, or production processes. Hence those managers whose attention is too firmly directed toward the marketplace and near-term profits may suddenly discover that their decision to make rather than buy important parts has locked their companies into an outdated technology. . . .

Long-term contracts and long-term relationships with suppliers can achieve many of the same cost benefits as backward integration without calling into question a company's ability to innovate or respond to innovation. European automobile manufacturers, for example, have typically chosen to rely on their suppliers in this way; American companies have followed the path of backward integration. The resulting trade-offs between production efficiencies and innovative flexibility should offer a stern warning to those American managers too easily beguiled by the lure of short-term ROI improvement. A case in point: the U.S. auto industry's huge investment in automating the manufacture of cast-iron brake drums probably delayed by more than five years its transition to disc brakes.

Process Development

In an era of management by the numbers, many American managers—especially in mature industries—are reluctant to invest heavily in the development of new manufacturing processes. When asked to explain their reluctance, they tend to respond in fairly predictable ways. "We can't afford to design new capital equipment for just our own manufacturing needs." is one frequent answer. So is: "The capital equipment producers do a much better job, and they can amortize their development costs over sales to many companies." Perhaps most common is: "Let the others experiment in manufacturing; we can learn from their mistakes and do it better."

Each of these comments rests on the assumption that essential advances in process technology can be appropriated more easily through equipment purchase than through in-house equipment design and development. Our extensive conversations with the managers of European (primarily German) technology-based companies have convinced us that this assumption is not as widely shared abroad as in the United States. Virtually across the board, the European managers impressed us with their strong commitment to increasing market share through internal development of advanced process technology—even when their suppliers were highly responsive to technological advances.

By contrast, American managers tend to restrict investments in process development to only those items likely to reduce costs in the short run. Not all are happy with this. As one disgruntled executive told us: "For too long U.S. managers have been taught to set low priorities on mechanization projects, so that eventually divestment appears to be the best way out of manufacturing difficulties. Why?

"The drive for short-term success has prevented managers from looking thoroughly into the matter of special manufacturing equipment, which has to be invented, developed, tested, redesigned, reproduced, improved, and so on. That's a long process, which needs experienced, knowledgeable, and dedicated people who stick to their jobs over a considerable period of time. Merely buying new equipment (even if it is possible) does not often give the company any advantage over competitors."

We agree. Most American managers seem to forget that, even if they produce new products with their existing process technology (the same "cookie cutter" everyone else can buy), their competitors will face a relatively short lead time for introducing similar products. And as Eric von Hipple's studies of industrial innovation show, the innovations on which new industrial equipment is based usually originate with the user of the equipment and not with the equipment producer. In other words, companies can make products more profitable by investing in the development of their own process technology. Proprietary processes are every bit as formidable competitive weapons as proprietary products.

The American Managerial Ideal

Two very important questions remain to be asked: (1)Why should so many American managers have shifted so strongly to this new managerial orthodoxy? and (2)Why are they not more deeply bothered by the ill effects of those principles on the long-term technological competitiveness of their companies? To answer the first question, we must take a look at the changing career patterns of American managers during the past quarter century; to answer the second, we must understand the way in which they have come to regard their professional roles and responsibilities as managers.

The Road to the Top

During the past 25 years the American manager's road to the top has changed significantly. No longer does the typical career, threading sinuously up and through a corporation with stops in several functional areas, provide future top executives with intimate hands-on knowledge of the company's technologies, customers, and suppliers. . .

In addition, companies are increasingly choosing to fill new top management posts from outside their own ranks. In the opinion of foreign observers, who are still accustomed to long-term careers in the same company or division, "High-level American executives. . . seem to come and go and switch around as if playing a game of musical chairs at an Alice in Wonderland tea party."

Far more important, however, than any absolute change in numbers is the shift in the general sense of what an aspiring manager has to be "smart about" to make it to the top. More important still is the broad change in attitude such trends both encourage and express. What has developed, in the business community as in academia, is a preoccupation with a false and shallow concept of the professional manager, a "pseudo-professional" really—an individual having no special expertise in any particular industry or

technology who nevertheless can step into an unfamiliar company and run it successfully through strict application of financial controls, portfolio concepts, and a market-driven strategy.

The Gospel of Pseudo-Professionalism

In recent years, this idealization of pseudo-professionalism has taken on something of the quality of a corporate religion. Its first doctrine, appropriately enough, is that neither industry experience nor hands-on technological expertise counts for very much. At one level, of course, this doctrine helps to salve the conscience of those who lack them. At another, more disturbing level it encourages the faithful to make decisions about technological matters simply as if they were adjuncts to finance or marketing decisions. We do not believe that the technological issues facing managers today can be meaningfully addressed without taking into account marketing or financial considerations; on the other hand, neither can they be resolved with the same methodologies applied to these other fields.

Complex modern technology has its own inner logic and developmental imperatives. To treat it as if it were something else—no matter how comfortable one is with that other kind of data—is to base a competitive business on a two-legged stool, which must, no matter how excellent the balancing act, inevitably fall to the ground.

More disturbing still, true believers keep the faith on a day-to-day basis by insisting that as issues rise up the managerial hierarchy for decision they be progressively distilled into easily quantifiable terms. One European manager, in recounting to us his experiences in a joint venture with an American company, recalled with exasperation that "U.S. managers want everything to be simple. But sometimes business situations are not simple, and they cannot be divided up or looked at in such a way that they become simple. They are messy, and one must try to understand all the facets. This appears to be alien to the American mentality."

The purpose of good organizational design, of course, is to divide responsibilities in such a way that individuals have relatively easy tasks to perform. But then these differentiated responsibilities must be pulled together by sophisticated, broadly gauged integrators at the top of the managerial pyramid. If these individuals are interested in but one or two aspects of the total competitive picture, if their training includes a very narrow exposure to the range of functional specialties, if—worst of all—they are devoted simplifiers themselves, who will do the necessary integration? Who will attempt to resolve complicated issues rather than try to uncomplicate them artificially? At the strategic level there are no such things as pure production problems, pure financial problems, or pure marketing problems.

Merger Mania

When executive suites are dominated by people with financial and legal skills, it is not surprising that top management should increasingly allocate time and energy to such concerns as cash management and the whole process of corporate acquisitions and mergers. This is indeed what has happened. In 1978 alone there were some 80 mergers involving companies with assets in excess of $100 million each; in 1979 there were almost 100. This represents roughly $20 billion in transfers of large companies from one owner to another—two-thirds of the total amount spent on R&D by American industry.

In 1978 *Business Week* ran a cover story on cash management in which it stated that "the 400 largest U.S. companies together have more than $60 billion in cash—almost triple the amount they had at the beginning of the 1970s." The article also described the increasing attention devoted to—and the sophisticated and exotic techniques used for—managing this cash hoard.

There are perfectly good reasons for this flurry of activity. It is entirely natural for financially (or legally) trained managers to concentrate on essentially financial (or legal) activities. It is also natural for managers who subscribe to the portfolio "law of large numbers" to seek to reduce total corporate risk by parceling it out among a sufficiently large number of separate product lines, businesses, or technologies. Under certain conditions it may very well make good economic sense to buy rather than build new plants or modernize existing ones. Mergers are obviously an exciting game; they tend to produce fairly quick and decisive results, and they offer the kind of public recognition that helps careers along. Who can doubt the appeal of the titles awarded by the financial community; being called a "gunslinger," "white knight," or "raider" can quicken anyone's blood.

Unfortunately, the general American penchant for separating and simplifying has tended to encourage a diversification away from core technologies and markets to a much greater degree than is true in Europe or Japan. U.S. managers appear to have an inordinate faith in the portfolio law of large numbers—that is, by amassing enough product lines, technologies, and businesses, one will be cushioned against the random setbacks that occur in life. This might be true for portfolios of stocks and bonds, where there is considerable evidence that setbacks *are* random. Businesses, however, are subject not only to random setbacks such as strikes and shortages but also to carefully orchestrated attacks by competitors, who focus all their resources and energies on one set of activities.

Worse, the great bulk of this merger activity appears to have been absolutely wasted in terms of generating economic benefits for stockholders. Acquisition experts do not necessarily make good managers. Nor can they increase the value of their shares by merging two companies any better than their shareholders could do individually by buying shares of the acquired company on the open market (at a price usually below that required for a takeover attempt).

There appears to be a growing recognition of this fact. A number of U.S. companies are now divesting themselves of previously acquired companies; others (for example, W.R. Grace) are proposing to break themselves up into relatively independent entities. The establishment of a strong competitive position through in-house technological superiority is by nature a long, arduous, and often unglamorous task. But it is what keeps a business vigorous and competitive.

The European Example

Gaining competitive success through technological superiority is a skill much valued by the seasoned European (and Japanese) managers with whom we talked. Although we were able to locate few hard statistics on their actual practice, our extensive investigations of more than 20 companies convinced us that European managers do indeed tend to differ significantly from their American counterparts. In fact, we found that many of them were able to articulate these differences quite clearly.

In the first place, European managers think themselves more pointedly concerned with how to survive over the long run under intensely competitive conditions. Few markets, of course, generate price competition as fierce as in the United States, but European companies face the remorseless necessity of exporting to other national markets or perishing.

The figures here are startling: manufactured product exports represent more than 35% of total manufacturing sales in France and Germany and nearly 60% in the Benelux countries, as against not quite 10% in the United States. In these export markets, moreover, European products must hold their own against "world class" competitors, lower-priced products from developing countries, and American products selling at attractive devalued dollar prices. To survive this competitive squeeze, European managers feel they must place central emphasis on producing technologically superior products.

Further, the kinds of pressures from European labor unions and national governments virtually force them to take a consistently long-term view in decision making. German managers, for example, must negotiate major decisions at the plant level with worker-dominated works councils; in turn, these decisions are subject to review by supervisory boards (roughly equivalent to American boards of directors), half of whose membership is worker elected. Together with strict national legislation, the pervasive influence of labor unions makes it extremely difficult to change employment levels or production locations. Not surprisingly, labor costs in Northern Europe have more than doubled in the past decade and are now the highest in the world.

To be successful in this environment of strictly constrained options, European managers feel they must employ a decision-making apparatus that grinds very fine—and very deliberately. They must simply outthink and outmanage their competitors. Now, American managers also have their strategic options hedged about by all kinds of restrictions. But those restrictions have not yet made them as conscious as their European counterparts of the long-term implications of their day-to-day decisions.

As a result, the Europeans see themselves as investing more heavily in cutting-edge technology than the Americans. More often than not, this investment is made to create new product opportunities in advance of consumer demand and not merely in response to market-driven strategy. In case after case, we found the Europeans striving to develop the products and process capabilities with which to lead markets and not

simply responding to the current demands of the marketplace. Moreover, in doing this they seem less inclined to integrate backward and more likely to seek maximum leverage from stable, long-term, relationships with suppliers.

Having never lost sight of the need to be technologically competitive over the long run, European and Japanese managers are extremely careful to make the necessary arrangements and investments today. And their daily concern with the rather basic issue of long-term survival adds perspective to such matters as short-term ROI or rate of growth. The time line by which they manage is long, and it has made them painstakingly attentive to the means for keeping their companies technologically competitive. Of course they pay attention to the numbers. Their profit margins are usually lower than ours, their debt ratios higher. Every tenth of a percent is critical to them. But they are also aware that tomorrow will be no better unless they constantly try to develop new processes, enter new markets, and offer superior—even unique—products. As one senior German executive phrased it recently, "We look at rates of return, too, but only after we ask 'Is it a good product?' ". . .

● ● ●

NO

John W. Kendrick

PRODUCTIVITY AND ECONOMIC GROWTH

. . . Both major political parties have embraced the objective of stimulating investment, productivity, and economic growth, as evidenced by the recent unanimous reports of the Joint Economic Committee and by the 1980 political platforms. It is recognized that stronger productivity growth will help attain other economic objectives. It will clearly make possible larger increases in planes of living. Although the effects of slower productivity growth on real income per capita were mitigated by increasing ratios of labor force to population from the mid-1960s, this trend will be reversed in the 1980s, making stronger productivity advance all the more essential to rising real income per capita. The associated higher growth of real GNP will also ease the burdens of rising national security outlays and of the higher investment ratios needed not only to accelerate productivity growth but to meet other social objectives, including greater energy independence.

An increase in the rate of productivity growth will also be helpful in bringing the rate of inflation down. To reduce the rate of inflation will require reducing the rate at which labor costs per unit of output rise. The rise of unit labor costs is compounded of the rates at which average hourly compensation and output per hour or productivity rise. Although no realistically forseeable acceleration of productivity will eliminate the need for slowing down the rise of hourly compensation, feasible acceleration of productivity will moderate the slowdown of compensation increases that is required and so make it easier to achieve.

Productivity growth is also related to employment rates. My studies show that in periods of slow productivity growth, unemployment rates are above average, and that when productivity increases more strongly, they are lower. This is because above average productivity growth is associated with higher rates of investment and growth of capital per worker, which stimulate the growth of demand, output, and employment.

From, "Curriculum for Economics 1981: Productivity and Economic Growth", *The AEI Economist* (November 1980) ©1980, American Enterprise Institute. Reprinted by permission.

IS THE DECLINE IN PRODUCTIVITY DUE TO MANAGEMENT?

Some observers assert that the higher growth of productivity in most other industrialized countries reduces the international competitiveness of the U.S. economy, and that this is another reason for promoting productivity growth here. Actually, much of the higher growth abroad has been due to a catching up with U.S. levels of technology. Productivity growth has slowed abroad in the 1970s and may slow further in the 1980s as the technological gap narrows further. But the underlying reasoning is questionable under a regime of floating exchange rates.

It should also be noted that in many countries factor prices have risen more than in the United States, resulting in a faster growth of unit costs and prices despite better productivity performance. Certainly, U.S. exports have expanded strongly despite the productivity slowdown. Yet it is true that domestic industries whose productivity growth has lagged the most have been most vulnerable to foreign competition. In addition, these industries often lose market shares to other domestic industries with superior productivity and price performance. But there will always be declining industries, and the possible role of government policy in these cases is a lively issue, addressed below. . . .

The Roles of the Private and Public Sectors in Growth

As Herbert Stein noted in his introduction to this series in the June 1980 *AEI Economist*, to an important extent the growth rate in our type of economy is the result of numerous decisions by individuals as members of households, firms, and private nonprofit organizations. Thus, choices between work and leisure affect labor force participation, employment rates, and hours worked. The allocation of income between consumption and saving, and the demand for money, as reflected in interest rates, affect the volume of tangible nonhuman investment.

Decisions to invest in oneself and one's children affect the rate of growth of human capital and thus the quality of labor input. Choices among goods and services result in resource reallocations, and decisions regarding relocation affect the rapidity of the adjustments of labor. Basic values and attitudes of individuals affect the intensity of their work efforts. But in all these areas, and others, the policies of governments condition the decisions and actions of households, firms, and other actors in the private economy.

The types and rates of taxation affect patterns of expenditure and decisions to work, save, and invest. Budget balances augment private saving when in surplus, and compete with private investment for funds when negative. Monetary policies affect interest rates and actual or expected changes in the general price level and thus the levels of private saving and investment. Government and credit institutions and loan guarantee programs affect the allocation and volume of lending, and industry-specific measures affect resource allocations generally. Across-the-board policies designed to promote private enterprise, and social regulations that impose costs, not only have generalized effects but also usually have different industry impacts affecting relative growth rates.

On the expenditure side of fiscal policy, the composition of outlays can have a major impact on productivity. A substantial portion of expenditures represents investments, tangible and intangible—for construction, equipment, natural resource development, education, training, health, safety, and mobility. The aggregates and composition of these developmental outlays affect productivity not only in the private economy but in government activities.

Finally, macroeconomic policies affect cyclical movements, and to the extent that the sum of public policies promotes, or retards, economic growth, they have an effect on economies of scale. One might also mention that the pronouncements of public officials, as well as their actions, affect private attitudes and plans. In particular, investment decisions of businessmen are influenced by their perceptions of the rationality, predictability, and probable effectiveness of government economic policies as a whole.

This quick review of the many types of public policies that affect growth, and the many causal forces that can be affected, indicates that even if it were considered desirable, governments could not pursue a strictly neutral policy with respect to growth, letting the achieved growth rate reflect the composite of relevant individual decisions. Further, in a democracy public officials have the legitimate function of trying to balance the various objectives of the electorate, including growth of productivity and real income per head, and to attain the optimum combination of the objectives.

Although there is a general agreement now that promoting the growth of productivity should rank higher in the scale of national objectives, this does not mean that everything that would speed up the growth of productivity should be done. In general the measures that might be taken would have some costs, and the more powerful measures would probably have

larger costs. Many of the costs show up in the budget, in the forms of lower tax revenues resulting from reduced taxes and of higher expenditures for such purposes as research and development.

These costs reflect a more fundamental problem. Speeding up growth will require use of more of the nation's output for investment, research, and education, and that means less for other purposes— consumption being the largest—at least until total output has grown substantially. The transfer of resource-use from consumption to investment is likely to involve a shift in the distribution of after-tax income to higher income people; some may regard this shift as a cost even though in time the incomes of everyone will be raised. Revision of some government regulations that impede growth may involve a cost in the form of more pollution or industrial accidents. Many other kinds of costs can be imagined in the growth-producing process. . . .

Labor Input

This country does not have a coherent population policy, although government policies affect birth, death, and immigration rates. Certainly labor force participation and employment rates are affected. Since the mid-1960s, growth of the labor force and, to lesser extents, employment and hours worked have accelerated, mitigating somewhat the impact of the productivity slowdown on real income per capita.

In the 1980s, however, labor force growth will slow significantly and the dependency ratio begin to increase. In view of the real income effect, and the increasing burden of social security retirement payments on the active population, policies to promote the growth of the

51

labor force and employment should be considered, particularly increased incentives to work and reduced incentives for early retirement.

The declining labor force participation of youth reflects increases in average years of schooling, which are presumed to enhance productivity. But the declining labor force participation rates of men over fifty-five and women over sixty-five could be slowed by a variety of measures. Legislation prohibiting employers from establishing a mandatory retirement age less than seventy was a step in the right direction, and the next step could be to eliminate blanket mandatory retirement requirements altogether. If the earnings test for old age benefits were also eliminated or further liberalized, more older people would choose to continue working. The degree to which resulting increases in general tax revenues would offset the increase in benefit payments cannot be precisely estimated, but it is substantial. Increases in the ages at which individuals become eligible for partial and full benefits from sixty-two and sixty-five to, say, sixty-four and sixty-eight, would also increase the proportions of older workers as well as lighten the social security burden. The expansion of part-time jobs, flexitime schedules, and job enrichment programs would encourage more oldsters, and others, to continue working, and further reduction of age discrimination would create more opportunities. Taxation of all or part of old age benefits would further increase the incentives to work, just as taxation of unemployment benefits would tend to reduce periods of unemployment and thus the unemployment rate. The increasing resistance to rising social security tax rates, rising longevity, and stagnant real take home pay suggest

that a social consensus might support a change in the old standards.

Saving, Investment, and Technological Progress

In recent years declines in saving ratios and in the growth of real capita per unit of labor have contributed measurably to lagging productivity advance. An important contributing factor has been the reduced rates of return on investment in the 1970s compared with the 1960s, when allowance is made for the erosion of book profits by higher inflation. High and unstable inflation rates have been a major deterrent to saving and investment in recent years. Among other things it has led to a recurrent cyclical process in which, first, cost increases gather momentum, and then an effort is made to curb the resulting inflation by restrictive monetary policy. This gives rise to a squeeze on profit margins in cycle peak years as well as to a credit crunch. The prospect of this is discouraging to private investment. Achieving a reasonable degree of price stability would be a major contributor to faster productivity growth. The July issue of the *AEI Economist* dealt with this. . . .

A basic problem—one that helps explain why the U.S. ratio of saving and investment to GNP is lower than in other industrialized nations—is that the federal tax system militates against saving and investment.* With some exceptions, the income out of which saving is made is taxed, and so, too, is the income from the investments into which saving flows. This represents a form of double taxation of

---

*[Eds. note]: The impact of Governmental tax policies on business is discussed further in Issue 8.

saving. The double taxation of dividends beyond the first hundred dollars is well known. The 70 percent top bracket tax rate on property income, compared with the 50 percent maximum on income from labor, represents further discrimination. . . .

There are other ways to promote technological progress: revising the patent system; expanding the dissemination of scientific and technological information; clarifying antitrust policy; using government procurement to stimulate innovation; promoting industry-university cooperation in R & D and generic technology centers; and fostering the formation and development of small innovative firms. President Carter made some proposals under these headings in his "industrial innovation initiatives" of October 31, 1979. Many have not been implemented, however, while others have been initiated on a very small scale. In 1981 the initiatives and proposals should be reviewed and expanded, with strengthened support for those that are most promising.

Returning to investment, further reductions in the capital gains tax, at least back to the pre-1969 rates, would provide further stimulus, particularly for formation of new businesses, one incentive for which is the possibility of capital gains. This effect is attested to by the surge of new incorporations in 1979 following enactment of the Steiger amendment. Revenues at reduced rates tend to rise, at least for a time, because of reduction of the "lock-in" effect on security holders with unrealized capital gains. More equitable would be the indexation of capital gains to avoid what is in effect a capital levy in inflationary periods.

Savings can be encouraged by a variety of measures in addition to increasing returns on investment: exemption of larger amounts of dividends and similar amounts of interest receipts from the personal income tax; expansion of the scope of tax-deferred saving and investment plans (such as the Keough and IRA plans); reduction of the maximum tax on property income; and, of course, reduced personal income tax rates generally. The last-named measure would be less effective in increasing saving than the others per dollar of revenue loss, since it does not change the incentive to save rather than consume. While reduced tax rates on property income would probably elicit more saving, the effects of lower rates on labor income on the supply of labor are not well known, as pointed out in the April 1980 issue of this publication. . . .

Resource Reallocations and Industry Policy

Shifts of labor and capital from uses and industries with below-average rates of remuneration to those that are above average have contributed to economic growth in the past. The contribution declined after 1973 in part because the shift out of agriculture slowed as that sector shrank and its relative rates of remuneration rose. But dynamic changes in the economy, reflected in shifts in industry demand and supply functions and relative price changes, are continually creating new opportunities for profitable resource shifts. The magnitude of the effects depends in part on the sensitivity with which the market price system reflects changes in the forces of supply and demand, and in part on the degree of mobility of resources and the speed with which they respond to price signals.

Vigorous competition is a major force driving the private economy to higher levels of productivity. Maintenance of a liberal international trade policy strengthens the forces of competition, of course. The antitrust laws are another way we try to preserve that competition. But we need to consider again whether those laws, as now drafted, interpreted, and administered, are sacrificing their basic objectives of competition and efficiency to the protection of existing interests and the perpetuation of groundless hostility against bigness. Policies with respect to mergers, patent rights, and collaboration on R & D are especially critical from this standpoint.

Even in the regulated industries the trend toward greater reliance by regulatory agencies on competition, free entry, and market pricing should be extended. Where regulation of natural monopolies is necessary, the rate-making power might be used more ingeniously to promote productivity—for example, by permitting a return somewhat in excess of the cost of capital when superior productivity results are demonstrated. This more closely approximates the outcome of competitive markets in providing rewards and incentives for innovation and efficiency. . . .

With regard to labor mobility, programs to train, retrain, place, and, where necessary, relocate displaced workers under the Comprehensive Employment and Training Act, on which tens of billions of dollars have been spent, need to be critically examined. Capital has always been quite mobile as investors seek to maximize rates of return consistent with other objectives. Lower capital gains taxes would reduce their lock-in effect, as noted above. Accelerated depreciation would promote the reallocation of funds invested in fixed capital. More flexible land-use laws, consistent with other ob-

jectives, would also raise total productivity. The mobility of both human and nonhuman resources is promoted by relatively full employment, discussed below.

In a predominantly free enterprise economy, changes in the industrial composition of GNP have generally been the result of market forces, reflecting changes in factor prices and productivity on the supply side, and in demand, particularly on the part of the sovereign consumer. Yet government has frequently intervened to assist particular industries, or to dampen the demand for the products of other industries. In the past year or so there has been a revival of discussions of industrial policy under various rubrics, sometimes called the Four Rs: reindustrialization, revitalization, renewal, and reelection!

To the extent that industrial policy comprises measures to promote productivity and economic growth generally, it involves the basic issues that this essay is all about. To the extent that it involves picking the potential winners, and assisting companies and industries with above-average prospects for increasing productivity and sales, the case for the policy depends on confidence in the superior ability of government to do the picking, which is in doubt, although there may be cases in which the government does have a special ability. The policy makes some sense subject to the constraint that the assistance be confined to the infancy stage of the industries and that it is then gradually withdrawn as they grow. This is the rationale behind tariff protection of "infant industries," assistance to small business by subsidized loans, procurement policies, and other means. But protection or assistance must be phased out as the companies or industries become competitive in order not to subsidize inefficiency.

To the extent that industrial policy involves assisting losers—companies and industries with below-average increases or declines in both productivity and sales—the policy does not make sense on a long-term basis. It can be defended as a short-term response to temporary problems, the solution of which would enhance the probability of competitive viability in the long-run. If, for example, the problems of Chrysler stem from the recent recession and the time-lags involved in converting facilities to production of a car that will revive the fortunes of the company as markets expand, assistance can be rationalized. Similarly, measures to assist the steel industry during an extensive modernization effort can be justified if the measures will enhance competitiveness in the long run. But unless the longer-term prospects are encouraging, assistance of declining firms and industries is a sure formula for retarding growth of productivity and output in the national economy. Again, the ability of the government to assess the future prospects of the industry better than private investors do is the critical requirement for success. The better approach is to facilitate the transfer of resources to expanding industries, as is now attempted for labor under the Economic Development Act. National security considerations may, however, dictate protection of a given minimum productive capacity in key industries concentrated in the most efficient firms and plants.

Macroeconomic Policies and the Government-Business Relationship

. . . With respect to the government-business interface, on the negative side there is no doubt that the proliferation of regulations since the late 1960s has increased real costs and inputs, but not measured output. It is doubtful if economic welfare has yet been raised by regulatory initiatives as much as the real costs have grown. But the public outcry, especially from business, has been so great that progress is being made in rationalizing regulations. Executive Order 12044 requires early public involvement before enactment of new regulations, coordination of agency activities, and improvement in methods for evaluation of proposed and existing regulations. Beyond that, efficiency and innovation would be promoted by greater reliance on economic incentives (for example, effluent taxes and fees) to accomplish regulatory goals. More emphasis should be put on performance standards rather than on regulating technology. The uncertainties of regulation should be reduced, and consistencies of measures increased. Beyond that, Congress might consider broadening the mandate of the various regulatory agencies to require them to consider the undesirable side-effects of their actions, with particular respect to innovation, productivity, costs, and product variety. Some critics propose regulatory budgets to force agencies to concentrate on measures that promise the greatest benefits relative to cost ceilings. The important point is that pressures must be kept on the new Congress and administration in 1981 and beyond to ensure that regulations continue only where it has been demonstrated that the benefits achieved are clearly worth their cost.

On the plus side, government renders valuable services to business and the broader community. It is important that investments in infrastructure be undertaken whenever the social rates of return exceed the rental cost of the capital. Even though Congress appears allergic to the public capital budget concept, business-like principles in selecting capital projects for approval should be applied. And as noted above, government administrators must be as diligent as company managements in continually seeking to improve the productivity of both the capital and the labor that are employed in the public service. . . .

As can be readily seen from the foregoing discussion, a great many aspects of government policy affect the growth of productivity. But all of the more powerful ones, at least, have important consequences other than their impacts on productivity. This creates a problem for the organization of the federal executive decision-making process to give due weight to the productivity objective. Obviously, responsibility for tax policy, education policy, research policy, competition policy, and so on cannot all be transferred to an agency whose primary or exclusive goal is more rapid productivity growth. For the agencies charged with these responsibilities productivity growth is only one of many objectives, and it is not likely to be a primary one. Attempts were made to remedy this situation during the 1970s by the establishment of successive multipartite commissions on productivity, including key government officials. These were not effective. For the official members, productivity growth was a remote and academic concern, and the commission staffs were too far out of the policy-making flow to have any influence. A better solution might be to charge a White House officer, possibly one of the members of the Council of Economic Advisers, with responsibility for representing the long-run interest in productivity. He could be a member of the group of five or six officials that seems inevitably to develop at the center of government to oversee economic policy, and he could make his case on policy decisions as they flow through the government. The main requirement for success will be that the president give weight to the objective of raising productivity growth, even though the benefits during his own term of office may be small.

It must be admitted that economists know all too little about the quantitative relation between policy actions and the growth of productivity. We cannot say if such and such an action is taken with respect to tax rates, or regulations, or research expenditures, for example, it will be followed by such and such a result in faster productivity growth. But there is little doubt that if certain measures are taken we can improve the growth of productivity. These measures will involve sacrifice for a time—most importantly, a slowdown in the rate of growth of consumption The counterpart of this sacrifice may have to be a slowdown of government expenditures of kinds that do not promote growth, deferral of tax reductions that mainly stimulate consumption, and even increases of taxes of kinds that restrain consumption. But it is my belief that this sacrifice would be of short duration and that within a few years per capita consumption would be higher than it would be in the absence of an effective growth-oriented program.

● ● ●

POSTSCRIPT

IS THE DECLINE IN U.S. PRODUCTIVITY THE RESULT OF A FAILURE OF MANAGEMENT?

Professors Hayes and Abernathy discount the conventional wisdom of the conservative-liberal camp on the grounds that declining productivity is a uniquely North American phenomenon. If our recent experiences could be traced to general economic conditions such as the worldwide inflation, the impact of OPEC or any number of other general economic events, then these same events should depress productivity in other parts of the world. They do not find this to be the case.

Thus Hayes and Abernathy look to management policy and practices as the root cause of our problems. They maintain that management's pursuit of three policies has led to our current situation. First, organizational decentralization with management's focus upon "profit centers," results in firms maximizing shortrun profits and avoiding at all costs even "a momentary dip in the bottom line." Second, the use of portfolio management—carefully monitoring rates of return—to judge the effectiveness of various diversified profit centers under one corporate umbrella, does not provide any "hands-on" experience for top management. This results in extremely cautious corporate behavior. Third, corporate concern with customers rather than products may lower short run risks, but this lower risk may be at the expense of superior products in the long run.

Professor Kendrick places no blame upon corporate management. Rather he asserts that declining productivity can be traced to i)government regulations which stifle initiatives and increase business costs; ii)a federal tax system which "militates against savings and investment;" iii)government expenditure programs which do not promote growth; and iv)general economic conditions such as high energy prices, inflation or the changing composition of the work force. The implications of this phenomenon are then detailed: Public policy must be designed to eliminate or at least minimize these market interferences.

Much has been written about productivity in recent years. Several excellent books by Edward F. Denison are ACCOUNTING FOR SLOWER ECONOMIC GROWTH: THE UNITED STATES IN THE 1970S (Brookings Institute, 1979) and ACCOUNTING FOR UNITED STATES ECONOMIC GROWTH, 1929-1969 (Brookings Institute, 1974). Another general reference is the National Commission of Productivity and Work Quality, *Fourth Annual Report* (March, 1975). Additionally, a series of three articles appeared in the October, 1980 *Wall Street Journal*. These articles were written by Ralph Winter and appeared as lead articles on October 13, 21, and 28, 1980. Lastly, Professor Abernathy, who is an expert on the automobile industry, has also written THE PRODUCTIVITY DILEMMA: ROADBLOCK TO INNOVATION IN THE AUTOMOBILE INDUSTRY (Johns Hopkins University Press, 1978).

ISSUE 3

HAS ANTITRUST POLICY GONE TOO FAR?

YES: Robert H. Bork, from THE ANTITRUST PARADOX: A POLICY AT WAR WITH ITSELF (New York: Basic Books, Inc. Publishers, 1978).
NO: John M. Kuhlman, from "In a Lifeboat with an Elephant", Perry Seminar, University of Missouri, Columbia (1979).

ISSUE SUMMARY

YES: Bork is persuaded that the basic premises upon which current antitrust policy is founded, are incompatible with competition. As a result, antitrust policy is "at war with itself."
NO: Kuhlman is convinced that current antitrust policy has not gone far enough. He likens the existence of large firms competing in the same markets with small firms to being in a "lifeboat with an elephant."

More than ninety years ago, Congress recognized that the economic power of the large corporation had to be contained. Thus they passed our first antitrust legislation, the Sherman Act of 1890. This Act and the Clayton Antitrust Act of 1914 were intended to impede the progress of the great merger movement which was dominating the economy at the turn of the century.

Combines of many large and small firms were pulled together in what became known as "trusts": the Whiskey Trust, the Sugar Trust, the Cotton-Oil Trust, the Standard Oil Trust, were names that dominated not only the headlines on the financial pages but also the front page news of many daily papers. The trusts, which provided a mechanism for firms to collectively reduce supply and increase price, were often controlled by a few financial groups and individual families such as the Morgans, the Rockefellers, the DuPonts, the Mellons and the Carnegies. The abuses inflicted on society by these firms were so in conflict with the tenets of a free market economy that immediate and decisive steps were needed.

However, although decisive steps may have been needed, decisive steps have not been taken consistently. As a result antitrust policy has a long history of vacillation. In its early years under President Theodore Roosevelt, a tiny staff made great progress in tackling corporate giants with the aid of public opinion. In the process they established the "rule of reason": monopolies were not considered illegal unless they established or exercised their market position in an "unreasonable" manner. After an initial burst of activity during the early 1900s, public opinion began to sway to the side of big business. It was not until the anti-business environment of the New Deal Era that new life was breathed into the antitrust movement. Under Franklin D. Roosevelt's administration, active prosecution of antitrust violations was pursued. This New Deal activism culminated in 1945 with the Aluminum Company Case. In this case, the Courts went beyond the "rule of reason" and stated that the mere existence of monopoly influences, even if this had been established in a reasonable fashion, is a violation of antitrust laws. Thus, "market structure" rather than "market conduct" became the critical issue in antitrust cases.

In the post World War II years, the antitrust activism begun by the Roosevelt administration has continued. The Celler-Kefauver Antitrust Act was passed in 1950 to strengthen the Clayton Act, the Brown Shoe case in 1962 severely limited the extent of vertical mergers (mergers of firms at different stages of production within one industry, such as merging a leather tanning firm with a shoe manufacturer or merging—as in the Brown Shoe Case—the manufacturer with a retail shoe chain). In a like manner, the 1967 Bethlehem Steel Case severely limited horizontal mergers (mergers of firms at the same stage of production within one industry, such as merging two steel manufacturers). And in the Electrical Equipment Case of 1961, the Court levied treble damages for price fixing. This does not mean that all issues in the antitrust area have been settled. The Courts, for example, have not developed a set of rules to deal with one of the most important types of mergers: "conglomerate mergers" (these are mergers between a firm of one industry with a firm of a totally different industry such as the merger of an oil company with a department store chain). Additionally, how do we explain the fact that the two hundred largest firms in the U.S. control two-thirds of all the assets in manufacturing? If we have had effective antitrust policy, how has this concentration of economic power occured?

Robert Bork, Professor of Law at Yale University, maintains that this concentration is most desirable, and attempts to reduce it would result in many inefficiencies. John Kuhlman, an academic economist from the University of Missouri is horrified at the prospect of industries which are characterized by the presence of a few large firms competing with a number of small firms.

YES
Robert H. Bork

THE CRISIS IN ANTITRUST

Improbable as the statement may seem, antitrust today is almost an unknown policy. It is ubiquitous: Antitrust constitutes one of the most elaborate deployments of governmental force in areas of life still thought committed primarily to private choice and initiative. It is popular: There is some intellectual but almost no political opposition to its main features. And it is even exportable: This supposedly peculiarly American growth has spread to and taken at least equivocal root in Europe and even in Asia. Yet few people know what the law really commands, how its doctrines have evolved, or the nature of its ultimate impact upon our national well-being. Even among the specialized and elite corps of lawyers who operate the antitrust system there is remarkably little critical understanding of the policy.

This state of affairs is curious, and certainly unfortunate, but perhaps it is understandable. Antitrust is a subcategory of ideology, and by the time a once militant ideology triumphs and achieves embodiment in institutional forms, its adherents are likely long since to have left off debating first principles. "The antitrust movement," as Professor Richard Hofstadter remarks, "is one of the faded passions of American reform." But Hofstadter goes on, and probably it is not a paradox—"the antitrust enterprise has more significance in contemporary society than it had in the days of T.R. or Wilson, or even in the heyday of Thurman Arnold." The very nearly simultaneous "collapse of antitrust feeling both in the public at large and among liberal intellectuals" and our arrival at a state of affairs in which "the managers of the large corporations do their business with one eye constantly cast over their shoulders at the Antitrust Division" are probably to be explained, though Hofstadter does not quite make the causality explicit, by the fact that "antitrust as a legal-administrative enterprise has been solidly institutionalized in the past quarter-century." The waning of fervor with the growth of organization, bureaucracy, and effective power is a familiar occurrence in both secular and religious movements. . . .

YES   Robert H. Bork

The full range of modern rules that significantly impair both competition and the ability of the economy to produce goods and services efficiently is discussed in detail in the remainder of this book. Generally, these rules ignore the obvious fact that more efficient methods of doing business are as valuable to the public as they are to businessmen. In modern times the Supreme Court, without compulsion by statute, and certainly without adequate explanation, has inhibited or destroyed a broad spectrum of useful business structures and practices. Internal growth to large market size has been made dangerous. Growth by merger with rivals is practically impossible, as is growth by acquisition of customers or suppliers. Even acquisitions for the purpose of moving into new markets have been struck down, as the law evolves a mythology about the dangers of conglomerate mergers. Cooperative ventures between independent businesses are outlawed through a misapplication of the sound policy against price fixing and market division. The Court has destroyed the most useful forms of manufacturer control over the distribution of products, requiring higher-cost modes of reaching the public. It has needlessly proliferated rules about pricing behavior that have the effect of making prices higher and markets less effective allocators of society's resources. The Court has done these things, moreover, on demonstrably erroneous notions of the economics that guide the law.

So far as the Supreme Court is concerned, we appear at the moment to be between cycles of antitrust expansion. Extensions of old doctrine to new fields have been relatively infrequent the last half dozen years or so, but there is scant

comfort in that. The situation will not last. A position based not upon settled ideology but rather upon an accidental equilibrium of forces is unlikely to prove stable. Unless the theory of antitrust is understood and the law brought into line with it, the law will surely move on again, becoming even more unnecessarily restrictive of business freedom. A majority of the current Supreme Court has recently taken a significant step toward reforming a part of antitrust, and prospects for an intelligible, proconsumer law may now be brighter than they have been for several decades. Still, there is a very long way to go. Existing case law incorporates principles that have not been extended to the full reach of their internal logic. Law grows by analogizing new situations to old, and antitrust may move still further away from a policy of competition simply by realizing the potentialities inherent in the principles it now espouses.

But there is more to fear than that, for the courts are of course not the sole generators of antitrust policy. A new era of antitrust expansion seems likely to begin in Congress, which is influenced by popular moods. There has always existed in this country a populist hostility to big business, a hostility that is currently reinforced by the suspicion that major corporations are somehow to blame for hardships that have their origin elsewhere, in the politics of OPEC, in federal regulation of natural gas prices—or in bad weather, for that matter.

The direction of new legislation is determined by the prevailing tone of public discourse. That discourse has in recent years been almost uniformly in favor of fresh antitrust assaults on business. Ralph Nader, though rather more voluble than most, expresses not untypical attitudes. "Antitrust," Mr. Nader

61

informed us a few years back, "is going to erupt into a major political issue because it is not just an esoteric issue for lawyers." Rather, it is "going modern and will shed more and more of its complexities." He was a true prophet: shortly thereafter, a Nader Study Group filed a report on something called "The Closed Enterprise System" which shed the complexities of antitrust so completely that the reader is given no hint of their existence. Indeed, both the tone and the message of the report are best paraphrased by Professor Richard Posner as suggesting "that if we would only stop thinking so much about the problem and throw the book at the bastards our monopoly problem would be solved. . . ."

Such attitudes have, of course, found reflection in Congress. Recently, for example, Congress enacted legislation allowing each state to sue on behalf of all persons residing within its borders for triple the damage done them by antitrust violations. The same legislation made mergers more difficult by requiring advance notification to government, and greatly expanded government's power to compel information without resort either to a lawsuit or a grand jury investigation. The Petroleum Industry Competition bill, which won astonishingly wide support in the Senate in 1976, was designed to destroy vertical integration in the major oil companies by requiring that each company confine itself to one of three phases of the industry: production, transportation, or refining and marketing. That bill is, as of this writing, scheduled for reintroduction, along with other bills that would prevent oil companies from entering or remaining in any other energy field, such as coal or solar energy. There is no reason to believe that the destruction of national wealth involved in the enact-

ment of these bills or other recent proposed legislation* would be compensated by any social gain.

We are urged, then, by persons in and out of Congress, to throw the antitrust book at business in order to improve the quality of American life. One could wish that those who want to throw the book had taken the time to understand it. In the pages that follow, I attempt to contribute to that necessary understanding by reading the antitrust book in light of the disciplines of law and economics, in order to show that the policy is not what it seems. Antitrust presents itself as a body of developed knowledge and principle worked out over years of investigation, thought, and litigation. That image is misleading. Antitrust is not all of a piece.

Because antitrust's basic premises are mutually incompatible, and because some of them are incorrect, the law has been producing increasingly bizarre results. Certain of its doctrines preserve competition, while others suppress it, resulting in a policy at war with itself. During the past twenty years or so, the protectionist, anticompetitive strain in the law has undergone a spectacular acceleration, bringing to pass what Ward Bowman and I have termed the "crisis in antitrust." The resolution of this crisis will determine antitrust's future. The law must either undergo a difficult process of

---

*A few years ago, the late Senator Philip Hart, then chairman of the Antitrust Subcommittee of the Senate Judiciary Committee, introduced a proposed Industrial Reorganization Act. Reflecting the current shibboleth that monopoly is everywhere, the bill would have directed antitrust attack at about 140 of the nation's largest 200 companies in seven industries. More recently, Senator Hart introduced a bill that would make it no defense in a civil monopolization action that defendant's monopoly power was "due to superior product, business acumen, or historic accident," thus proposing a break up market positions based on superior efficiency.

reform, based upon a correct under- standing of fundamental legal and economic concepts, or resume its descent to the status of an internal tariff against domestic competition and free trade. . . .

A consumer-oriented law must employ basic economic theory to judge which market structures and practices are harmful and which beneficial. Modern antitrust has performed this task very poorly. Its version of economics is a melange of valid insights and obvious- ly incorrect—sometimes fantastic—as- sumptions about the motivations and effects of business behavior. There are many problems here, but perhaps the core of the difficulty is that the courts, and particularly the Supreme Court, have failed to understand and give proper weight to the crucial concept of business efficiency. Since productive efficiency is one of the two opposing forces that determine the degree of consumer well- being (the other being resource misal- location due to monopoly power), this failure has skewed legal doctrine dis- astrously. Business efficiency necessarily benefits consumers by lowering the costs of goods and services or by increasing the value of the product or service offered; this is true whether the business unit is a competitor or a monopolist. When ef- ficiency is not counted, or when it is seen as a positive evil, it appears that no business structure of behavior has any potential for social good, and there is consequently no reason to uphold its legality if any remote danger can be imagined. The results could not have been worse, and would probably have been better, if the Court had made the opposite mistake and refused to recog- nize any harm in cartels and monopolies. Yet neither mistake need have been

made. The hopeful development in the current Supreme Court's approach to antitrust, referred to a few pages back, is a single case weighing in favor of a business practice its capacity to create efficiency. That approach seems obvious, but against the background of the juris- prudence of the last two decades it appears revolutionary. Applied general- ly, it could save antitrust as useful and respectable policy. It is too soon to tell whether the Court will follow up its new beginning. . . .

The reader will find in this book from time to time a note of dismay or of dis- appointment about the path that antitrust has taken. Since it may seem odd or inappropriate that emotion should be expended on such a topic, perhaps I had better explain why antitrust seems to me worth study and concern. If this were a law having to do only with the efficiency of one sector of the economy, if its sole function were to make consumers mar- ginally richer, the law's current plight would hardly be a matter for even "faded passion." At best it would be a stimulating intellectual puzzle. But antitrust is much more than that. Its mystique, its legends, its celebration by all branches of the federal government constitute an excep- tionally potent educative force that af- fects our thought, for better or for worse and in ways we do not fully realize, about all the aspects of society the law touches. I have referred to it as a subcategory of ideology; it is not far-fetched to view antitrust as a microcosm in which larger movements of our society are reflected and perhaps, in some small but significant way, reinforced or generated. The walls of ideological subcategories are per- meable; battles fought and won or lost in one are likely to affect the outcome of parallel struggles in others. It is important, therefore, to recognize the aspects of society upon which this law impinges.

Antitrust is, first and most obviously, law, and law made primarily by judges. We are right to be concerned about the integrity and legitimacy of that lawmaking process, both for its own sake and because ideas about the power and discretion proper to courts in one field of law will inevitably affect their performance elsewhere. At issue is the question central to democratic society: Who governs? . . .

● ● ●

NO

John M. Kuhlman

IN A LIFEBOAT WITH AN ELEPHANT

A Broad Overview of the Economy

The economic system of the United States is a collection of different types of markets, ranging from the very competitive to those which are highly monopolistic in nature. In agriculture, most of the markets are quite competitive. By this I mean that the suppliers have no influence on price, in contrast with some obvious instances in which the buyers exercise control over the price. Agriculture is an industry of many small firms without market power. In many respects the nation's retail industry is similar to agriculture, but within the past four decades we have seen the development of large retailers such as Sears and J.C. Penny, plus RCA which controls Hertz, Mobil Oil which owns Montgomery Ward, etc. The service industries are, for the most part, made up of many small firms but even here, some industries such as accounting and banking are dominated by a few very large firms.

In manufacturing, the picture is considerably different. In automobiles, there are two large domestic manufacturers and two small (and marginal) firms. Competition in the automobile industry is largely from foreign producers. In farm machinery, a small number of firms dominate the manufacture of heavy agricultural equipment—tractors and combines. In basic metals, a few firms dominate. There are three manufacturers of commercial aircraft;

From, "In a Lifeboat with an Elephant", presented at Perry Seminar, University of Missouri — Columbia. Reprinted by permission of the author, and Agricultural Experiment Station, University of Missouri — Columbia.

three of typewriters (including Exxon); two of telephones (although the number may now be increasing); and so on.

Using output, sales, employment, or nearly any other measure that one may choose except numbers, large economic units dominate a major portion of our economic life. This has had a major impact on our educational system. Colleges of Business train future bureaucrats rather than future entrepreneurs. Colleges of Agriculture tilt toward agri-business and away from the family farm. More and more of our undergraduates aspire to a nice bureaucratic position with a large firm or the government. And it may be that many of our college-educated entrepreneurs are those students who majored in some subject that did not enable them to get a job with General Dynamics, General Electric, General Foods, General Mills, General Motors, or the General Services Administration.

Who Owns What?
Who Controls What?

It is possible, in the case of local businesses or farms, to determine just who owns a particular piece of property or business. You know whom you are dealing with or whom you are working for. This is not true in the case of large economic units. Since Berle and Means wrote their masterpiece of many years ago, *The Modern Corporation and Private Property,* there has been a continuing dispute about who controls the modern corporation and in whose interest it functions.

In 1973 the Committee on Government Operations undertook a study of corporate ownership. The relationships it found between corporations and the banking system are impressive. Some people tell me that there is nothing wrong with Chase-Manhattan's being the largest (or one of the largest) stockholders in four different airlines. These securities are, it is true, in trust accounts and the banks are supposed to vote them in the interest of the trustees. As a practical matter, most are voted for the incumbent management.

But this is only one bit of evidence. The interlocking directorates between the nation's major banks and the manufacturing concerns would bring out the same picture. Or one might examine the use of wholly-owned subsidiaries in petroleum and the grain trade. Or one might choose to examine the use of corporate acronyms rather than intelligible names and the use of brand names in advertising without reference to the corporate name.

All of these serve to "fuzz over" the question of ownership and control. Whom are you doing business with when you use your VISA card? Who is your employer when you work for Shell Oil or Hertz? Who is responsible if your car bursts into flames when hit in the rear? Who is minding the store?

The Amoral Society

Our traditional ethical teachings all involve person-to-person relationships. Do unto others as you would have them do unto you. Do not covet your neighbor's property. These and many more tell us how to behave toward some other person. But we have no ethical teachings as to how we should behave toward the large social unit and, in particular, the large corporations that I so sketchily describe.

We can't convert the above into rules for our conduct *vis-à-vis* the large corporations. Should we behave toward the Ford Motor Company as we expect them to behave toward us? Are we under the same ethical obligation to tell American Express the truth as our next-door neighbor?

Most of us would call it to the attention of a waitress if she gave us too much change but never check to make sure that all of the VISA sales slips come back. I suspect that most of us make sure that those that do come back are legitimate, but if there are some that are lost, that would seem to be VISA's problem. We see a little old lady or a cute young child pushing a grocery cart—miles away from the store—and we grab our camera for a contest-winning photograph rather than calling the police. It must be theft, but theft from whom?

It is my hypothesis that the hired man on the farm works harder than the employee in the large organization. The farmer knows who the employer is. He is the fellow whom he is working next to in the hayfield. But the employee of the large firm knows his supervisor and maybe one or two people above that level—but the company—oh, it is located in New York, or Chicago, or Paris, or somewhere. The employee in the small enterprise can see the relationship between his productivity and the success or failure of the firm. In the large enterprise, that relationship is not discernable to even the most discerning. Can a society continue to exist in which there is a large group of amoral relationships coexisting with a group of moral, interpersonal relationships? It looks to me as though there is a very strong chance that the amoral relationships between the individual and the anonymous corporation will spill over into the interpersonal relationships. The way I treat Exxon may become the way I treat Joe Smith. If I don't have ethical obligations to the firm I work for, will my ethical obligations to other people also disappear? Unfortunately, I think that this is likely to happen, if it is not already happening.

The Corporation
as a Planning Agency

Gailbraith and Heilbroner, among others, have commented that the United States has been moving, and continues to move, toward a system of planning and away from a market system. Large firms don't respond to the market as small firms do. Large firms orchestrate their demand through advertising. They then use their resources in such a way as to meet the objectives they have created.

When small firms make mistakes, few people outside the firm are hurt. When large firms make errors, short and long run consequences may extend far beyond the boundaries of the firm. There are many examples. General Motors, Firestone, and two oil companies financed National City Lines, a company which bought up street car systems in the 1930s. As a condition of the financing, National City Lines bought its buses from General Motors, its tires from Firestone, and its petroleum products from the oil companies. With out expert hindsight, we now recognize that it was probably unwise to move from a mass-transit system to an automobile-oriented system. But it was a good business decision, just a bad planning decision.

In the 1950s, the oil companies convinced the Eisenhower administration that quotas were needed on imported oil. The argument for a limitation of imports was simple: we should not be dependent upon foreign sources of oil. It was certainly in the short-run interest of the oil companies but may not have been in the long run interest of the country.

As corporations increase in size and number, greater reliance is placed on internal financing as a source of funds for new capital expansion. We get the funds for financing expansion from the purchaser of the product rather than from the capital market. This is a part of the planning process.

Large social organizations make large errors. They might be compared to the supertankers. They need lots of room to manuever. And when there is an accident, it will be a large accident. Small ships and small social institutions cannot have large accidents. And so it is with the corporations as planning agencies. They plan. They make large errors, but the cost of those errors will be the burden of society—either directly through government bail-outs or indirectly through higher costs and less efficient utilization of resources.

Corporations, Savings, and Productivity

The common cry, and I am afraid it is widely accepted, is the present need for increased saving which, in turn, is trans-lated into increased investment in capital plant and equipment which, in turn, means increased productivity. In this scenario, believe it or not, the public turns out to be the culprit. We are consuming too much—that is, we are using too much of the nation's resources to produce goods for consumption. We do not leave enough to produce capital goods.

One might think that the obvious solution would be to reduce consumption. America's business community spends tens of billions of dollars a year encouraging people to consume. Why don't the large corporations spend a fraction of their present advertising budget to encourage people to save—that is, not to consume—and then to purchase stock in those companies or buy their bonds? The problem with that approach is obvious. If people cut back on their consumption, sales and profits would fall, and unemployment in the corporate sector would increase.

So let's cut the corporate income tax. The corporations will have a greater amount of after-tax income that can be used to finance capital expansion. It will be an internal decision rather than a market decision. But can we have capital expansion without a reduction in consumption if there are few unemployed resources? The answer, to me at least, would appear to be rather dubious. Reducing corporate income taxes on the assumption that it will lead to increased investment and productivity will, in times of nearly full employment, only lead to further increases in prices.

Information

In a competitive market such as agriculture, market information is pretty much a public good. Let me explain. A competitive market generates a series of transactions and associated with each there will be a price and quantity. A by-product is also generated. It is market information. Most of the parameters of the transaction are known to the public. Agricultural reporting services supplement the market data by issuing crop forecasts and figures on inventories. With some exceptions, all of the traders then have the same information. And that information is costless to them. Thus they can trade more or less as equals.

I should say a word about the exceptions in agriculture. A handful of very large companies dominate the world's trading in grain. These firms do acquire information that is not generally available in the market and that gives them an advantage in trading. (This trading in grain is vividly described in Morgan's GRAIN MERCHANTS.) But even these grain merchants encountered trouble in trading with the Soviet Union with its penchant for secrecy.

But what is an exception in agriculture may be much more common in that part of the economic system dominated by large firms. Take, for example, the large oil companies. From the time the oil is taken from the ground to the time it is put in your tank at the company-owned service station, there is no public price. We don't know what transfer prices the integrated companies put on the product. We can only hope they are using the market prices.

It is difficult to formulate public policy in the field of petroleum since we have so little reliable information. As a matter of fact, we know little more than the companies choose to tell us.

In general, as companies get larger and larger more and more information is internalized and not generally available to the public. Large companies with consolidated accounting statements simply generate no market information that would cause resources, outside the company, to move. No one outside P&G, for example, can know the profit on Tide. If we did, resources might move into the production of detergents.

In the case of large companies, we are hardly in a position even to answer the basic question—"Are they efficient?" There is no shortage of self-testimonials. Mr. Bork, in THE ANTITRUST PARADOX, happily assumes that they are efficient; otherwise they would not be so large. I would personally prefer, however, that the market work sufficiently well that the efficiency or lack of efficiency would be apparent to all.

Although I fear that I am being too dismal and pessimistic, I can't see any change in the direction of improvement. More and more information will become private information. It is not at all apparent to me that we can get the proper kind of resource response in such a situation. . . .

Competition as a Viable Public Policy

Competition has both economic and noneconomic values. As far as the first is concerned, it stimulates efficiency. If excess returns are being earned, resources will flow toward those higher returns, just as resources will move away from areas where returns are too low. Competition promotes innovation. Insofar as noneconomic values are concerned, competition diffuses power over a large number of economic units rather than concentrating power in a small number of units. This is consistent with the political philosophy inherent in our Constitution and the federal form of government.

But competition would be an impossible goal if there were widespread economies of scale in the economic system. If bigger farms are always more efficient than smaller farms, the most efficient method of organization would be one large farm. No one believes this to be the case. There is, however, a rather warm disagreement about how large an automobile company needs to be in order to be efficient. Or a steel company, airline, railroad.

As it stands, we don't really know how many firms in any given industry are needed, as judged by either efficiency or democratic pluralism as criteria. I offer these suggestions as tentative kinds of thoughts:

First, in most industries I would prohibit horizontal mergers between all but the very smallest of firms. I wouldn't, for example, object if two small quarries or two local grocers merged but if two regional groups merged, I would object.

Second, I would sharply limit vertical mergers—that is, mergers where buyer and seller merge—if either of the firms is greater than some minimum size.

It is much preferable that firms grow through internal expansion rather than merger, since industry capacity increases with internal growth as contrasted with merely changing ownership.

Third, I would simply prohibit growth through mergers for all large companies. I can't really believe that the consumer is better off because Mobil Oil purchased Montgomery Ward or Exxon purchased Reliance Motor. Conglomerate firms such as ITT probably yield few benefits to the public that would not be equally likely under some other structure.

Fourth, I would continue to prosecute with vigor such offenses as price fixing, predatory pricing, market sharing agreements, tying agreements, and other types of anticompetitive practice. I think that it was a great step forward when the federal government provided funds for the establishment of antitrust units in the offices of the attorneys general at the state level. Adding forty-some new antitrust enforcement agencies will do a great deal to discourage anticompetitive practices at the state and local level.

Fifth, we should carefully examine our tax laws as to their effect on the structure of industry. Certainly, many of the mergers of the 1950s were a result of the tax code and it is likely that the present movement is similar. Two possibilities strike me as being worthwhile. One would be the use of a graduated corporate income tax so that larger firms would pay a higher tax rate than smaller firms. This would provide an incentive for firms to spin off divisions or subsidiaries instead of continually expanding. A second possibility would be to eliminate the corporate income tax and then tax all profits as though they were paid to the stockholders. This would result in profits being distributed as dividends and then the firms would have to go into capital markets to obtain the necessary capital.

Sixth, we should carefully examine our tariff policy. At the turn of the century, the tariff was rightly called the "mother of trusts." The only chance for competition in automobiles, steel, heavy farm equipment and the like is from foreign competitors. We should not yield to pressure to protect domestic industry from foreign competition.

Deregulation

In 1887, Congress passed the Interstate Commerce Commission Act, a piece of legislation which established a utility-type regulation for the railroads. Later legislation extended a similar type of regulation to pipe lines, airlines, electric utilities, telephonic communications, and trucking. All were based on the assumption that the industries in question were natural monopolies; that is, the economies of scale were of such a magnitude that one firm was more efficient than two. Thus, these industries were regulated in terms of both price and the quality of service.

But a natural monopoly is a product of the existing technology. In 1887, there was no substitute for railroad transportation for much of the country, and especially the Midwest. Now there is an abundance of substitutes. Competition is now a very real alternative.

But competition, as we have seen over the past two years, will work in airlines. It will also work in trucking. It will probably work in the case of long distance lines in telephonic communications. We do not need regulation in the wholesale power industry. In short, much of our public utility regulation could be dismantled—

but only if we are willing to enforce a policy of competition.

Conclusion

It is very easy to say that the "other fellow" ought to compete. Competition is the accepted national policy—for the other fellow. We want that policy enforced—but always against the other fellow. There are always good reasons why competition should not prevail in medicine, farming, automobiles, insurance, trucking—you name it.

But immediate self-interest aside, competition does have virtues. First, it provides a tremendous stimulus for efficiency. Prices will tend to reflect costs. Second, it does have certain democratic values. In a competitive system, power is not concentrated. Young people have a greater chance to enter business as independent entrepreneurs. And, finally, the competitive markets work in an impersonal manner without the benefit of any bureaucracy, public or private.

At this stage the following question might fairly be asked. Would a policy of competition solve the problem of inflation? I think that the answer would be that it is doubtful that it would. But an increased reliance upon competition would, at a very minimum, increase the chances that we would see some increase in productivity. It would increase the likelihood that prices would fall when demand falls. It would mean that there would be a greater incentive to weed out the inefficient producers.

I don't believe that controlling the money supply or fine-tuning the system through taxes and spending will solve the problem of inflation if either of those policies is followed without any consideration of the structure of the economy. If we move toward a more competitive economy, our traditional monetary and fiscal controls would at least have a chance of coping with inflation.

• • •

POSTSCRIPT

HAS ANTITRUST POLICY GONE TOO FAR?

Two aspects of current antitrust policy are most disturbing to Bork. First Professor Bork finds that an antitrust philosophy or "mystique" is imbedded in the actions of all branches of the Federal government. This ideology constitutes "an exceptionally potent educative force" that lends credence to and helps shape current and future policy toward the business community. Second, antitrust developments have far reaching implications for the "political fate of the competitive, free-market ideal." Bork fears that the "capture of the field by anti-free-market theories" will have lasting and devastating effects on economic freedom.

Kuhlman takes a typical liberal-antitrust stance. He maintains that imperfect competition cannot be ignored. The existence of large dominant firms in an industry destroys the benefits of competition. In order to reap these benefits those large firms must be controlled by antitrust policy.

Kuhlman admits that there is some uncertainty as to how many firms are needed in an industry to insure the benefits of competition. But he knows that we can't make that judgement on economic efficiency grounds alone. In our Constitutional, Democratic society, he warns that we must be watchful that economic power is not concentrated in the hands of a few. One way to diffuse this economic power is through effective competition in the market place. Antitrust policy can achieve this end.

Whether you side with Bork or with Kuhlman will depend upon what priority you place on economic efficiency and how you view the impact of imperfectly competitive markets. To help you make your decision, we suggest that you read George Stigler, "The Economics of the Antitrust Laws," *Journal of Law and Economics* (October, 1966), Wesley Leebeler, "Market Power and Competitive Superiority in Concentrated Industries," *UCLA Law Review* (August, 1978) and Sam Peltzman, "The Gains and Losses from Industrial Concentration," *Journal of Law and Economics* (October, 1977). These selections lend support to Bork's assertion that antitrust policy has gone too far. Kuhlman's position is supported in Walter Adams' THE STRUCTURE OF AMERICAN INDUSTRY, 5th edition (Macmillan, 1977), F.M. Scherer's, INDUSTRIAL MARKET STRUCTURE AND ECONOMIC PERFORMANCE (Rand McNally, 1971), and Willard Mueller's, "Social Control of Economic Power," in ALTERNATIVE DIRECTIONS IN ECONOMIC POLICY, Bonello/Swartz ed., (Notre Dame Press, 1978).

ISSUE 4

"SHOULD THE FEDERAL GOVERNMENT DEREGULATE AMERICAN BUSINESS?"

YES: **Murray L. Weidenbaum,** from "The Changing Nature of Government Regulation of Business," *Journal of Post Keynesian Economics* (Spring, 1980).

NO: **Mark Green and Norman Waitzman,** from "Cost, Benefits, and Class," *Working Papers* (May-June, 1980).

ISSUE SUMMARY

YES: Weidenbaum asserts that government regulations cost the U.S. more than $100 billion per year. He implores policymakers to employ cost-benefit analysis to justify current and future government regulations.

NO: Green and Waitzman contend that Weidenbaum grossly exaggerates the private costs of public regulation. They go on to challenge the underlying assumptions of Weidenbaum's benefit-cost analysis.

No one single issue is more on the cutting edge of the free market economists' attack on government intervention than their campaign to eliminate or at least reduce substantially the regulation of private enterprise. They contend that this regulation results in higher consumer prices, reduced worker productivity, declining innovation and investment, rising unemployment rates, reversals in our balance of payments position, increases in our federal budget deficit and just about every other problem that can be found in our economic system. They are exercised about this issue because government intervention, particularly intervention that effects directly the productive process, is in direct violation of the precepts set down by Adam Smith and his fellow classical economists.

This has been a growing problem for the free market economist, since

Congress has markedly increased regulatory activity during the late 1960s and early 1970s. In order to offset this new wave of regulations, a counter offensive was spear-headed by organizations such as the American Enterprise Institute, an organization which author Weidenbaum served as President. These groups have provided Congressional testimony, initiated their own journal called *Regulation*, written numerous popular and professional articles, received growing financial support from the business community, established endowed professorships at a number of universities, and above all they have had a direct influence on public opinion. Perhaps nothing is more telling than the comic strips which line Weidenbaum's office walls. In his words: "When it (government overregulation) begins to be the topic of humor, then you know this thing is getting big."

The free market economist's impact does not stop with comic strips. The Democratic Congress which supported and sponsored many of the government regulations that raised the ire of their conservative counterparts, is the same Congress that began to dismantle these regulations in 1979 and 1980. Legislation was passed to deregulate the airlines, trucking and natural gas. The Occupation Safety and Health Administration (OSHA), the Equal Employment Opportunity Commission (EEO), and the Environmental Protection Agency (EPA) came under close scrutiny. All in all, the tide has turned and the free market economists can rejoice in their past triumphs and their likely future triumphs under the Reagan Administration.

Perhaps too late, the liberal economists recognized the ground swell which was engulfing their programs. They reacted by engaging in their own rhetorical battles. But their emotional appeals to protect life and limb fell on deaf ears. Green and Waitzman represent an attempt to move the debate beyond rhetoric. Their paper, which systematically attacks the Weidenbaum arguments, lays the foundation for the defense of government regulation.

In the following selections, Weidenbaum outlines the basic arguments which are used by the free market economists to discredit government regulation. Green and Waitzman then subject these arguments to a close examination.

YES   Murray L. Weidenbaum

THE CHANGING NATURE OF GOVERNMENT REGULATION

This article is a paper presented to a conference sponsored by the American Assembly of Collegiate Schools of Business and Washington University, St. Louis, on July 11, 1979. It draws heavily on a study being prepared for the Hoover Institution at Stanford University and on the author's book, THE FUTURE OF BUSINESS REGULATIONS (New York: Amacom Press, 1979).

The unprecedented expansion in government regulation of business in the United States in recent years has altered fundamental aspects of business-government relations. This article considers some of the implications of that change; it does not attempt to evaluate the worthiness of the regulatory programs themselves. Rather, the impacts are examined from the viewpoint of the business firm. The cost of business compliance with government regulation is a factor that properly enters into any reasonable benefit/cost analysis of regulation, as one factor among many that must be weighed in the policy process.

The concept of a regulated industry has, in a way, become archaic. We now live in an economy in which every industry is feeling the rising power of government regulation in each major aspect of its day-to-day operations. Virtually every company in the United States knows the impacts of a vast array of government involvement in its internal decision making.

If we could accurately measure the pervasiveness of government intervention, I doubt that we would find the economists' favorites—electric utilities and railroads—at the top of the list. More likely, we would encounter such giants of the manufacturing sector as automobile, aerospace, and chemical companies, with the oil industry not too far behind. Because of the rapid proliferation of government regulatory activity in the past two decades, it is difficult to understand the totality of the process that is still under way. This article is an attempt to provide an initial overview.

The Pervasive Impacts
On the Business Firm

It is hard to overestimate the rapid expansion and the great variety of government involvement in business now occurring. Most of the recent

From, "The Changing Nature of Government Regulation." Reprinted from Journal of Post Keynesian Economics, Spring 1980, by permission of the publisher, M.E. Sharpe, Inc., White Plains New York 10603 ©1980.

regulation does not issue from the traditional independent agencies, such as the Interstate Commerce Commission, the Civil Aeronautics Board, and the Federal Communications Commission. Rather, the expansion of government power over business has been carried out through the use of the operating arms of government—the departments of Agriculture, Commerce, Energy, Health, Education, and Welfare, Interior, Justice, Labor, Transportation, and Treasury.

Indeed, when we attempt to look at the emerging business-government relationship from the business executive's viewpoint, we find a very considerable public presence in what historically have been private matters. No business, large or small, can operate without obeying a myriad of government restrictions. Entrepreneurial decisions fundamental to the enterprise are becoming subject to more governmental influence, review, or control—decisions such as what lines of business to go into, what products and services to produce, which investments to finance, how to produce goods and services, where to make them, how to market them, what prices to charge, and what profit to keep.

Virtually every major department of the typical American corporation has one or more counterparts in a government agency that influences its internal decision making. There is almost a "shadow" organization chart of public officials matching the organizational structure of each private company. For example, the scientists in corporate research laboratories now do much of their work to ensure that the products they develop are not rejected by lawyers in regulatory agencies. Engineers in manufacturing departments must make sure the equipment they specify meets the standards promulgated by labor department authorities. Marketing staffs must follow procedures established by government product safety agencies. Location of business facilities must conform with a variety of environmental statutes. Activities of personnel staffs are increasingly geared to meet standards of the various agencies concerned with employment conditions. Finance departments often bear the brunt of the rising paperwork burden imposed on business by government agencies.

In short, there are few aspects of business activities that escape some type of government review or influence. Moreover—and most important—the impacts of regulation go far beyond general requirements for corporate results; they increasingly permeate every facet of internal business operations.

Important internal adjustments are taking place in the structure and operation of the typical corporation. Each of the major business functions is undergoing an important transformation. These changes tend either to increase the overhead costs of doing business or to deflect management and employee attention from the conventional tasks of designing, developing, producing, and distributing new, better, or cheaper goods and services. As Arthur F. Burns stated in his Frances Boyer Lecture in December 1978, "as things stand, many corporate executives find so much of their energy is devoted to coping with regulatory problems that they cannot attend sufficiently to the creative part of their business . . . .

The role of top management is undergoing a fundamental metamorphosis as it responds to the changing external environment. The outlook of key corporate executives is shifting from primary concern with conventional production and marketing decisions to coping with a host of external and often strange policy considerations, frequently motivated by groups with nonbusiness and noneconomic priorities. Members of the senior management group may become as attuned to the desires of those new interests as to their traditional accountability to shareholders.

It is not surprising that numerous chief executives report that one-third or more of their time is now devoted to governmental and public policy matters—dealing with the many federal, state, and local regulations that affect the company, meeting with a wide variety of civic and special interest groups that make "demands" on the organization's resources, and participating increasingly in the public policy arena.

Some of the most fundamental impacts of governmental intervention are discernible in the research and development area, although the ramifications are likely to unfold only over a long period of time in the form of restrained product and process innovation. A rising share of corporate R&D budgets is being shifted to so-called defensive research, that is, to meeting the requirements of governmental regulatory agencies, rather than to designing products with greater customer appeal. This trend is most advanced in the automotive industry, where the head of General Motors' research laboratory has stated: "We've diverted a large share of our resources—sometimes up to half—into meeting government regulations instead of developing better materials, better manufacturing techniques, and better products. . . ." A similar trend appears in the chemical industry, in response to a plethora of new laws and regulations, all

ostensibly designed to yield a cleaner or safer environment. The government, by means of the regulatory process, is building what has been referred to as a "legal envelope" around existing technology.

The combined impacts of the rulings of the Environmental Protection Agency (EPA), Occupational Safety and Health Administration (OSHA), Food and Drug Administration (FDA), and Consumer Product Safety Commission (CPSC) are also altering major aspects of the manufacturing function of the typical American business firm. One result of the pressures to meet government environmental and safety requirements is that a major share of company investment—about one-tenth at the present time—is being devoted to these required social responsibilities rather than to increasing the capacity to produce higher quantities, or improved quality, of material output, at least as conventionally measured. Coupled with the many factory closings due to regulation, the result of these socially imposed requirements is a smaller productive capacity in the American economy than is generally realized.

Virtually every aspect of the marketing function of business is affected by government. Advertising is now subject to greater scrutiny by the Federal Trade Commission. The details of product warranties are also closely controlled. Labeling and packaging are now regulated by the Federal Trade Commission, the Food and Drug Administration, the Consumer Product Safety Commission, and the Department of Agriculture. Motor vehicle producers must include mileage ratings in advertising; cigarettes must display statements about their probable link to cancer; appliances must be labeled according to energy usage;

and processed foods must list ingredients in specified order. The most severe restrictions, however, relate to the power of government agencies to refuse to permit the production of products not meeting their standards, or requiring the recall of products already sold (the latter is a process that is often referred to euphemistically as "reverse distribution").

The primary thrust of many personnel departments has shifted from serving the staffing needs of their companies to meeting the requirements of government agencies. Maintaining complete familiarity with applicable regulations, filling out agency forms, and preparing reports to the government have literally been elevated to major end products of this traditional corporate function. One astute observer of the Washington scene has pointed out the adverse, albeit unintended, impact of these regulatory activities: "It has become considerably more expensive to employ anyone."

It is corporate finance departments that often bear the brunt of the almost insatiable demand for paperwork from government agencies; such finance units tend to react mostly to external demands for information, rather than primarily meeting the corporation's own data requirements for internal planning, reporting, and control. This reflects a change in the locus of corporate decision making whereby a variety of outside organizations and considerations figure very actively.

Expansions in specialized staff operations often constitute the most direct company response to the widening role of government in business. Virtually every company is developing some capability to inform itself about and evaluate present and future government developments as they relate to its activities. Firms of substantial size generally maintain headquarters planning staffs and Washington offices, while smaller companies rely primarily on their trade associations and on Washington-based attorneys and consultants. In some cases, substantial changes are made in the corporate organizational structure. A major headquarters office on government relations may be established by a company, with direct ties to each of its operating departments, as well as to offices in Washington and state capitals.

Douglas North contends that the key margin of decision making in our society today is access to government influence. As he describes the matter, the predictable result "is to shift the locus of the investment of resources into attempts to favorably influence the strategic governmental official or to prevent the enactment of governmental policies that will adversely affect the interest of groups." The point may be overstated. There are still many more opportunities for private undertakings. Moreover, the adverse public reaction to massive use of business resources in politics would, under present circumstances at least, be overwhelming. Nevertheless, North is indicating an important emerging development, especially in the case of the larger business organizations.

Measuring the Effects

First- and Second-Order Effects. Government imposition of socially desirable requirements on business through the regulatory process may appear to be an inexpensive way of achieving national objectives. The practice would seem to represent no significant burden on the consumer. However, the public does not get a free, or even a low-cost, lunch when government imposes requirements on private industry. In large measure, the costs of regulation show up in higher prices of the goods and services that consumers buy. These higher prices represent a "hidden tax" imposed on the public. In effect, the real level of federal taxation—in terms of the government burden imposed on the public—is higher than is generally realized. (To be sure, at a given output level an accommodating monetary policy is required to attain these results.)

The phenomenon of the regulatory tax is most visible in automobile regulation. The newly produced automobile in the United States carries a load of equipment that the federal government has mandated must be installed, ranging from catalytic converters to heavier bumpers. All in all, there was approximately $666 in government-mandated safety and environmental control equipment in the typical 1978 passenger automobile. For the 10 million cars sold that year, that amount totaled $6.7 billion in the form of higher auto prices paid by the American consumer.

But examination of the visible costs, such as to the motorist, provides only the initial or "first-order" effects of government regulation. It is the indirect or second-order effects that are truly huge—the various efforts involved in changing a company's way of doing business in order to comply with government directives. One indirect cost of regulation is the growing paperwork imposed on business firms: the expensive and time-consuming process of submitting reports, making applications, filling out questionnaires, and replying to orders and directives.

The most serious second-order effects flowing from government regulation are

the losses of productivity that result from the various federal restrictions. Coal production per worker per day declined 32 percent between 1969 and 1976, a sharp reversal from the growth in productivity during the preceding seven years. There is widespread agreement that the basic cause of this decline was the change in mining procedures made to comply with the Coal Mine Health and Safety Act of 1969.

Government regulation can also have strongly adverse effects on employment. This fact has been demonstrated in the minimum wage area, where teenagers tend to be priced out of labor markets. One study has shown that, because of the 1966 increase in the statutory minimum wage, teenage employment in the United States totaled 225,000 lower in 1972 than it otherwise would have been.

It is difficult, of course, to obtain an aggregate measure of the total cost involved in complying with governmental regulations. A pioneering effort along those lines was made at the Center for the Study of American Business at Washington University in St. Louis. We culled from the available literature the more reliable estimates of the costs of specific regulatory programs. Using a conservative procedure, we put the various dollar figures on a consistent basis and aggregated the results for 1976. The total annual cost of federal regulation was shown to be approximately $66 billion, consisting of $3 billion of taxpayer costs to operate the regulatory agencies and $63 billion (or twenty times as much) for business to comply with the regulations (Weidenbaum and DeFina, 1978). Thus, on the average, each dollar that Congress appropriates for regulation tends to result in an additional $20 of costs imposed on the private sector of the economy.

Applying the same multiplier of twenty to the budget figures available for more recent years, we can come up with some current approximations of the private sector's cost of compliance. On that basis, the expenses of the regulatory agencies themselves, as well as the costs they induce in the private sector, come to a total of $102.7 billion for 1979, or almost $500 per capita (Weidenbaum, 1978). That is a substantial hidden tax imposed by federal regulation.

Third-order effects. Yet, the most fundamental impacts of governmental intervention are the "third-order" induced effects on the corporation. These are the actions the firm takes to respond to the direct and indirect effects of regulation. Included are such negative actions as cutbacks on research and development, and on new capital formation because of the diversion of funds to meet government-mandated social requirements. The basic functioning of the business system is affected adversely by these cumulative impacts, notably in a reduced pace of innovation, a lessened ability to finance growth, and ultimately a weakening of the capability of the firm to perform its central role of producing goods and services for the consumer. These elusive induced impacts may, in the long run, outweigh the more measurable direct costs resulting from government oversight of private-sector decision making.

For example, the governmental decision-making process can have adverse effects on capital formation by introducing uncertainty about future regulations governing new processes and products. It is a trial of sorts for American companies to move ahead with building any new energy facilities. It took the Standard Oil Company of Ohio (Sohio) more than four years to obtain the 703 permits required to construct a delivery terminal and a pipeline from Long Beach, California, to Midland, Texas, plus approval by the voters in a local election. The company temporarily abandoned the project while it was awaiting a favorable tax ruling from the Internal Revenue Service.

In the newer, high-technology areas, the adverse impact of regulation on new undertakings is even more striking. A cogent example is furnished in the report by a task force of the President's Energy Resources Council dealing with the development of a new synthetic fuel industry.

The task force stated, for example, that a major uncertainty was the length of time that a project would be delayed, pending the issuance of an environmental impact statement that would stand up in court. They noted that the cost of such delays—additional interim financing and further cost increases in labor and equipment—is an obvious potential hazard for any new project. The task force provided the following evaluation of the overall impact of government regulatory activity: "In summary, some of these requirements could easily hold up or permanently postpone any attempt to build and operate a synthetic fuels plant."

Where the impact of government is less dramatic, it may be no less profound. A significant but subtle bureaucratization occurs in the corporate activity that is undertaken. The Employee Retirement Income Security Act of 1974 (ERISA) has shifted much of the concern of the management of pension funds from maximizing the return on the contributions to following a more cautious approach of minimizing the likelihood that the fund managers will be criticized or sued for their investment decisions. It thus becomes safer, although not necessarily more desirable to the employees covered, for the pension managers to keep more detailed records of their deliberations, to hire more outside experts (so that the responsibility can be diluted), and to avoid innovative investments. The federal rules also tend to make the pension fund manager unwilling to invest in other than blue-chip stocks, thus depriving smaller, newer, and riskier enterprises of an important source of venture capital. . . .

The Implications for Academic Thinking

Impetus for most of the expansion in government power over business does not come from the industries being regulated; generally, they have shown minimum enthusiasm for EPA, OSHA, EEOC (Equal Employment Opportunity Commission), ERISA, etc. If anything, they protest that the "benefits" to them are negative. The pressures for the new style of regulation come, rather, from a variety of citizen groups concerned primarily with noneconomic aspects of our national life—environmentalists, consumer groups, labor unions, and civil rights organizations. What is needed is a more comprehensive theory of the relationships among the regulators and the regulated, an approach that tries to assess the changing relations among public and private interest groups.

To talk or write about the regulated industry "capturing" its regulators is, to put it kindly, a rather quaint way of viewing the decisive shift in business decision-making power from private managers to public officials. Yet, the core of the economist's version of the "capture" theory still holds—public policy

tends to be dominated by compact organized pressure groups who attain their benefits at the expense of the more diffused and larger body of consumers (Stigler, 1976). But the nature of those interest groups has changed in recent years. Rather than the railroad baron (a relatively easy target), the villain of the piece has become a self-styled representative of the public interest, who has succeeded so frequently in identifying personal prejudices with the national well-being. In contrast, the business firm, in performing the traditional middleman function, typically serves the unappreciated and involuntary role of proxy for the overall consumer interest.

The changing nature of regulation can be diagrammed as in Chart 1. The vertical lines show the traditional relationship between the old style of regulatory commission (the ICC, CAB, etc.) and the specific industry that it regulates. The great bulk of the economy, however—the manufacturing, trade, and services sectors—is virtually exempt from that type of regulation.

In contrast, the horizontal lines show the newer breed of regulation—the EPA, EEOC, OSHA, CPSC, etc. In the case of these relative newcomers to the bureaucracy, jurisdictions extend to the great bulk of the private sector and at times to activities in the public sector itself. It is this far-ranging characteristic that makes it impractical for any single industry to dominate these regulatory activities in the manner of the traditional model.

Yet, in comparison to the older agencies oriented to specific industries, the newer regulators operate in a far narrower sphere. They are not concerned with the totality of a company or industry, but only with the limited segment of operations that falls under their jurisdiction. If there is any special interest that may come to dominate such a functionally oriented agency, it is the one that is preoccupied with its specific task—ecologists, unions, civil rights groups, and consumer organizations.

When we turn to the proposals for change in government-business relations, we also find a need for updating professional thinking. Pleas for deregulation are frequent. Indeed, they may be appropriate in those relatively few cases where market competition is thwarted by regulation, notably the ICC, CAB, and FERC (Federal Energy Resources Commission). But the proliferation of regulation is occurring elsewhere, primarily in those programs designed to deal with the externalities of environmental pollution and work place and product hazards (where the unregulated market fails to deal with these factors). Here, the prospects for regulatory improvements have been adversely affected because the issue has been posed in terms of the free market versus dirty air.

A Marginal Approach?

The serious question, of course, is not whether government should deal with those market failures, but which techniques and approaches are most effective. The tools of analysis used to evaluate proposed investments of government resources—such as benefit/cost tests and cost/effectiveness studies—may provide a more satisfactory alternative to setting regulatory policy than the emotional statements that often dominate policy discussions in the regulatory field.

To an eclectic economist, government regulation should be carried to the point where the incremental costs equal the incremental benefits, and no further. Those who are concerned that this approach justifies a considerable amount of government intervention in the economy may find some solace in the words of Friedrich von Hayek in his CONSTITUTION OF LIBERTY (1960): "a free market system does not exclude on principle . . . all regulations governing the techniques of production. . . . They will normally raise the cost of production, or what amounts to the same thing, reduce overall productivity. But if this effect on cost is fully taken into account and it is still thought worthwhile to incur the cost to achieve a given end, there is little more to be said about it. The appropriateness of such measures must be judged by comparing the overall costs with the gain; it cannot be conclusively determined by appeal to a general principle."

• • •

NO

Mark Green and
Norman Waitzman

COST, BENEFIT, AND CLASS

A rubber plant is currently emitting 25 units of sulfur dioxide into the air daily. Our best estimate of the medical effects is that three people become sick for each unit of pollution, and it costs $50 to treat each patient. The cost to the firm is as follows:

Amount of Reduction	Cost of Removing Unit	Total Cost of Removing Pollution by This Amount
1st unit	$40	$40
2nd unit	$60	$100
3rd unit	$100	$200
4th unit	$200	$400
5th unit	$350	$750

QUESTION: What is the optimal amount of pollution from society's point of view?

—Freshman Economics Exam

Let's see now. Damage to the three sick people costs society $150. Therefore the firm should spend up to $150 to eliminate each unit of pollution. The chart shows that after the third unit of pollution is removed, the cost begins to outweigh the benefit. Okay, remove three units: let the twenty-two remaining people keep getting sick, and pay them each $50. Next question.

From, "Cost Benefit and Class", *Working Papers*, Vol. Vii, No. 3, May/June, 1980. Reprinted by permission.

It is hardly surprising that freshman economics is so faint a proxy for reality. What *is* surprising is that this stuff is having very wide influence. Cost-benefit analysis scarcely more refined than the freshman exam is taught in universities and used in the corporate campaign against health and safety regulation. And it is being taken seriously.

Freshman economics students are taught to excuse the unreality of model-building by chanting the magic incantation *ceteris paribus* (other things being equal). But when their professor flies into Washington to testify, *ceteris* and *paribus* get left behind in Cambridge.

Consider what the exam question assumes. Science presumably can provide perfect knowledge of the health hazard. Every potential victim is presumed not only aware of the hazards, but easily identified and treated. The polluting firm can presumably choose from a precise range of available technologies, using a smooth cost curve. Pollution presumably does not build up over time (as in ozone decay or seepage from a chemical dump). And there are supposedly no cumulative or synergistic effects, such as those from lead or cotton dust or asbestos poisoning, or nuclear pollution. Harm to workers is somehow assumed to be analogous to harm to the general public. In short, known benefits trade off neatly against known costs, and the "correct" expenditure is a mathematical expression, obvious to anyone but a pointy-headed bureaucrat.

To its credit, this dismal exercise at least seeks to factor in benefits. Generally the corporate diatribes against regulation fail to acknowledge benefits at all. Instead there is a steady stream of pseudoscientific studies, which are in turn distilled into corporate advertising, all conveying the dire warning that red-tape is strangling American industry. The best known of these is Murray Weidenbaum's "The Cost of Government Regulation of Business," which has been widely cited as a dispassionate, factual study.

Weidenbaum, an assistant secretary of the Treasury in the Nixon Administration, is a prototype of the new corporate academic. He is currently in residence at the American Enterprise Institute, on leave from Washington University in St. Louis, where he directs something called the Center for the Study of American Business: both institutions are heavily funded by major corporations.

Though the form of Weidenbaum's research is scholarly, the content is unblushing polemic; and the methodology is dubious. He places the 1979 cost of complying with government regulation at $102.7 billion. He gets into the $100 billion stratosphere by multiplying his computation of government's administrative costs for fifty-five agencies in 1979 ($4.8 billion) by twenty, on the theory that complying with regulation costs, on average, twenty times government's direct costs. This ratio is based on a handful of studies of several agencies' compliance costs, which give Weidenbaum his average multiplier of twenty that he then applied on a weighted basis to fifty-five agencies.

Using this approach, Weidenbaum is able to take agencies (such as the Interstate Commerce Commission) that have low administrative costs or high compliance ratios, and extrapolate their ratio to the entire government, thus grossly inflating his final number. Another major reason for the magnitude of both his multiplier and his final compliance figure is that Weidenbaum counts IRS paperwork as a cost of regulation. The function of IRS, of course, is to raise revenue. Filling out income tax forms may be a time-consuming nuisance, but it is hardly "regulation" in the usual sense.

The astronomical size of the final number delights Professor Weidenbaum. "You know, " he told a business audience recently, "people think I'm in my second childhood. When they walk into my office what do they see? Tables, charts, statistics? No. I've got my walls lined with comic strips. All say the same thing: Government is overregulating. Now, this is a very important phenomenon. When it begins to be the topic of humor, then you know this thing is getting big."

One of the reasons it is getting so big, of course, is that Weidenbaum and other allies of business have made it their business to persuade public opinion that regulation is oppressive and that cost-benefit analysis is a scientific way to measure its value. With Weidenbaum's assistance, the American Enterprise Institute now publishes a slick journal, *Regulation*, which analyzes regulatory issues from a generally antiregulation perspective, and helps publicize tracts like Weidenbaum's. . . .

The cruder sort of polemic, which finesses the question of benefits by simply ignoring them, is not the only problem with cost-benefit analysis. A somewhat more subtle fallacy is the lumping together of health and safety regulation with economic regulation. Where health and safety regulation is usually devised to protect the public or the worker, economic regulation often operates primarily to serve the regulated industry.

Economic regulation in the interest of economic cartels, far from producing net costs to the industry, produces benefits to the industry and costs to the public. The history of the capture of regulatory agencies by regulated industries is well known. Regulation of the capital markets by the Securities and Exchange Commission operates in the interest of buyers and sellers of securities. The regulation of banks to limit interest rates paid to small savers operates in the interest of banks. Many airlines opposed deregulation of air fares and routes, because they knew it would open this sheltered industry to competition and fare reductions. And the American Truckers Association is currently waging a hilarious advertising campaign warning against the perils of deregulation. So it is extremely presumptuous of the Business Roundtable to count these benefits as costs.

Perhaps this sort of legerdemain is only to be expected in research sponsored by the Business Roundtable and its ideological allies, whose purpose is overly political. But even more refined, purportedly objective, cost-benefit analysis raises troubling methodological and ethical questions. And it tends to be more insidious, because there is no apparent political motive. Because cost-benefit analysis is widely taught and used in the policy debate, it deserves the most careful examination—and rebuttal. . . .

There are, of course, factors outside the cost-benefit equation that public policymakers must address, such as procedural fairness and distributional equity. But suppose we concede Crandall's point and try to make cost-benefit accounting explicit. An immediate problem is to find a common currency to measure *all* the costs and benefits—to the regulated industry, to the potential victims, and to "society." Is it really logical (or possible) to measure all costs and benefits in a common coin?

In standard economic analysis, trade-offs require comparability. In the case of compensation, for example, what is lost must be comparable to what is replaced. The *ceteris* must be *paribus*. For example, when a bicycle is stolen compensating the victim is nearly as satisfying a strategy to the victim as preventing the theft. Except for any sentimental attachment to the old bike, the victim can be restored to his original position through the purchase of a new bike, just as if he had freely agreed to an exchange. Society can measure the cost of reimbursement (or insurance premiums) against the costs of increased policing or antitheft technology, and arrive at an optimum. This is sometimes tricky, but fundamentally reasonable, and even useful in clarifying options.

But try to extend this approach to health and safety regulation. What, exactly, is health "worth"? How does one reasonably trade off profit against safety? Is my health worth more than yours? Is Murray Weidenbaum's worth more than a retired coal miner's? Textbook economics do not help, because costs and benefits are far from comparable and unequal power relationships intrude on transactions that are supposed to be voluntary. Pressed on the point, the cost-benefit people can become quite ghoulish—and revealing—in their calculations.

The economists' concept of optimality, from which cost-benefit analysis is derived deliberately ignores distributional questions. Consequently, even the most sophisticated methods produce logical absurdities that violate commonsense ideas of justice and equity.

Two widely used methods that attempt to measure costs against benefits are the Discounted Future Earnings approach (DFE) and the Willingness To Pay approach (WTP). It should be noted that each type of benefit measurement requires data that are inherently hard to obtain and quantify.

The Discounted Future Earnings approach values a person's life based on society's valuation of his labor: lifetime earnings lost from premature death define—by inference—the individual's worth. As a refinement, lost future earnings are "discounted" in order to translate them into current dollars. Other "costs" are often added on to the DFE base to reflect the diversion of other resources. The National Highway Safety Administration's $359,000 value for "societal loss" per fatality includes, in addition to discounted future earnings, losses to family and community, loss of production of co-workers, consumption losses, medical expenditures, funeral expenses, and legal fees. Similarly, the benefit of averted injury is calculated as the present value of lost earnings plus the cost of treatment. But this logic immediately runs into problems worthy of Jonathan Swift's famous "modest proposal" to solve Irish overpopulation and English hunger by serving Irish children at the dinnertables of English aristocrats. For example, since medical treatment can be extremely expensive, an auto accident which kills a seriously handicapped person, in this methodology, may produce a net benefit to society.

Because valuation of life is based on earnings potential, the results are biased against the poor and the old. The lives of those who can expect no future income, like the severely handicapped or the elderly, are valued at next to nothing. One DFE index placed the value of an eighty-five-year-old black woman at $128.

The policy implications in a world of scarce resources allocated by a DFE analysis are obviously troubling. Save the rich man before the poor man, the unionized before the nonunionized, the white male before the black female. Indeed, save the people facing the least risk before those confronting the most severe risks.

The choice of discount rate is another difficult yet crucial factor in weighing cost against benefit. Funds now invested in emissions controls could have been invested in different portfolios yielding different rates of return. How are the benefits of such an investment, which accrue over a lifetime, or many lifetimes for that matter, to be weighed against alternate investment projects? Economist Otto Eckstein emphasizes that market signals will simply not generate the appropriate rate. Yet, in 1975, the National Highway Traffic Safety Administration employed a weighted average of rates of time and savings bonds, corporate bonds, and other assets to arrive at a 7.3 percent discount rate for societal loss per fatality.

Finally, the DFE approach is inadequate to appraise the benefits of health and safety regulation because it cannot appraise the benefits of avoiding damage to property and things of aesthetic value. Only if damage has direct impact on economic variables—lost productivity, lost income, the creation of other expenses—can a corresponding social benefit be computed.

The Willingness To Pay method of measuring benefits attempts to correct for both the incompleteness of the DFE method and its narrow basis in society's value of an individual's labor. This method computes the value of life based on the individual's own valuation of it as a "good."

Of course, people are willing to pay an infinite sum to avoid certain death, and the richer you are, the more you can afford. The relevant question, as Ezra Mishan has observed, is how much are you willing to pay to avoid the added risk of death, injury, disease, and damage to property and aesthetic goods? Willingness to pay, in effect, is the risk-benefit variation of cost-benefit analysis.

How do you estimate how much people are willing to pay to avoid an added risk? One way is to take a survey—go out and ask people how much the lowering of risks to life and health is worth. A second approach is the "surrogate market," which reveals what premium people actually place on lowered risk. For example, one ambitious surveyor, Jan Acton, asked.

> Let's suppose that your doctor tells you that the odds are 99:1 against your having a heart attack. If you have the attack, the odds are 3:2 that you will live. The heart attack program would mean that the odds are 4:1 that you will live after a heart attack. How much are you willing to pay in taxes per year to have this heart attack program which would cut your probability of dying from a heart attack in half (i.e., the chances are 1,000:2 you will have a heart attack and be saved by the program this year).

The responses to this worked out to a value for life of $28,000.

One problem with the survey approach is that people may not be honest, for a variety of reasons. "The difficulty with asking people questions such as 'How much for your grandmother?' " said J.G.U Adams, "is that they generally do not give honest answers."

Going further, there is a problem over the extent to which people can imagine a risk they've never experienced, and then put a value on it. The acceptance of an added risk may also hinge on how other people will react to it. Whether friends will still want to vacation with you in the mountains if the air is less likely to be clean, for example, will be an important factor in your own decision, but it will add to uncertainty when responding alone to a questionnaire. Adams, of course, is distressed when his subjects cannot play the role his methodology requires. And when 95 percent of the answers in a WTP poll fit into the "I don't know" category, Adams, rather than blaming his methodology, blames the educational system. "This very widespread inability to perform the calculations to convert lives into money is a very worrying reflection of the unworldly nature of the educational system in this country."

Indoctrinating people in WTP methodology, however, would probably have very little impact on the success of the survey. Responses to a different questionnaire by Michael Jones-Lee, for example, regarding higher or lower airplane fares for lower or higher risk of fatal crash, produced a $5 million value for life. Such an outrageous range of values ($28,000 to $5,000,000) seems less a reflection on human intelligence than an indication of the plain illogic of the survey approach. The respondents have a far surer grasp on reality than the researchers.

Acknowledging the complications that arise with surveys, economists have turned to surrogate markets, especially the labor market, to estimate how much people do, in fact, value life and limb. Labor market theory assumes that a worker is faced with a range of risk-wage trade-offs. If he doesn't like the risk, he can voluntarily take a cut in pay for a lower risk. It also assumes that workers are well-informed about risks. But, in practice, choices are so limited that the entire approach is suspect.

Most importantly, the labor market does not offer the same trade-off to everyone. Those who are better educated and those who receive higher incomes may not face a real trade-off between wages and risk at all, while the poor face both the highest risks, and the least attractive trade-offs.

Economists justify this approach on the grounds that the population is large enough for life to be statistical life rather than individual life. But the results of the studies demonstrate that the risk-wage trade-off exists only among some segments of the population. Obviously, workers in hazardous occupations face greater risks than the general population, as does anyone who lives near a plant emitting hazardous waste. The less random the distribution of risk, the weaker the justification for use of the WTP approach.

Income plays a central role in the trade-off of risks and costs, not because the poor are ignorant, but because they cannot afford risk avoidance. Residents of Triana, Alabama, for instance, eat fish from the Tennessee River with levels of DDT fifty times the amount the Food and Drug Administration considers carcinogenic because they cannot afford anything else. According to authorities at TVA, the contamination of the river is caused by an Olin Corporation chemical plant. This fish, however, is not served on the dinnertables of Olin executives. As United Steelworkers President Lloyd McBride observes sagely, "I think we'd find that the worker lives downwind and downstream from the manager."

Again, the decision to leave a job because it is too hazardous can never be a one-issue decision. It may involve giving up pension rights, abandoning a home, leaving acquaintances, and relocating a family. Nor does a worker necessarily see that there is a decision to be made. Nicholas Ashford, assistant director of the Center for Policy Alternatives at MIT, notes that many workers "are convinced of the necessity of performing [certain hazardous jobs] in order to earn their livelihood.

In short, class has raised its head. All of these methodologies stumble on the unpleasant truth that the poor simply have fewer choices. Implicitly, cost-benefit analysis condones this by suggesting that the "choice" of accepting a higher risk is purely voluntary, when in fact it is often a necessary result of economic conditions. Income distribution is not a concern of this supposedly value-free methodology. If the outcome is that poor people have to take more of the risks, that is outside the scope of cost-benefit analysis.

As Yale Law Professor Guido Calabresi has pointedly observed, "The willingness of a poor man confronting a tragic situation to choose money rather than to [avert the risk] always represents an unquiet indictment of society's distribution of wealth."

Even if the thorny distributional and ethical problems with cost-benefit analysis could be solved by refining the methodology or the logic (and in our view they can't), there remains the insurmountable problem of measurement. Despite the mighty efforts of the cost-benefit accountants to wring all subjectivity out of their balance sheets, many of the things being measured remain inherently subjective. And they cannot be measured by inferring value from people's actual choices in the marketplace, because many of these "decisions" are not voluntary decisions at all, but the result of coercive economic circumstance.

The worker who contracts byssinosis in a textile mill cannot buy back his health, no matter how lavishly he is compensated. For a violinist who loses a finger in a lawnmower accident, dollar compensation does not provide comparability.

For the DES daughter with vaginal cancer, or the asbestosis victim, indemnification in the form of dollar payment does not restore the victim to the original position. Free choice has become permanently supplanted.

Health, safety, and environmental protection, in other words, are *prerequisites* for full appreciation and enjoyment of all "economic goods." Sacrificing them for short-term production is like using the walls of one's house for firewood on a wintry night. Preservation of such primary goods is an investment in the basic freedom of choice of every other economic good, and an essential precondition to the competitive market of economic theory.

According to standard theory, each successive market exchange is a snapshot, entirely separate from the previous one. Health, safety, and environmental damage, however, are not amenable to this kind of exchange. They tend to create dynamic effects which rebound on the market and distort it—distortions that tend to linger for years and reverberate for generations. This was the case with Thalidomide and DES. It is also the case with Love Canal, thousands of other potential Love Canals, and the Kepone contamination of the James River by Allied Chemical Corporation.

Responding to these gross costs, new industries blossom to produce compensatory rather than primary goods. Health care is the nation's largest, fastest growing "industry," and one of the most inflationary. It accounted for $12 billion in 1950, and $200 billion today. It was 4 percent of GNP in 1955, and 9 percent today. These increasing costs, in part, are the result of a deteriorating environment—80 to 90 percent of the 400,000 annual cancer cases are complicated by some environmental factor. In short, these expenditures do not produce wealth, but compensate for lost health.

The multibillion dollar legal and insurance industries are also getting healthier as the condition of the nation's health and environment deteriorates. Product liability suits multiply and insurance premiums rise with unsafe products and an unhealthy environment. According to *Business Week*, liability insurance for manufacturers and retailers cost $2.75 billion in 1978. But should the burgeoning health care, legal, and insurance "industries" be the conceptual equivalent to industries that produce real products like electronics, food, or transport? Should we applaud when production in compensatory industries increases?

The dynamic effects of health and safety damage on production itself are simply not comparable to the production of real products, despite the economists' exhortation to measure all goods equally. According to the Bureau of Labor Statistics, workers lost more than 250 million working hours in 1977 as a result of occupational injuries alone. Such a loss translates into a $3.4 billion loss in output for that year. Noise can contribute to decreased productivity. The effects of black lung disease reduce the productivity of labor in underground coal mining by 20 to 30 percent. The disability program of the Social Security Adminis-tration currently costs $11 to $13 billion every year. According to a study sponsored by the Department of Labor in 1978, 3 million of the 15 million people with a disability traced it to their jobs. Over a million were prevented from working at all because of their conditions, while 9.5 million were restricted in the type of job they could perform.

Pollution also deteriorates capital input. Sulfur oxides accelerate corrosion. Just with respect to metals, increased maintenance costs, preventive measures, and more frequent replacement because of air pollution cost $1.45 billion in 1970, according to one study. Acid rain, 50 percent of which is caused by the noxious chemical sulphur dioxide spewed forth from coal-fired power plants in the United States, could sound the death knell for all fish and plant life in 48,000 lakes in Ontario, Canada, as well as in 300 lakes in New York's Adirondack Mountains. Architectural damage from sulphur dioxide is placed at $12 billion every year. Textile damage is placed at more than $2 billion every year from air pollution. And vegetation losses ran over $200 million in 1970 for mobile source emissions alone, according to the National Academy of Sciences.

Unlike the market for products, the "market" for pollution prevention before-the-fact is morally and economically preferable to compensation afterward. Prevention of Love Canal would have run $4 million in 1979 dollars; so far, $23 million in tax revenues from the State of New York and $4 million from EPA have been funneled into the cleanup. Proper disposal of PCBs in Raleigh, North Carolina, would have cost $100,000; proper cleanup could cost between $2 million and $12 million. The Environmental Protection Agency estimates that it would cost *$8 billion* to clean up the James River, but adds that it may be impossible to restore the river to its former state—at any cost. A $200,000 investment by Allied Chemical could have put an end to the episode before the first toxic domino fell. And Ford, of course, contributed to extensive deaths and injuries because the company refused to put a safety shield costing $11 into the Pinto.

Economic efficiency requires informed choice, but outside the realm of theory, information is often imperfect. Risks in the workplace, the marketplace, and the environment defy well-informed choice. As Dr. Irving J. Selikoff of Mt. Sinai Medical School bluntly put it, "We will not know for another twenty years whether the chemicals introduced in the 1960s are hazardous. We need better methods than we have now without waiting to see the dead bodies in the streets." Time lags in the reaction to toxic substances have become their brutal trademark. It was impossible for the 500,000 to 2 million women given DES between 1945 and 1955, for example, to know that they were increasing their daughters' chances of developing vaginal or cervical cancer. Nor can laboratory tests be relied upon to produce the necessary information. Twice as much exposure to radiation is not necessarily twice as hazardous, and tests do not predict the "dose-response curve" with certainty.

In one laboratory study, there was significant increase of tumor development for those exposed to DES at levels of 6.25 part per billion (ppb) and above 50 ppb, while those receiving dosages in between, 12.5 ppb and 25ppb, did not exhibit significant departure from the tumor development rate of the controls. Such results challenge the assumption of a threshhold below which ingestion is safe; it also challenges the belief that greater exposure necessarily means greater risk, that dose and response are related in a smooth, continuous curve.

A different set of epidemiological data required for informed choice is even more difficult to test in the lab: the data for interaction between drugs. Women exposed to DES, for example, should avoid any further exposure to estrogens because cancer-causing effects tend to accumulate. Many interactions have synergistic rather than purely cumulative effects. For asbestos workers who smoke, lung cancer is ninety-two times more frequent than for the nonsmoking population. Amphetamines are ten times more toxic under noisy conditions than under normal stress.

Risk identification is one matter; deliberate identification with risk is another. Well-informed, rational choice requires consumers and workers to understand the risks they undertake. "It doesn't do any good to write on a menu that if you have bacon you run a one times ten to the minus nine probability of getting cancer," says economist Allen Ferguson, head of the Public Interest Economics Center. A recent survey showed that only 18 percent of those interviewed felt that there was even a one in ten likelihood of their being in an accident the following year. Fifty percent felt that the probability was less than one in three hundred. The actual probability? One in five.

To the economist, the solution is to provide more information. But, given the nature of the information, one wonders whether people will or can calculate the multiple probabilities of injury or death for the many products they buy daily. Consumers are not actuaries.

Industry manipulation of consumer options also restricts informed choice. What John Kenneth Galbraith has termed "induced demand" limits free choice, and undercuts the basic premise of market economics by making the response of the consumer a function of the activity of the supplier. Thus, based on the auto industry's advertising emphasis, consumers have been free to choose the color or style of car they want but not whether it has air bags or bumpers that can survive a five-mile-an-hour impact.

One could easily write an entire book about the costs imposed on society by the *failure* to regulate. The demand for health and safety regulation did not materialize out of thin air. Nor is it, as Irving Kristol and Paul Weaver wrote in *Public Interest* magazine, a conspiracy by "Naderites" who seek to replace a "society shaped by voluntary commercial transaction among consenting adults" with a "more powerful government, in which they have positions of authority." The transactions that cause the maiming of millions of Americans yearly are often neither informed nor voluntary. Historically the periodic bursts of health and safety regulation have not been orchestrated by conspiring Naderites, but rather come from public indignation about adulterated meat, hazardous drugs, flammable children's pajamas, carcinogenic chemicals, and all the other evidence of industrial negligence dating back to Upton Sinclair's THE JUNGLE and the Pure Food and Drug Act of 1906.

Although the drug industry regularly complains about the testing procedures required by FDA to prove safety and effectiveness, the Thalidomide episode grimly demonstrates how essential this regulation is to the public's safety. Indeed, countless dangerous drugs and devices that slipped through FDA's net, from Chloramphenicol to DES to the Dalkon shield, prove reminders that FDA procedures are, if anything, far too lax.

The current drug industry campaign is attempting to persuade public opinion that FDA red tape is keeping the public from the next generation of miracle drugs—cancer cures, elixirs of youth—that would pour forth from the test tubes if only the FDA got out of the way. What they fail to point out is that FDA regulation requires only what a prudent manufacturer would do anyway—assure safety and effectiveness—were it not for the temptation to beat the competition to production.

Industry notoriously exaggerates the costs associated with regulation it opposes, precisely because regulation is a political process. The higher the alleged cost, the more credible is the case against regulation. As the Moss subcommittee of the Senate has observed, "The most significant factor in evaluating a cost-benefit study is the name of the sponsor."

A case in point is the proposed OSHA standard to control the dust and fumes created in processing beryllium, which poses a cancer threat for more than 25,000 workers. Beryllium is used in the production of nuclear weaponry. Relying strictly on the $150 million cost-of-compliance estimate from industry, former Energy Secretary James R. Schlesinger maintained that the standard was a potential threat to national security because it would allegedly shut down plants. Less than three weeks after Schlesinger wrote to Secretary of Labor Ray Marshall warning of the security threat, Energy Department officials conceded that the industry estimate was "a gross estimate based on rule of thumb."

Actual cost? Between $3.7 and $4.6 million.

In the early 1970s the chemical industry estimated its compliance cost with a proposed vinyl chloride standard to be 200 times higher than what it turned out to be. When members of Congress requested the raw data, they were told that it had been destroyed according to a prior agreement among the participating firms.

The Securities and Exchange Commission found that the U.S. Steel Corporation kept two sets of data on compliance costs with environmental standards: one for investors and another, higher, one for the media and the public.

The American Petroleum Institute (API) recently pegged the costs of complying with environmental regulations on oil and gas drilling at $45.5 billion per year, a cost which prompted a *Wall Street Journal* editorial entitled "EPA Runs Amuck." The API estimate, however, was based on implementation of an elaborate monitoring system, which was not included in the proposed regulation, but which comprised over 98 percent of the estimate. According to EPA's then-Assistant Administrator for Water and Waste Management, Thomas C. Jorling, API knew that the cost estimate was "patently untrue." Furthermore, he states, "there is substantial double counting here since several proposed EPA requirements are already required by existing regulations in some states and on federal lands.

In a May 29, 1974, letter to the U.S. General Accounting Office, Volvo, the Swedish automaker, noted that most of the data released by U.S. automobile manufacturers on the cost of meeting federal regulations was based on and "aimed purely at resisting regulation."

Using price information supplied by auto companies, the Bureau of Labor Statistics compiled data on auto price increases attributed to safety standards. How much "price" data diverges from "cost" of compliance data is illustrated by information supplied to BLS on the price of shoulder harnesses. Industry attributed a $25 increase in the price of a 1968 model car to the shoulder harness. Through a private investigation conducted by then-Senator Walter Mondale and Senator Warren Magnuson, however, it was revealed that cost of compliance for the auto manufacturers was less than $5 per car. In other words, industry reaped every year an extra $100 million in profit disguised as the cost of the safety device.

Cost-benefit analysts often assume away any learning curve—that is, the rate at which the cost of pollution control and safety goes down as engineers gain experience with new methods and as the standard becomes part of the normal production process. And once regulations become designed into the production process rather than just a departure from a competitive market, as cost-benefit analysis assumes, their true impact on the economy becomes next to impossible to isolate. Regulation has fueled the growth of the pollution control and chemical industries, whose investments, in turn, have become vital links in the circular flow of goods and services in the economy. They are far more real than the compensatory industries that grow out of society's failure to regulate.

All of the limits of the market, in other words, become the biases of cost-benefit analysis—biases which invariably lead to an overstatement of costs and an understatement of benefits.

Class dismissed.

● ● ●

POSTSCRIPT

SHOULD THE FEDERAL GOVERNMENT DEREGULATE AMERICAN BUSINESS?

Although Weidenbaum is concerned about all government regulation, he is most concerned about the "new style" of regulation that has occurred during the past fifteen years. These regulators, such as OSHA, EPA, and EEO, are concerned with specific activities of a firm or industry and are totally uninterested in the other activities of these firms or industries. In their zest to monitor their specific tasks, these regulators can cause immense damage to those they regulate. Weidenbaum therefore asks that each regulation pass a simple test: Do the extra benefits associated with this regulation exceed the extra costs of imposing this regulation? Green and Waitzman challenge the validity of Weidenbaum's test. They find that the application of this benefit-cost rule overstates the costs and understates the benefits. In addition, they assert that benefit-cost analyses are biased toward the affluent in society and penalize those of lesser means.

Recent professional and popular literature contain many articles on government regulation. The impact of the free market economists is apparent in this literature. Nearly all of it is critical of government regulation. Murray L. Weidenbaum is one of the most visible contributors to this growing body of books, pamphlets and articles. His work with Robert De Fina, THE COST OF GOVERNMENT REGULATION OF ECONOMIC ACTIVITY (American Enterprise Institute, 1978) and his book THE FUTURE OF BUSINESS REGULATION (Anacorn Press, 1979) are excellent examples of the anti-regulation mood that has swept the country. Pro-regulation articles are now beginning to appear in the literature. For example, Daniel Fusfeld responds to Weidenbaum in a short piece entitled "Some Notes on the Opposition to Regulation," *Journal of Post-Keynesian Economics* (Spring, 1980), Sam Zagoria in "Making Consumer Products Safer," *Federationist* (February, 1980), details the types of unsafe products which would appear on the market if regulation did not exist, and Alasdair MacIntyre's "Regulation - A Substitute for Morality," *The Hasting Report* (February, 1980) asserts that regulation provides a minimum ethic for the community.

Since Weidenbaum and Green/Waitzman are quite persuasive, how you will judge the validity of their arguments depends in part on the value that you attach to economic efficiency, equity and stability.

ISSUE 5

DO FIRMS EXPLOIT WORKERS AND LOCAL COMMUNITIES BY CLOSING PROFITABLE PLANTS?

YES: Barry Bluestone and Bennett Harrison, from "Why Corporations Close Profitable Plants," *Working Papers* (May-June, 1980).
NO: Richard B. McKenzie, from "Frustrating Business Mobility," *Regulation* (May-June, 1980).

ISSUE SUMMARY

YES: Professors Bluestone and Harrison assert that large modern corporations, particularly conglomerates, systematically milk profits from healthy firms, mismanage them, fail to maintain them, and then shut them down on the grounds that they are inefficient.
NO: Professor McKenzie argues that in a healthy market economy it is natural and necessary for some plants to move and others to close in order to achieve the great benefits of economic efficiency.

No one denies that economic efficiency in a market economy is achieved by the application of the "survival of the fittest rule." Inefficient firms are driven out of the market place by their efficient competitors. Thus the ever present threat of market failure makes each firm strive for the maximum degree of economic efficiency.

The fact that the market metes out this blind justice to the inefficient firm is one of the first lessons in an introductory economics course. It is the mechanism which allocates resources. That is, when an inefficient firm fails, this increases the supply of factors of production which were previously employed by this inefficient firm. The increase in the supply of factors of production results in factor prices falling. These lower factor prices now make these factors attractive purchases for other, presumably efficient, firms. Thus resources are "freed" from inefficient firms and "absorbed" by efficient firms.

The current controversy does not take exception to this notion of economic justice. Although some economists challenge the underlying assumptions of this allocation mechanism—such as, the downward flexibility of wages, the ability to substitute a unit of labor in alternative occupations or the mobility of labor—the current critics challenge the viability of this mechanism in today's highly concentrated industrial sector. They are concerned with two basic issues: the impact of large enterprises on local communities and the legitimacy of the allocation process when multiplant firms and multiproduct firms dominate the marketplace.

Critics such as Bluestone and Harrison stress the fact that the marketplace is characterized by firms that are totally different from the firms of Adam Smith's day. If one of the modern day firms closes its doors, large numbers of individuals can suddenly become unemployed and flood the labor market of that region. Total income in that community falls. This sets off a multiplier effect which reduces business demand and income of local businesses which provide goods and services to those workers who are now unemployed. Additionally, the impact of a plant closing on the local tax base cannot be ignored. Not only does the local community lose the property tax assessment of the closed plant—they are rarely sold and renovated for alternative uses—but it loses property tax assessments on worker homes as the supply of housing increases and home prices fall when workers attempt to flee the community. This decline in property tax collections coupled with falling sales tax and income tax collections can leave a community financially strapped just when increased demands are placed upon it due to its high unemployment rate. Thus closing a modern day plant with its 500, 1000, or 5,000 employees is dramatically different than closing Adam Smith's pin factory with its six employees.

The second concern of critics is perhaps more fundamental. Multiplant firms and multiproduct conglomerates can work outside the realm of the traditionally conceived marketplace. That is, profits earned in one plant can be siphoned off for the benefit of a totally unrelated activity. This phenomenon forms the crux of this issue.

Professor McKenzie argues that the allocation of funds from one part of an enterprise to another part of the same enterprise is totally consistent with the classical economist's profit maximization rule. Professors Bluestone and Harrison argue that these transfers violate the internal logic of classical economics and in the process these transfers work immense hardships on the workers these firms employ and on the communities where they are located.

Public policy to encourage or to discourage plant relocations hinges upon the outcome of this debate. Should firms be granted tax concessions for investments in plant and equipment that replicate old plants in another part of the country? Should firms be relieved from retirement program obligations when these production facilities are no longer profitable? Should tax write-offs be allowed for firms which close down a marginally profitable plant? These and other policy questions can be resolved only when the debate between McKenzie and Bluestone/Harrison is settled.

YES

Barry Bluestone and Bennett Harrison

WHY CORPORATIONS CLOSE PROFITABLE PLANTS

Plant closings are becoming a grimly familiar story. The parent conglomerate, usually from a remote home office, announces one day that a well-established local factory is no longer competitive. Typically, the handwriting has been on the wall for years. The machinery is outmoded; the company's more modern factories are using newer equipment—and nothing foreshadows a shutdown like failure to reinvest. The workers have been told to hold down wages, or the plant will have to move; the town has been warned that property taxes must be abated or they will lose the plant altogether. Often these demands have been met.

But the dread day arrives anyway. Hundreds of jobs will be lost; the tax base will be devastated. The town elders wring their hands. Workers with seniority (those with roots in the community) are invited to pull up stakes and take lower wage jobs in company plants out of state.

A last ditch effort by workers to buy the plant fails; they can't raise the necessary capital. Although the factory is obsolete, oddly enough it is worth a king's ransom. Anyway, it must be a real lemon, or why would the company shut it down?

Why indeed?

The editorial pages of the *Wall Street Journal* suggest the reasons for plant relocation are obvious. Don't credit the sunbelt's climate, says the *Journal*. The real cause of the sunbelt's economic growth is its superior attitude toward business. Labor costs (translation: wages) are lower; tax burdens (translation: public services) are lower. Plants must relocate, therefore, because in the high-cost Northeast and Midwest workers have greedily demanded decent wages, and communities have insisted on adequate school, police, fire, and sanitation services.

And anyway, plant closings, despite their human toll, mean that the system is performing the way it should. Capital mobility is an essential ingredient in our free-market economy. The profit-maximizing entrepreneur must be free to invest capital where it will return the highest possible yield. Otherwise, we

From, "Why Corporations Close Profitable Plants", *Working Papers*. Vol. Vii, No. 3, May/June 1980. Reprinted by permission.

are sanctioning inefficiency: letting the economy as a whole operate below its optimum potential means allowing lower productivity and falling wages. And we surely don't want that.

Again and again, trade unions and state legislatures grappling with plant closings listen to business executives insist that plants close because they've ceased to be profitable: "If it could make money, do you really think we would shut it down?"

The contention seems plausible at first but, like so much in textbook economics, it simply fails to describe real life. Large modern corporations—and conglomerates in particular—will and frequently do close profitable branch plants or previously acquired businesses. They may do so for a variety of reasons that flow from the way conglomerates are organized. Centralized management and control produces pressure to meet corporate growth objectives and minimum annual profit targets; it also siphons off subsidiaries' profits to meet other corporate needs. Sometimes management by "remote control" actually creates the unprofitability of the subsidiary that eventually leads to shutdown—as when the home office is far removed from the production site or unfamiliar with the industry in which a subsidiary competes. Again, the textbook model of competition among entrepreneur-owned and -managed businesses utterly fails to explain why plants relocate.

Modern industrial theory says large corporations are under constant pressure to grow, to expand their market share. Stability is often seen as a sign of decline, no matter how well run and steadily productive the plant. In a letter to an executive of the K-Mart discount department chain, Paul McCracken, former

head of the President's Council of Economic Advisors, wrote: "History suggests that companies which decide to 'take their ease' are apt to be on the route to decay."

This pressure is reinforced by the corporation's need to offer growth stock in order to attract equity capital. Investors in growth stocks make their money from capital gains realized when they sell their stock rather than from steady dividends paid out by the firm. The purchase price of the stock is thus high in relation to the dividends it earns. However, only by growing can a company keep the price-to-earnings ratio high, and continue to attract investors to its stocks. In many situations it is easier for a corporation to boost its price-earnings ratio by acquiring efficient and profitable businesses—often in unrelated markets—than by developing new ventures or expanding existing operations. This option was particularly attractive during the mid-1960s and the late 1970s when the stock market tended to undervalue real assets. Then a corporation or conglomerate seeking to expand could acquire those assets at "bargain" prices.

Plants must also meet target rates of return. Many companies that are divisions or subsidiaries of parent corporations or conglomerates are now routinely required to meet minimum annual profit targets as a condition for receiving finance or executive "perks" from the home office. Many are ultimately shut down because they cannot achieve what the managers describe as the parent corporation's current "hurdle rate."

At Cornell University, studies of conglomerate destruction of viable businesses have found many cases in which conglomerates abandoned going concerns that did not meet the specified target rates of return. For example,

> The Herkimer [New York] plant, producing library furniture, had been acquired by Sperry Rand in 1955. The plant had made a profit every year except one through the next two decades, and yet Sperry Rand decided to close the plant and sell the equipment [in part because it] was not yielding a 22 percent profit on invested capital. That was the standard used by this conglomerate/management in determining an acceptable rate of return on its investments.

Another example is the experience of the Bates Manufacturing Company, a leading Maine textile operation. After several changes of ownership after World War II, all the mills except the one at Lewiston were sold to textile conglomerates. The Lewiston facility, along with a coal and energy business Bates had acquired, was then sold to two New York investors. At the time, Bates offered a steady but low return of 5 to 7 percent. The energy business, however, promised a 15 to 20 percent return. As one long-time manager at Bates put it, "These boys were not textile men, they were money men." And sure enough, they decided to close the textile plant in 1977, in order to put all their money into the energy business.

Again, in the lower Pioneer Valley of central Massachusetts, the Chicopee Manufacturing Company was generating an estimated 12 percent rate of return on its apparel products. The parent firm, Johnson & Johnson (whose principal line is pharmaceuticals), was dissatisfied with anything short of a 16 percent minimum, and announced that Chicopee would be shut down.

As times change, the hurdle rate may rise. In textiles and apparel, for example, Royal Little, the founder of Textron, told a Congressional investigative committee in 1948 that his conglomerate generally insisted that each of its subsidiaries earn 10 percent on total invested capital before taxes or risk being shut down. By the late 1970s, according to its own corporate reports, another clothing conglomerate, Genesco, was imposing a 25 percent hurdle rate on its various companies.

Whatever the target rate in a particular company at a particulat time, the existence of the corporate hurdle rate means that in the era of monopoly capital, viable businesses can be closed even though they are making a profit—because it is not enough of a profit. Perhaps the most dramatic example of this phenomenon involved Uniroyal's closing of its eighty-seven-year-old inner tube factory in Indianapolis in 1978. The *Wall Street Journal* reported the story in the following way:

> The factory has long been the country's leading producer of inner tubes. It operates profitably. Its $7 million to $8 million annual payroll sustains the families of nearly 600 employees.
>
> The company, in a formal statement, cited "high labor costs" and "steadily declining demand." Union and management officials who worked at the plant tell another story. They say that Uniroyal could have kept the plant operating profitably if it wanted to but that under pressure from the securities markets management decided to concentrate its energy on higher-growth chemical lines. Interviews with securities analysts support this theory. Richard Haydon, an analyst at Goldman, Sachs and Co., says: "You have

one very large entity looking at a very small entity, but the small entity being very large to those people that work there. I think it's a truism that many companies have grown too big to look at the small market.

One consultant advises his corporate clients that, when the wage bill as a percent of sales rises, or when the rate of return on investment falls below some standard—he proposes the current money market interest rate—it is time to think about shutting down. "If capital does not work for you effectively, it should be invested elsewhere."

The case histories of Bates, Chicopee, and Uniroyal all have happy endings of one kind or another. Jobs at Bates were saved when the mill workers and some of the former managers chose to buy it. They were able to do so through an Employee Stock Ownership Plan arrangement, and in the first year after it was bought Bates earned a 17 percent after-tax profit. (See "Employee Ownership: How Well Is It Working?" by Daniel Zwerdling in *Working Papers* May/June 1979). To keep Chicopee from closing, twenty-one savings banks in the Pioneer Valley created a fund for high-risk business development. This enabled Chicopee's management to buy the company. And Uniroyal factory workers saved their jobs with the help of the presidents of the Indianapolis City Council and the Rubber Workers Union. They persuaded local financiers to put up the capital to purchase the plant from Uniroyal. The profit forecast for the first year of operation predicts that $500,000 will be distributed among the workers, and another $500,000 invested in new machinery. At the moment, all three plants are operating in the black, reconfirming that the cor-

porations had been about to shut down basically profitable enterprises.

Subsidiaries' profits are prey to corporate appropriation. Not only do many parent companies deny their branches and conglomerate subsidiaries the power to establish their own performance criteria, but the profits they *do* earn are generally repatriated to the parent firm, to be reallocated according to the latter's priorities. For example, in one subsidiary of a Fortune 500 corporation, the profits from its local specialty paper products operation are taken by the parent, which returns only enough capital to the mill to meet Environmental Protection Agency and basic maintenance requirements. "In fact, only 5 percent of capital expenditures over the past five years have gone for growth. In that period net assets have declined 26 percent and employment has declined 9 percent . . ."

A healthy subsidiary that generates excess capital is sometimes a "cash-cow." An example of this would be a regional industry that has run out of opportunities for local growth: the New England market for department store sales is thought by industry leaders to be more or less saturated. Therefore, "the local [New England] units of national holding companies and department store chains are made to serve as cash-cows for [stores in other] areas of the country."

The appropriation of a subsidiary's or a branch's surplus by the parent corporation introduces potentially severe structural imbalance into a plant's operations During years when sales are good, the profits accrue to the parent. When times go bad, the operating company has been stripped of its revenues, and may be forced to go into the local capital markets for a loan. However, lack of control over its own future profit stream makes the servicing of this loan uncertain, and local banks or other leaders will deal with this uncertainty by charging a higher interest rate—and of course the parent firm may not even permit the branch or subsidiary to borrow on its own.

Thus, by becoming the banker to its various constituent plants or companies, the centralized corporation is able to enforce its own growth goals. At best, the subsidiaries are forced to compete directly with one another for access to their own profits. But in fact, conglomerates (and, since 1976, more and more large single-product corporations) have tended to place the capital so obtained into other, often totally unrelated, acquisitions instead of reinvesting in the sector—let alone the specific company—from which the surplus was redistributed.

The managers of K-Mart, for example, believe that their continuing operations will be throwing off far more cash than the department store business has traditionally been able profitably to absorb. As a result, industry sources estimate that by 1981 fully one-quarter K-Mart's available cash will have no place to go. One executive told *Fortune* magazine: "Time is running out and we are aware of it. K-Mart must search out new directions."

Yet at the same time—just to show the chaos and irrationality of the economic era in which we now live—Mobil Oil Corporation used a substantial part of its post-1973 inflated international oil profits not to expand domestic petroleum production, but to purchase Montgomery Ward, an established department store chain!

The diversification in the steel industry that led to the famous shutdown in 1977 of the Campbell plant of the Youngstown Sheet and Tube Company in Ohio began early in the decade. Between 1970 and 1976 the steel industry as a whole paid out 43 percent of after-tax profits in dividends. This rate was above average for all industry, yet the steel industry was simultaneously complaining that required pollution-control expenditures prevented them from upgrading their old plants and equipment. Some Wall Street analysts have seen the high dividend rate as a strategy for holding on to investors while developing a plan for diversifying into new fields. In the late 1970s the industry has done just that—it has shifted capital into cement, petrochemicals, coal, natural gas, nuclear power plant components containers and packaging, and real estate.

According to U.S. Steel's annual reports, for example, the share of that corporation's annual plant and equipment investment going into actual production of steel fell from 69 percent in 1976 to just over half in 1979. For every dollar of old plant and equipment written off, only $1.40 in new investment was undertaken (in fact, the ratio of new capital spending to depreciation in the steel operations fell by 100 percent, from 2.9 to 1.4). But for every dollar of capital depreciation in its nonsteel operations, U.S. Steel spent nearly three dollars in new capital investment. By 1978, 44 percent of U.S. Steel's total worldwide assets were in nonsteel operations.

Youngstown Sheet and Tube Company was not owned by U.S. Steel, but by a New Orleans-based conglomerate, the Lykes Corporation. Lykes purchased it in 1969, when Sheet and Tube was the nation's eighth largest steel-making firm. The acquisition was financed mainly by a major loan package, which Lykes promised to pay off out of Sheet and Tube's very substantial cash flow. During the next eight years, Lykes used Sheet and

Tube's cash to amortize that debt and to expand its nonsteel operations. Figure 1 shows pre- and post-merger annual capital investment in Youngstown. Before the merger, investment in plant and equipment averaged almost $10 million a year. After the acquisition by Lykes, the average fell to about $3 million per year, and would have had a *zero* trend if not for a few investment projects that were quickly abandoned during the 1975-76 recession. Clearly, Lykes was pursuing a pattern of planned disinvestment in its recent acquisition. This has led most financial analysts to agree that "Lykes must bear responsibility for a good deal of the failure at Youngstown Sheet and Tube." *Business Week* put it in its October 3, 1977, issue: "The conglomerators' steel acquisitions were seen as cash boxes for corporate growth in other areas." In a rather absurd postscript to the closing—which cost 4,100 Ohio workers their jobs—Lykes merged in 1978 with the owners of the nation's *next* largest steel-maker, the conglomerate Ling-Temco-Vought. The argument used in court by Lykes and LTV to overcome antitrust objections to the merger was that their steel business was "failing," and could only be rescued by achieving financial scale economies through merger! The merger now makes Lykes-LTV the nation's third largest producer of steel. Thus does corporate profit appropriation encourage economic concentration.

This concentration in turn makes it possible for management to impose other costs by "remote control." Centralized control by a home office can impair the profitability of a newly acquired branch or subsidiary, and can even make the business actually unprofitable.

Sometimes the home office requires its new acquisition to carry additional management staff from headquarters, staff the subsidiary did without before and that are probably redundant. For example, in a recent issue of a New England trade magazine, a small manufacturer with 40 percent of the domestic hypodermic needle market was offered for sale by its conglomerate parent. The market analyst notes that "the parent corporation, a Fortune 500 company. . . . has imposed an excess of staff and other requirements which add nonproductive costs to the operation. A *pro forma* [simulated balance sheet] eliminating this overlay of corporate expenses shows a much better picture." Recently freed from its former parent (the Esmark conglomerate), the Peabody tannery in Massachusetts projects a reduction in overhead and administrative support services of almost $500,000 during its first year.

In 1978, the New England Provision Company (NEPCO) of Dorchester, a Boston neighborhood, had its meat-packing operations shut down by the same LTV conglomerate that recently merged with the Lykes Corporation. The firm had been consistently profitable prior to its acquisition by LTV in the late 1960s. One factor turning profits into losses seems to have been LTV's insistence that NEPCO pay a fee to the parent for management services. This practice was also found to be present in the case of the Colonial Press in Clinton, Massachusetts, acquired in 1974 by Sheller-Globe, primarily a maker of auto parts, school buses, and ambulances, and closed three years later, in 1977. Colonial was charged an average of $900,000 a year in corporate overhead charges. Some months it was charged $200,000.

There was little justification for these

charges. The Press was being forced to pay the costs of larger corporate activities from which it did not benefit. For example, Sheller-Globe maintained an entire department that was solely responsible for security. Given the conditions in the automotive industry there was some justification for these costs. However, Sheller-Globe's corporate policies meant that the security department applied the same systems to all divisions. The corporation built a link fence around three sides of the Colonial Press plant and hired twenty-two security guards. Upon exiting the plant, employees would often be searched for stolen goods. The level of theft at the Press could not possibly justify the cost of the fences and guards, yet Colonial Press was forced to bear part of these costs.

Sometimes the parent firm forces the subsidiary to purchase from particular distant providers, even if the subsidiary's managers could cut costs by purchasing locally. In the NEPCO case,

> the firm was required to buy the meat it processed and packaged from [another LTV subsidiary, Wilson Foods and Sporting Goods] at inflated prices; and an inept marketing company was hired . . ., the result of a "sweetheart" contract arranged for the benefit of a former LTV executive vice-president. . . .

Lykes imposed the same burden on Youngstown Sheet and Tube. According to the Senate hearings, YST ended up paying more for raw materials (coal and iron ore) from Lyke's mines after the merger than it would have paid on the open market. After the merger, YST began purchasing parts and equipment, which had previously been supplied locally, from a Lykes subsidiary at higher

rates. This arrangement cost YST $60 million a year.

To tax the subsidiary in order to subsidize the operations of the headquarters (or its friends) is bad enough. But perhaps most serious of all are the cases where home office policy actually *creates* the unprofitability of the (previously profitable) subsidiary, through clumsy interference with the local managers who know the situation best. William F. Whyte's case study of the Library Bureau, a furniture plant in Herkimer, N.Y., revealed just such a problem.

> The plant had always had its own sales force and was not dependent upon Sperry Rand for its market. In fact, being part of the conglomerate imposed serious barriers in marketing. For example, it was a rule of Sperry Rand that the Library Bureau salesmen could not call on any customers served by Sperry Rand. While this left the Library Bureau its main markets with public and educational institution libraries, the rule barred the plant from selling to a large number of industrial and business firms that used library equipment. The [subsidiary] could only enter these markets through Sperry Rand salesmen who were unfamiliar with Library Bureau products and had more important things to sell. The handicaps were similar in the export field. . . . [According to the former] head of sales for the Library Bureau . . . "We were not officially barred from exporting, but to sell anything outside of the country, we had to send our proposal to the international division, and it would just die there. We would never hear anything back.

Similarly, after its acquisition of the Colonial Press, Sheller-Globe immediately brought in outside management that, except for the newly installed president, had no experience in the publishing industry. Yet this outside group was given control over the most important decisions. In particular, Sheller-Globe wanted to change Colonial's orientation from sales to manufacturing. It wanted to emphasize producing books more efficiently rather than satisfying more clients. This decision impaired long-standing relations with the publishing companies that were Colonial's clients (these included Reader's Digest and Random House), since Sheller-Globe believed there was not a great deal of difference between "producing a steering wheel and producing a book."

Flexibility to accommodate customer's publication schedules was reduced. Colonial was no longer allowed to offer free warehouse space to publishers. The customer service and order departments were merged, resulting in misplaced orders and deteriorated customer relations. An expensive computerized management information system was installed, which so fouled up operations that "books were lost and there was often general confusion about what materials there were and where they were located." Publishers were no longer given itemized cost estimates, and in general, the management under Sheller-Globe mistreated its customers. As a result of all this, "the publishing industry became alienated and sales declined. . . . Decisions which were appropriate to the automotive industry proved disastrous in the book-printing industry."

This disaster has been somewhat mitigated by the reopening of the Press in 1979, as the Colonial Cooperative Press. With the help of the Massachusetts Community Development Finance Corporation and the Industrial Coopera-

tive Association, the press was sold to the workers as a full-scale cooperative. However, it is a much smaller enterprise and it isn't clear whether or not it will succeed. The Colonial Press had over 1,000 workers. Colonial Cooperative Press has 75. Furthermore, in the two years it took to reorganize the plant, the Press lost many of its customers.

Whether or not it survives, this worker-purchase is another example of an ad hoc solution pulled together by the workers and their community as the conglomerate-owner abandoned them. There is no institution in the U.S. economy to which viable businesses can turn when they are sold out by a parent-corporation. Each plant must find its own solution within its particular local economy. Unlike the Chrysler Corporation they cannot turn to the federal government. But, also unlike the Chrysler Corporation, many of these conglomerate subsidiaries do not *need* to be bailed out, for they were not actually losing money to begin with. What they need is assistance in setting up autonomous, decentralized, locally owned operations.

The conventional wisdom about highly centralized management is that it makes possible a higher degree of efficiency in information and personnel management than ever before. But the evidence suggests that the managers of the giant corporations and conglomerates frequently "overmanage" their subsidiaries, milk them of their profits, subject them to strenuous or impossible performance standards, interfere with local decisions, and are quick to close them down when other, more profitable, opportunities appear. In 1975-76 Gulf and Western almost dumped the Brown Paper Company of Holyoke, Massachusetts, a leading producer of quality papers, and

105

actually did sell off its most profitable product line to a Wisconsin competitor. By 1977 the plant's sales were up again to over $450 million.

Highly centralized organizations like Gulf and Western and Textron have positioned themselves so as to be able to make a profit either from a subsidiary's success or from failure that requires divestiture (since it can be treated as a tax loss and used to offset profits earned in other operations). From the point of view of capital asset management this may be the pinnacle of capitalist institutional creativity. But from the perspective of economic stability for working people and their communities, these clever capitalist giants are a disaster. The much-discussed trade-off between efficiency and equity turns out to mean capital management efficiency, but tremendous inefficiency at the level of actual production, to go along with the inequities imposed on workers and communities.

In short, modern monopoly capitalists will sell off or shut down profitable businesses if they think they can make even more money somewhere else. This strategy is not a recent one, nor have its harmful effects ever been unforeseeable. Here is Emil Rieve, president of the Textile Workers Union of America before a Congressional committee thirty years ago:

> Mr. Little is a capitalist, but in the field of finance rather than the field of production . . .
>
> I say this in the same sense that Hitler and Stalin are in the tradition of Napoleon and Alexander the Great. We have changed our attitude toward financial conquerors, just as we have changed our attitude toward military conquerors. Success is not the only yardstick.
>
> I do not know whether Mr. Little has

broken any laws. But if he has not, our laws ought to be changed.

"Mr. Little" is Royal Little, founder of Textron, the Rhode Island conglomerate that first developed many of the strategies now in use. Textron was initially a textile company. This year the Securities and Exchange Commission has charged it with paying over $5 million in bribes to officials in eleven foreign countries in order to "stimulate" sales of its Bell Helicopters. Its chairman at the time was G. William Miller, the current Secretary of the Treasury.

Just as the law in other areas has gradually evolved over the years to recognize that property rights, though dominant, are not absolute, the law must be changed to temper arbitrary plant relocation. Fifty years ago, tenants had no rights arising from their occupancy of a building. Today, the law stipulates that a landlord must keep the building habitable, that he must provide heat and hot water, and that tenants may not be arbitrarily evicted. Some communities have authorized rent control and even rent strikes when the property is not kept in good repair.

Family law has undergone a similar evolution. A wife is no longer her husband's property, and a couple's tangible property is no longer assumed to be the fruits of the husband's labor. Even banking law has been amended to deny banks the right to shut down when the community would be denied essential banking services.

But laws dealing with plant relocation are back in the eighteenth century. Profitability is considered an absolute right, not a relative one; and the right of a plant to relocate in the name of greater profitability is still sacrosanct, even where management's judgment or motive is specious.

As Emil Rieve observed thirty years ago, laws that sanction promiscuous relocations must be changed. A handful of states are considering requiring a year's notice before companies may shut down plants. Legislation is also under discussion to require severance pay, as well as compensation to the community. Companies could be required to pay back all tax abatements; labor contracts could also demand that the parent company not shift the production to other plants; tax write-offs for shutdowns could be prohibited. The proposed legislation to require federal chartering of the largest corporations could also include a range of sanctions against arbitrary relocations.

Far from interfering with industry's "right" to use capital optimally, these sanctions could force parent companies that acquire independent firms to operate them efficiently. As things stand now, conglomerates are being rewarded for running their subsidiaries into the ground—and the employees along with them.

● ● ●

NO

Richard B. McKenzie

FRUSTRATING BUSINESS MOBILITY

Business mobility—the mirror image of the free play of economic forces—is a normal, indeed inevitable, feature of any dynamic and growing economy. Nonetheless, particular moves (plant closings, relocations, and the like) can and do evoke protests by the communities and workers left behind. They see themselves as somehow "wronged." And among the political remedies they seek are restraints on business mobility by government fiat.

Cities are worried about losing employers and tax revenues to the suburbs, the Snowbelt is worried about losing both of those and skilled workers as well to the Sunbelt, and politicians everywhere seem attracted to the notion that economic stability in their areas can be ensured by putting a check on management's freedom to pull up stakes. Two years ago when American Airlines announced its decision to move its headquarters from New York to Dallas, for example, New York Mayor Edward Koch termed it a betrayal, and a taxi union vowed to stop serving the airline's New York terminals. Fortunately for the airline and its passengers, as well as the cabbies, the threat was never made good. And American's headquarters was moved.

In recent years, bills that would seriously restrict business mobility have been introduced in the U.S. Congress and a number of state legislatures.* The scheme is also the centerpiece of Ralph Nader's current campaign to "democratize" corporate America, to make major corporations more responsive to the "general interest." (His vehicle is the Corporate Democracy Act of 1980, H.R. 7010.) If such a measure became federal law, it would substantially increase government intervention in business decision making, alter our national economic system in fundamental ways, and be, on balance, detrimental to the regional and local economies of the country in the bargain.

*At last count eleven, including the northeastern states of Connecticut, Maine, Massachusetts, New Jersey, New York, Pennsylvania, and Rhode Island, plus Illinois, Michigan, Ohio, and Oregon.

From "Frustrating Business Mobility", *Regulation.* May/June 1980 ©1980, American Enterprise Institute.

The "Runaway Plant Phenomenon"

The general purpose of the restrictive legislation, which already has been enacted in Maine, is to remedy what has been called the "runaway plant phenomenon." Typically, the bills provide for a government agency to investigate business moves and rule on their appropriateness. For example, the National Employment Priorities Act, a 1977 proposal that was reintroduced in the House last August, by Representative William Ford (Democrat, Michigan) and sixty-one co-sponsors, would set up a National Employment Priorities Administration within the U.S. Department of Labor to investigate plant closings, to report its findings on the economic rationale for the decision and on employment losses and other impacts on the affected community, and to recommend ways of preventing or mitigating these harmful effects. (In the 1977 version, the investigation would determine whether "such closing or transfer" was "without [and presumably also "with"] adequate justification.") A bill pending since 1978 in the New Jersey General Assembly would vest similar responsibilities in a state agency called the Division of Business Relocation.

A second typical feature of bills designed to curb business mobility is the levying of penalties on firms that move. The Ohio bill, for instance, would require such firms to dole out to the employees left behind severance pay equal to one week's wage for each year of service and to pay the community an amount equal to 10 percent of the gross annual wages of the affected employees.

Under the Ford bill (H.R. 5040), a business that moved or closed would have to pay the workers left jobless 85 percent of their last two-years' average wage for a period of fifty-two weeks, less any outside income and government assistance. Besides, the firm would have to make a year's normal payments to any employee benefit plan and cover relocation expenses for employees who decided to move to any other company facility within the next three years. Workers over age fifty-four at the time of a move or closing would be entitled to full retirement benefits at age sixty-two instead of sixty-five or seventy. Failure to comply with the act would carry severe penalties—a combination of fines and the denial of tax benefits associated with a move. Finally, the local government would be owed an amount equal to 85 percent of the firm's average tax payments for the last three years. If the firm moved abroad and an "economically viable alternative" existed in the United States, the firm would have to pay "damages" equal to 300 percent of any tax revenue lost to the U.S. Treasury. Any payment required under the act, not met by the firm, and paid by the federal government would become a debt owed by the firm to the federal government.

Third, the kind of legislation under consideration here generally provides for government assistance to the people and entities adversely affected. Under the Ford bill, for instance, the U.S. secretary of labor, with the advice of a relocation advisory council, would be empowered to provide financial and technical assistance to employees who lost their jobs, to the communities affected by plant relocations, and even to businesses themselves—those that might decide not to relocate if government assistance were available. Assistance to employees would take the form of training programs, job placement services, job search and relocation expenses, in addition to such existing welfare benefits as food stamps, unemployment compensation, and housing allowances. Federal grants for additional social services and public works projects would go directly to the community. Assistance to businesses would be given as technical advice, loans and loan guarantees, interest subsidies, and the assumption of outstanding debt, but only if the Secretary of Labor were to determine that the aid would "substantially contribute to the economic viability of the establishment." The New Jersey and Ohio proposals provide for similar community and employee aid.

Fourth, under the various bills, firms are required to give advance notice of their plans to move or close—up to two years' notice in the Ohio bill and in the proposed Corporate Democracy Act of 1980. The prenotification requirement in the Ford bill varies with the size of the anticipated loss in jobs: two years for firms expecting the loss to be greater than 500, one year for 100 to 500, and six months for less than 100. The legislation proposed in New Jersey requires only a one-year notice. Exceptions could be made, of course, but generally only if the firms can show that meeting the requirement would be unreasonable.

Fifth, the various bills usually require that businesses offer their employees, to the extent possible, comparable employment and pay at the new location. And finally, each of the bills contains some minimum-size cutoff point. The proposed National Employment Priorities Act, for example, would apply only to firms with more than $250,000 in annual sales. But it should be noted that many McDonald's restaurants do that much business in a year. The bills' reach, typically, is both wide and deep.

Drawing the Battle Lines

In describing the changing regional structure of the U.S. economy, *Business Week* magazine observed: "The second war between the states will take the form of political and economic maneuver. But the conflict can nonetheless be bitter and divisive because it will be a struggle for income, jobs, people and capital" (May 17, 1976). And so it promises to be. When he introduced the original National Employment Priorities Act in 1977, Representative Ford gave us a preview of the economic rationale of the political battle lines and some flavor of the ensuing debate:

> The legislation is based on the premise that such closings and transfers may cause irreparable harm—both economic and social—to workers, communities, and the Nation. . . . My own congressional district suffered the effects of the runaway plant in 1972 when the Garwood plant in Wayne moved and left 600 unemployed workers behind. . . . [T]he reason these firms are moving away is not economic necessity but economic greed. For instance, the Federal Mogul Company in Detroit signed a contract in 1971 with the United Auto Workers and 6 months later announced it would be moving to Alabama. A spokesman for the company was quoted as saying that they were moving "not because we are not making money in Detroit, but because we can make more money in Alabama."

Two years later, in introducing his significantly revised 1979 bill, Representative Ford stressed that business movements from the Northeast during the last decade had resulted in a million lost jobs in manufacturing and pointed to studies showing the suicide rate among workers displaced from their jobs by plant closings at thirty times the national average. He also noted,

> It is well established that the affected workers suffer a far higher incidence of heart disease and hypertension, diabetes, peptic ulcers, gout, and joint swelling than the general population. They also incur serious psychological problems, including extreme depression, insecurity, anxiety, and the loss of self-esteem.

A veritable chamber of horribles!

So it should come as no surprise that the campaign for government restrictions on business mobility adopts the rhetoric of war. Phrases like "second war between the states," "counter-attacks," and "fierce and ruinous state warfare" fill popular accounts of regional shifts. The economic conflict at the heart of attempts to control business relocations is viewed as "us" against "them"—North versus South, the Snowbelt versus the Sunbelt.

Such rhetoric may serve transient political purposes. But it distorts public perception of economic conditions in different parts of the country and hides nonsensical arguments behind the veil of "urgency" as to government action. Thus, it is instructive to examine the major arguments made to support restrictive legislation.

Changes in Population

The contention is made that southward business movements have increased the rates of population growth in the South and Southwest. The corollary is that the North is actually losing people, especially highly educated workers, and that the population shifts that have been occur-

Table 1
POPULATION GROWTH RATES, BY REGION, 1950-1977

Region	1950-1960	1960-1970	1970-1977
Northeast	13.2	9.8	0.4
New England	12.8	12.7	3.3
Middle Atlantic	13.3	8.9	-0.4
North Central	16.1	9.6	2.3
East North Central	19.2	11.2	2.0
West North Central	9.5	6.1	3.4
South	16.4	14.3	11.2
South Atlantic	22.6	18.1	11.8
East South Central	5.0	6.3	8.0
West South Central	16.6	14.0	12.3
West	38.9	24.2	12.7
Mountain	35.1	20.9	21.0
Pacific	40.2	25.2	10.1
U.S. Total	18.5	13.4	6.4

Source: Adapted from Richard B. McKenzie, *Restrictions on Business Mobility* (Washington, D.C.: American Enterprise Institute), Table 1.

ring are larger than can be accommodated by existing political institutions.

What do the data actually show? First, as is evident in Table 1, the population growth rates of the Northeast and North Central regions have indeed declined significantly since the 1950s, but so have the population growth rates of *all* regions, including the South and West. (Only the Middle Atlantic states experienced a net decline in the 1970-1977 period, and that decline was very modest.) Further, and here Table 2 is in point, these changes in population growth rates have

Table 2
AVERAGE ANNUAL GROWTH RATES IN POPULATION BY REGION AND CAUSE, 1960-1970 AND 1970-1976

Region	Population		Natural Increase		Net Migration	
	1970-1976	1960-1970	1970-1976	1960-1970	1970-1976	1960-1970
Northeast	0.1	0.9	0.4	0.9	-0.3	0.1
North Central	0.3	0.9	0.6	1.0	-0.3	-0.1
South	1.5	1.3	0.8	1.2	0.7	0.2
West	1.6	2.2	0.8	1.3	0.8	1.0
U.S. Total	0.9	1.3	0.7	1.1	0.2	0.2

Source: McKenzie, *Restrictions on Business Mobility*, Table 2.

been caused as much or more by "natural" factors—changes in family life styles, the costs of rearing children, the widespread use of contraception, and the legality of abortions—as by net outmigration.

Second, aggregate data on population shifts blur the complex picture of who moves and for what reasons. Many of the people who moved south in the 1970s are the same people who moved north in the 1950s and 1960s. Others (for example, retirees) have moved south for reasons wholly unrelated to business location. Still others have moved because of new and expanding industries in the South, not because of relocations from elsewhere. It is also interesting to note that a major source of the above average population growth of the South Atlantic states (11.8 percent in the 1970-1977 period) has been the extraordinary growth of a single state, Florida (over 25 percent).

Third, a favorite argument in support of restrictions on business mobility is that the South and West are gaining a disproportionate share of highly educated and highly skilled workers, leaving the North and Midwest with a preponderance of uneducated, unskilled, and thus low-income workers. Now the new wave of outmigration from the North of course includes many highly educated and skilled people; but the proponents of restrictive legislation greatly exaggerate the quite undramatic facts. For instance, in the 1975-1977 period substantially more unemployed male workers moved from the Northeast to the South, (23,000) than from the South to the Northeast (14,000), and virtually the same pattern held for unemployed female workers. (The Northeast also exported more unemployed workers to the West than it imported from the West.)

Other considerations are equally revealing. Far more people below the poverty line migrated from the Northeast to the South (133,000) than vice versa (39,000) in the 1975-1977 period. (Much the same point can be made about the migration of low-income people between the Northeast and West.) In addition, while more people with one or more years of college migrated from the Northeast to the South (151,000) than from the South to the Northeast (102,000), those with *some* college education were a significantly greater proportion of the southern migrants to the North (56.3 percent) than the other way around (40.3 percent). (The same cannot be said about the migration of college-educated people between the Northeast and the West.) In short, it simply is not clear that the South or the West is receiving from the North a disproportionate number of highly trained, high-income people. Some—but no tidal wave.

Finally, most people move within a region, not among regions—and mostly they stay within the same state. Indeed, of the people who moved to a different house in the 1975-1977 period, approximately 60 percent stayed in the same county! Hence, if business relocation rules are seen as a means of restraining migration, *and insofar as migration results from business relocations at all,* these rules will in fact restrain migration *within* regions and states more than *among* regions. And insofar as such rules are designed to retard the economic development of the South and West by restricting the migration of people and jobs, it follows in all likelihood that they also will restrict the economic development of *all* regions, the North along with the rest.

Changes in Income

Edward Kelley, in a position paper of the Ohio Public Interests Campaign, claims that business movements are reducing individual incomes and the tax collections of governments in the North: "As the manufacturing base of the [northern] economy declines, so does the tax base. There are fewer taxable industrial locations and fewer people paying taxes" *(Industrial Exodus: Public Strategies for Control of Runaway Plants,* 1977). Yet in fact individual incomes in the North have been rising over the years. It is also true that individual incomes have been growing faster in the Southeast, Southwest, and West. What is happening, as the accompanying figure clearly shows, is that the relative incomes of the

regions are converging. Personal income in the North has decreased relatively (while increasing absolutely), but it still averages 25 percent higher than personal income in the South. In short, if business movements owe something to the disparity in regional incomes and if regional incomes are converging, it would seem that Representative Ford and Mr. Nader have proposed a solution to a problem that is being solved anyway, and predictably so, by normal market forces. In fact, because of the convergence of regional incomes, business mobility is likely to be less dramatic in the future than it was in the past.

The movement of businesses to the South does not necessarily mean that the North is made worse off, absolutely, or that improvement in living standards

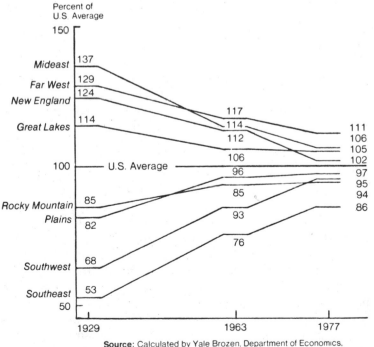

INDEX OF REGIONAL PER CAPITA DISPOSABLE INCOME

Source: Calculated by Yale Brozen, Department of Economics, University of Chicago

113

there has been retarded. Indeed, the converse may be reasonably argued—namely, that the movement of people and industry south has contributed to an improved standard of living in the North. By moving south where production costs are lower, businesses are able—at least in the long run—to provide goods to northern markets at lower prices than if they had stayed in the North. And they can expand production at lower cost. In not too many years, this increases both national income and, because the prices of goods are lower, the purchasing power of *all* workers' incomes, including those in the North.

The Decline in Northern Manufacturing Jobs

The claim that the North has lost a million or so manufacturing jobs in the last ten years suggests an economic problem serious enough to justify severe restrictions on entrepreneurial freedom. In fact, however, the claim misinterprets the actual state of employment opportunities in the North. The narrow focus on *manufacturing* employment hides the very important fact that *total* employment in the North has risen continually and significantly during the last several decades.

As Table 3 shows, manufacturing employment in the Northeast and East North Central regions did indeed decline by about 1 million jobs between 1969 and 1979; but in the same period total nonagricultural employment grew substantially, by 4.5 million jobs, reflecting the strong upward trend in service and government employment during the period. Moreover, since 1975 even manufacturing employment in the North has begun to move up again. If business

Table 3

NONAGRICULTURAL EMPLOYMENT IN THE NORTHEAST AND EAST NORTH CENTRAL REGIONS, 1965-1979

(in thousands)

Year (monthly average)	Total Employment	Manufacturing Employment
1979 (Dec.)	38,100	10,172
1978	36,331	10,153
1977	35,408	9,886
1976	34,288	9,601
1975	33,376	9,396
1974	34,826	10,423
1973	34,506	10,533
1972	33,358	10,093
1971	32,803	10,027
1970	33,249	10,936
1969	33,358	11,201
1968	32,384	11,055
1967	31,589	11,007
1966	30,867	11,034
1965	29,464	10,472

Note: The Northeast and East North Central regions include Maine, Vermont, New Hampshire, Connecticut, Rhode Island, Massachusetts, New York, Pennsylvania, New Jersey, Ohio, Indiana, Illinois, Michigan, and Wisconsin.
Source: *Statistical Abstract of the United States,* 1965-1977, and *Employment and Earnings,* 1978 and 1979.

relocation rules are designed to thwart the movement of manufacturing jobs generally, they may well have the ironic effect of choking off this recent reversal of the long-term downward trend in northern manufacturing jobs.

Finally, it must be stressed that only a very small percentage of the 1 million lost manufacturing jobs in the North can be attributed to business migration in any case. A study by Peter Allaman and David Birch of the Massachusetts Institute of Technology shows that just 1.5 percent of the North's job losses in the 1969-1972 period stemmed from the outmigration of firms, while a recent extension of that study by James Miller of the Department of Agriculture puts the figure at 1.6 percent for the 1969-1975 period. In other words, as Miller concluded, the impact of firm migration on the reallocation of manufacturing employment among regions "was trivial compared to the net effect of starts, closures and stationary firms."

An added inducement to this alleged movement south, it is often argued, is the "wage-attraction" of the South. However, it is more illuminating to assess the impact of "wage-push" in the North. From the wage-attraction perspective, it may appear that low-paid workers in the South are stealing business from and causing economic harm to the North. But the wage-push perspective suggests that wages in the North are higher and on the rise for such classical economic reasons as competition for workers from the developing service sector in the North. In other words, manufacturers are forced to pay higher wages or risk losing their labor force to more rapidly expanding sectors of the economy. Firms that move south are "pushed" south, having been outbid for labor resources in the North. From this perspective, industrial movements to the South are a consequence of gains made by many workers in the North—and the "runaway plant phenomenon" is a positive force in the dynamic and growth economy, South *and* North.

Even if northern manufacturing firms were to be restricted from moving south by legislation, the movement of manufacturing jobs to the South, though impeded, would not be stopped. Firms move because costs of production in the new location are lower—and anticipated profits higher. Restrictions on business mobility would cause new firms to spring up in southern locations and existing southern firms to expand by more than they otherwise would. Because of cost disadvantages, firms in the old northern locations would be induced by natural market forces—*which relocation rules attempt to override*—to contract their operations or to go out of business.

Comparative Cost Advantages

And this of course is the key, this ill-conceived attempt to improve on "nature" by those who urge regulation to restrict business mobility. Even at the risk of accentuating the obvious, it is helpful to return to a first principle or two. People in different parts of the country trade with one another because differences in their costs of production make it to their mutual advantage to do so. Specialization in trade leads to maximum output from the resources available to the community as a whole. And, because the conditions of production—the availability of resources, technology, consumer preferences for work and for goods—continually change, so do the comparative costs from region to region. What once was relatively advantageous to produce in the North may, for any number of reasons, become less costly to produce in some other region. This constantly shifting calculus of costs can be altered by changes in the relative scarcity of resources, worker education levels, or regional preferences for services. Whatever the reason, the cost of producing any particular good in one region can go up and, as a consequence, the production of that good moves elsewhere—all, to repeat, very "naturally."

Pinning down the precise reasons for changes in regional economic structures is difficult in the best of circumstances. In recent decades, however, the comparative advantages of the North have indeed changed, and for two principal reasons. First, the demand for services in the North has increased rapidly, more so than in other parts of the country; and this in turn has increased the cost of resources, including labor, for all other sectors of the northern economy. Also, environmental legislation has placed more severe restrictions on industrial production in the congested North than in many other parts of the country and has increased the relative costs of manufacturing there. The unavailability of "pollution rights" in the North has caused many firms to look to locations with less present pollution and less stringent immediate pollution-control standards—to the South and West, for example.

Undeniably, these changes in regional production costs, and the economic adjustments that result from them, can and do cause hardship for some. But restricting business mobility is a cure worse than the disease. Such restrictions would force employers to lock labor and other resources into comparatively inefficient uses—resources that could and should be moving into expanding sectors of various regional economies. Thus, governmental rules that impede the movement of manufacturing industry out of the North would not only retard the development of industry in the South (or elsewhere) but, by the same token, would retard the development of the service sector in the North. The overall result would be increased nationwide production costs and reduced national production and income.

The Worst of Worlds

States and communities that are mulling over business mobility restrictions may believe they would be protecting their economies by protecting their industrial bases, but in fact they would be hurting them—and themselves. What company would want to move into an area that had substantial economic penalties for moving out? What entrepreneur would want to start a business in a community or state that had penalties for changing locations? Companies interested in profits will always try to settle in those areas that leave them free to make the basic decisions on when to shift among products, when to close, and when to move. States or communities that do not impose restrictions will obviously have a competitive advantage over those that do—which makes it equally obvious why Representative Ford and others, who want restrictions in their own areas, are seeking through federal legislation to have all areas of the country abide by the same rules. And this simply tightens the squeeze on U.S. industry in world markets and provides yet another marginal inducement for U.S. firms to locate their production facilities in foreign countries where such restrictions are not in place.

Indeed, viewed from whatever perspective, restrictions on business mobility constitute an idea whose time one hopes will never come. Predictably, restrictions would tend to reduce the efficiency of resource allocation; reduce national and regional income levels; and reduce the ability of the economy to respond to changes in people's tastes and to changes in technology, in the availability of resources, and in the mix of demand for particular goods and particular services. In short, they represent a bad bargain all around—for the communities and workers affected (in spite of the appearance of near-term relief), for Representative Ford's constituents as much as everyone else, for the U.S. economy generally, for entrepreneur and taxpayer alike.

• • •

POSTSCRIPT

DO FIRMS EXPLOIT WORKERS AND LOCAL COMMUNITIES BY CLOSING PROFITABLE PLANTS?

Professors Bluestone and Harrison find that there are several common threads contained in recent plant closings undertaken by a number of large conglomerates. That is, excess funds are milked from one enterprise and transferred to a totally unrelated enterprise. This may result in disinvestment in the "cash cow" and the eventual reduction in its profitability. Third, the parent corporation may assign an unwarranted share of the conglomerate's common costs to one enterprise. This added burden will reduce its profitability. Fourth, management may force the firm to purchase its supplies from other subsidiaries of the conglomerate, even if these supplies are more costly than other sources. The end result is that a potentially profitable plant may be run "into the ground—and their employees along with them."

Professor McKenzie argues that the movement of industry from the Northeast to North Central states to the Sunbelt is a natural economic phenomenon which should be encouraged rather than discouraged. Plant closings in the North and the movement South and West is a function of differentials in factor costs. As long as these differentials exist, the migration will continue. Second, the labor freed from the industrial plants which are closed in the North can now enter the growing service sector in the North. Prior to the Sunbelt migration, the Northern service sector competed with the Northern industrial sector for labor. This drove the price of labor up and pushed industrial firms out of the North. Third, Northern consumers are benefited by the migration of firms South and West. Since production costs are lower, these firms can sell their output at lower prices.

Professor McKenzie's arguments are fully articulated in his recent book, RESTRICTIONS ON BUSINESS MOBILITY: A STUDY IN POLITICAL RHETORIC AND ECONOMIC REALITY (American Enterprise Institute, 1979). An interesting complementary piece to McKenzie which discusses the weaknesses of worker-owner takeovers of closed plants is "Youngstown Sheet and Tube—A Classic Takeover Case," *The Center Magazine* (November-December, 1979). Professors Bluestone and Harrison will further develop their case in their forthcoming book CAPITAL AND COMMUNITIES: THE CAUSES AND CONSEQUENCES OF PRIVATE DISINVESTMENT. Arthur Shostak examines the private costs of displaced workers in his article "The Human Costs of Plant Closings," *Federationist* (August, 1980). Lastly, many of the problems articulated by Bluestone and Harrison are contained in the U.S. Senate, Committee on the Judiciary, *Hearings on Mergers and Industrial Concentration, 95th Congress* (Government Printing Office, 1979).

ISSUE 6

ARE WE PROVIDING TOO MUCH SECURITY IN OUR SOCIAL SECURITY PROGRAM?

YES: Peter J. Ferrara, from "Abolish the Social Security System," *Inquiry* (January 12 and 26, 1981).
NO: Larry Smedley, from "Maintaining the Balance in Social Security," *AFL-CIO American Federationist* (February, 1979).

ISSUE SUMMARY

YES: Attorney Ferrara is persuaded that society will be unable and/or unwilling to pay for all the social security benefits that we are now promising to pay current and future retirees.
NO: Labor representative Smedley responds that society not only stands ready to insure the current rights of our retired workers but is ready to expand those rights in certain areas.

Out of the throes of the Great Depression of the 1930s emerged America's first attempts at social legislation. The reality of unemployment at the time, which included as much as twenty-five percent of the workforce and the resultant human suffering, immense uncertainties and loss of confidence in the system mandated that Congress act quickly and decisively. Thus on August 14, 1935, President Roosevelt signed the Social Security Act into law.

This legislation, which only a few years earlier would have been unthinkable politically, attempted to place a floor under those who were devastated by the failing economy. Since many had lost their savings when their banks failed and others had lost their homes when they could no longer meet their mortgage payments, many faced retirement both pennyless and homeless. Social Security was to be the answer for these families.

But the U.S. society was not ready for a massive welfare program. We had had a long history of being fiercely self sufficient. Thus the only way that social security was acceptable to Congress, was to establish it as if it were an annuity insurance system. That is, Congress established a trust fund which received payments from those actively in the labor force and paid out benefits to those who retired.

However, unlike an annuity, the payments made by those in the labor force did not remain in the trust fund to earn interest until the individual retired. Instead those payments were used to support the benefits of those who were retired. As a consequence, the system was placed on a "pay-as-you-go" basis not on a "pay-before-you-go" basis.

Although we called social security taxes "contributions," referred to the program as "insurance" not welfare, and encouraged the notion that the benefits were "earned," it was not, and could not have been set up as an annuity program. Those who were left pennyless and homeless by the Great Depression and were retired or about to retire needed help right away. They could not reenter the work force and spend 25 years building an annuity program. Thus the original Act of 1935 was amended and the trust fund began to pay out benefits by 1940.

This presented no serious problem for the social security system as long as the number of persons in the work force grew faster than the number of retired persons. This is exactly what happened. World War II pulled every able body into the workplace. The end of World War II saw the veterans return and a boom in the birth rate. Eighteen years later the "baby boom" began to hit the job market and this was followed by the women's movement which again swelled the workplace with new entrants. Even though individuals retired earlier and lived longer, and even though retirement benefits were steadily increased, there was no serious difficulty in paying benefits to those who were retired.

But times change. The "baby boom" was replaced by the "baby bust." We can no longer look forward to a labor force which will grow faster than the number of retired workers. As the ratio of retired workers to active workers increases and as retirement benefits are increased to keep pace with inflation, the burden placed on today's workers gets heavier and heavier.

Ferrara believes that this burden will get so heavy that the system will collapse. He maintains that this collapse will be hastened by funding the system partially or totally with general federal revenues. Smedley, on the other hand, believes that with a few modifications which include general revenue funding, the system can and will continue to provide "social security" for our retired workers.

Who is right and who is wrong has dramatic implications for each of us. How much will we have to pay for our retirements? Will the generation behind us be willing to pay for our retirements? Scarey stuff this social security system!

YES

ABOLISH THE SOCIAL
SECURITY SYSTEM

There was a time when the only harsh words for the social security system came from the lunatic right. For the rest of us, it was the goose that laid the golden eggs. But when the latest social security tax hike took effect two weeks ago, harsh words were probably spoken all over the country. It was, after all, the third social security tax increase in three years. Nine more such increases have already been scheduled for the rest of this decade. And despite all these massive infusions of cash—social security consumes 25 percent of all taxes the federal government collects—the system continues to flounder. Its board of trustees, in the latest report, says social security will run out of money this decade, possibly as early as 1982.

One of the very first matters President Reagan ought to be concerned with is reversing this Carter legacy of ever higher, but still inadequate, social security taxes. Reagan, after all, campaigned on an antitax platform, and he even promised to appoint a commission to study ways to avoid a future conflict between the generations that incessant social security tax increases might cause. Reversing this legacy, however, will take more than some Band-Aids: it requires fundamental reforms in the current structure of the social security system.

Conservatives, who have never liked the program, will of course fall in behind Reagan. What may surprise him, though, is that liberals too will be on his side. In fact, they're already spearheading the reform drive.

Conventional liberals have long been concerned with the social security tax, which is simply a flat-rate levy on all wages below a certain maximum taxable amount. It's a terribly regressive tax because (1) it applies only to wages, rather than including investment income, and (2) the ceiling on taxable income means that the wealthy pay no social security tax on most of their money, although low-income workers are taxed on everything they make. The enormous increase in social security taxes in recent years has made the problem much worse; today a lot of working people pay more in social security taxes than in income taxes.

Because of these concerns, many liberals have advocated funding social security partially or even entirely with general federal revenues, which come primarily from more progressive tax sources like the individual and corporate income taxes. As early as 1968, the Brookings Institution published a comprehensive study of the entire social security program which concluded by advocating just such a reform. Another persistent proponent of this strategy has been *New York Times* columnist Tom Wicker. And most recently, presidential candidate` John Anderson suggested something similar.

This may be the one liberal reform effort that has a better chance of success after the conservative landslide of November than it had before. The massive social security tax increases of recent years have aroused considerable taxpayer resentment. An ABC News-Harris poll in 1980 showed that 50 percent of Americans favor rolling back the 1977 payroll tax increases and substituting general revenues instead; 35 percent are opposed. With the latest large increase earlier this month, the margin can only grow, especially as taxpayers become aware that virtually annual tax increases are already scheduled for the rest of the decade.

The prospects for reform are even further brightened because social security is in such bad shape financially. The recent recession caused a sharp drop in social security tax revenues at the same time that inflation was increasing benefits dramatically under the automatic inflation adjustment formula. The 1980 annual report of the board of trustees for the social security trust funds admitted that there won't be enough money to meet obligations by 1982 or 1983—and another major recession would advance that critical date.

Already devastated by the continuing, massive social security tax increases legislated in 1977, taxpayers are unlikely to accept more harsh payroll tax increases in response to yet another social security financing crisis, especially in the middle of yet another recession. Since social security benefit cuts are also politically impossible, the only choice for Congress would be partial general-revenue financing.

It is true that old-line conservatives have opposed all moves toward general revenue financing in the past. The Ford administration, for example, rammed through a payroll tax increase to head off social security financing problems in the mid-1970s, firmly rejecting general revenue use. But the new President has been openly critical of Social Security throughout his public life and has been conspicuous in urging consideration of fundamental changes in the program. President Reagan would certainly lose much of his new blue-collar support if he followed in Carter's footsteps and sanctioned a social security tax increase that would hit those workers the hardest. Moreover, the populist, antitax wing of the Republican party, which gained the most in the 1980 campaign, is beginning to see general revenues as a means of reducing the high payroll taxes. If these new elements brought about a change in Republican sentiment, then the liberal goal of at least partial financing from general revenues would become not only likely, but inevitable.

Having opened the Pandora's Box of social security reform, would liberals be able to quickly close it without further changes? Can one fundamental element of the program be radically changed without further changes? Probably not.

The social security payroll tax is now the cornerstone of public acceptance of the program. Most people view the tax as a sort of premium for a government-run insurance program. Thus they see social security benefits as something they've paid for, rather than unearned, free, welfare handouts funded by the general public. This perception has been deliberately fostered by the government to make the system politically attractive to both taxpayers and beneficiaries; it also makes cutting benefits virtually impossible, for such cuts appear to be taking away earned and paid for entitlements. But with a large portion of social security benefits financed from general revenues, this perception of social security benefits as investment earnings will be shattered. Rather than receiving benefits they think they have paid for and earned, people will be getting handouts from general revenues.

Once the program is perceived as a dole, further structural changes are inevitable. And one inescapable question will tirelessly haunt the program—why should younger working people who are struggling with new careers, families, and homes be taxed through general revenues to provide free retirement benefits not only to those older persons in need, but to all retired individuals, including those who are fairly wealthy? Doctors, lawyers, top corporation executives, movie stars—they all retire, usually with large estates, and they can all collect social security. As it shifts to a welfare program paid out of general revenue there will be a public outcry over this— why should, say, Farrah Fawcett-Majors

be able to collect welfare payments?— and some sort of income test will be established for recipients.

This will create a snowball effect; the admission that social security is in fact a welfare program for the less fortunate will lead a lot of people to point out that it hardly makes sense to use a regressive payroll tax that falls most heavily on the poor in order to finance a program for the poor. And as more and more of the program is financed from general revenues, there will be more and more demands to make the income test stricter so that the only eligible recipients are truly needy. Eventually social security will become just another redundant welfare program, with all the insurance functions of the program fully privatized. One day, as part of a general welfare reform, social security will be consolidated with other programs and disappear altogether.

This is precisely why Nobel laureate Milton Friedman, who has long opposed social security and favored reliance on private alternatives, supports any moves toward general revenue financing. This is also why Wilbur J. Cohen, one of the original architects of the program and one of its staunchest supporters, and the Social Security Administration, with an obvious interest in self-perpetuation, oppose all such moves. It is also precisely why one Franklin Delano Roosevelt insisted that the entire program be funded solely through the payroll tax.

New Deal liberals might initially cringe in horror, but President Reagan and the conservatives would probably be quite comfortable with it. Yet with a few additional elements, reform can be acceptable to both. Suppose the substitution of general revenue financing for the payroll tax was combined with a new system of tax exemptions for retirement investments. Each individual would be allowed to set aside and invest each year, in his own retirement account, the full amount he would otherwise have paid in social security taxes under the current system, a total equivalent to both the employer and employee shares of the tax. All investments made through such an account would be fully tax-free so that the account would receive the full rate of return. This would not reduce total tax revenues, however, because social security taxes are not invested now. So the investment returns that would not be taxed under the new system are not even being generated under the current system.

To make the transition to the new system, we would (1) eliminate the present payroll tax and use general revenues to pay for social security, and (2) freeze the system so that people already in it would continue to get whatever benefits they've already paid for but no new obligations would be accepted. In the short run this would be expensive, but in a few years the number of recipients of social security benefits and the total outlay would radically decline.

This reform should appeal to today's liberals because it eliminates the regressive payroll tax. But more intriguing is that it may provide a rebuttal to supply-side economics and the tax revolt.

This new political phenomenon is the most serious threat to liberal orthodoxy on the political scene today. From Proposition 13 to capital-gains tax cuts to the Kemp-Roth bill to the landslide election of Ronald Reagan, the adherents of this new economic analysis have accumulated growing political clout. And no wonder. The tax burden grows heavier every year, and it is crushing incentives and stultifying the economy. Not only are taxpayers understandably annoyed, but

our nation's savings and capital supply have been badly hurt. The United States has one of the lowest rates of savings and capital accumulation of all developed nations, which is devastating for all dimensions of the U.S. economy. The supply-siders' response to these concerns is simple and direct: Cut taxes and regulatory burdens sharply, especially in ways which are most likely to stimulate economic activity.

Conventional liberals do in fact share many of these same concerns. But they remain wary of supply-side economics and the "tax revolt" because they fear that the tax cuts and other policies associated with these views would primarily benefit the rich. And they worry that if economic growth is not sufficiently stimulated to generate more tax money—if the Laffer curve is wrong—the tax cuts will require cuts in publicly funded social programs, hurting the poor.

The reform proposal we're discussing, however, would be a supply-side tax cut par excellence without any of these accompanying problems. Social security taxes are running close to $150 billion a year, and if individuals were suddenly allowed to save and invest these amounts in lucrative, tax-free retirement accounts, the resulting increase in savings and capital accumulation would be enormous. Yet, since each individual would be allowed to save in his tax-free account only the amounts he would otherwise have paid in social security taxes, the direct monetary benefits would be distributed relatively equally throughout the entire population.

Social security reform along these lines could thus be the liberal approach to supply-side tax cuts. It would offer a powerful answer to some of the problems addressed by supply-siders while avoiding what liberals *see* as the usual pitfalls in supply-side solutions. It would allow liberals to once again flow with the tide of public opinion.

A byproduct of this reform that should appeal to liberals is that it will widen access to ownership of America's business and industry and lead to a more equal distribution of national wealth. Every individual's retirement trust fund will represent his ownership interest in the country's productive assets. Economists estimate that if individuals saved and invested in such accounts all that they currently pay in social security taxes, over 40 percent of the nation's wealth would be held in this widely distributed form and the nation's concentration of wealth would be reduced by at least one-third. It is regrettable that the social security system has in effect discouraged the average person from accumulating a substantial stake in the nation's productive enterprises. Reversing this effect of the program will not only deconcentrate wealth, but will also give the average person a greater voice in corporate decision making.

These side effects should have great appeal to liberals as well as conservatives, but the primary result would still be the solution of many serious problems plaguing social security.

First, social security has a number of powerful, severely negative effects on the nation's economy. Worst of all, the program seriously discourages private saving, which substantially reduces the nation's capital supply. Why save for retirement, a worker asks; I'm doing that through social security.

Yet, because social security is operated on a pay-as-you-go basis (taxes paid in are not saved and invested for the future, but are immediately paid out to current beneficiaries), the program does not accumulate any returns to offset the loss in private saving. The result is an enormous loss in savings and a comparable loss in the nation's capital supply, which means a severe brake on economic growth and national income.

If social security reduces private savings by the full amount of social security taxes, then private savings in 1979 would have been reduced by about 45 percent. If we assume that social security reduces private savings by only 35 percent, the program in 1979 would still have cut the GNP by $450 billion, or about $2000 per person. Our reform proposal would reverse this.

It would also counteract the increasing lack of appeal of the program compared to private alternatives. A pay-as-you-go social security program has two separate and distinct phases—a start-up phase and a mature phase. In the start-up phase, the first generation of retirees paid little or nothing in past taxes into the program, but got full benefits. Thus they received very high, above-market returns on the taxes they did pay. But as the program matures, eventually, retiring individuals will have paid social security taxes all of their lives. Since these taxes have not been saved and invested, the money will not have earned a return that would allow the payment of more in benefits than was paid in taxes. Such a return thus entails increasing taxes on current workers.

It is true that with a constant payroll tax rate, the amount of taxes collected will increase naturally as population and wages increase. Consequently, a pay-as-you-go system can pay a "rate of return" equal to the sum of these two. But this artificial "rate of return" has historically been less than one-third of what would have been the full, before-tax rate of return on capital investment. Recent declines in birth rates and persistently slow wage growth indicate that the discrepancy will grow even worse.

A straightforward invested system can earn the higher rate of return because the investments actually increase production, which leads to a higher return. Because no investments are made in a pay-as-you-go system, however, there is no ripple effect, and the only returns such a system can pay must come at the expense of others through increased taxes.

America's social security system is just evolving from the start-up phase into the mature phase. Those who retired in the early years of the program certainly did receive very high, above-market returns, but those in the future will receive returns well below market rates. This is especially true for young people entering the program today. If these young workers were allowed to save and invest the amounts they would otherwise pay in social security taxes into a tax-free retirement account, they could earn far greater retirement benefits than they would ever receive under social security.

Our reform proposal would also protect retired people from temporary downswings in the economy. Since the current program operates on a pay-as-you-go basis, any adverse economic development like an increase in inflation or a deep recession threatens to upset the delicate balance of taxes and benefits and cause a shortfall in revenues. Similarly, adverse demographic developments like a decline in birth rates can also cause serious problems for a pay-as-you-go system.

The future of current social security financing arrangements is clouded by

both eventualities. Besides the short-term economic problems we've already examined, the Social Security Administration's own projections of expected economic performance over the next seventy-five years suggest that tax revenues will not grow fast enough in the future to meet soaring benefit demands. In addition, birth rates in recent years have fallen to their lowest levels in U.S. history and the Social Security Administration projects that by the time young people entering the work force today retire, there could be as many as 63 beneficiaries for every 100 workers, compared to 31 per 100 today. By 2035, when many of today's young workers will still be in retirement, the same projections indicate that there could well be 73 beneficiaries per 100 workers.

As a result of these and other factors, by the time today's young workers retire, social security payroll taxes will have to consume 25 percent or more of taxable payrolls to pay the promised benefits, based on projections in the 1980 board of trustees' Annual Report. It's a safe bet that taxpayers will not tolerate such incredible tax rates—people have other things they want to do with their lives besides pay taxes. Thus, social security benefits may soon be not merely inadequate, but invisible.

But if each individual is financing his own benefits with his own accumulated reserves, future benefits will not be threatened by changes in the fertility and birth rates or by the volatile economic factors that can devastate a pay-as-you-go system. Retirees in the new system will also not have to worry about the willingness of the public to continue to support the program politically and financially.

Another flaw in the current social

security system is that it discriminates against minorities. Women, blacks, and the poor have all demonstrated how the program discriminates against them and the Supreme Court in recent years has struck down some of the program's most blatantly discriminatory provisions. But ultimately these groups are fighting a losing battle. Since social security forces all individuals to participate in one standardized insurance program, that program will be tailored to the typical, average individuals who constitute the majority of participants. Members of minority groups and those who pursue alternative lifestyles find that the provisions of the program are poorly suited to them. One typical example: Blacks tend to join the work force earlier in life, and their life expectancy is shorter. Thus they pay in more to the system and take out less. Allowing each individual to purchase a package of insurance protection suited to his own needs from among the varied alternatives available in the marketplace would meet this objection too.

A final problem to note, although there are many others, is that social security does indeed entail a serious loss of liberty. Conventional liberals inexplicably never consider this. All individuals are forced to participate in social security regardless of their preferences. They are forced to purchase one particular type of insurance protection from one "seller"—the federal government. As a result, they lose control over a substantial portion of their own incomes. This hardly seems just in what is supposed to be a free country. Even if the reform were to include a requirement that individuals save a certain percentage of their incomes each year, they would still be free to choose their own investments and insurance purchases in the market.

A move toward general revenue financing of social security, combined with the other reforms suggested above, is thus a course that liberals should support. Such changes would greatly improve the system and would advance other traditional liberal goals. Indeed, if reason and principle are to prevail over symbolism and inertia, then such fundamental changes in the social security program should become the next liberal *cause célèbre*.

With strong liberal support a possibility, President Reagan should quickly embrace this reform proposal as a top priority. In doing so, he would not only solve one of our country's major problems and bring about changes conservatives have long advocated, he just might become the next liberal hero as well.

● ● ●

NO
Larry Smedley

MAINTAINING THE BALANCE
IN SOCIAL SECURITY

At a time the social security system still enjoys unprecedented popularity, it is also a topic of widespread criticism and concern. Part of the problem is a misunderstanding of the principles that have been the basis of the social security program since its inception almost 50 years ago:

- *Individual equity:* Benefits should be provided to both the rich and poor as a matter of right, not charity, and should be related to wages earned and contributions paid to the system, but only on a certain portion of income (wage base).

- *Social adequacy:* At the same time, social security accepts the principle that low-income persons require larger benefits proportional to earnings than high-income people.

These principles represent two different concepts about how benefits should be allocated among beneficiaries. Individual equity holds that contributors should receive benefits related to their wage levels and amounts of contributions. Social adequacy holds that benefit levels should provide all beneficiaries with a minimum level of living. These two principles are balanced in uneasy coexistence within the system.

If totally dominant, the individual equity principle would create a system with the characteristics of a private insurance company—more benefits to those who can afford to buy more coverage—and such a mechanism would be incapable of meeting social purposes. Conversely, total dominance of social adequacy would create a welfare type program resulting in many of the same problems that plague our welfare programs today. As long as neither principle becomes dominant, both the well-off and the poor will feel they have a stake in the system. This is a major factor in the popular acceptance of social security.

Because of these limitations, many object to social security playing any major role in eliminating poverty because they claim it is inefficient. In other words, given expenditures through other programs would make a greater

From, "Maintaining the Balance in Social Security", *AFL-CIO American Federationist*, the official magazine of the AFL-CIO, February, 1979. Reprinted by permission.

impact on poverty at less cost since they can be targeted to reach only the poor. The issue should not be decided solely on efficiency but on which programs will secure public acceptance and will do an acceptable job of reducing poverty. Enhanced prospects for legislative approval and receipt of benefits with dignity are two good reasons that social security is preferable to a means test approach to poverty prevention as long as the basic principles of the program are not impaired.

Though the objectives of social security are much broader than preventing poverty, it has been one of the most effective programs in doing so. More than 12 million beneficiaries are kept out of poverty by their social security benefits. But the program alone cannot be expected to resolve the nation's poverty problems, which require a multiple program approach and the more effective each individual program, the more circumscribed the problem and the more amenable to total resolution.

The supplemental Security Income Program (SSI) is a good example of the multiple program approach. This program established a uniform federal supplemental minimum benefit program for the adult categories (aged, blind and disabled) in place of the state welfare programs for those groups and transferred the administration of these programs to the Social Security Administration. Other forms of income such as dividends, interest, pension and social security benefits are subtracted from the minimum and any deficiency is covered by a supplemental federal payment from general revenues.

Though still inadequate—some states are above the federal minimum and are required to maintain supplemental

programs in order to maintain previous benefit levels—the program comes close to lifting all the adult categories out of poverty. By establishing minimum benefits for the first time in all parts of the nation, the legislation has clearly laid the foundation for a guaranteed income program above the poverty level for the aged, blind and disabled. One major priority of sound security of the future should be to raise the SSI benefits to at least the poverty level.

General Revenue Financing

A major factor in the popular acceptance enjoyed by the social security program is that all beneficiaries earn protection by working and by paying contributions on earnings. Thus, both the public and beneficiaries look upon benefits as an earned right.

Critics say the social security contribution rate is regressive because workers with low earnings pay a larger percentage of their total incomes than higher paid employees. They concede the benefits are progressive since they are weighted in favor of low-income workers but emphasize that contributions paid by low-wage workers bear heavily on already low incomes during the long period of their working years. The AFL-CIO, like these critics, is concerned about the burden of the social security tax on low-and middle-income workers during their working lives.

The best way to relieve the payroll tax burden and to secure additional funding would be to use general tax revenues with these revenues raised as much as possible by progressive taxation. It seems inevitable that Congress will have to resort to some general revenue financing. A major causative factor will be pressures on the payroll tax arising from the low birthrate. The fertility rates of recent years are expected to stabilize at a rate that will eventually produce zero population growth. In the future, this means a sizable increase in the number of retired workers relative to active workers. The 1977 ratio of approximately 3 workers for each beneficiary may decline to about 2 to 1 in the next century. In short, fewer people at work will have to support more retired people than in the past.

But the extent of the economic burden has been exaggerated. In any society, the working population has to support those who can't work: the children, disabled, unemployed and the like. This future dependency ratio will change little—and in fact may be more favorable—than it is at present. This ratio will include more older people but fewer in the other categories. In short, the economic burden for active workers will not change much. For the economy as a whole, increased costs for supporting the elderly will be largely offset by a decline in costs for the other sectors of the non-working population, particularly children. Expenditures will decline for schools, day care and child-related services and these savings can be used to support the larger retiree population.

These compensating gains are not reflected in increased income to the social security program itself. For the total economy the cost problems are not that serious but it is a serious problem for the social security program because of the circumscribed manner in which it is financed. Exclusive reliance on the payroll tax would require major tax increases and would place the entire increased burden on a reduced proportion of wage earners. The problem is how to shift these compensating gains from a declining

birthrate to the social security program to help pay for the increased costs for the greater number of retirees. General revenue financing is the most feasible way to transfer to the program these financial gains elsewhere in the economy and at the same time provide greater tax equity.

Many European countries supplement employer-employee contributions by providing general revenues to their social insurance systems. The idea of using general revenue contributions for social security has also long been contemplated in the United States. The Committee on Economic Security, the group which drafted the original Social Security Act, anticipated the system would eventually need general revenue financing. Almost every Social Security Advisory Council has recommended some general revenue financing. Such contributions are already being used to meet a significant portion of program costs, wage credits for military service, hospital insurance for the non-insured, matching funds for the Medicare premium and for special benefits at age 72.

However, we believe that proposals to finance the disability and Medicare programs totally from general revenues without any worker contribution would undermine the social insurance principle of benefits as a matter of right. If adopted, it could in time lead to income and means tests. A major factor in social security's popularity is the absence of a welfare stigma. The public looks upon benefits as an earned right because workers have made contributions during their working lives. Therefore, organized labor historically has opposed general revenue financing of any of the social security programs that does not maintain the contributory principle—although labor strongly favors general revenue supplementing payroll taxes.

An excellent source of additional revenue would be to tax the full payroll of employers. The wage base is necessary to determine the employee contribution and the average wage on which benefits are based but it plays no role in the employer's tax. An employer's responsibility for the welfare of employees should be based on the total payroll, not just a portion of each worker's earnings. Employees must pay federal income tax on their contributions to social security but employers deduct their tax as a business expense. Thus there is every reason the employer should pay social security tax on the entire payroll.

Social Security and Private Pensions

Few of the aged have significant supplemental sources of income. Though about half of U.S. workers in private jobs are currently covered by private pension plans, only about 24 percent of those over 65 are receiving private pension payments. For the foreseeable future, social security will be the only retirement system for a majority of the retired population.

A major issue since the inception of the program has been the future relationship between social security and private pensions—whether the program should be made more adequate for those earning average and above-average wages, and thus reduce the role of private pensions.

A national public retirement system is the most socially efficient way to provide for pension protection. Private pensions tend to have defects that make it difficult, if not impossible, to effectively achieve major worthwhile social objectives. Most private pension plans, for example, (1) hold workers to jobs and reduce labor force mobility, (2) do an inadequate job of providing income for survivors, (3) prevent portability of benefits, and (4) have major difficulties in keeping benefits up-to-date with increasing wages or the cost of living.

Pension plans have been established by most large employers and major industries, particularly those characterized by strong unions. Thus, the future growth of private pensions will depend largely on the willingness of small employers to start pension plans. But most lack a strong financial base and union pressure to provide pension protection. Though the vesting and other standards of the new pension reform law will insure that more pension plan participants receive entitlement to benefits, the law may also discourage the creation of new pension plans since its requirements, though laudable, create additional costs and burdens to employers.

Recent social security improvements and the growth of private pensions are no guarantee that the next generation of beneficiaries will be any better off than the previous generation. They will receive higher benefits than the earlier generation but in comparison with their customary standard of living these benefits may still be just as inadequate. . . .

Even if inflation is slowed or prices stabilized, the economic status of the aged will decline relative to those at work since the wages of workers increase in accordance with productivity and those who are retired do not share in these increased living standards. Thus, the greater the economic growth and the longer the retirement period, the wider the gap becomes in the economic position of the elderly relative to the working population. In short, the elderly now have a shorter worklife in which to accumulate savings, experience more rapid erosion of the value of these savings than in the past, both during and after their worklives, and must make provision to spread them over a longer retirement period. Such problems can be effectively balanced only by a national public system such as social security.

The social security program should be the primary retirement system for the nation's retired population. Clearly, private pensions will remain a significant factor in the overall retirement picture but their primary purpose should be to supplement social security benefits. The nation needs to discard the myth that social security benefits are only a minimum floor of protection and that the typical retiree can fill any gap by income from pension, investments and savings. Social Security benefits should be increased until older people can maintain a decent standard of living on these benefits alone.

Early Retirement

At the beginning of the century only one out of three males aged 65 or over had left the labor force. Now more than two out of three do so. The ratio between work and nonworking time depends primarily on a nation's level of economic development—on labor productivity and the ability to which an economy can support its citizens in nonworking pursuits. Thus, labor force participation is greatest in agricultural nations and lowest among the economically advanced.

Labor force participation continues to decline in industrial countries not only because of earlier retirement but also

because of greater education and training given the young before worklife begins. At the same time, improved health services that accompany industrialization also increase life expectancy. In fact, for the first half of the 20th century in the United States, both the working and nonworking lives of men increased and only in the second half has there been a decline in the time spent in the labor force by men.

The length of the retirement years is growing with more and more workers retiring early. In 1978, about 60 percent of U.S. working men who retired on social security did so "early" or before age 65. Since wives usually retire somewhat earlier than their husbands, many people now spend one-fourth, or even one-third of their lives in retirement. . . .

The trend toward early retirement has resulted in pressure for an across-the-board reduction in the age 65 requirement for full benefits since a large majority of workers retire before that age. Such legislation, it is urged, would assist in meeting the overall problem of unemployment, would help a large group of persons who are unable to maintain the production pace of younger workers, and would help the many older persons who have chronic ailments not severe enough to qualify for disability benefits but severe enough to restrict their ability to secure and hold a job.

Obviously, when a worker should retire depends on many interrelated factors that vary greatly from one individual to another. Because of the physical demands of the job, the retirement decision of a laborer or coal miner may differ substantially from that of a white-collar worker. During their later working years, many older workers find the pace of their jobs beyond their physical ability. Large numbers of them also suffer from chronic ill health. The figures show that a large majority of workers who retire early do so involuntarily—a majority because of poor health and another large group because of layoff or discontinuance of jobs.

The social security system should provide more adequate protection for the victims of these problems. By introducing a greater degree of flexibility, the system could facilitate coordination with retirement and disability programs achieved through collective bargaining as well as other forms of social insurance so the special problems faced by many older workers could be more easily resolved.

The large number of early retirements because of ill health clearly demonstrates the need for improvements in the disability program. At the present time, the definition of disability is very stringent, requiring that workers who frequently suffer from chronic ailments, are unable to work in their usual occupations, and cannot secure other employment because of age and ill health.

They are disqualified for disability because theoretically they might be able to work in some kind of job, no matter how unrelated to their previous occupation or how unavailable such a job is. A change in the definition of disability should be made to allow older workers to receive benefits if their impairments bar them from their regular occupation. Permitting older workers the right to receive disability benefits when unable to engage in their usual occupation—if coupled with provisions allowing retirement at age 60 at less than a full actuarial reduction—would, in effect, establish a zone of retirement after age 60.

This approach would also allow older workers more rational choices in retirement decisions based on their own individual circumstances. And it would avoid the problems of wholesale retirement at earlier ages that would develop from adoption of an across-the-board age reduction. The intent is to target program benefits to deal with social problems and avoid encouraging healthy workers to retire early.

In 1961, social security first began paying actuarially reduced benefits, permitting men to collect benefits at age 62 instead of age 65 if they were willing to accept permanently reduced monthly benefits. More men retired on reduced benefits than on regular benefits during the first year. The proportion of early retirees has increased so that now 60 percent of men retire on social security before age 65. And, as mentioned, more than two-thirds of them do so for two reasons: 54 percent because of poor health and 13 percent because of layoff or discontinuance of jobs.

These individuals would be the primary victims of raising the age of benefit eligibility. The solution is effective economic policies that will enable people to work. The result would be more income for the trust funds and more older workers remaining in and reentering the labor force from voluntary choice and not from economic coercion.

Women and Social Security

Recently, several Supreme Court decisions have done much to correct differential treatment between men and women by the social security law. But there is still a lot that can and should be done to improve the situation.

The various provisions of the Social Security Act relating to the treatment of men and women can be divided into two categories. Those that contain specific reference to sex for the deliberate purpose of treating men and women differently, and those that make no specific reference to sex but indirectly result in differing treatment of men and women because of economic and social conditions extraneous to the law.

With regard to specific reference to sex, the AFL-CIO has long taken the position that all legal rights that flow from a worker's wage should be the same whether that worker is male or female. Therefore, the AFL-CIO recommends that all differences in the benefit treatment of men and women should be removed from the law. This would insure equality of treatment for all benefit purposes and would mean improved benefits for men as well as women.

The second category is much more difficult to deal with. It is difficult, in some cases impossible, to modify the Social Security Act to deal with all the socio-economic imbalances that have arisen for reasons unrelated to social security.

Provisions which make no distinction as to sex still have a much different impact on women than on men. They reflect the economic and cultural differences of our society—some fair, some unfair. As society changes and discriminatory practices are eliminated, so will the impact of these provisions change. However, a number of improvements can be made that are desirable for all beneficiaries but at the same time strengthen social security protection for women. In the interest of furthering this objective, the AFL-CIO recommends the following changes:

● Eliminate the recent current work test (generally 20 out of 40 quarters) to qualify for disability insurance. The insured status requirements for disability particularly affect women. Because

women frequently have interrupted employment due to child-bearing and child-rearing responsibilities, most do not qualify for disability protection. Only about 40 percent of women are covered by disability insurance compared to about 90 percent of men.

● Make disabled widows and disabled surviving divorced wives eligible for social security without regard to age and without an actuarial reduction in benefits. (This would also apply to males in the same categories.) This is no justification for withholding benefits until a disabled widow (or widower) reaches age 50 and then actuarially reducing them from each year prior to age 62. The reduced benefit amounts payable under these provisions are in many cases so low as to be of little help to the disabled beneficiary. Also, in many cases, the need of the younger disabled widow may be greater than that of the widow between age 50 and 60, since the wage earner who dies at an early age, leaving a younger widow, would have less opportunity to accumulate assets that might provide some resources for the widow.

● Provide benefits to disabled spouses of beneficiaries. A wife of a retired or disabled social security beneficiary who has not herself reached retirement age and is not caring for a young child is capable of working and supporting herself. This is not the case for a wife who is totally disabled. In many cases the husband's social security benefit is practically the only income available to help meet living costs of the couple.

● Modify the present benefit formula by increasing the number of drop-out years to better relate benefits to more current earnings. In calculating the average wage on which benefits are based, the social security law allows

133

dropping out only five years of low or no earnings. This can be very harsh on workers who are for periods of time out of the labor market—particularly married women workers with children. Additional drop-out years would be particularly helpful to women workers who are unemployed or marginally employed for part of their working careers.

● Provide for optional computation of benefits based on the combined earnings of a working couple with a 20-year record of covered earnings after marriage but not in excess of the maximum wage base. Such a proposal was once adopted by the House Ways and Means Committee in 1972. It is possible for a working couple to receive less in benefits than another couple with only the husband working, even though both couples have the same earnings and paid the same amount in payroll taxes. This inequity should be corrected and would be of help to working couples, particularly to working wives.

Retirement Test

The retirement test is one of the most controversial and least understood provisions of the Social Security Act. This text provides that social security benefits are payable in full if a person's annual earnings remain below an exempt amount—$4,500 for those over 65 and $3,480 for those under 65. This amount is automatically increased periodically in accordance with increases in covered wages. If earnings exceed that level, the social security benefit is reduced $1 for each $2 of earnings in excess of the exempt amount. Many economists oppose the retirement test on the grounds it has an adverse impact on labor force participation. . . .

It is true that the retirement test applies only to earned income. By paying benefits regardless of other financial resources, social security serves as a base on which other forms of protection such as investments, savings, insurance and private pensions can be built. Withholding benefits because of sources other than nonwork income would reduce incentive for savings and would make it impossible for most people to make provisions for a more financially secure old age than would be possible by social security benefits alone. It would also jeopardize the eligibility of private pension recipients to receive social security benefits. It might also increase the danger of the introduction of a means test for social security recipients.

Repeal of the retirement test would increase the cost of the social security program by billions of dollars a year now and more in future years. But only a very small percentage of total retirees have any benefits withheld under the retirement test. Its elimination would benefit inordinately that small group of people who would be eligible for benefits even though they are working full time.

As mentioned earlier, the large majority of aged persons are unable to work because of poor health or lack of employment opportunities. Obviously, this is a group for whom full-time work cannot be expected to be a satisfactory means of supplementing social security benefits. More adequate cash benefits are what is needed. This would help all beneficiaries including the large majority who do not work after retirement and would not be helped by elimination or undue liberalization of the retirement test.

● ● ●

POSTSCRIPT

ARE WE PROVIDING TOO MUCH SECURITY IN OUR SOCIAL SECURITY PROGRAM?

Attorney Ferrara argues that recent developments will eventually lead to the elimination of—or at least a substantial reduction in—our social security system. Ferrara's rather extraordinary assertion is founded upon the implications of past and future social security tax increases. He is convinced that these increases will excite an immediate and intense taxpayer resentment.

To hasten the demise of the social security system, Ferrara endorses the substitution of general revenues for payroll taxes. Ferrara contends that this substitution would eliminate once and for all, the insurance analogy. No longer could individuals "view the tax as a sort of premium for a government-run insurance program." Rather they would have to view social security payments as "unearned, free, welfare handouts funded by the general public."

Smedley of course rejects the very essence of Ferrara's position. Smedley maintains that if the two basic principles of the social security system—1) benefits are a right and should be partially related to the worker's earnings history; 2) all workers are entitled to benefits which are socially adequate regardless of the earnings history—are balanced, the system will continue to enjoy a broad, popular support.

Smedley recognizes that the system is not free of problems. Foremost among those problems is the question of the payroll tax burden. Smedley supports Ferrara's attempt to substitute general revenues for at least a portion of the payroll tax. Unlike Ferrara, however, Smedley does not believe that this will undermine the insurance analogy or that it will lead to the eventual demise of the system.

Much has been written of our social security system. One important source of information is contained in the written reports of the Advisory Council on Social Security which is appointed every four years under the Social Security Act. The Advisory Council reports generally support the position taken by Smedley. This position is also well articulated by Henry Aaron of the Brookings Institute. See: SOCIAL SECURITY: PERSPECTIVES FOR REFORM (Brookings, 1968), WHY IS WELFARE SO HARD TO REFORM (Brookings, 1973) and "A Debate on Social Security" *Across the Board* (July, 1980). This does not mean that Ferrara is alone in his position. A. Haeworth Robertson has echoed Ferrara's concerns in his essay "A Debate on Social Security" *Across the Board* (June, 1980). Additionally, Robert S. Kaplan's FINANCIAL CRISIS IN THE SOCIAL SECURITY SYSTEM (American Enterprise Institute, 1976) and J.W. Gorkom's SOCIAL SECURITY: THE LONG TERM DEFICIT (American Enterprise Institute, 1976) share Ferrara's perspective.

ISSUE 7

IS THERE AN ENERGY CONSPIRACY?

YES: John M. Blair, from "Seven Sisters in a Castle Built on Collusion" *Business and Society Review* (Spring, 1977).
NO: Stephan Chapman, from "The Gas Lines of '79" *The Public Interest* (Summer, 1980).

ISSUE SUMMARY

YES: The late John Blair contended that with the assistance of government, the major oil companies have conspired to prevent the appearance of "distressed oil" on the open market.
NO: Stephan Chapman responds that the oil shortages of 1973-74 and 1979 were not the product of a conspiracy among the seven major international oil companies.

North America has long been blessed, with cheap energy. The abundant natural resources found on this continent—vast stands of trees, swift moving rivers, enormous quantities of coal, and what appeared to be endless supplies of natural gas and oil—were supplemented by the importation of inexpensive oil from other parts of the world, particularly the Middle East. As far as energy went, life was easy from the time of the Industrial Revolution all the way up to the early 1970s. There were moments of concern such as World Wars and flare-ups in the Middle East, but by and large we were confident that we were energy independent.

Any time the price of an item remains low for long periods of time, there is a tendency to increase the usage of that item. Oil is no exception. We've substituted it for other sources of energy. We've designed our industries to depend upon it. Our homes and our cars consume it lavishly. In short, until the early 1970s, there was no incentive to either conserve energy or to develop renewable sources of energy. As a consequence, our consumption of energy, particularly oil, increased at a rapid rate during the post World War II period.

During this same period, the price we paid for the oil we purchased from the Organization of Petroleum Exporting Countries (OPEC) remained remarkably stable. (The price rarely rose above $2.00 a barrel.) Thus OPEC was faced with a declining level of income as import prices increased over time and its export prices stayed constant. Since these countries were forced to forfeit larger and larger quantities of oil to obtain a given quantity of imports, it is understandable that they attempted to force the world price of oil upwards.

And force the price of oil upward they did! Beginning in 1973, OPEC sharply increased the price of oil. Since the first shock waves, which were felt all across the world, oil prices have risen from the pre-cartel level of $2.00 a barrel to an average price of $35.00 a barrel in early 1981. Considering the fact that the production costs remain well below 50 cents a barrel, immense profits have accrued to the Persian Gulf countries.

Why has OPEC been able to engineer this eighteenfold increase in the price of oil? Some contend that it is the natural result of runaway demand for energy in Western countries, notably in the U.S. Journalists like Stephen Chapman argue that there is nothing mysterious, and certainly nothing conspiratorial about these rapidly rising prices. When OPEC chooses to restrict supply there is no way that the large international oil companies can offset these reductions. Given the mounting demand for this oil, the end result must be price escalation. Blair countered with assertions that there has been a conspiracy and that this conspiracy continues today. He maintained that the only way OPEC could organize and operate a highly complex and unstable cartel was with the cooperation and support of the "Seven Sisters."

Whether or not these major international oil companies have conspired to improve their profit position is critically important for public purposes. The rate of increase in oil prices must be slowed. If these increases are not slowed, the market will generate the perverse result of ever decreasing supplies of oil in the market place. That is, profit maximizing oil suppliers will find it to their advantage to withhold oil as long as the rate of increase in oil prices is greater than the current interest rate. They will simply watch their oil reserves increase in value. Holding their reserves earns them a greater return than alternative investments. How this cycle of ever rising prices and ever falling supplies is broken depends upon whether or not there is an oil conspiracy which includes the Seven Sisters (British Petroleum, Exxon, Mobil, SoCal, Royal Dutch Shell, Texaco, and Gulf).

YES

John M. Blair

SEVEN SISTERS IN A CASTLE BUILT ON COLLUSION

Although the world became aware of the energy crisis when it burst on the scene in 1973, the fact is that the supply of world oil has been under tight control for a long time. Documents obtained by the Federal Trade Commission from the files of the major international oil companies reveal unmistakabley evidence over both marketing and production in international oil. Specifically, it shows the manner in which the international majors joined together to exploit on a common or joint basis, the first area of oil production in the Middle East, namely Iraq, through the Iraq Petroleum Company, and how this joint activity among the Seven Sisters was continued as oil was discovered in Iran, Kuwait, Saudi Arabia, Abu Dhabi, and the other major oil-producing countries of the Middle East.

Not surprisingly, a number of other companies have tried to enter the international oil business. When one looks at the price-cost margin that has prevailed in the sale of that resource, one can well understand its attractiveness: the cost per barrel, including both the operating and development costs, has been placed below 20¢ a barrel, while the lowest price at which oil has been sold in many years was about $1.30 a barrel. Of course it is now more than $12 a barrel.* One reason why other companies—independents, including some sizable domestic majors—have not become producers of Middle East oil has been that they were, in effect, induced not to do so by the U.S. State Department. The recent hearings of Senator Church's multinational corporation subcommittee revealed the role played by the State Department in pursuing American firms, some of them of very respectable size, to stay out of the Middle East. That is, not to take concessions that were in dispute between the Middle East government and one or the other of the jointly owned operating companies of the Seven Sisters. I find this role played by the State Department most interesting. Quotations from these documents, which I've included in the book, should cast a very considerable light on what

[*Eds. note:] As of May 1981, the price of OPEC oil had reached the $35.00 level.

really happens behind the scenes in Washington when a government agency with far-reaching powers associates itself with, and becomes an arm of, a group of huge privately owned enterprises.

The success of the Seven Sisters has been almost unbelievable. The key to the maintenance of price, particularly in a product such as oil, is control over production: the avoidance of what the industry refers to as "distressed oil," which is oil that has been produced in excess of the quantity that can be taken by the market at the given price. It happens that since World War II the production of oil by the countries that now make up the Organization of Petroleum Exporting Countries has risen at the rate of about 9½ percent a year. Indeed, the deviations from that 9½ percent growth rate are so slight as to be almost a matter of disbelief. Particularly when one considers the fact that this production by the OPEC members as a whole has each year been made up of countries some of whose output is rising at a very rapid rate, and others whose output is declining. When one looks at the trends in the individual countries, the only impression one can have is one of utter chaos. And yet, their total outputs have been orchestrated in such a manner as to bring about this absolutely miraculous 9½ percent annual growth rate which has been, apparently, enough to meet the expanding needs of the oil and, at the same time, avoid the appearances of oil producing in excess of what the market would take at the existing price.

With Help from Their Friends

The output in the domestic United States has, for many years, been closely controlled in a manner somewhat similar

---

Who Are The Seven Sisters?

Of the seven major international oil companies, five of them are American: Exxon, Mobil, SoCal, Texaco, and Gulf. The other two Sisters are Royal Dutch Shell and British Petroleum. It is hard to comprehend the enormity of these enterprises. Exxon, the biggest of them, has annual revenues of approximately $50 billion. Seven of the largest fifteen U.S. corporations are oil companies. Nine of the largest twenty are oil companies. Senator Gaylord Nelson has pointed out that if Exxon "retained its crude oil and exploration facilities alone, it would still be the largest privately owned company in the world."

---

to that which has existed in the world oil trade. But here there has been greater reliance upon the use of government, both federal and state, to prevent the appearance of distressed oil. Actually, compared to some industries like the breakfast cereals or automobiles, the domestic production of oil is not among those highly concentrated industries. And that fact has made it necessary for domestic oil companies to enlist the support of the government if they are to avoid price-weakening surpluses, which is precisely what they did. There was established a very intricate domestic control mechanism under which the Bureau of Mines would, each month, estimate the demand for oil for the following month; then, in effect, a consensus was arrived at among the various oil-producing states through the instrumentality of the Interstate Oil and Gas Compact Commission as to the amount of that total that would be produced by each of the oil-producing states. Then the various oil-producing states had differing types of systems by which their share was allocated, in effect, out to the various producing wells within the state. In the State of Texas, that was done by what we refer to as prorationing administered by the Texas Railroad Commission. In the State of Louisiana it was done through a more sophisticated technique known as unitization. In each case, however, the objective was the same: to prevent the appearance on the domestic market of distressed oil.

The very fact that domestic production was limited by these instrumentalities in order to maintain the price served in two ways as a stimulus for some of the lesser majors and the larger independents to seek their own sources of foreign oil. They could then bring it back into the United States where the price was considerably above the world market price. Also, the production costs abroad were generally lower than the production costs in the United States. So, for those two reasons, obtaining your own source of foreign oil became a very desirable and understandable economic objective. And enough of this "uncontrolled" oil began to be imported into the United States in the mid-1950s to bring about a significant weakening of the domestic price structure. The profit rates of the major oil companies began to decline. Protests were heard from various oil-producing states, particularly Texas, that the United States was favoring foreign oil over domestic production. As a consequence, there was imposed what has been called a mandatory import quota system.

Under the import quota system the price in the United States was maintained generally at a level of about $1.25 above the world price. The quota permitted only

12 percent of the U.S. consumption to be supplied by foreign sources, and most of that came from Canada and Venezuela.

This quota was particularly injurious to the long-range interests of the United States, and not merely because of the excessive prices that were charged to American consumers, which amounted to around $5 billion a year. But, important as that may seem, it really pales into insignificance as compared to the fact that it forced the United States to use up its own rapidly diminishing reserves at the very time when oil from abroad was being offered to the United States in unlimited quantities at very low prices—as low as $1.30 a barrel. For that same oil we are now paying $12 a barrel or more. Hence, the fact that we are now rapidly running out of oil is due in good part to the fact that for this entire fourteen-year period that the quota was in effect, we kept out foreign oil and used up our reserves.

At the time, a few petroleum geologists and economists voiced concern in congressional hearings or in the pages of academic journals. Little, if any, attention was paid to them. I can say this with some meaningfulness since I was among those whose warnings, if you may call them that, were apparently regarded by the House as something from the lunatic fringe. But one can understand why congressmen and senators did not pay too much attention to their warnings, because shortly after the import quota was imposed the petroleum geologists of private research organizations supported by energy interests began to raise their estimates of the amount of oil that remained to be discovered in the United States. The higher these estimates were, the less persuasive was the argument that we should not have an import quota because the import quota would result in an acceleration of the depletion of our own reserves. I think that most authorities, including some of the major oil companies, are now pretty much in agreement that these forecasts were inflated. It is now generally recognized that the total supply of oil deposited in the United States by nature, was, more or less, roughly about the level that these reserves were estimated to be before this inflation took place.

Along Came OPEC

The fantastic OPEC price increases of the seventies changed the international oil business. The oil companies, in my opinion, used the increases as a handy opportunity to accomplish two objectives. First was to shift the locus of profit-making downstream toward refining and marketing. For many years the oil companies had followed a pricing structure under which most of the profit was made in the actual production of crude oil. The reason was simply that it was at that stage that the tax benefits—percentage depletion, the expense of intangible drilling costs—could be applied. Obviously, it only made good sense to take your profit at that stage where one could maximize the tax advantages. But the oil companies, looking down the road, could see that this heavy historical reliance on production was probably dangerous for two reasons.

First, there were complaints being increasingly heard in Congress about these forms of preferential tax benefits. Indeed, the percentage of depletion was cut from 27½ percent down to 23 percent. To the extent that the tax advantages were removed, or reduced, the making of profits at the stage of produc-

A Victim of Prejudice

Three of the Seven Sisters—Exxon, Mobil, and SoCal—are direct descendants of the giant Standard Oil Trust organized by John D. Rockefeller late in the nineteenth century. Rockefeller started out as an oil refiner in Cleveland during the Civil War. As his business grew he realized, like all oilmen after him, that the price of oil is particularly vulnerable to fluctuations of supply. In order to keep "distressed" or "uncontrolled" oil from the market, Rockefeller organized the oil monopoly which made his family one of the richest in the world.

John Blair's current book about the oil oligopoly had its forerunner in Rockefeller's time. Ida Tarbell's *History of the Standard Oil Company* is still famous for its account of Rockefeller's rise, although John D. dismissed it as "without foundation." Rockefeller, who prided himself on his moral character, discounted such criticism by noting that "great prejudice exists against all successful business enterprise—the more successful, the greater the prejudice."

tion ceased to make good sense. A second factor was that throughout the world the members of OPEC were increasingly embarking upon nationalization schemes; they were saying that they would demand control over their own natural resources. Now, to the extent that the oil companies' position was shifted from that of a concession-holder to that of a purchaser of oil from a sovereign state, a very valuable tax advantage was lost. This was the foreign tax credit, under which taxes paid to a foreign government can be used as a dollar-for-dollar offset against other taxes on other foreign income owed to the United States Treasury. To the extent that the oil companies were paying for their oil in the form of taxes rendered to the host country—really royalties disguised as taxes—then they could have the advantage of taking these payments to the foreign countries and using them as offsets against taxes and other foreign income owed to the United States Government. But they could not, conceptually at least, make the same use of purchases. These are not a tax. Purchases are a deduction rather than a dollar-for-dollar offset; in terms of tax savings, they're worth only half as much as a tax credit.

Because of these changes, the oil companies needed to lessen their dependence on the production stage for making profits. By various devices and price-cost determinations, the downstream stages of refining and marketing became more profitable than they had been in the past. I call this "shifting the locus of profit-making downstream."

The second thing done by the oil companies was to use the OPEC price rise as a handy occasion to raise what economists refer to as their target rate of return. For example, in a statement to a congressional committee early in 1974, Exxon stated that its rate of return on its net worth had not varied by more than a half a percentage point above or below 12 percent for ten years. Exxon added that for various reasons the company regarded that as too low, and that it felt it necessary to raise the target rate from 12 percent to a minimum of from 14 percent to 16 percent.

The target return during the period 1963 to 1972 at Exxon had averaged 12.8. In 1974 Exxon exceeded the target return, attaining the profit rate of 21.3%. In that year, all of the target objectives of the six companies for which figures were obtained averaged 15.9 percent, and they actually attained an average of 19.0. Now the profit rates fell several percentage points below that in the recession of 1975 but it appears, in most cases, that they would be close to attaining their new target rates. This is not a matter which the oil companies are trying to hide. It is an explicit statement.

There's a common, widespread misapprehension that all that the companies have done since the price explosion is simply pass on the increase. If they had done nothing but pass on the increase, their profit rate would be unchanged. That their profit rate has risen substantially above the preprice-explosion level must mean that any cost incurred by the company as a result of the price explosion must have been more than offset by the revenues that they obtained in the sale of refined products. The major oil companies don't sell very much crude oil to one another. What they do sell is refined products. Unless there had been that more than passing on of cost increases to them, their profit rate could have risen.

Moreover, the Seven Sisters have had a hand in supporting OPEC and keeping prices higher. The OPEC cartel has not broken down basically because OPEC production was reduced substantially. There are only two parties who could have brought about that decrease in production: OPEC or the major companies. It is very doubtful that OPEC is equipped to carry on such an intricate and difficult undertaking. Not only would the total amount of reduction have to be determined, but it would then have to be apportioned among the various OPEC countries.

Now there are members, such as Venezuela, who have long urged that the central body of OPEC be granted the authority to limit production and allocate the allowables to the various producing countries. This authority has never been granted. So since it is very unlikely that OPEC is equipped either by delegated powers, by expertise of staff, or by the other factors involved in carrying out this procedure, some other party must have been responsible. And that must have been the companies. If the companies had not reduced production in the OPEC countries in 1974, the result would have been the production of distressed oil. The resultant saving to the consumer, to the underdeveloped countries of the world, would have been enormous. But it didn't break down and the reason it didn't is because the companies make more money by maintaining and enhancing the OPEC price structure than they do by bringing about reductions in the OPEC structure.

This is why the relationship between the companies and the countries is not of an adversary character with the companies being in the role of large buyers demanding greater discounts, lower prices, as Sears, Roebuck seeks to get lower prices for tires that it sells under its brand. The relationship is not adversary, it is symbiotic. We have here a new form of economic organization where it's not buyers and sellers so much as it is parties, both of whom benefit from higher prices. For their part, the companies simply reduced their production of oil in an amount sufficient to prevent the appearance of distressed oil during the recession. For their part, the OPEC countries have, from all the evidence I can gather, abstained from selling oil to independents at discount prices which would enable the independents to break the price structure for refined products.

A Bad Situation

Fortunately, there are some legal remedies to help prevent a bad situation from becoming worse. They would not prevent the United States from running out of oil, but they could reduce the extent to which the public interest is adversely affected by the monopolistic exploitation of the tight supply situation.

Now there are two ways which the remedies of law can be brought to bear: either through direct regulation of price as in the regulation of public utilities, or through the steps designed to infuse a greater degree of competition into the industry. For the oil industry in a number of respects lends itself readily to traditional public utility rate regulations. That is, the government could establish a maximum profit rate allowed to the oil companies. It could then determine the level of price that, in view of costs prevailing, would be required to yield that specified profit rate. And it could see to it that the prices did not exceed the levels that had been specified by its rate-making authority. So the oil industry does not present problems unsuited to traditional public utility rate-making. Where they do present a problem is in their enormous political influence. And here what is involved is the extent to which the American people would support their government in its efforts to control an industry which has never yielded very nicely to the imposition of controls in the public interest.

But many experts in the area feel that the best remedy of all would be in the injection of greater competition. That can be done in several ways. One step that the

143

government ought to inquire into is the question of whether the reductions in output made during the 1974-75 recession, to which I alluded earlier, were brought about as a result of conspiracy, collusion, or a planned common course of action in violation of Section 5 of the Trade Commission Act. The collusive restriction of production has, for a half century or more, been regarded as simply illegal. The Federal Trade Commission would not be required to establish that those restrictions were done with an unlawful intent. It wouldn't be necessary for those agencies to show that they were accomplished through the use of monopolistic practices. It would be simply enough if the agencies were able to establish that these restrictions in output were brought about through a common course of understanding or through an agreement which need not be in writing, but could consist merely of implied understandings.

Another step that I think ought to be taken is to require the large companies which are importing oil to set aside a portion of that oil for sale to independent refiners. The Small Business Administration has had for years the power to require the Defense Department to set aside portions of military contracts for the exclusive use of small business. That same principle could well be established with respect to the oil imported by the big companies.

Divestiture

Finally, of course, there is the much-discussed remedy of divestiture. This would require the oil companies to determine whether they wish to stay in production, refining, or marketing. They would then have to divest themselves of their holdings in other areas. To divestiture's supporters, the central issue is the destruction of competition inherent in companies which are not only of immense size but vertically integrated from wellhead to pump.

More important than reducing the size or increasing the number of sellers would be changes in motivation. No longer would those majors electing to remain in production afford to calmly accept (if not welcome) OPEC actions raising the cost of crude, secure in the knowledge that they could pass it along in the prices of refined products. And since they could not look for profits at other stages, those majors remaining in refining could be expected to exert a continuous downward pressure on their own costs. Moreover, since producers would have to sell to refiners, and refiners to marketers, the task of preventing the appearance of distressed oil would become infinitely more difficult. And that task is what the Seven Sisters have been dedicated to in their control of oil.

● ● ●

NO

Stephen Chapman

THE GAS LINES OF '79

Fascination with conspiracies, real or imagined, appears to be an inherited American taste. Satanic conspiracies often figured prominently in the sermons of colonial New England ministers; later Satan was replaced by more worldly but no less malevolent agents. In his famous essay, "The Paranoid Style in American Politics," Richard Hofstadter noted that at various points in the Republic's history, dark conspiracies have been attributed to Masons, Catholics, slaveholders, international bankers, munitions manufacturers, and the House of Hapsburg. Hofstadter called such thinking "paranoid" because "no other word adequately evokes the qualities of heated exaggeration, suspiciousness, and conspiratorial fantasy I have in mind." It was the characteristic of the conspirator in each of these theories, wrote Hofstadter, that "[he] wills, indeed he manufacturers, the mechanism of history himself, or deflects the normal course of history in an evil way. He makes crises, starts runs on banks, causes depressions, manufactures disasters, and then enjoys and profits from the misery he has produced."

Does that suspect description bring anyone to mind? Of course it does; the oil companies, objects of general suspicion and distrust ever since the Arab oil embargo of 1973-74, which coincided with a quadrupling of oil prices at the decree of the newly emergent Organization of Petroleum Exporting Countries. It was largely overlooked by various organs of the American news media, particularly the television networks, that Western-based petroleum firms had not been treated kindly in many of these nations, where ruling governments had discovered expropriation of foreign assets to be the path to social justice and national self-determination. What caught everyone's attention instead was the jump in oil-company profits that followed OPEC's seizure of control of the world oil market. The taxable income of all American oil firms, which was only $3.2 billion in 1972, rose to $6 billion in 1973 and $23.5 billion in 1974. In the same period the average return on shareholders' equity climbed from

From, "The Gas Lines of '79", *The Public Interest*, Summer, 1980. Reprinted with the author's permission from *The Public Interest*. No. 60, Summer, 1980. Copyright ©1980 by National Affairs, INC.

IS THERE AN ENERGY CONSPIRACY?

10.8 percent to 19.6 percent. The popular reasoning was *post hoc, ergo propter hoc:* Inasmuch as the embargo, the emergence of OPEC, and shortages in the United States had been accompanied by startling increases in oil-company profits, those events must have been part of a carefully orchestrated scheme by the oil companies to increase their profits. The average American, not understanding complexities of international oil economics, substituted as explanation a cabal of pin-striped corporate moguls. And thus was born the most cherished of contemporary villains: Big Oil.

Even though oil-company profits settled back to levels comparable to those of most other American industries in the five years following the embargo, and even though the price of gasoline remained stable in real terms, the popular resentment of Big Oil simmered. Then in spring 1979, it boiled over once again. The reason was another gasoline shortage, complete with long lines, cursing motorists, and one or two homicides committed against drivers violating accepted queue etiquette. The shortage struck first in California, lingered a few weeks, and then vanished, only to reappear in Washington, D.C., having mysteriously bypassed all of the area in between. From there it made raids against several East Coast cities, and it was even spotted in what used to be the oil capital of the world—Houston, Texas. For a good three months the gasoline lines dominated the headlines and provided endless footage for the television news programs. What quickly became clear from numerous polls and hundreds of curbside interviews was that no one believed the official government explanation for the shortage—namely, a reduction in supplies

from Iran. Everyone "knew" the real reason gasoline was so hard to find: The oil companies had gotten greedy once again and had manufactured a phony crisis to jack up prices and profits.

The Conspiracy Theory

In no time at all, the belief that the shortage was purely fraudulent became an unchallenged article of popular faith. Given the unsavory reputation of the oil companies, this was not surprising. And the popular superstition rapidly gained credence among several established muckrakers in the nation's press, who were able to locate a few stray facts and statistics to provide a patina of intellectual respectability to the gut feelings of the public. The case against Big Oil has been made, with only slight variations, by several advocates, including Fred J. Cook of *The Nation,* Jack Anderson of *The Washington Post,* author Robert Sherrill in *The New York Times Magazine,* and several staff writers of *Newsday* in a long article condensed and reprinted in *Reader's Digest.* The conspiracy theory goes something like this: The halt in oil production by Iran last winter did not create a shortage of oil in the world because other countries more than made up the difference. World oil production actually *rose* in the first quarter of 1979. Nor was there any shortage of available crude oil in the United States, since imports of oil were higher than the previous year. If one includes oil stored in the Energy Department's Strategic Petroleum Reserve, the nation had the largest stocks of oil in history at the beginning of 1979. Supplies were hard to find only because the oil companies planned it that way. While Iran's oil fields were lying fallow, American producers cut production substantially and refiners slowed their production of gasoline by running at less than capacity. While the nation was suffering long gasoline lines, the oil companies were increasing *exports* of oil. In conclusion, there was, in Anderson's words, "a conspiracy by the oil companies to extract huge profits from the American public's belief in a shortage that was in fact a phantom."

This conclusion is utterly mistaken, to judge from all reliable evidence. In fact the very statistics cited by those who suspect a gigantic fraud, when examined more than superficially, suggest precisely the opposite conclusion—that the shortage was in fact real, that the oil companies were not to blame, and that the crisis was aggravated by the very people at the Department of Energy who were supposed to alleviate it.

The increase in American imports of oil during the first half of 1979 is the most incriminating piece of evidence offered by the prosecution. It is also the most misleading. It is true that in each of the months from January through June, imports of crude (excluding those designated for the strategic reserve) were at least 200,000 barrels per day higher than in the corresponding month of 1978—an increase of about 3 percent. *But the reason 1979 imports were higher than in 1978 is that imports in 1978 were abnormally low.* To understand why one must go back all the way to the winter of 1976-77, one of the coldest winters in modern history, which caught many heating oil suppliers short. In the latter part of 1977, the oil companies stockpiled huge inventories of crude oil and refined products. This hoarding reflected three factors: normal precautions against another unusually cold winter; the expectation of a nationwide coal strike that would in-

crease the demand for other fuels (and which did happen); and the anticipation of an increase in the price of OPEC oil (which did not). As a result, stocks of crude in January were extraordinarily high—nearly 14 percent higher than the previous January. Storing crude oil is expensive, so the oil companies spent most of the rest of 1978 drawing on their bloated inventories, which meant they imported less oil. In April 1977, for example, the nation imported an average of 8.7 million barrels per day; the following April imports were only 7.4 million barrels per day, a decline of nearly 15 percent. Only in September did imports finally regain the previous year's level. But during these months the demand for oil products continued to grow at a predictable rate. By the end of the summer crude stocks were back down to normal levels. But the fall proved to be unusually warm, stimulating Americans to drive more than they normally would. Demand for gasoline in the months of September, October, and November was 3.3 percent higher than in the same period of 1977. By January crude stocks, depleted somewhat by this surge in demand, stood at 303 million barrels, only 3 percent higher than two years before.

In normal times those inventories could have been rebuilt without any problem. But 1979, it turned out, was no normal year. On December 27, an oil-workers strike shut down Iran's production, which would not resume for more than two months. Total world oil production dipped from 62.1 million barrels per day in December to 59.7 million in January. More important for American drivers, U.S. imports of oil fell from an average of 8.9 million barrels per day in December to 8.3 million in February and remained low, bottoming out at 7.7 million in

IS THERE AN ENERGY CONSPIRACY?

April—down 13 percent from December. It is true that imports remained above those of the previous year throughout the first half of 1979—about 5 percent above. But that was not enough to make up for the depleted inventories and the natural increase in demand. What is important is the total available supplies of oil in its various forms, not merely the level of imports. The Energy Department, in a July report exonerating the oil companies, calculated that there was only 95 percent as much petroleum available from February to May as in the same period of 1978.

One mistake made by the conspiracy theorists is including oil in the Strategic Petroleum Reserve in calculations of total stocks. It is true that the nation's crude stocks, including the reserve, were not unusually low but rather the highest in history. But the oil stored in the reserve might as well not have existed, for all the good it might have done. The Energy Department unfortunately pumped the oil into underground caverns and salt domes without installing equipment to get it back out. So the oil was of no use. Excluding the reserve, the nation's stocks of crude in January were below the level the Energy Department regarded as the acceptable minimum. There was no room for a disruption in the flow of oil from abroad. But a disruption is what happened.

Rationing by Wait

The loss of supplies from Iran would have caused fewer problems if, as is claimed, demand in the United States had declined in the first half of 1979. In fact, this is not quite the truth. Gasoline consumption in January and February was higher than in the same two months

of 1978, and fell off only in March and April. Normally a drop in consumption is the same thing as a drop in demand—demand being the amount of a product consumers will buy at a given price. But in this case there was less gasoline available than consumers wanted at the established price. In a normal market the price would have risen to the point where demand was equal to the available supply. But gasoline prices were—and are—regulated by the government to prevent them from rising in this fashion. So instead of rationing gasoline according to who is willing to *pay* for it, the government forced service stations to ration it according to who was willing to *wait* for it—hence the long lines. Consumption did drop in March and April, but only because there was less gasoline available than consumers wanted to buy.

So oil refiners found themselves in a bind. On the one hand, demand for gasoline was increasing—but inventories were low and the needed supplies of imported oil simply weren't there. One source of crude during the shortage was the spot market, where a small portion of the world's oil is sold at whatever price is bid on a given day (unlike most sales, which are made under long-term contracts). But the Energy Department exhorted the oil companies not to buy on the spot market, in the hope that such restraint would hold down the soaring spot prices. The Department of Energy got its way. American refiners mostly stayed out of the spot market. But prices continued to climb anyway, and in May DOE finally told them to go ahead and get whatever they could. By this time it was too late to do much good.

Several other statistics are crucial to the argument that the shortage was privately contrived. One is that U.S. domestic crude production fell during the very period when Iran's oil fields were producing nothing. Energy Department statistics show that U.S. output fell from 8.8 million barrels per day in October to 8.5 million in February. There is nothing mysterious about this decline. American oil production normally peaks in the summer or fall and declines in the winter, due to hindrances imposed by bad weather. During the same period in 1977-78, American wells reduced their output by 200,000 barrels per day. The decline in the winter of 1978-79 was slightly larger, but not so much as to make much difference. In fact, production in both January and February of 1979 was higher than in the same months of 1978—even though U.S. oil production has declined steadily since 1970, when it reached an all-time high of 9.6 million barrels per day. If anything, the production in the winter of 1978-79 was surprisingly high.

It is also true that U.S. refineries operated at less than full capacity in the first six months of 1979. This is taken as additional proof that oil companies were doing their best to keep supplies of gasoline off the market. But in fact one can reasonably assume that the slowdown in refinery operations (from 91 percent in November—which is regarded as the maximum—to 83 percent in March) was a natural precautionary reaction to the loss of supplies from Iran. Refiners worried about getting supplies of crude had to be careful to keep adequate inventories on hand, particularly with the practical ban on spot-market purchases. Otherwise they ran the risk of having to shut down completely, which requires halting production for as long as two weeks before the refinery can resume normal production. This is a very expen-

sive process. It is considerably cheaper to run slightly below capacity continuously than to run at full capacity for a couple of weeks and then shut down for another couple of weeks before starting up again. Of course by the spring the refiners' fears had been realized: Crude was hard to find and they could not have operated at peak capacity in any case. (This is also normally the time for routine preventive maintenance, which also reduces output.) It is getting things backward to suggest that lower operating rates reflected an attempt to create a shortage. The refineries had to run at less than capacity because there was already a shortage.

The charge that American oil companies actually exported more oil during the shortage than in the previous year is accurate. It is also meaningless. Total exports are trivial in volume—1 or 2 percent of total U.S. consumption. And in any case, virtually the only exports allowed by U.S. law are barrel-for-barrel exchanges of different types of crude oil or refined products—in other words, exports that do not reduce the nation's supply of oil.

So one is left to conclude that the gasoline shortage was not somehow contrived by the nation's oil companies. How then does one explain it? There can be no doubt that the upheaval in Iran was the root cause. But the primary effect of the revolution and the accompanying halt in oil production was not to reduce available supplies in the world, though it did that briefly, but to increase worldwide *demand* for oil. After Iran stopped producing, everyone expected a shortage, so everyone—refiners, middlemen, speculators, and governments—began buying up every available barrel of oil. Even after Iran began exporting oil again (at less than half the level of the previous year), its turbulent political climate created widespread worry that it might cut off production again—or worse, that its Islamic revolution might stir up political trouble in other Arab oil-producing countries. The reason spot-market prices rose so high was that buyers of all sorts were stockpiling crude oil against the possibility of more upheavals in the Middle East—rather like people rushing to the grocery store upon hearing forecasts of heavy snow. As it turned out, oil production in the Middle East remained reasonably stable for the rest of the year, which meant all the stockpiling wasn't really necessary. But it would have been seen as a smart policy if Iran had quit exporting again, or if Colonel Qaddafi had carried out his threat to cease producing for a few years, or if the Saudi monarchy had been overthrown. If there are wars or revolutions in the Middle East in 1980, stockpiling may yet be vindicated.

The shortages of gasoline in some American cities owed something to the same kind of panic psychology. One reason service stations were short of gasoline was that drivers were, in effect, stockpiling it—in their fuel tanks. It was reported during the shortage in California, for example, that the average credit card purchase of gasoline amounted to only three dollars. The Energy Department aggravated anxiety among drivers by issuing frequent apocalyptic warnings, and among oil company executives, by warning that refiners would have to begin shifting production to heating oil earlier than usual (normally this shift takes place around the end of July) to protect against a possible shortage of heating oil in the coming winter. (This protected the President in February's New Hampshire

primary.) As a result refiners had to keep their inventories of gasoline higher than they might have otherwise, to make sure they would have enough to last through the summer and fall driving seasons.

Making the Uncomfortable Unmanageable

But it nonetheless appears clear that there was simply less gasoline around than people wanted. The Energy Department estimates, rather roughly, that imports of oil were about 800,000 barrels a day less than was needed to keep supplies at their 1978 level. In other words, the nation had only about 95 percent as much oil on hand during the shortage as it had had the previous year—an uncomfortable situation, but not an unmanageable one. What made the shortage unmanageable was the Energy Department.

The gasoline lines owed their existence mainly to the government allocation system, which dictated where, and in what quantity, supplies of gasoline would go. The allocation rules effectively freeze supply patterns by requiring that all dealers supplied by a refiner receive the same percentage of gasoline. If a refiner is shipping only 80 percent of what he shipped the previous year, then he has to provide each dealer with 80 percent of the supplies he received at a particular point in the past. At first, DOE's allocations were based on supply figures for 1972. So a station whose business had been cut in half in those seven years would receive the same allocation as one whose business had doubled. Later DOE changed the base period to 1978, which brought allocations a little closer to current patterns of consumption but still made no allowances for stations—or cities—whose gasoline needs had risen in the intervening year. In places, such as urban areas, where the population has been growing, the allocations provided too little gasoline. In places where it has been declining, such as rural areas, it provided too much. In addition, the allocation rules channeled gasoline to where it had been consumed in past, normal years—for example, resort areas. But fears of being stranded kept vacationers away from those places, where the gasoline was plentiful, and at home, where it wasn't.

There is another reason that network camera crews found no gasoline lines in small towns in Kansas or Texas. Under the DOE allocation system, farmers were designated as "priority users" (as were state governments, hospitals, and a few other types of consumers). These priority users were guaranteed all their "current requirements" of gasoline, which meant they got as much as they wanted. Unfortunately, there was no way to tell if farmers were getting more gasoline than they actually needed—i.e., stockpiling— or if they were using in the family car fuel meant for farming. A July 24 report by the Energy Department concluded ruefully that "some priority users took advantage of their priority status to obtain more gasoline than needed, resulting in larger shortages for others."

The special treatment of "priority users" also explains why a 5-percent shortage translated into cutbacks of 15 to 25 percent in the amount of gasoline supplied to dealers. Before they could make their shipments to dealers, refiners first had to provide priority users with all the gasoline they wanted. Only then could they calculate how much to supply to ordinary drivers. In practice, about 15

percent of the available gasoline went to these privileged buyers.

The allocation system was needed only because of the price controls on gasoline. In a normal market, supplies would have been divided according to who was willing to pay the most—in other words, by demand. The price controls foreclosed this sort of bidding. Dealers had no incentive to bid for gasoline because they couldn't increase their prices above a certain fixed level anyway. Without the allocation rules, refiners might have simply cut off everyone but their own brand-name stations. The rules, one should note, are not designed to protect consumers. They are designed to protect dealers by guaranteeing them access to supplies.

The crucial fallacy in the conspiracy theory is assuming that if oil-company profits rise, then oil companies must have simply decided to raise them. But if the oil companies can effectively control the market for oil products, why didn't they move sooner to increase their profits? Between 1974 and 1978 the real price of gasoline in the United States actually declined slightly. If the oil companies had the stranglehold on American consumers suggested by Cook, Anderson, et al., then clearly they would not have tolerated this state of affairs. The gasoline shortage obviously did prove profitable for oil producers. The 25 leading American companies enjoyed a 74-percent increase in profits in the first nine months of 1979 over the previous year. The previous year, however, was not a particularly good one. Earnings of the top 25 companies were 22 percent lower in real terms than in 1974. The gas lines here did increase earnings by making it possible to charge higher gasoline prices (insofar as the price controls allowed), which increased the profit margin on each gallon sold. The sharp increase in world oil prices also raised the value of oil company inventories and reserves of crude oil. But most of the higher earnings came from foreign operations and thus had nothing to do with the shortage here.

The gasoline shortage was not the product of a conspiracy. It grew out of several factors—the revolution in Iran, the panic buying that followed it, and the federal government's mismanagement of the subsequent reduction in oil supplies. The pattern closely resembles the first shortage in the winter of 1973-74. And

the pattern of the next shortage will be roughly the same.

There is little our government can do to prevent Arab populations from overthrowing their governments, or to prevent such upheavals from throwing the world oil market into disarray. But it can act to avoid the gasoline lines caused by its own price controls and allocations. So far, though, Congress and the President alike have insisted on keeping both, which means that the next disruption in the world oil trade is guaranteed to create shortages and gasoline lines here at home. But that isn't a conspiracy. That's a government policy.

● ● ●

POSTSCRIPT

IS THERE AN ENERGY CONSPIRACY?

John Blair's case for a conspiracy among the major international oil companies is fully developed in his book THE CONTROL OF OIL (Pantheon, 1967). In his book and in this short article, which was his last writing before his death, he argued that OPEC could not have established its cartel, let alone kept it in operation, without the cooperation and support of the Seven Sisters. OPEC and its price increases, provided a convenient screen to cover increases in the oil companies target rates of return. Oil companies have not remained neutral. As OPEC raises its price, the Seven Sisters pass that increase—along with their own increase—on to the consumer. The net result is an increase in the profitability of the "big oil companies."

Chapman finds Blair's contentions to be utterly groundless. In support of his position, he examines the most recent energy crisis: 1979. In 1979, several events occurred simultaneously. There was a gasoline shortage in the U.S. However, the U.S. still reduced its production of gasoline. Secondly, U.S. exports of oil increased. Thirdly, the profitability of U.S. oil firms skyrocketed. These factors taken together appear to indicte a conspiracy.

Chapman, however denies that there is a conspiracy. He asks the reader to examine each of these events. First, the most incriminating evidence is the increase in oil imports. But 1979's increase of 3 percent over 1978, is due only to the fact that 1978 was an abnormally *low* year for oil imports. This 3 percent increase was not enough to restore depleted inventories or to meet rising demands. Second, demands were rising, but consumption was falling. This perverse phenomenon occurred because government-regulated prices forced service stations to ration their limited supplies and some consumers were unwilling to wait to get their gas. Third, the decline in production of gasoline was a natural precautionary reaction to the interruption of crude oil from Iran. It is far less costly for firms to run at less than full capacity than it is to run at full capacity and then to completely shut down. Lastly, the charge that exports of oil actually increased during the shortage is correct. But the increase was so small that it had no impact on the situation. Chapman concludes that the shortage cannot be traced to a conspiracy. Rather it can be traced to the interruption of oil production in Iran. This touched off a wave of panic buying which sent prices upwards.

There has been much written about the energy crisis. One standard reference is Peter R. Odell's OIL AND WORLD POWER: BACKGROUND TO THE OIL CRISIS, Third revised edition (Taplinger, 1975). Several other excellent books are: Gus Hall, THE ENERGY RIP-OFF: CAUSES AND CURES (International Publishing Co., 1974) and Burton Kaufman, THE OIL CARTEL CASE: A DOCUMENTARY STUDY OF ANTITRUST ACTIVITY IN THE COLD WAR ERA (Greenwood Press, 1978).

ISSUE 8

WILL A DECREASE IN TAXES STIMULATE PRODUCTION AND EMPLOYMENT?

YES: Jude Wanniski, from "Taxes, Revenues, and the 'Laffer Curve'." *The Public Interest* (Winter, 1978).
NO: Donald W. Kiefer, from "An Economic Analysis of the Kemp/Roth Tax Cut Bill, H.R. 8333." (Government Printing Office, 1978).

ISSUE SUMMARY

YES: Former *Wall Street Journal* editor Jude Wanniski uses the concept of the Laffer Curve to argue that current tax rates are in the "prohibitive range for government" and, therefore, reductions in these rates will lead to increases in productive activity.
NO: Economist Kiefer holds that the Laffer Curve is too simplistic a device upon which to base a tax cut and the effects of a tax cut depend on a number of factors which are not a part of the Laffer Curve construct.

In 1977, Representative Jack Kemp (R) of New York and Senator William Roth (R) of Delaware introduced legislation in Congress which, if passed, would lead to dramatic decreases in taxes. Immediately a debate developed concerning the likely consequences of the sharp cut in tax rates, a debate which continued into the Presidential election of 1980. Kemp and Roth and their supporters, including President Reagan, argued that the legislation would stimulate saving, investment, production, and employment. These positive effects, it was maintained, would occur without an acceleration in the rate of inflation. Opponents of the Kemp/Roth legislation, identified as H.R. 8333, including then President Carter, argued that the major consequence of such sharp tax cuts would be a rapid acceleration in the rate of inflation.

At the heart of this disagreement are alternative views regarding the theoretical justification for the Kemp/Roth legislation. This conceptual base is the Laffer Curve. Thus, in order to understand the disagreement on Kemp/Roth, it is necessary to understand the alternative views on the Laffer Curve. The two articles included here take opposite positions on the Laffer Curve. Wanniski supports the Laffer Curve and Kemp/Roth. He begins by describing the Laffer Curve, the reasons why the relationship should hold, and then offers several historical examples where tax decreases led to increases in production and employment. Kiefer's presentation represents the negative. He underscores the simplistic nature of the Laffer Curve: it ignores too many factors to be a useful guide to tax rate policy.

It is useful to put the tax cut issue into the context of basic economic philosophies. Normally the notion of tax reductions would seem to be consistent with the conservative-free market philosophy associated with the Republican party. However, as Wanniski indicates, until Kemp/Roth, Republicans have been reluctant to endorse tax reductions. This reluctance can be traced to another concern of the Republican party, the need for a balanced budget. Thus the Republicans have hesitated to support tax cuts for fear that the cuts would either create a budget deficit or make an existing deficit larger. So rather than support tax cuts because they give consumers and producers more economic freedom, the Republicans resisted tax cuts for budgetary reasons. Liberal-Democrats have over the recent past typically endorsed tax cuts. Their support follows less from their concern with economic freedom than from their belief that the tax cuts will promote production and employment.

The question then is; if Republicans normally resist tax cuts while Democrats typically favor them, why has there been a reversal of usual positions on the Kemp/Roth reductions? The answer to this question is, again, the Laffer Curve. The Republicans believe that with the tax cuts the increase in economic activity will be so large that tax collections will actually increase. The Democrats believe that the effects of tax cuts, given the current state of the economy, will be primarily on prices and not on production and employment. And increased rates of inflation will work mainly to the disadvantage of low and middle income groups. The Laffer Curve because it ignores such things, as Kiefer points out, as the current state of the economy, is therefore not a reliable guide to policy actions.

Clearly in understanding the Kemp/Roth legislation as well as the position of the two political parties, knowledge of the Laffer Curve is important. These two articles get to the heart of the matter and indicate the central positions of proponents and opponents.

YES

Jude Wanniski

TAXES, REVENUES, AND THE "LAFFER CURVE"

As Arthur Laffer has noted, "There are always two tax rates that yield the same revenues." When an aide to President Gerald Ford asked him once to elaborate, Laffer. . .drew a simple curve, shown on the next page, to illustrate his point. The point, too, is simple enough—though, like so many simple points, it is also powerful in its implications.

When the tax rate is 100 percent, all production ceases in the money economy (as distinct from the barter economy, which exists largely to escape taxation). People will not work in the money economy if all the fruits of their labors are confiscated by the government. And because production ceases, there is nothing for the 100-percent rate to confiscate, so government revenues are zero.

On the other hand, if the tax rate is zero, people can keep 100 percent of what they produce in the money economy. There is no governmental "wedge" between earnings and after-tax income, and thus no governmental barrier to production. Production is therefore maximized, and the output of the money economy is limited only by the desire of workers for leisure. But because the tax rate is zero, government revenues are again zero, and there can be no government. So at a 0-percent tax rate the economy is in a state of anarchy, and at a 100-percent tax rate the economy is functioning entirely through barter.

In between lies the curve. If the government reduces its rate to something less than 100 percent, say to point A, some segment of the barter economy will be able to gain so many efficiencies by being in the money economy that, even with near-confiscatory tax rates, after-tax production would still exceed that of the barter economy. Production will start up, and revenues will flow into the government treasury. By lowering the tax rate, we find an increase in revenues.

On the bottom end of the curve, the same thing is happening. If people feel

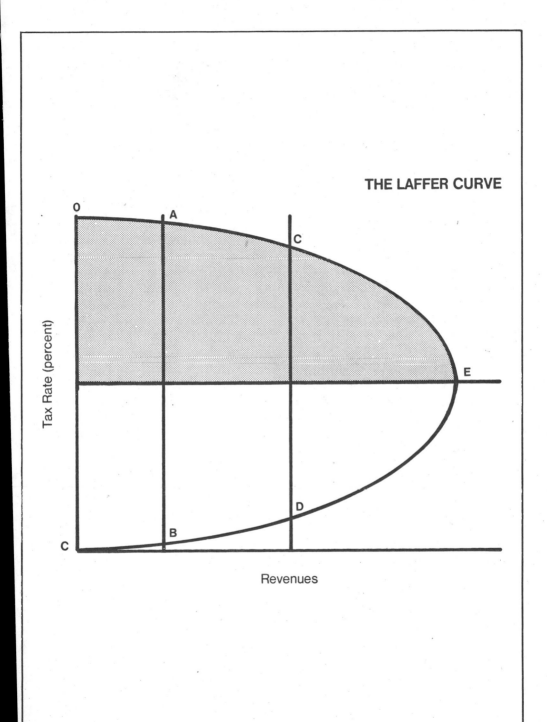

THE LAFFER CURVE

that they need a minimal government and thus institute a low tax rate, some segment of the economy, finding that the marginal loss of income exceeds the efficiencies gained in the money economy, is shifted into either barter or leisure. But with that tax rate, revenues do flow into the government treasury. This is the situation at point B. Point A represents a very high tax rate and very low production. Point B represents a very low tax rate and very high production. Yet they both yield the same revenue to the government.

The same is true of points C and D. The government finds that by a further lowering of the tax rate, say from point A to point C, revenues increase with the further expansion of output. And by raising the tax rate, say from point B to point D, revenues also increase, by the same amount.

Revenues and production are maximized at point E. If, at point E, the government lowers the tax rate again, output will increase, but revenues will fall. And if, at point E, the tax rate is raised, both output and revenue will decline. The shaded area is *the prohibitive range for government,* where rates are unnecessarily high and can be reduced with gains in *both* output and revenue.

Tax Rates and Tax Revenues

The next important thing to observe is that, except for the 0-percent and 100-percent rates, there are no numbers along the "Laffer Curve." Point E is not 50 percent, although it may be, but rather a variable number: *It is the point at which the electorate desires to be taxed.* At points B and D, the electorate desires more government goods and services and is willing—without reducing its productivity—to pay the higher rates consis-

tent with the revenues at point E. And at points A and C, the electorate desires more private goods and services in the money economy, and wishes to pay the lower rates consistent with the revenues at point E. It is the task of the statesman to determine the location of point E, and follow its variations as closely as possible.

This is true whether the political leader heads a nation or a family. The father who disciplines his son at point A, imposing harsh penalties for violating both major and minor rules, only invites sullen rebellion, stealth, and lying (tax evasion, on the national level). The permissive father who disciplines casually at point B invites open, reckless rebellion: His son's independence and relatively unfettered growth come at the expense of the rest of the family. The wise parent seeks point E, which will probably vary from one child to another, from son to daughter.

For the political leader on the national level, point E can represent a very low or a very high number. When the nation is at war, point E can approach 100 percent. At the siege of Leningrad in World War II, for example, the people of the city produced for 900 days at tax rates approaching 100 percent. Russian soldiers and civilians worked to their physical limits, receiving as "pay" only the barest of rations. Had the citizens of Leningrad not wished to be taxed at that high rate, which was required to hold off the Nazi army, the city would have fallen.

The number represented by point E will change abruptly if the nation is at war one day and at peace the next. The electorate's demand for military goods and services from the government will fall sharply; the electorate will therefore desire to be taxed at a lower rate. If rates are not lowered consistent with this new lower level of demand, output will fall to some level consistent with a point along the prohibitive side of the "Laffer curve." Following World War I, for example, the wartime tax rates were left in place and greatly contributed to the recession of 1919-20. Warren G. Harding ran for President in 1920 on a slogan promising a "return to normalcy" regarding tax rates; he was elected in a landslide. The subsequent rolling back of the rates ushered in the economic expansion of the "Roaring Twenties." After World War II, wartime tax rates were quickly reduced, and the American economy enjoyed a smooth transition to peacetime. In Japan and West Germany, however, there was no adjustment of the rates; as a result, postwar economic recovery was delayed. Germany's recovery began in 1948, when personal income-tax rates were reduced under Finance Minister Ludwig Erhard, and much of the government regulation of commerce came to an end. Japan's recovery did not begin until 1950, when wartime tax rates were finally rolled back. In each case, reduced *rates* produced increased *revenues* for the government. The political leader must fully appreciate the distinction between tax rates and tax revenues to discern the desires of the electorate.

The easiest way for a political leader to determine whether an increase in rates will produce more rather than less revenues is to put the proposition to the electorate. It is not enough for the politician to propose an increase from, say, point B to point D on the curve. He must also specify how the anticipated revenues will be spent. When voters approve a bond issue for schools, highways, or bridges, they are explicitly telling the politician that they are willing to pay the high tax rates required to finance the bonds. In rejecting a bond issue, however,

the electorate is not necessarily telling the politician that taxes are already high enough, or that point E (or beyond) has been reached. The only message is that the proposed tax rates are too high a price to pay for the specific goods and services offered by the government.

Only a tiny fraction of all government expenditures are determined in this fashion, to be sure. Most judgments regarding tax rates and expenditures are made by individual politicians. Andrew Mellon became a national hero for engineering the rate reductions of the 1920's, and was called "the greatest Treasury Secretary since Alexander Hamilton." The financial policies of Ludwig Erhard were responsible for what was hailed as "an economic miracle"—the postwar recovery of Germany. Throughout history, however, it has been the exception rather than the rule that politicians, by accident or design, have sought to increase revenues by lowering rates. . . .

The Politics of the "Laffer Curve"

The "Laffer curve" is a simple but exceedingly powerful analytical tool. In one way or another, all transactions, even the simplest, take place along it. The homely adage, "You can catch more flies with molasses than with vinegar," expresses the essence of the curve. But empires are built on the bottom of this simple curve and crushed against the top of it. The Caesars understood this, and so did Napoleon (up to a point) and the greatest of the Chinese emperors. The Founding Fathers of the United States knew it well; the arguments for union (in *The Federalist Papers*) made by Hamilton, Madison, and Jay reveal an understanding of the notion. Until World War I—when progressive taxation was

159

sharply increased to help finance it—the United States successfully remained out of the "prohibitive range."

In the 20th century, especially since World War I, there has been a constant struggle by all the nations of the world to get down the curve. The United States managed to do so in the 1920's, because Andrew Mellon understood the lessons of the "Laffer curve" for the domestic economy. Mellon argued that there are always two prices in the private market that will produce the same revenues. Henry Ford, for example, could get the same revenue by selling a few cars for $100,000 each, or a great number for $1,000 each. (Of course, Ford was forced by the threat of competition to sell at the low price.) The tax rate, said Mellon, is the "price of government." But the nature of government is monopolistic; government itself must find the lowest rate that yields the desired revenue.

Because Mellon was successful in persuading Republican Presidents—first Warren G. Harding and then Calvin Coolidge—of the truth of his ideas the high wartime tax rates were steadily cut back. The excess-profits tax on industry was repealed, and the 77-percent rate on the highest bracket of personal income was rolled back in stages, so that by 1925 it stood at 25 percent. As a result, the period 1921-29 was one of phenomenal economic expansion: G.N.P. grew from $69.6 billion to $103.1 billion. And because prices fell during this period, G.N.P. grew even faster in real terms, by 54 percent. At the lower rates, revenues grew sufficiently to enable Mellon to reduce the national debt from $24.3 billion to $16.9 billion.

The stock market crash of 1929 and the subsequent global depression occurred because Herbert Hoover unwittingly contracted the world economy with his high-tariff policies, which pushed the West, as an economic unit, up the "Laffer curve." Hoover compounded the problem in 1932 by raising personal tax rates almost up to the levels of 1920.

The most important economic event following World War II was also the work of a finance minister who implicitly understood the importance of the "Laffer curve." Germany had been pinned to the uppermost ranges of the curve since World War I. It took a financial panic in the spring of 1948 to shake Germany loose. At that point, German citizens were still paying a 50-percent marginal tax rate on incomes of $600 and a 95-percent rate on incomes above $15,000. On June 22, 1948, Finance Minister Ludwig Erhard announced cuts that raised the 50-percent bracket to $2,200 and the 95-percent bracket to $63,000. The financial panic ended, and economic expansion began. It was Erhard, not the Marshall Plan, who saved Europe from Communist encroachment. In the decade that followed, Erhard again and again slashed the tax rates, bringing the German economy farther down the curve and into a higher level of prosperity. In 1951 the 50-percent bracket was pushed up to $5,000 and in 1953 to $9,000, while at the same time the rate for the top bracket was reduced to 82-percent. In 1954, the rate for the top bracket was reduced again, to 80 percent, and in 1955 it was pulled down sharply, to 63 percent on incomes above $250,000; the 50-percent bracket was pushed up to $42,000. Yet another tax reform took place in 1958: The government exempted the first $400 dollars of income and brought the rate for the top bracket down to 53 percent. It was this systematic lowering of unnecessarily high tax rates that produced the German "economic miracle." As national income rose in Germany throughout the 1950's, so did revenues, enabling the government to construct its "welfare state" as well as its powerful national defense system.

The British empire was built on the lower end of the "Laffer curve" and dismantled on the upper end. The high wartime rates imposed to finance the Napoleonic wars were cut back sharply in 1816, despite warnings from "fiscal experts" that the high rates were needed to reduce the enormous public debt of £900 million. For the following 60 years, the British economy grew at an unprecedented pace, as a series of finance ministers used ever-expanding revenues to lower steadily the tax rates and tariffs.

In Britain, though, unlike the United States, there was no Mellon to risk lowering the extremely high tax rates imposed to finance World War I. As a result, the British economy struggled through the 1920's and 1930's. After World War II, the British government again made the mistake of not sufficiently lowering tax rates to spur individual initiative. Instead, the postwar Labour government concentrated on using tax policy for Keynesian objectives—i.e., increasing consumer demand to expand output. On October 23, 1945, tax rates were cut on lower-income brackets and surtaxes were added to the already high rates on the upper-income brackets. Taxes on higher incomes were increased, according to Chancellor of the Exchequer Hugh Dalton, in order to "continue that steady advance toward economic and social equality which we have made during the war and which the Government firmly intends to continue in peace."

From that day in 1945, there has been no concerted political voice in Britain arguing for a reduction of the high tax rates. Conservatives have supported and won tax reductions for business, especially investment-tax income credits. But while arguing for a reduction of the 83-percent rate on incomes above £20,000 (roughly $35,000 at current exchange rates) of earned income and the 98-percent rate on "unearned income" from investments, they have insisted that government *first* lower its spending, in order to permit the rate reductions. Somehow, the spending levels never can be cut. Only in the last several months of 1977 has Margaret Thatcher, the leader of the opposition Conservative Party, spoken of reducing the high tax rates as a way of expanding revenues.

In the United States, in September 1977, the Republican National Committee unanimously endorsed the plan of Representative Jack Kemp of New York for cutting tax rates as a way of expanding revenues through increased business activity. This was the first time since 1953 that the GOP had embraced the concept of tax cuts! In contrast, the Democrats under President Kennedy sharply cut tax rates in 1962-64 (though making their case in Keynesian terms). The reductions successfully moved the United States economy down the "Laffer curve," expanding the economy and revenues.

It is crucial to Western economic expansion, peace, and prosperity that "conservative" parties move in this direction. They are, after all, traditionally in favor of income growth, with "liberals" providing the necessary political push for income redistribution. A welfare state is perfectly consistent with the "Laffer curve," and can function successfully along its lower range. But there must be income before there can be redistribution. Most of the economic failures of this century can rightly be charged to the failure of conservatives to press for tax rates along the lower range of the "Laffer curve." Presidents Eisenhower, Nixon and Ford were timid in this crucial area of public policy. The Goldwater Republicans of 1963-64, in fact, emphatically opposed the Kennedy tax rate cuts!

If, during the remainder of this decade, the United States and Great Britain demonstrate the power of the "Laffer curve" as an analytical tool, its use will spread, in the developing countries as well as the developed world. Politicians who understand the curve will find that they can defeat politicians who do not, other things being equal. Electorates all over the world always know when they are unnecessarily perched along the upper edge of the "Laffer curve," and will support political leaders who can bring them back down.

● ● ●

NO

Donald Kiefer

AN ECONOMIC ANALYSIS OF THE KEMP/ROTH TAX CUT BILL

The "Tax Reduction Act of 1977," H.R. 8333,[1] better known as the Kemp/Roth tax cut bill, has become the subject of substantial interest in Congress and the nation at large in mid-1978. The bill and its underlying philosophy, largely embodied in the so-called "Laffer Curve," have been the subject of considerable Congressional discussion and debate, numerous articles in the popular press and programs in the electronic media, and a large number of requests to the Congressional Research Service for information and analysis. This paper is intended as an overall response to those requests. . . .

Description of the Tax Cuts in the Kemp/Roth Bill and Their Direct Economic Effects

H.R. 8333 would cut individual and corporate income taxes through three separate devices, all conceptually simple. Individual income taxes would be cut through reductions in the statutory tax rates applicable to each taxable income bracket. Corporate income taxes would be reduced by a cut in the normal corporate tax rates and an increase in the surtax exemption. . . .

The "Laffer Curve" and Supply Side Fiscal Response

The general contention that a sizeable tax cut will have large supply side effects through stronger incentives to work, save, and invest has most often been voiced by the Kemp/Roth proponents through reference to the so-called "Laffer Curve," named for its originator, Professor Arthur Laffer of the University of Southern California. The most extensive presentation of the Laffer Curve has been made by Jude Wanniski in an article in THE PUBLIC INTEREST. . . .

---

[1] The bill was introduced July 14, 1977, and proposes tax cuts beginning in calendar 1978. For analytical purposes this paper assumes the tax cuts would still begin in 1978 even though nearly a year has passed since its introduction.

From, "An Economic Analysis of the Kemp/Roth Tax Cut Bill, H.R. 8333."

WILL A DECREASE IN TAXES STIMULATE PRODUCTION?

Laffer Curve adherents, including Professor Laffer, argue that the United States is now in the "prohibitive range" of taxation. This claim. . . [is] the rationale for arguing that the Kemp/Roth tax cut, or presumably any tax cut, would increase Government revenue rather than reduce it.

The Laffer Curve obviously has a certain amount of intuitive appeal. However, it is also an overly simplistic approach which ignores very complex economic relationships, and therefore falls considerably short of providing information directly relevant to policy formulation. A brief analytical review of the concept is provided below in outline format.

1. Central to the Laffer Curve is the notion that there is something which can be called a "tax rate" for the overall economy, and that for each tax rate a given amount of tax revenue will be raised. But what is this tax rate? There are literally hundreds of different taxes imposed by the Federal Government and State and local governments; they apply to personal income, corporate income, wages, sales, property, and myriad other tax bases. Their structures vary; some are flat-rate taxes; some have elaborate exemptions and deductions. It is impossible for one tax rate to characterize this complex tax structure in the U.S. . . .

2. The Laffer Curve represents a gross simplification of a major portion of macroeconomics into a single curved line. Countless books and articles have been written to conceptualize, identify, and measure the impact of taxation and fiscal policy on the U.S. economy, and despite all of this effort and research there are still many important issues which are unresolved. However, it is known that the effect of a tax cut or tax increase on the economy, and in turn on tax revenues, depends on a multitude of factors and their complex interrelationships. These factors include the level of employment and unemployment, the level of capacity utilization, the level of investment, interest rates, inflation rates, the savings rate, the posture of monetary policy, levels of consumer and business confidence, the size of the Federal deficit, the budget position of State and local governments, and the level of the foreign trade balance, to name only a few. . . .

All of these factors and many more are involved in understanding and assessing the potential economic impact of a tax cut. To subsume all of these economic effects into a single line on a graph is to ignore much of the substance of responsible tax policy.

3. The notion behind the Laffer Curve depends almost entirely on the response of work, savings, and investment behavior to levels of taxation. The assertion is that higher taxes lead to reduced incentives and lower levels of economic activity; lower taxes increase incentives and economic activity. The Laffer Curve asserts that as taxes are increased from 0 to 100 percent, at some point the effect on tax revenue of the diminished economic activity overwhelms the effect of the higher tax rates, and tax revenue begins decreasing rather than increasing. This assertion is no doubt true, but because the Laffer analysis concentrates on economic responses at or near the end points—tax rates of 0 and 100 percent—it is not very relevant. The relevant issue is the incentive effect of small tax rate changes within the range of feasible alternatives to present policy. Analysis of these incentive effects is much more complex and leads to different conclusions, than suggested by the Laffer Curve.

4. By concentrating primarily on in-

centive and supply side effects, the Laffer Curve largely ignores the actual mechanism by which fiscal policy exerts its biggest and most immediate impact—demand side effects. The most immediate impact of a tax cut is that individuals and businesses have more disposable or after tax income. The largest percentage of this after tax income will be spent rather rapidly, thus raising aggregate demand in the economy. If there are unemployed workers and idle productive resources, this higher aggregate demand will lead to more jobs and higher GNP; if unemployment is slight and there is little idle capacity, the increased demand will be inflationary and destabilizing.

Thus, the timing of a tax cut is very important. However, the Laffer Curve analysis does not include an explicit consideration of the state of the economy at the time of a tax cut. It asserts that we are in the "prohibitive range" of taxation, and offers the faith that supply side effects will create the capacity for higher output and the incentives for higher work effort. However, capacity creating investment is not planned, financed, and constructed overnight; it takes years. But the demand side effects of a tax cut are immediate, reaching full effect within a few calendar quarters. Therefore, the effects of a substantial tax cut enacted when excess capacity is low, based on Laffer-type faith, would be a rapid increase in demand, which would quickly accelerate price increases and raise interest rates, thus choking off the hoped for increase in investment.

5. Professor Laffer and the adherents to his concepts claim that the United States is presently in the "prohibitive range" of the Laffer Curve, i.e. that the "tax rate" is so high and stiffling of incentives that an across-the-board tax cut

would actually increase revenues rather than reduce them. However, there is virtually no evidence to support this assertion. If this assertion were true one would expect effective tax rates to have risen dramatically in the U.S. in recent years; however Federal taxes as a percentage of GNP or personal income have remained virtually constant over the last quarter century.[2] If this assertion were true one might also expect to find that the U.S. tax burden considerably exceeds that of the other developed countries of the World; however, total taxes in the U.S. as a percent of GNP are lower than the average for the OECD countries. Some countries which have higher productivity growth than the U.S., for example Germany and Sweden, also have higher overall tax burdens. . . .

6. Part of the intuitive appeal of the Laffer Curve derives from the interpretation of point E on the curve. This point is the crossover point to the "prohibitive range" of the Laffer Curve where incentives are so bruised that higher taxes yield lower revenues. It is also claimed to be the point at which the electorate desires to be taxed, in other words, an optimal size for government at which just the right amount of public services is provided. It is an easy deductive leap from the asserted coincidence of these two points to conclude that if government becomes only slightly larger than the electorate would prefer, then we enter the prohibitive range and taxation becomes oppressive.

However, there is no reason to believe that these two points are the same. The desired level of government services in the U.S. is not determined by raising

---

[2]Total Federal, State and local taxes have increased about percent as a portion of GNP over the same era.

taxes until higher tax rates produce lower revenues; if so tax rates would undoubtedly be much higher than presently. The desired level of government in this country is determined through the political process, and there is nothing which suggests that the size of government produced by that process is the maximum possible which can be imposed without suppressing productive enterprise. In fact, the overwhelming evidence is to the contrary. In the United States the determinants of the optimal size of government have more to do with the desire for personal freedom and a preference for private production of goods and services, than with diminishing returns from higher levels of taxation. Thus, the optimal size of government in this country is probably very small compared to point E on the Laffer Curve, and the relatively small variations in government size around the optimal point which result from the political decision making process do not currently appear to run the risk of entering the "prohibitive range" of taxation on the Laffer Curve.

7. The Kemp/Roth advocates have contributed an important observation regarding the effect of taxation on incentives. Recently, considerable attention has been focused from many quarters on the effect of taxation on capital formation and incentives to invest. However, the Kemp/Roth proponents have added to this discussion the observation that the individual income tax has become more of a general economic disincentive over the past 13 years because taxpayers have been pushed into increasingly higher marginal tax brackets. . . .

The last tax cut in the United States which was achieved by reducing marginal tax rates was the 1964 tax cut.[3] In the intervening years there have been several tax reductions affecting the individual income tax (in 1969, 1971, 1975, 1976, and 1977), but all have been accomplished by increasing the standard deduction or the personal exemption, or by creating new devices such as the general tax credit or the low income allowance. However, these changes have not been sufficient to prevent a general movement of taxpayers into higher tax brackets, and since the tax rates have remained constant, the marginal rates experienced by many taxpayers have increased. . . .

[3]This statement ignores the reduction in tax rates which occurred when the surtax expired in 1970.

● ● ●

POSTSCRIPT

WILL A DECREASE IN TAXES STIMULATE PRODUCTION AND EMPLOYMENT?

According to Wanniski, a reduction in taxes as embodied in the Kemp/Roth legislation will stimulate production and employment. At the same time these tax cuts will lead to increases in government revenues so no budget deficit fears need impede support of the cuts. Kiefer believes that tax cuts can stimulate the economy but whether this stimulus translates into actual gains in production and employment or increases in price depends on a number of factors including the state of the economy. More simply put, Wanniski accepts the Laffer Curve as an appropriate basis for policy while Kiefer believes it is too simplistic a device for the determination of tax rates.

Because of the length of the debate and its importance in the policy arena, the issue has been joined by a number of persons. A useful compilation of alternative views has been edited by Arthur B. Laffer and Jan P. Seymore, THE ECONOMICS OF THE TAX REVOLT: A READER (Harcourt Brace and Jovanovich, 1979). Besides Kiefer's complete analysis "An Economic Analysis of the Kemp/Roth Tax Cut Bill, H.R. 8333: A Description, An Examination of Its Rationale, and Estimates of its Economic Effects" (Library of Congress, Congressional Research Service, 1978), a detailed analysis of Kemp/Roth was completed by the Congressional Budget Office, "Analysis of Kemp/Roth" (1978).

ISSUE 9

CAN WAGE AND PRICE CONTROLS HELP SOLVE OUR INFLATION PROBLEMS?

YES: Gar Alperovitz and Jeff Faux, from "Controls and the Basic Necessities," *Challenge* (May/June, 1980).
NO: Albert Rees, from "Controls," *Across the Board* (May, 1980).

ISSUE SUMMARY

YES: Alperovitz and Faux, co-directors of the National Center for Economic Alternatives, support wage and price controls because inflation has been concentrated in the essential sectors of housing, food, health care and energy and because all other anti-inflation policies have failed.

NO: Economist Rees disapproves of controls for they prevent prices from performing important short run and long run functions, and besides they haven't worked very well in the recent past.

During a speech to the nation on August 15, 1971, then President Nixon said to a surprised nation: "I am today ordering a freeze on all prices and wages throughout the United States for a period of 90 days." Thus began the most recent experience with wage and price controls. This experiment proceeded through several phases with varying degrees of rigidity including a return to a price freeze during the summer of 1973. The controls ended in 1974.

It is important to distinguish between freezes, controls, and guidelines, all of which may be grouped under the title of incomes policies. A freeze means that wages and prices must remain at a fixed level; controls mean that wages and prices may change but only in accordance with some explicit rule; and guidelines are controls which do not carry the force of law, that is, to ignore guidelines is not illegal. The U.S. has actually experimented with all three of these incomes policies; indeed, all three types of incomes policies were used during the 1970s.

The use of incomes policies, whether in the form of freezes, controls, or guidelines, is predicated on the belief that more conventional economic actions to achieve, simultaneously, price stability and full employment will be unsuccessful. So rather than rely exclusively on monetary and fiscal policies, policymakers turn to income policies primarily as a mechanism to slow down inflation. Each of the three types of actions is, of course, more drastic. Guidelines, because they carry no legal penalties, may be ignored. So the real questions focus on controls and the most severe form of controls is represented by freezes. Can they achieve their goal of helping resolve our inflation problems?

In addressing this issue, Alperovitz and Faux argue that controls are necessary because all other anti-inflation policies have failed. Putting controls into place would stop the inflation, giving the government an opportunity to put into place programs which will improve price performance in those sectors where the inflation is worse. Rees views the important roles prices play in the economy. He argues that without the freedom of prices to fluctuate, industries that should be growing will not, decreases in the production of certain commodities will not occur, and the flow of labor to certain occupations may diminish.

Restructuring the yes and no positions in terms of basic economic philosophies, we find that the yes side is generally associated with the liberal view while the no side is typically the position of free market advocates. Even so, the preceeding discussion indicates that it was a Republican and not a Democratic administration which imposed the more rigid incomes policies. During the last twenty years Democratic presidents—Kennedy, Johnson, and Carter have not ventured beyond guidelines while the Republican Nixon used both freezes and controls. In explaining the Nixon anomoly, practical considerations resolve the paradox. At the time he imposed the controls, Nixon's concern was that efforts to promote employment through monetary and fiscal policies would exacerbate the inflation problem. The solution appeared to be the temporary imposition of constraints on prices and wages. And when things returned to normal the controls would be lifted. Nixon's own words in that same August 15, 1971 speech seem to maintain this Republican aversion to controls:

> Let me emphasize two characteristics of this action. First it is temporary. To put the strong, vigorous American economy into a permanent strait-jacket would lock-in unfairness; it would stifle the expansion of our free enterprise system, and second, while the wage-price freeze will be backed up by government sanctions, if necessary, it will not be accompanied by the establishment of a huge price-control bureaucracy.

As Alperovitz and Faux indicate, the cry for controls has arisen again. The question is, will they work and if so, at what costs. Alperovitz and Faux do not believe these costs are too high. Rees believes they are.

169

YES

Gar Alperovitz and
Jeff Faux

CONTROLS AND THE
BASIC NECESSITIES

There has been a dramatic shift in the debate over anti-inflation policy in recent months—a shift which preceded President Carter's balanced budget proposals of March 14, [1980] and which is likely to continue. Barry Bosworth, former Director of the Council on Wage and Price Stability, initiated the change in February when he abandoned the gradualist administration tactics he had helped design, and said it was time for wage-price-profit controls. Bruce K. MacLaury, Brookings Institution President (and former Minneapolis Federal Reserve Bank Chief) followed suit. Otto E. Eckstein, former member of the Council of Economic Advisers under President Johnson, testified about the same time that mandatory controls now "deserve a serious look." And as the Consumer Price Index (CPI) hit an annualized rate of 18.2 percent during the last week in February (and the prime rate broke 20.0 percent), House Banking Committee Chairman Henry Reuss, and Henry Kaufman, Chief Economist for Salomon Brothers, all joined, in one way or another, the call for controls. Kaufman, a leading conservative financial oracle, said it was time for the President to declare a "national economic emergency."

Liberal economists John Kenneth Galbraith, Robert Lekachman, and James Tobin, of course, have been urging controls for some time; and the AFL-CIO has been calling for an equitable controls plan since October 1978. But the new shift in opinion marks an erosion of the consensus among economists who had supported the Carter administration's policies of budget-cutting, tight money, and ultimately planned recession. They have been forced to acknowledge that these hold virtually no hope of bringing inflation under control. As Bosworth put it, only a major recession in which the jobless rate would rise to 10 percent or more would have any significant effect on prices. He urged instead that virtually every source of income—wages, prices, profits, and rents—be brought within limits of 5 to 6 percent.

The trend in professional opinion is, in fact, playing catch-up with the public. Despite a steady drum beat of ideological argument against government intervention, the public has long sensed that controls are the only way to halt the extraordinary costs and personal pain of double-digit inflation. The Gallup Poll, taken February 11, found a solid majority in favor of wage-price controls. The administration's latest package may momentarily hold the public's eye, but it is highly doubtful that it will make any significant dent in inflation. The Congressional Budget Office estimates that the budget cuts will at best shave a few tenths of a percent off inflation in 1981— and even Charles L. Schultz acknowledges that the 10-cent-a-gallon gasoline price increase and higher interest costs will *add* to inflation this year.

Confidence in administration strategies is, accordingly, likely to continue to erode, and it is a sure bet that significant numbers of people in the economics profession will slowly get off the fence and move toward endorsing controls in the coming months. As this process unfolds, three fundamental questions need to be faced: (1) Why are wage-price controls necessary now? (2) Will they work? (3) What is the larger meaning for the 1980s of the failure of the Carter administration's gradualist policies?

Why Wage-Price Controls Now?

The most revealing question is the first: Why has what the late Arthur Okun called "muddle-through" conventional economic strategy failed? Here, despite the tremendous outpouring of rhetoric on inflation, most analysts have failed to grapple with the real issues. They have stubbornly persisted in viewing high prices primarily as an issue of generalized inflation. Popular prescriptions have for this reason aimed at cutting the budget, tightening the money supply, and holding down wages across the board to reduce overall inflationary pressures.

The problem is that inflation has not been primarily the result of generalized pressures. It has, in fact, been extremely concentrated in a few key sectors of the economy. Final figures for 1979, for instance, show that virtually the entire increase in the inflation rate last year (as compared to 1978) was caused by the rising prices of the "basic necessities"— food, housing, energy, and medical care. In 1978, the combined rate for these items was 10.8 percent. Last year it skyrocketed to 17.6 percent.

Meanwhile, for everything else measured by the Consumer Price Index— what can loosely be termed the non-necessities—the inflation rate changed only from 6.5 to 6.8 percent. In 1976 when President Carter was elected, "necessities inflation" stood at 3.7 percent. In 1977 it rose to 8.3 percent. The escalation in 1978 to 10.8 percent, and in 1979 to 17.6 percent has been unyielding. Yet, during the same four-year-period, the non-necessities stayed in the 6.5-to-7.0 percent range, except for 1977 when they were 4.7 percent. Thus, freezing all prices and wages could halt the moving picture of general inflation, but it would not deal with the fact that very different factors are causing the problems in the leading sectors.

The unusual concentration of inflation began in 1973-74 when major upward "jolts" in food and energy prices hit the United States. Both were symptomatic of a new era in which world markets for these commodities have become increasingly tight. The quadrupling of

171

crude oil prices by OPEC resulted in a 44 percent increase in U.S. energy prices in 1973-74. At the same time, simultaneous poor harvests in several areas of the world (especially in the Soviet Union) led to heavy demands on U.S. grain supplies. Because the United States—unlike virtually every other major industrialized country—did not have a policy of insulating the domestic food economy from the effects of short-term world shortages, U.S. food prices rose 35 percent in the same 1973-74 period. The two jolts were the sector-specific initiators of much of the more general inflationary price-wage spiral of the rest of the decade. As the Council of Economic Advisers put it: "The dominant influence was the rise in fuel and food prices. It's force was not limited to direct effects. The pass-through of cost increases into other prices broadened the inflation, and the rise in consumer prices led to efforts by wage earners to recover lost real income." In 1975 the worst recession since the thirties somewhat moderated the portion of inflation that was simply attributable to the cycle of wages chasing prices chasing wages, but it has continued to the present day. More important, however, it has been supplemented by additional special factor increases in all four basic necessity sectors.

In the past two years energy and food prices have again been major contributors. Energy rose 37.4 percent in 1979 alone, and food prices rose 23 percent in 1978-79. Over the last six years the annual inflation rate for medical care has averaged 10.0 percent, and has never dropped below 8.8 percent. Though there is a statistical debate over precisely how to measure housing costs, all experts agree they have gone up dramatically,

rising 17.4 percent alone in 1979 by the most commonly used index.

The sum total of the food and energy jolts of 1973-75 and 1978-79, and the more structural inflation in medical care and housing, have resulted in a combined rate of inflation for these items of 101 percent from 1973 through 1979. In that period, energy prices rose 171 percent, food prices 92 percent, housing costs 90 percent, and medical care 87 percent. During the same period these price rises (and the subsequent wage increases they led to) resulted in some increases in other goods and services, but they were much less substantial. In contrast to the 101 percent necessities increase, the combined prices of non-necessities rose only 55 percent from 1973 through 1979.

Much current economic thinking has tended to view inflation in the key sectors as "temporary aberrations." Wage earners are supposed to absorb the special factor increases and then the economy will resume its normal path. This is the meaning of Alfred Kahn's repeated argument that although "the desire to keep pace by catch-up increases is certainly understandable . . . unfortunately it is not possible. . . ." Federal Reserve Board Chairman Paul Volcker has put the case more bluntly: "The standard of living of the average American has to decline."

The difficulty is that the policy of ignoring the special sectoral problems is at a dead end. The necessities account for 60 to 70 percent of the spending of four out of five families; they are 90 percent for the lowest 20 percent of society, and even more for the poor (who must go constantly in debt to pay for groceries and rent). Real spendable earnings declined over 5 percent last year. There may be some modest fat in family budgets, but it is both politically and economically absurd, and morally unconscionable, to expect family budgets to absorb the entire 17.6 percent inflation rate in basic necessities—a rate which in 1979 was virtually double the average 8 to 9 percent wage settlement. This, however, has been precisely the premise of most of the Carter administration's anti-inflationary strategy.

The answer to our first question, then, is straight-forward: wage-price controls are now necessary because everything else has failed. It had to. Not only is it becoming impossible to squeeze family budgets any further, but cutting the federal budget will do nothing about food or fuel prices; and tightening the money supply will increase, not decrease, business costs and monthly mortgage payments. It will also increase the long-term inflationary problems in housing by reducing investment. Moreover, the administration's energy policy, with its price decontrol strategies (and now, with the additional 10-cent-per-gallon import fee on gasoline), has deliberately pursued price-increasing policies. Only through its weak hospital cost containment proposals, and its support for a slight expansion of assistance to health maintenance organizations, did the administration seriously attempt to target a basic necessity sector, but its approach has been half-hearted. Besides, its efforts have been counteracted by its simultaneous support for an inflationary health insurance plan that centers only on catastrophic illness.

Wage-price controls are now being advocated because in the absence of a targeted sectoral program, increases in the basic costs of living are "spilling over" into higher wage demands and then into higher prices. Voluntary wage guidelines no longer suffice and a very deep reces-

sion is the only way to prevent the "spill" from becoming a massive tidal wave of price hikes.

Will Wage-Price Controls Work?

Undoubtedly the answer to this question is that they *can* work to one degree or another. First, they could break or moderate the cycle of price-wage inflation psychology. Many critics cite the difficulties of the recent Nixon experience as evidence that controls must necessarily fail. Experts disagree on precisely how much of the inflation reduction during that period can be attributed to controls, but it is clear that the Nixon administration's inability to deal with the special food and energy problems undermined much of the effort. Most of these same experts agree that in the Truman era, controls were more successful. Conservatives, however, never tire of arguing that once the lid is taken off we will inevitably see a re-explosion of prices. They are right—unless the underlying problems that are fueling inflation in each sector are dealt with. But this is just the point: *before, during, and after controls, we must face up to the fundamental problems, not the superficial ones.*

The difficulties in the basic necessity sectors are not aberrations, but are structural and long-term in nature. Can anyone believe that the trend for energy prices will go anywhere but up during the 1980s, [since] President Carter decided to allow domestic energy prices to rise to OPEC cartel-determined levels? The same holds true for food with current policies. Food expert Lester Brown points out that the growing gap between world food demand and supply "takes us to the bottom line: a promise of future food-price rises that may dwarf those of the

173

recent past." What can we look forward to but spiraling health care costs as the population ages, and as medical science develops new wonder technologies which the present financing system prevents from being subjected to a hard cost-benefit analysis? By driving interest rates high enough we may succeed in making it impossible for young couples to own a home, but how will we prevent the rent increases that will result from forcing poor people out of theirs?

Only if we deal directly with the special sectoral problems do we have a chance of undercutting the price part of the price-wage cycle. In health care, we still need tough hospital cost containment legislation, and limits on physicians' fees. But again, controls alone do not deal with the fundamental dynamics of the system; limits on hospital spending could lead to rationing of care—and medical professionals could increase the quantity of services to compensate for limits on individual fees. We need to change the wasteful incentives of the fee-for-service system, and the financial irrationalities of third-party insurance programs in which virtually any cost is easily passed on to the consumer or the government. This requires an expansion of prepaid health care and health maintenance organizations employing salaried professionals. We also need to devote far more of our national health resources to health education and other public and occupational health measures.

The longer-term issue in housing requires us to expand the supply to bring it into line with growing demand. Current tight money strategies aim only at dampening short-term speculation, and run contrary to the more fundamental problem: we are now in the midst of a massive surge in new household forma-

tions as the post-war baby boom has become a family boom, and as more people (divorcees, young people, and the elderly) have begun to live alone. In the 1980s we will need a phased program of expanded supply which allocates credit and investment to the housing sector, steering it especially toward low- and moderate-income housing investment. We will have to give priority to the rehabilitation of the existing housing stock in urban areas. Additional construction of public housing will be necessary. It is virtually impossible to impose controls on the selling prices of homes and condominiums, and unless we directly undertake a considerable expansion of the basic housing supply, rent controls alone may hasten the loss of available shelter for people with low and moderate incomes.

In energy, there is likely to be considerable controversy. We believe, however, that the United States can no longer afford the tremendous inflationary cost of energy price decontrol. We do not believe that the American people will follow OPEC to any price level the Arab sheiks demand in the 1980s. Will we stop at thirty-five dollars a barrel? Forty-five? Seventy-five? The recent Canadian election showed strong public feelings there against constantly rising energy prices. The U.S. public will also probably draw the line in due time.

This means reimposition of controls to keep domestic prices below the world cartel price. In fact, recontrol is probably inevitable; the real question is whether it will come as part of a coordinated policy, or just be imposed helter-skelter when costs become absolutely intolerable. Once this principle is recognized, it is clear that direct measures to achieve energy conservation are vital. Gasoline rationing is one. We would also benefit from much more aggressive presidential leadership in developing tough automobile mileage standards and more meaningful solar, gasohol, and insulation and weatherization programs. (The [Carter] administration's March package *reduces* funds for solar and conservation efforts.) Getting people out of their cars and into an expanded system of mass transit and passenger railroads would also reduce our need for Mideast oil—and probably provide the United States with far more national security than putting money into railroads for MX missiles. There are opportunities for diversification of supply sources in non-OPEC countries, such as Mexico, and for long-term commitments to develop heavy crude as, for instance, in Venezuela. The elements of a coherent program which both stabilizes basic energy prices, such as home heating oil and drive-to-work gasoline, and achieves *direct* conservation have been offered by numerous experts. They could be part of an overall strategy that does not put anti-inflation and energy policies at loggerheads.

The obstacles to solving our underlying food inflation problems are more political than economic. We do not have the shortages here that we do in energy. Relative to its domestic needs the United States is the richest agricultural nation in the history of the world; we export more than half our grains. As noted previously, a fundamental problem stems from our failure to insulate domestic markets from short-term world shortages. During the last period of wage-price controls we foolishly placed price controls on beef, while at the same time we allowed feed prices to explode—an extremely short-sighted policy which, by exacerbating the cattle cycle, contributed ultimately to much of the beef-led food inflation even in 1978-79. A system of export management could stabilize domestic grain prices and thereby also reduce fluctuations in meat supplies. International agreements on grain reserves must also be pursued. For the decade of the 1980s as a whole, it would not be difficult to sketch the outlines of a modern version of the Brannon plan which would put ceilings on farm prices and floors under them. Then we could use expanded deficiency payments to maintain adequate farm income levels. The main question is one of leadership to shape a new political consensus on food policies: a focus by the President on the economic and moral priority of the "necessities of life" could set a context in which many specific political difficulties could be overcome. Over the longer run, some basic restructuring to eliminate the wastes of excessive concentration in the processing and marketing sectors will be needed, but for now, strictly enforced wage-price-profit controls would eliminate much of the inflation originating there.

Focus on the Sectors

To return to the second question: Will wage-price controls work? Only if appropriate measures to deal with the special sectoral problems are developed during the period they are in place. In fact, unless we focus on the sectors, we will squeeze family income even further while wage-price controls are in effect. This has already happened under the voluntary program, but it will worsen if key items in the family budget—fuel oil and food, for example—are allowed to skyrocket while wages are held down with the force of law. We could see a replay of the Nixon administration's controls pro-

175

gram, described by the man in charge, Arnold Weber, as a mechanism to "zap labor." A program of wage-price controls which did not deal with underlying pressures in the key sectors—far worse now than in 1971-73, and growing—would do more than "zap labor." It would put family income up against the wall and systematically crush the average household budget.

Some commentators have identified wage-price controls as the strategy of the "liberals." But as the Nixon experience should make clear, controls are inherently neither liberal nor conservative. Nixon's Treasury Secretary, John Connally, backed them; and many conservatives now urge controls as part of a comprehensive package of budget-cutting, tax reductions for business, and wage roll-backs. What might be termed a "necessities-conscious" controls package could either be shaped neutrally or progressively as to ultimate impact on the distribution of income—depending upon the degree of stabilization of key prices relative to wages.

Beyond the fundamental equity issue lies a practical one. If a Nixon-style scenario were to be played out, wages— and then prices—would explode again after controls were lifted, as families attempted to catch up with the real income they lost while the controls were in effect. Then we would almost certainly see a replay of the last six years: a worsening inflationary spiral, then an attempt to engineer a recession, and probably reimposition of controls because everything else had failed.

To be sure, there will inevitably be inefficiencies with wage-price controls. But they are miniscule, we believe, when measured against the extraordinary costs of the above scenario. Arthur Okun

estimated that $200 billion of real GNP is lost for each percentage point decrease in the underlying inflation rate achieved by deliberate slow-growth policies. It is only in comparison with the hundreds of billions of dollars in lost output which the failing muddle-through strategy entails in practice that the far smaller inefficiencies of controls can rationally be assessed.

The Larger Implications

Which brings us to our final question: What are the larger implications of the collapse of the Carter administration's economic policies? The experience of the 1970s teaches us that some form of planning will obviously be needed if inflation is ever to be controlled—especially vis-a-vis the basic necessity sectors. We can continue to ignore the changes in family formation rates that affect the housing industry—or we can get ahead of the problem by ensuring adequate new housing investment. We can continue to allow a hundred billion dollars a year of our national wealth to be shunted to the OPEC nations (as Felix Rohatyn points out, this amount is the monetary equivalent, in five years, of more than half the stocks listed on the New York Stock Exchange). Or we can recognize that a serious conservation and rationing program is well within our capacity. Here, and in food and health care as well, the underlying fundamentals all point towards the need for a more coherent integration of our economic policies.

Planning, however, has been a dirty word in the language of American economics. Instead we prefer doing nothing, allowing problems to build up, and then groping towards a crisis solution like *unplanned* wage-price controls. Government intervention is the likely result of the process in either event, and once this is understood, the central issue facing the economy in the coming decade comes sharply into focus. The economic performance and rates of productivity growth in Germany, Japan, and a number of our other industrial competitors have been outpacing us for some time. In the period from 1967 to 1978, for instance, output per man hour in manufacturing increased 28 percent in the United States, but 75 percent in Germany and 113 percent in Japan. U.S. manufacturing productivity growth was the lowest of eleven industrial nations—trailing even Great Britain. Our productivity rates turned negative during 1979. If the next decade repeats this performance, the effects of compounding guarantee that the very heart of our industrial economy will be threatened as we stagger in productivity, while our major competitors race forward.

Much of our failure has been due to the obvious fact that we live in a stop-go economy. No intelligent executive plan for long-term investment in high productivity equipment unless confidence exists that a growing market can be counted on. And yet, the nature of the new jolts the economy recurrently faces—and the uncertainties caused by our policy responses—force most financial advisors into a prudent, retrenchment stance. Moreover, in a continually uncertain economy, we build in supply bottlenecks which *must* prevent future expansion. To the extent investment is limited by expectation of weak performance, future inflation is guaranteed when an upward swing is throttled by limited capacity—itself the inevitable result of stop-go expectations.

Our only real alternative for the 1980s is to break this pattern and to resume an upward growth plan. The Japanese, three times as dependent as we are on imported energy, achieved a 5.6 percent real economic growth rate last year, and an 8.3 percent increase in productivity. Rather than slowing the economy in a futile attempt to control an energy-induced inflation, we should be planning a carefully phased expansion of output to pay for our higher import bills (and of course, we should reduce our need for foreign oil as quickly as possible).

It is precisely at this point that popular remedies for inflation are most at odds with the realities of the 1980s. Tightening the monetary screws another notch—when many businesses are paying 20-percent interest rates for working capital—is fast becoming a prescription for economic suicide, especially for the innovative small business sector. Broad-brush calls for "fiscal restraint" are more likely to weaken a strategy of careful expansion than they are to help control inflation. Despite its political appeal, in fact, "budget-cutting" contributes very little to the solution of our new inflation problems. Viewed in the larger perspective of the sector-specific problems of the 1980s, generalized calls for tax reduction can create large budget deficits while contributing little to a strategy of planned growth.

There is much discussion these days of "supply-side economics" as the conservative answer to our economic woes. Usually this means across-the-board tax breaks to business in hopes of increasing productivity. But most executives make large investment decisions because of confidence in a future market, not because of tax breaks. The Congressional General Accounting Office, assessing the impact of investment tax credits granted in 1978, found they made very little difference in actual investment decisions—at a huge budgetary cost of $19 billion! A "supply-side economics" *is* necessary, but one that is carefully targeted to the problem sectors—and integrated into an overall plan which can offer confidence in resumed growth. To achieve this we will have to make long-term commitments to invest in ways which simultaneously deal with such big inflation issues as housing construction, conservation, renewable energy development, and transit and railroad revitalization.

Under the umbrella of wage-price controls, the job creation involved in a coherent, targeted program of this kind could become the basis of a committed economic strategy for the 1980s which also deals with the economic needs of American communities. But this can only happen if we face up to the fact that we simply have no choice but to break decisively with the stop-start pattern of the 1970s. To resume productivity growth in the uncertain world of the 1980s also requires a strategy which is equitable to all the key players. No consensus on broad economic issues can be achieved without a workable incomes policy. Organized labor has demonstrated considerable moderation in its wage demands in light of the rate of non-wage-based inflation. Various proposals for tax relief as part of an anti-inflation wage package could help solve some problems of transition caused by the failures of the 1970s. But a long-term consensus involving wage moderation will hold only if the special problems of the sectors most important to the average family budget are resolved. The AFL-CIO, in fact, has consistently declared its willingness to compromise on key points if food, housing, energy, and health care issues are dealt with.

This brings us full circle to the crucial role of the basic necessities. The emerging dialogue over the nature of wage-price controls is far more significant than many realize. What actually happens while controls are in place will determine much of our economic strategy for the 1980s. If the traditional nostrums of budget cutting, tight money, and tax write-offs are the basic ingredients of a comprehensive controls package, we will have learned very little from our mistakes. If, on the other hand, we confront the specific issues facing us, sector by sector, we have a chance both of controlling inflation and resuming an upward growth path. Viewed in this light, the real question we are beginning to debate is whether the United States must continue to be on the defensive economically—or whether we are willing to set a positive course for our economic future.

● ● ●

NO

Albert Rees

CONTROLS

Whenever inflation becomes severe, some political leaders advocate the imposition of wage and price controls. This view commands wide support from the public because of its simplicity. If prices are rising too fast, why not just pass a law to hold them down?

A few professional economists share this view, but they are in a distinct minority. The majority of economists feel that controls cannot halt inflation for long, and that they will themselves create other serious economic problems. Why do economists differ so sharply on this important issue? What are the leading arguments on each side?

The leading advocate of wage and price controls among professional economists is John Kenneth Galbraith, Professor Emeritus of Economics at Harvard University and former United States Ambassador to India. Galbraith held an important position in the Office of Price Administration during World War II. Shortly thereafter he wrote two important articles defending controls in leading professional journals.

In one of these he wrote the following:

> The simple fact is that price control has worked. If it hasn't worked well, it has at least worked to the extent of preventing a wholesale deterioration of values. And prices have been fixed in the context of a large and continuing excess of aggregate demand over supply.

More recently, Galbraith has expressed the view that controls would work as well in peacetime as they did in wartime provided that they were administered by people who believed in them. In his judgment this was not true of the controls that were in effect in the period 1971-74.

By saying that controls work, Galbraith means that they can slow down the rate of inflation as measured by such broad price indexes as the Consumer Price Index or the gross national product deflator. However, such indexes are less meaningful in the presence of controls. The indexes measure the posted ceiling prices, but not all transactions take place at these prices. Some take place on illegal or black markets, where prices are not reported to the government and do not get recorded in the price indexes. The indexes therefore understate the rate of inflation and overstate how well controls work by some amount that is very hard to estimate.

One of the basic functions of prices is to ration scarce commodities. If the supply of a particular item decreases, its price will rise. Suppose, for example, that the supply of raisins is reduced by a crop failure. Prices will shoot up, and only those consumers who have the strongest preference for raisins will continue to buy the same amount at the higher prices. Others will cut back their purchases so that the new price will clear the market— the amount demanded will be equal to the smaller amount available.

Under controls, prices cannot perform this rationing function and other devices are needed. If the government does not institute coupon rationing, sellers will do the rationing themselves. As a leading economics textbook puts it:

> Goods may be kept under the counter and sold only to regular customers, for example. In wartime Britain, a person who moved from one town to another lost his important status as a "regular" in many stores. Unless one was a regular, it was very difficult indeed to obtain cigarettes and beer, both of which, though unrationed, were subject to price control.[1]

Because rationing of consumer goods by sellers is often unfair, the United States government introduced coupon rationing during World War II for many scarce items, including meat, shoes, and gasoline. To buy meat required not only money but red stamps. Galbraith has written:

> Price control under conditions of excess demand in markets that approximate pure competition *must* be supplemented by rationing. . . . Meat rationing in particular showed the indispensability of rationing for price control.[2]

The question of how the government can ration fairly is not a trivial one. If gasoline is to be rationed, should each licensed driver of a car get so many gallons per month, or should there be so much for each car? Should there be further distinctions based on place of residence (rural versus urban) or occupation? No answers to these questions are fully satisfactory. However, advocates of controls point out that rationing by price is also inherently unfair because the rich can afford to buy more of scarce commodities than the poor. Of course, this state of affairs prevails even in periods of peacetime and stable prices. There is always some inequality of income and consumption in all modern societies, though inflation can make the inequalities worse. In contrast, the inequities of rationing seem artificial rather than normal and may therefore be unacceptable.

As Galbraith points out, government rationing of supplies is not needed in the case of industrial commodities, such as steel and aluminum, that are produced by a few large firms. The producers will allocate the available supplies to their usual customers in proportion to past purchases. This may be entirely satisfactory for short periods, but has the undesirable effect in the longer run of keeping new firms from entering the fabricating industries because the entrants cannot get access to scarce supplies of materials.

---

[1] Richard G. Lipsey and Peter O. Steiner, *Economics,* fourth edition (New York: Harper and Row, 1975) p. 107.

[2] "The Disequilibrium System," op.cit., pp. 300-301. Emphasis in the original.

The power of producers to allocate supplies can also be used to impose disguised price increases. For example, in 1973 when there were shortages of primary aluminum at the controlled price, some fabricators of aluminum felt obliged to sell their aluminum scrap to their primary metal suppliers at less than its market price in order to be assured of continued supplies of primary metal.

We have been discussing the effect of controls on the rationing function of prices. In the long run, this is not the most important function that prices perform in a free market economy. They also have the task of guiding the expansion and contraction of production. In wartime this task may be taken over in large part by priorities set by the government. In peacetime, prices give signals to producers to make more of the things that people want most, because these are the most profitable goods to produce. A producer who turns out articles that are no longer in demand will be unable to charge prices that cover his costs.

A dramatic example of this function of prices was recently seen in the market for automobiles. The rising price of gasoline has caused a shift in demand from large to small cars. Small cars, sold at their full sticker price, are profitable to manufacture, while large cars sell at a substantial discount and are unprofitable. Producers thus have a strong incentive to convert to small cars as quickly as possible. Government controls on average miles per gallon of a manufacturer's car production are working in the same direction, but more slowly.

Prices in a free market also tend to reflect costs of production. If the costs of making a particular product rise more than costs in general, producers of that product will raise their prices more,

inducing some of their customers to substitute other products.

Price controls can interfere with some of these long-run functions of market prices. For example, during the price control program of 1971-74 the price of broiling chickens was originally controlled, but the price of grain for feed, a raw agricultural commodity, was not. When grain prices rose, broiler production became unprofitable at controlled prices, and many broiler producers could no longer stay in business. The resulting shortages of broilers were eliminated by declaring broilers also to be a raw agricultural commodity, exempt from price controls. Their prices rose more than 50 percent, production increased, and prices soon fell again.

A similar shortage caused by controls took place in the summer of 1973 when meat prices were first controlled and later decontrolled. The decontrol was announced some weeks before its effective date. During this period cattle were held on feedlots putting on unwanted fat, while meat counters were empty and consumers ate poultry, fish, or spaghetti.

Advocates of controls would argue that able and experienced administrators of a price control program could avoid such costly errors. Because the 1971-74 controls were temporary, the staff did not reach the size or perhaps the levels of competence that could be expected of a more permanent program. But any staff whose primary mission is to hold down prices is likely to err in the direction of understating the need for price increases and of permitting them only after the delays required by bureaucratic processes.

Wages play the same role in allocating labor to employers that prices play in allocating goods. However, there has

181

been relatively little discussion among economists of the effects of wage controls on the allocation of labor. There is some evidence that during World War II wage controls contributed to severe labor shortages in some jobs with poor working conditions—for example, refuse collection and hot, heavy work in steel mills and foundries. I know of no such evidence for peacetime wage controls. In part this is because low-wage workers have been exempted from peacetime wage controls, and wide labor shortages have their earliest and greatest effect on low-wage jobs. Employers and union negotiators have also been generally free under peacetime controls to increase wages for scarce skills when the skilled workers in question are only a small part of an employee unit.

The more common complaint against wage controls by union leaders and labor economists is that they can create inequities among workers. For example, different rules applied to collective bargaining agreements negotiated before and after November 14, 1971 (the beginning of Phase II of the Nixon controls). A local union bargaining with two employers who had always paid the same wage rates might suddenly find a wage differential created by the fact that its agreement with one employer was signed November 10 and that the other was signed on November 20. The union members who had received the lower wage would have felt aggrieved and blamed their leaders. Many such problems were solved by government administrative action, but only after long delay.

Some economists have also been concerned about the administrative costs of wage and price controls. The direct costs to the government are perhaps the

least of these. There are substantial costs to businesses and unions—the time of executives, the cost of record-keeping, and extra fees to lawyers and accountants.

The economists who advocate controls are well aware that controls have costs. They point out, however, that alternative measures to control inflation also have costs.

Economists opposed to controls generally advocate checking inflation by the use of monetary and fiscal policy to reduce aggregate demand. Their argument goes something like this: If the Federal Reserve System persistently restricts the quantity of money, and if the Federal government balances its budget or runs a surplus, the growth of aggregate spending will be restricted. If demand grows less rapidly than the potential supply of goods and services, sellers will develop excess capacity, buyers will reduce their purchases when prices rise, and further price increases will be discouraged. As the public comes to expect a lower rate of inflation, interest rates will fall, money wages will begin to rise less rapidly, and the process of deceleration of inflation will become cumulative.

This scenario has a large and very obvious price—it will require fairly high rates of unemployment (perhaps 7 percent or more) for a considerable period of time. The advocates of controls or policies that resemble controls, such as wage-price guidelines, argue that this is simply too high a price to pay. They also emphasize that the price of increased unemployment is paid most heavily by unskilled and minority workers.

Are the costs of persistent monetary-fiscal restraint higher than the costs of controls? As yet, no one can be sure. In the first place, the costs of controls are hidden and extremely hard to measure. We have only fragmentary evidence, often anecdotal, of their extent. Advocates of controls tend to estimate them as far smaller than opponents do.

More important, the policy of persistent restraint of aggregate demand has not been tried in the postwar U.S. economy. Full employment has been the overriding objective of national economic policy. Whenever unemployment has exceeded 6 percent, monetary or fiscal stimulus has been applied promptly to bring it down again. The postwar recessions have not had much effect in restraining price increases, perhaps because they have been so brief.

From this experience different economists draw opposite conclusions. Advocates of controls conclude that big business and big labor have so much market power that restraining aggregate demand to produce slack in the economy no longer has any effect in restraining wage and price increases, and therefore controls are needed. Opponents of controls argue that restraining demand has never been given a fair trial because restraint has always been relaxed at the first sign of a recession. Restraint must be maintained long enough to bring down the rate of inflation appreciably, they argue. Once inflationary expectations have disappeared, the rate of unemployment need be no higher than it was while prices were rising rapidly.

In my opinion, the experience with wage and price controls in 1971-74 was disappointing and argues strongly against trying them in peacetime again. I cannot accept the view that controls failed because they were administered by people who did not believe in them. It is true that some economists who were high officials in the Nixon Administration, including Treasury Secretary George P. Shultz and Herbert Stein, Chairman of the Council of Economic Advisers, were always skeptics. But others, including John T. Dunlop, Chairman of the Cost of Living Council, did believe in controls and tried hard and ably to make them work. Prices rose for reasons that were almost entirely beyond their control, such as the crop failures that caused farm prices to leap upward in 1973 and a tight labor market that brought unemployment below 5 percent.

In 1970, the year before controls were imposed, the Consumer Price Index rose 5.5 percent. By 1973, the last full year of controls, it rose 8.8 percent, and it rose 12.2 percent in 1974, the year in which controls were lifted.

It is impossible to know for certain whether prices would have risen still more in the absence of controls, but it seems unlikely. No doubt much of the 1974 rise would have taken place sooner, but the rise over the whole period would probably have been about the same.

The most careful statistical study of the Nixon controls supports this conclusion. It finds that by February 1974 the controls had lowered the price level by about 1.4 percent, but that the "catch up" after April 1974, according to the estimates, carried the price level slightly above what it would have been in the absence of controls. This suggests that if controls are to have a lasting effect, they must be permanent.

Rather than reimposing controls now, it seems more promising to me to try prolonged monetary and fiscal restraint, as the Board of Governors of the Federal Reserve System and the Carter Administration have committed themselves to do. During the period of restraint the victims of unemployment will require help.

CAN CONTROLS HELP SOLVE OUR INFLATION PROBLEM?

However, the mechanisms for helping them, such as unemployment insurance and food stamps, are already in place. New expenditure programs or temporary tax cuts are not needed, and to resort to them would be an unfortunate signal that the determination to end inflation had eroded.

● ● ●

POSTSCRIPT

CAN WAGE AND PRICE CONTROLS HELP SOLVE OUR INFLATION PROBLEMS?

Even though Alperovitz/Faux and Rees are on opposite sides of this issue, there are several points on which they agree. Both sides feel strongly that something must be done in order to reduce the rate of inflation; that past experiments with wage and price controls haven't been successful; and that recent monetary and fiscal policies designed to alleviate price pressures and reduce the money supply have not had the desired impact. But on the central issue of the usefulness of wage and price controls there is strong disagreement.

In their arguments in support of controls, Alperovitz and Faux proceed through a series of related points. First, is the notion that the current inflation is not truly general, but concentrated in the basic necessities sectors of the economy. Second, they do not propose permanent controls. Rather wage and price controls would be imposed while government takes action to cure the structural problems that are causing the rapid inflation in the basic necessities sectors. Third, they argue that the reason the Nixon controls program did not work was because the structural problems which then existed were not attacked.

Rees can see why wage and price controls might appear as appealing; however, he is strong in his opposition. He offers a series of examples to illustrate the inefficiences and difficulties which arise during periods in which controls actually existed. He also raises a basic question which must be answered under any control regime: how can government deal fairly with the shortages that must surely arise? Rees would rather use monetary and fiscal policies as the anti-inflation mechanisms. These policies will work if extended over a long enough period. This may mean rising unemployment but the program of unemployment compensation already exists and, according to Rees, is an effective antidote to this undesirable side effect.

A number of discussions of the Nixon controls exist. IN PURSUIT OF PRICE STABILITY (Brookings, 1973) by Arnold R. Weber offers an insider's view of the program. Also see "The Life Cycle of Wage and Price Controls" in ECONOMIC POLICY BEYOND THE HEADLINES (Norton, 1977) by George P. Schultz and Kenneth W. Dam. An excellent review of incomes policies over the 1947-1971 period is offered in EXHORTATION AND CONTROLS (Brookings, 1975) edited by Craufield D. Goodwin. For a description of recent efforts to control inflation including the use of guidelines see: 1980 ECONOMIC REPORT OF THE PRESIDENT pp. 75-90 (Government Printing Office, 1980).

ISSUE 10

SHOULD THE GOVERNMENT BE RESPONSIBLE FOR ACHIEVING AND MAINTAINING FULL EMPLOYMENT?

YES: Lane Kirkland, from "Full Employment: An America That Works," *American Federationist* (June, 1980).

NO: G.C. Wiegand, from "Thirty Years of 'Full Employment' Policies and Growing Unemployment," *Vital Speeches* (June 1, 1977).

ISSUE SUMMARY

YES: AFL-CIO President Kirkland holds that full employment yields benefits to individual workers and to the larger society. Government, because of its size, because of the structure of the economy, and because of democratic responsibility, must commit itself to the achievement of full employment.

NO: Former economics professor Wiegand believes that full employment cannot be achieved by government action and certain policies may have actually helped to increase unemployment by raising the costs of employment, thus making unemployment more attractive.

During the 1930s the American economy collapsed. Unemployment rates soared to twenty-five percent as productive activity fell by thirty percent. Although economists still debate the causes of the great depression, it did mark a turning point in the views of many regarding the appropriate role of government in the economy. With the reality of the great depression and a theoretical framework provided by Lord John Maynard Keynes, the view that government should actively intervene in the economy in order to promote employment, came to be commonly accepted.

This position is initially expressed in legislation in the Employment Act of 1946. In its declaration of policy, the act states:

> The Congress hereby declares that it is the continuing policy and responsibility of Federal Government to use all practical means consistent with its needs and obligations and other essential considerations of national policy; . . . to coordinate and utilize all its plans, functions, and resources for the purpose of creating and maintaining, in a manner calculated to foster and promote free competitive enterprise and the general welfare conditions under which there will be afforded useful employment opportunities, including self-employment, for those able, willing, and seeking to work, and to promote maximum employment. . .

There are no specific numerical objectives mentioned in this legislation nor are there any details concerning what actions should be taken.

This general policy stance was reaffirmed by the Full Employment and Balanced Growth Act of 1978, the so called Humphrey-Hawkins Act. In general, this more recent legislation maintains the same language in its declaration of policy, but explicitly uses the term "full employment" rather than "maximum employment." It goes on to define what is meant by full employment, an unemployment rate of three percent for individuals aged twenty and over and an unemployment rate of four percent for individuals sixteen and older. The 1978 legislation also lays out procedures to be followed in deciding what actions are to be taken but does not specify exactly what actions should be taken.

Reading the 1946 and 1978 acts, one might conclude that the issue has been settled and settled in the affirmative. However, this is not the case. Because both pieces of legislation do not detail what actions should be taken by government to achieve the full employment objective, debate always occurs over means. For example, liberals like Kirkland might argue for increased government spending while the conservative approach represented by Wiegand would support decreases in taxes. The disagreement may become even more fundamental with conservatives arguing against a liberal supported recommendation on the basis of the language in both the 1946 and 1978 acts. That is, conservatives may argue against an action because it is perceived as not "fostering or promoting free competitive enterprise."

As might be expected the fight over both pieces of legislation represented a clash between liberal and conservative views. As an example of the conflict, the words "full employment" were deleted from the original version of the 1946 act and the words "maximum employment" substituted as a compromise. In 1978, the stance of conservatives against the initial version of Full Employment and Balanced Growth Act led to major changes in the final version. So even though legislation exists which seems to endorse the "yes" side of this issue, the clash remains and with the so-called swing to the right in political opinion the debate will be joined again, perhaps with even more intensity.

YES   Lane Kirkland

FULL EMPLOYMENT: AN AMERICA
THAT WORKS

In expressing its views to the platform committees of both political parties,
the AFL-CIO wishes to stress the importance of platforms. A platform should
forthrightly state what a party stands for, not simply what it opposes. It should
advance in clear, precise language the programs the party and its candidates
will seek if elected.

Platforms should emphasize themes that unify, rather than divide. They
should raise reasonable expectations for performance, not just promise.
Rather than weaving rhetoric through a collection of single issues promoted
by narrow interests, platforms should present what each party believes is best
for all Americans and, thus, provide the electorate an opportunity to make an
informed choice based on issues rather than personalities. Public participation in elections is enhanced by responsible discussion of the issues that
confront the nation. That requires positive statements, not political polemics.

Growing nonparticipation in the electoral process is directly related to
greater emphasis on the politics of image and the failure of political parties to
address the issues directly. Too many citizens ask: "What does it matter?" A
platform can tell a voter what matters.

That is why we have prepared identical statements for presentation to both
parties. We have not sought to tailor our program to any preconceived notion
of what a particular party's platform may be or to fit it to any potential
candidate or ideology. The American labor movement rejects both
ideologues and demagogues.

Our program—"An America That Works for Everyone"—is the product of a
representative democratic process that reaches into every state and virtually
every community in the nation. It is the sum of concerns about their nation and
the world raised by working people through their unions. It is a hopeful,
optimistic document, because American workers want to believe in their

From, "Full Employment: An America that Works", *AFL-CIO American Federationist*, the official magazine of
the AFL-CIO, June, 1980. Reprinted by permission.

country, its institutions and its people. They ask both parties to construct platforms for building an America that works for everyone.

The United States is a beacon of freedom and opportunity for the world. Endowed with tremendous natural resources, an enduring political system and blessed with a population blended with all races and nationalities, America has always looked to the future with a goal of improving on the present. Indeed, the American dream remains what it has been for more than two centuries—to make life better for one's children and their children's children.

This commitment to the future requires a growing, healthy, expanding economy. For individuals and society, jobs are the key to the future. Meeting the common needs of life—food, shelter, clothing and medical care—is dependent upon the income produced by employment. Fulfilling the opportunities afforded every individual—to live in decent neighborhoods, to educate their children, to enjoy leisure time, and to enrich themselves through the arts—also requires a paycheck. Individuals who seek to advance to the limits of their own skills and initiative find the room to grow in a full employment economy, which is continually creating new jobs, the need for greater skills and the chance for promotion.

Work in America should be a rewarding experience—in terms of the wages that provide the wherewithal to enjoy life in this country, and, equally important, in terms of individual fulfillment. Work expands individual horizons, provides a sense of accomplishment and an expression of human worth. There is satisfaction in producing goods and services, and a

confidence in the future that results from productive work.

Society, too, has an important stake in full employment. From wages come the tax revenues that operate government, providing services that people need and creating new opportunities. The dynamic American economy rests on consumer purchasing power and the principle that workers are able to enjoy the goods and services they produce.

In other words, America works best when all Americans are working. Therefore, the AFL-CIO seeks an unequivocal commitment from both parties to full employment—a job opportunity for each person able and seeking work. Full employment is the cornerstone of our domestic program. And full employment is essential to building a strong America capable of meeting its commitments around the world.

Full Employment

Full employment is the only economic policy that would simultaneously fight inflation and the inequities that inflation causes. It would attack inflation through increased production of goods and services and more effective use of productive capacity that now lies idle. It would provide a better balance between tax revenues and expenditures by turning the unemployed into taxpayers instead of tax users.

Unlike other economic policies which fight inflation by increasing the inequities faced by those at the lower end of the economic spectrum, full employment is not a gimmick. Full employment is not the symbolic and unworkable solution proposed by the budget balancers. It is a workable economic policy which is based on more than statistical legerdemain.

189

Economic theories that ignore the integral role of the federal government in the economy in order to fit neatly into the dogma of a particular political ideology are doomed to failure. Government is more than an institution of governance; it is also a consumer and an employer. The government buys the goods and services it needs from private businesses, and the people who are employed by the government are also consumers. Reductions in government spending to reach some artificial numerical limit have a recessionary impact. Government assistance—particularly for the unemployed, retirees, and the poverty stricken—also has the beneficial effect of sustaining consumer purchasing power which is so vital to the economy.

Just as government should not be spendthrift, neither should the blind pursuit of a contrived balance between revenues and expenditures in all times be the preoccupation of economic policy. Of far greater benefit to the economy and society would be a balanced budget achieved through full employment. Such a balanced budget is both legitimate and desirable. It would be a budget based on the people's needs and the revenues generated by a healthy economy.

Spending reductions that increase unemployment actually widen the deficit. Each 1 million workers who become unemployed cost the federal government $25 billion in added social costs and lost tax revenue.

There are no acceptable tradeoffs between inflation and unemployment or between defense and those programs that make this society worth defending. Those who have borne the heaviest burden of inflation—the unemployed, the poor, the elderly, the handicapped and the minorities—must not be asked to sacrifice again through severe cuts in programs designed to ease their burden. The fight against inflation demands equality of sacrifice, not the sacrifice of equality. Further widening of the gap between the "haves" and "have nots"will only compound the ills of the economy and society.

Those who espouse a balanced budget regardless of economic circumstances are mixing anti-government political rhetoric with an economic theory that fails to recognize the current inflation does not fit the classic definition of too many dollars chasing too few goods.

Government is not the enemy of the people or the economic system. Government is the people; it is their agent, so designed by a democratic process. It must meet the obligations conferred on it by the people in the Preamble to the Constitution: "(to) establish justice, insure domestic tranquility, provide for the common defense, promote the general welfare, and secure the blessings of liberty to ourselves and our posterity."

The annual budget is the repository of all government actions to fulfill these obligations—obligations that are not conditioned by the phrase "but only if the budget is in balance." Nor is the government directed to "provide for the common defense" at the expense of programs to "promote the general welfare." It must meet both needs.

The danger of the balanced budget mania is not confined to the anti-government demagoguery surrounding it; it is also bad economics. The current budget deficit did not cause inflation, and eliminating the deficit overnight will not cure inflation. Even its strongest adherents admit that balancing the budget is a psychological or symbolic gesture. The nation does not need the psychology of unemployment or the symbols of un-employment lines.

The specific causes of inflation—energy, interest rates, housing, food and medical care—will continue unrestrained and unimpressed by the "symbol" of a balanced budget. Rather than a psychological ploy, America needs firm policies that will deal with those sectors of the economy that are contributing the most to inflation. Reducing interest rates, eliminating dependence on imported petroleum, controlling commodity speculators, containing hospital costs and increasing the housing supply would have a much greater effect on reducing inflation.

Much more will be needed to restore economic health, full employment and balanced growth. The nation must begin a comprehensive program designed to reindustrialize America. The nation cannot afford to be a service-based economy dependent upon other countries for both finished goods and vital raw materials. Too much of American technology is exported abroad; too many plants are obsolete; too many urban areas are becoming waste lands. The nation's transportation system is either inadequate or in disrepair. Reindustrialization will require a massive, coordinated national effort directed at areas of greatest need. Such an effort will require federal leadership and the participation of labor and management.

In a world that practices fair trade, a revitalized American industry can compete. International trade tactics—such as dumping, state-controlled export mechanisms, unfair barriers to U.S. products and government subsidies—only serve to stifle America's economic growth.

The nation needs a fair and equitable program committed to achieving full employment, and we look to the political parties to present such a positive program.

The AFL-CIO believes the American dream has currency; workers have the right to continue to seek a better life. In a democratic society, it is wrong for one group to impose lower expectations on another group, to demand a degree of sacrifice not demanded of all, to permit exploitation of some for the profit of others. The nation agreed with this principle when it enacted laws prohibiting child labor, establishing a fair minimum wage, promoting safety and health in the workplace, protecting prevailing pay standards and, most importantly, permitting workers to freely join unions and bargain collectively with their employers.

This body of law sets the ground rules for employer conduct. It is the sine qua non which sets the American free enterprise system apart from that practiced in other nations. Human life and dignity are not commodities that can be sold, traded or bartered.

Resolving the inevitable conflicts between employer zeal for profits and the determination of workers for fair compensation is never easy in a democratic society. The quick solution, of course, is government compulsion, but democracy is not designed to be convenient; it is supposed to give the participants the opportunity to live their own lives.

In recent years as inflation accelerated, those who have always opposed safeguards for workers and their rights have stepped up their attack on these protections. They hope that a public concerned about inflation will accept any proposals to reduce employer costs and ignore the consequences of life and liberty. They couldn't be more wrong.

191

This society places too great a value on human life to jeopardize the health and safey of workers in order to increase corporate profits in the dubious hope that corporate largesse will reduce prices.

The American people also know that if businesses are permitted to continue to flout the labor laws with impunity, such disrespect for the law soon undermines "domestic tranquility." Present labor law simply does not work effectively. Rather than serving as an instrument to provide industrial democracy, it has become a tool to frustrate workers' rights.

Laws that protect workers protect all of society. Unemployment insurance benefits not only the workers who lose their jobs, it also cushions the economy from a total loss of purchasing power. Workers' compensation insures society against having to assume the burden of the care of injured workers and their families. Trade adjustment assistance for workers injured by foreign trade also helps their communities adjust to the loss of jobs and maintain a skilled workforce.

The AFL-CIO asks both parties to commit themselves and their standard bearers to protecting and improving these programs and laws that are vital to workers and to everyone.

Inflation

Inflation and recession have halted progress to achieving equal rights and equal opportunity. Thus, it is no longer sufficient for the political parties to blandly pledge support for laws prohibiting discrimination against minorities and women. There must be aggressive, positive efforts to eliminate the discrimination and segregation through rates of pay and job classification.

Discrimination based on economic class is no more desirable than discrimination based on race or ethnic origin. Economic discrimination—because it traps greater percentages of black and Hispanic Americans in poverty—has racial overtones resulting from past failures of our society. To ignore that fact is to subscribe to discrimination, but under a supposedly more enlightened and color-blind premise.

Equal employment opportunity must not mean an equal chance to stand in the unemployment line. High mortgage interest rates must not subvert the purpose of fair housing laws. Statutory and legal rights to equality must not become empty promises, because the right to eat in a restaurant is valueless if the person cannot afford to pay the check.

Ratification of the Equal Rights Amendment must have the high priority and unswerving support of both political parties. Equality should be a constitutional right, and not the sum of piecemeal legislative efforts.

In the final analysis, however, the depth of commitment to civil rights in the platforms of the political parties must be measured by their proposals for the economy and, in particular, the federal budget, because the budget defines what the role of government will be in enhancing social justice and providing equal opportunities.

Much work remains to be done to improve the operation, administration and funding of the social programs that are important to the daily lives of millions of Americans and to the achievement of economic and social justice for every American. These programs are the bulwark of a society with a social conscience.

The status quo—the simple continuation of these programs—is not good enough. Social Security has been good for America and for its senior citizens, but it can be improved and strengthened. Free public education has made America great, but there must be more of it, accessible to more people. Medicare and Medicaid have helped millions of Americans, but now is the time to extend that help to everyone through comprehensive national health insurance.

Effective government—responsible to and representative of the people—is essential in a complex, democratic society. Government provides order, ministers to the common needs, protects the weak from exploitation by the powerful and nurtures individual rights and liberty.

The administration of government can be improved, but it will not be improved if those who work for government are treated as second class citizens or made scapegoats. Public participation in the electoral process can be enhanced, but that will not happen so long as millions of Americans are discouraged from participation by restrictive registration practices. Democracy can be strengthened, but not by continuation of such undemocratic procedures as the filibuster or the perpetuation of a system of campaign financing that makes dollars more important than votes.

Government cannot function properly if it is denied adequate funding as a result of statutory or constitutional measures that arbitrarily and mechanistically limit the budgeting process. The representatives elected by and accountable to the people must have the flexibility necessary to adopt budgets that meet the needs of the people as well as changing world conditions.

Poverty, exploitation and a lack of freedom burden the people of much of the world, and the United States must actively seek solutions to these problems.

The foreign policy of the United States must be based on the promotion of human rights and democratic values and institutions, including the strengthening of free trade union movements throughout the world.

Because of its political and economic importance, its treaty obligations and its support of human rights, the United States must continue to assume its leadership responsibilities in partnership with other nations that share our dedication to peace and freedom.

The Western Alliance has never faced tests as grave on as many fronts as it faces today. From the Persian Gulf to the Caribbean Sea, the Soviet Union is pursuing military, political and diplomatic initiatives which endanger peace and freedom. Economic warfare, too, has become a part of the complex international picture and a constant peril to Western economies.

Despite the growing military power of the Soviet Union, Western democracies maintain an unchallenged lead in economic resources and productive capacity. What is needed now is the will to harness that capacity to resist the totalitarian assault on vital Western interests and to promote democratic economic development in the Third World and other impoverished nations.

The United States and its allies must develop in concert the appropriate military capability to meet the Soviet challenge wherever it is presented. Industrial democracies must work more vigorously to achieve coherent and coordinated economic policies, including a critical reexamination of the growing dependence of Western economies on the Soviet Union. The Western Alliance, and particularly NATO, must resist Soviet diplomatic, political and economic efforts to

193

drive a wedge between the United States and its allies.

The continuing shift in the overall military balance to the disadvantage of the West must be corrected, by strengthening NATO and by modernizing and improving the readiness of U.S. military forces.

The United States must forge enduring international relationships for the coming years. The Camp David agreement provides a framework for peace in the Middle East and should be pursued. The Panama Canal Treaties provide a foundation for improved relationships with Latin American countries. Continued consultations with industrial democracies in Europe and Asia on economic issues offer hope for positive results.

The United States and its allies must not be found wanting or lacking in resolve in facing the challenges to peace and freedom.

The complex problems confronting the United States require strong leadership, deep commitment and firm resolve.

Both parties must address these issues in their platforms. The parties must present their proposals squarely, honestly and factually, and bind their standard bearers and legislative leaders to keeping the party's word as set forth in its platform. Such action is necessary to restore public confidence in the political institutions of this country.

Issues, and not personalities, should be the basis on which the American people determine their vote in November. Issues will be the sole determinant for the AFL-CIO. We shall examine and evaluate the platforms of both parties and report to our union members the positions of the parties on the issues of concern to working people.

● ● ●

NO

G.C. Wiegand

THIRTY YEARS OF "FULL EMPLOYMENT" POLICIES AND GROWING UNEMPLOYMENT

For thirty years the struggle for "full employment" has colored, if not determined, public policies in the United States and much of the free world. According to Senator Proxmire unemployment is "the cruelest problem of all problems;" Congressman Hawkins regards unemployment as "one of the great moral issues of our time;" and the Humphrey-Hawkins bill of 1976 blamed most social ills—"the proliferation of physical and psychological illnesses, drug addiction, crime, and social conflict"—on the "substantial and increasing unemployment."

In Germany, the leader of the Socialists, Helmut Schmidt, campaigned in 1972 under the slogan "rather five percent inflation than five percent unemployment." He won the election;—and during the following three years the German federal debt increased by 95 percent,—while unemployment continued to rise. Only belatedly, in 1977, did the Germans apparently realize that one cannot lick the unemployment problem by creating more fiat money,—a wisdom most other countries have not yet discovered.

Unemployment is no doubt one of the major problems of our time, partly— or largely—because the governments of the West, in trying to achieve "full employment," have actually created more unemployment by undermining the very foundations of the socio-economic system which is creating productive jobs on an unprecedented scale.

As a socio-economic problem, as we understand it today in the Western world, unemployment is only about half a century old. While there was widespread unemployment in Europe and many parts of the world during the 18th and 19th centuries and throughout history, it was regarded as a rule as an individual rather than a socio-economic problem. And this distinction is important. Those who could not find jobs in Europe, and had the will to better themselves, emigrated to the United States or other overseas countries, and many of them, or their children, acquired affluence. And what is called today

From. "Thirty Years of 'Full Employment' Policies and Growing Unemployment", *Vital Speeches of the Day.* Volume 43, #16, June 1, 1977. Reprinted by permission.

the "underprivileged youths," those who could not find jobs in New York, were told "go West, young man, go West."

Webster's Dictionary of 1859 defined "Unemployed" as "Not being in use, such as unemployed capital or money." No mention whatever of unemployed workers. In the subsequent Academic Edition, Mr. Webster did not even mention the word "Unemployment." In the 1880 edition of the Oxford Universal English Dictionary "Unemployed" is defined as "a state of leisure—temporarily out of work," and in 1940 Webster speaks of "not employed at any paid labor." Unemployment during the 19th century had two aspects. It was either a sign of the Calvinist sin of individual laziness, or the cause of poverty which in turn was partially alleviated through private charity.

Today, on the other hand, we look upon unemployment as a defect in the socio-economic system against which the individual is supposedly powerless, and which can be remedied only through government action. A remunerative job has become a "right" of the individual to be provided by the government, and if the government cannot provide the proper jobs, it supports the unemployed through various forms of direct payments. Being without a job no longer means "poverty" as far as the great majority of the unemployed is concerned, although it usually means a lowering of the standard of living, and often entails difficulties in paying past debts incurred during periods of high employment.

The change of regarding unemployment as primarily a social rather than individual problem did not occur until after the first World War, and in the U.S. not until the 1930's; and the notion of "full employment" did not develop until the mid-1940's. Reality—the fact that

people are unemployed—has changed little during the past 200 years, but our attitude has changed and this gives the problem an entirely new, and potentially dangerous dimension. While the 19th century, in the prevailing spirit of individualism, underestimated the socio-economic aspects of unemployment, our own age of the so-called "social conscience" has swung to the opposite extreme by under-emphasizing the responsibility of the individual to support himself, and by assuming that most social ills will be cured once the government provides jobs for all.

How Did It All Get Started?

As the second World War drew to a close, with the mass unemployment of the 1930's still a vivid memory, governments on both sides of the Atlantic, especially in Britain and the United States, were seriously concerned about the dangers of a major postwar depression. No fewer than 300 public and private agencies and organizations were developing postwar plans in the U.S., most of which dealt with the potential threat of mass unemployment.

Some eleven million American men and women were in the Armed Forces; about a third of the labor force was directly or indirectly involved in the war effort; and the returning veterans were not likely to be satisfied with a meager role. If the American economy could produce tens of thousands of tanks and planes, why should it not be possible to produce equally large quantities of consumer goods, provide jobs for all, and assure a rising standard of living!

The theory that government intervention could assure a high level of employment had first been suggested by Keynes in the mid-1930s and by the mid-1940's Sir William Beveridge's "Full Employment in a Free Society" and Henry Wallace's "Sixty Million Jobs" had become bestsellers. And both authors literally meant "full employment." As Beveridge put it: "Full employment . . . means having always more vacant jobs than unemployed men . . . The labour market should always be a sellers' market rather than a buyers' market." And in the U.S. a Federal Reserve study placed the expected labor force as of 1947 at 60.5 million;—hence Wallace's "60 Million Jobs."

To have a good job had suddenly become a "right" of every American. In his State of the Union Message of January 1944, President Roosevelt spoke of a "second bill of rights," which was to include "the right to a useful and remunerative job in the industries or shops, farms or mines of the nation."

Why Unemployment?

Since then, the number of employed workers has grown by about 50 percent, or at about the same rate as the population; and the per capita disposable income in fixed dollars has risen by about 160 percent, reflecting the rising affluence of the American people. The U.S. certainly did not suffer from a lack of purchasing power during the past 30 years. Yet unemployment, according to official statistics, never dropped below 4 percent except during the Korean and Vietnam wars.

FDR still spoke of a "useful job" in the private sector. But the number of jobs in the private sector grew by only about one third during the past 30 years, while the number of public employees who have to be supported by taxes or with the help of the printing press has risen by about 150 percent. Without the tremendous technological progress, financed by huge capital investments, the private sector could not have carried the growing burden of the public sector and provided the American consumer with an unprecedented increase in the average standard of living.

But there is a limit to "economic miracles," and since the early 1970's these limits have become more clearly visible. The dual drain on the economic resources by the top-heavy public sector and excessive private consumption have reduced the available savings needed for the necessary expansion of productive resources, so that the economy can no longer meet the inflated public and private demands—natural gas, oil, and the railroads are just three striking examples—nor provide jobs for the swollen number of jobseekers.

Without adequate aggregate demand, production will lag and workers will be idle. This is the established Keynesian wisdom, which in itself is perfectly true. But there is a second, equally important truth: without the necessary capital investments, the economy cannot produce the needed goods nor employ all the people looking for jobs. And the latter has been the case in the U.S., certainly since the beginning of the 1960's.

The notion of a perfectly balanced machine—the economy—of which the 18th century economists wrote, seems very old-fashioned today in an age of interventionism. Yet there exists a delicate balance between consumption, savings and investments, as Keynes himself emphasized, and this balance has been gravely disturbed during the past 15-20 years through government intervention and inflation.

SHOULD GOVERNMENT BE RESPONSIBLE FOR FULL EMPLOYMENT?

The result has been stagflation—chronic unemployment and at the same time, steadily rising prices. In 1960 government social spending was equal to 10.5 percent of the GNP, by 1976 it had risen to 20.6 percent. In 1976 alone, close to $170 billion which would have been available for job-creating investments if the ratio between welfare and the GNP had been maintained, were turned into social consumption, resulting in increased demand, while hampering and hence job opportunities.

The Ideological and Theoretical Confusion

From the very outset the "full employment" debate suffered from a basic confusion of objectives. It is the task of a well-functioning economy to produce the largest quantity of goods and services of a high quality at the lowest possible price. The creation of jobs is not the primary goal of economic activity, but the logical concomitant of a high rate of production. The emphasis should thus be on "full production" rather than "full employment." This is not a mere question of semantics, but of a fundamental cause-and-effect confusion which has plagued American policy for more than 30 years. Washington is officially promoting "full employment," while at the same time preventing "full production" through a crushing and irrational tax system; a fantastic growth of laws and regulations which hamper production; the emphasis upon consumption, especially public consumption, which impedes desperately needed capital formation; and above all through a policy of chronic inflation which drives savings into nonproductive inflation-shelters at home or abroad, and thus reduces productive investments and the creation of job opportunities.

How can Governments Assure Full Employment?

The rising rate of unemployment during the past five years should not have come as a surprise to Washington. In 1961, for instance, when the country was embarking full force on its prosperity-through-fiat-money scheme, a Congressional committee published a carefully documented report, "Employment in a Dynamic American Economy," in which the authors warned that "we are on the eve of an increase in the number of Americans who will be in the job market." Since then the number of gainfully employed has actually increased from about 64 million to 85 million, an increase of about 32 percent, while the population grew by only about 20 percent. The report further emphasized that "Congress makes its basic contributions not through the volume of its own spending, but by promoting conditions favorable to the exercise of individual enterprise and private effort." The warning fell on deaf ears. During the subsequent 16 years, federal spending rose from $92 billion to $394 billion, and an unprecedented mass of government regulations increasingly strangled the private sector.

The "New Frontier" and "Great Society" spending may have been politically expedient, but it was based on the basically false economic assumption that a government can create prosperity and maximum employment through the issuance of fiat money, and it accustomed millions of Americans to the notion that Washington can provide free lunches indefinitely.

The pseudo-Keynesian notion that

governments can create full employment through deficit spending and easy credit no doubt played a role in the wording of the "Employment Act of 1946!" "The rate of federal investment and expenditure may be varied to whatever extent and in whatever manner the President may determine to be necessary for the purpose of assisting in assuring continuing full employment." But the Keynesian philosophy did not take over in full force until the early 1960's, and it was not until 1975 that the Humphrey-Hawkins bill proposed to provide government jobs for all adult workers who could not find jobs in the private sector, above a basic 3 percent adult unemployment rate.

But one should not blame all the foolish policies of the past thirty years exclusively on Keynes. When the GENERAL THEORY was published in 1936 the world suffered not only from large unemployment and idle productive resources, but also from an accumulation of vast idle savings. The excess reserves of the American commercial banking system piled up in the Federal Reserve would have permitted the expansion of credit in an amount equal to the total national debt. Keynes proposed, therefore, to "mobilize" these idle savings through deficit spending;—which was a perfectly logical solution for the problems of the 1930's.

During the past 35 years, however, the situation has been radically different. Instead of accumulating "idle savings," the world has financed its rapidly rising standard of living through a fantastic expansion of public and private, domestic and international debts. Between 1946 and 1976 commercial bank credit in the U.S. increased by 420 percent, while the output of goods and services rose by only 166 percent. And the disparity was much greater in the Third World.

With the idle savings of the 1930's largely consumed during the war years, or off-set by the sharp increase in public indebtedness, the full-employment-through-deficit-spending scheme of the postwar years could be financed only with the help of the printing press which meant chronic inflation; first creeping at 1-2 percent a year, and more recently at a fast trodding pace of more than 10 percent. Yet as late as 1967, Walter W. Heller, one of the chief architects of the policy of accelerating inflation, wrote: ". . . We have at last unleashed fiscal and monetary policy for the aggressive pursuit of those objectives (full employment and maximum growth) . . . This is not the creation of a 'new economics' but the completion of the Keynesian Revolution . . . In political economics, the day of the Neanderthal Man—indeed, the day of the pre-Keynesian Man—is past."

The results are obvious. Since the second edition of Heller's "New Dimensions of Political Economy" appeared, in 1967, i.e., in about ten years, the federal debt has risen from $286 billion to $665 billion, and the dollar has lost almost 40 percent of its domestic purchasing power.

But Congress continues to "fine-tune" the economy a la Heller through ever larger deficits.

During the "full employment" debate of the 1940's, some members of Congress warned of the potential inflationary threat;—and Beveridge himself realized the danger, but simply suggested a system of wage and price controls, if his "full employment" scheme resulted in rising prices. He was thus quite willing to destroy the market economy, which had made first Britain and then the United States the leading and most prosperous countries in the world. "The list of essential liberties" he argued, "does not include the liberty of private citizens to own the means of production and to employ other citizens in operating them at a wage."

And the so-called "Liberals" in America thought along similar lines. As one writer of the *Nation* put it in 1946: "We on the Left agree with . . . the Soviet Constitution that the socialist organization of the national economy is the one certain way to guarantee full employment. We are not yet ready to state dogmatically that it is impossible to have both full employment and private enterprise . . . (but) free enterprise as it existed before the war was incompatible with full employment . . . The independent businessmen will be wise to do less worrying about sacred-cow words like "free enterprise.' "

The "full employment" advocates of the 1970's are less outspoken in their advocacy of a managed socialist society, and some may not even realize that their policies promote such an end, but there is actually very little difference between the so-called "Leftists" of the 1940's and the so-called "Liberals" of the 1970's.

The threat of inflation, which finally overtook the country in the early 1970's, was repeatedly and emphatically stressed by a minority in both houses during the "Full Employment" debate of 1946, but the majority prevented any mentioning of price stability in the Act itself.

As Dr. Keyserling, who became the head of the Council of Economic Advisors, argued; "A specific statement (regarding price stability) would run the risk of causing useless controversies over the meaning of a desirable degree of price stability and of making price stability and a goal that competed with the objective of maximum employment." That was the

time when Paul Samuelson argued in his famous textbook that "if price increases could be held down to, say, less than 5 percent a year, such a mild steady inflation need not cause too much concern. . . . An increase in prices is usually associated with an increase in employment. In mild inflation the wheels of industry are well lubricated and total output goes up. Private investment is brisk, and jobs plentiful. Thus a little inflation is usually to be preferred to a little deflation. The losses to fixed-income groups are usually less than the gains to the rest of the community."

This was the economic "truth" which was taught to literally millions of students throughout the world. (By 1958 Professor Samuelson had reduced his definition of a "mild inflation" from 5 percent to 2 percent, but the students were still told that "mild inflation" represented a "lubricant" for the wheels of industry.) Since the late 1940's when Paul Samuelson's "Economics" became an educational bestseller, and Dr. Keyserling argued that it was useless to discuss the desirable degree of price stability, the dollar has lost 55 percent of its domestic and an even larger share of its international purchasing power;—yet the rate of unemployment is materially higher today than it was in the 1940's and 1950's.

There is obviously something wrong with a policy which after 30 years has not only failed to achieve its goal, but has had serious adverse effects on the country and the entire world.

Yet the "full employment" arguments have changed little in the past 30 years. "The essential idea" as Henry Wallace put it in the mid-1940's "is that the Federal Government is ultimately responsible for full employment"—not the individual worker. Twenty years later, Walter Heller argued that "the Federal government has an overreaching responsibility for the nation's stability and growth." Since "private enterprise left to its own devices cannot," as *The New York Times* argued in 1946; "provide sufficient employment" the government has to step in; and Walter Heller agreed in 1966: "The economy cannot regulate itself. We now take it for granted that the government must step in to provide the essential stability at high levels of employment and growth that the market mechanism, left alone, cannot deliver."

"A free economy is risky, uncertain, and inherently unstable" wrote Professor Alvin Hansen, the leading American Keynesian of the 1940's, in one of his textbooks. "Thus it has at last become necessary for the government to take positive action designed to provide a stable and adequate flow of total expenditures to assure full employment."

With the wisdom of thirty years of hindsight we know today, what the experts and Congress should have known in the 1940's, that in a free society the government cannot produce full employment by creating additional fiat money. Yet Congress, even today, wants to continue the same policy, only on a larger scale with more government planning and more intervention in the market place.

What is Wrong with the "Full Employment" Policies?

What have been the basic defects of the "full employment" policies of the past 30 years? There are at least three:

(1) The unemployment problem in its present dimension, and in its impact on public opinion, rests to a large extent on misleading statistical aggregates.

(2) The situation is made worse through seemingly well-meaning—and politically expedient—measures taken by the government, including the job-destroying fiscal system.

(3) The solution of the unemployment problem is made virtually impossible because of the still widely held, but basically false notion, that governments can create jobs by creating more fiat money.

Full employment by government fiat is possible—at least in theory—in a planned totalitarian society where workers are assigned to jobs at rates of pay determined by the government, whether the workers like the jobs or not, and whether the jobs are economically justified or not. Given the choice between a concentration camp and cleaning the streets of New York at $1.50 an hour, most Ph.D's will probably prefer the latter form of "full employment." The Russian Constitution promises "full employment," and there is little or no unemployment in Moscow and Leningrad—although there is a great deal of underemployment in the vast Asian parts of the USSR,—but where is the American advocate of "full employment"—aside from the Leftists of thirty years ago—who is willing to tell the American people that to achieve "full employment," the U.S. may have to copy the Russian socio-economic and political system?

The Statistical Confusion

There is no scientific or quantitatively reliable definition of the three basic variables involved in the "full employment" debate: the size of the labor force;

201

the number of unemployed; and what constitutes "full employment."

The labor force is not a constant percentage of the population. In 1950, it constituted about 42 percent of the total population, in 1976 45 percent, which in itself represents almost a million additional men and women supposedly seeking jobs. The labor force expands and contracts due to a variety of exogenous forces and changes in definition. It is reduced—artificially—if workers are forced to retire at 62, 65 or 68, or whatever age the politicians decide. It is also reduced through child labor laws. On the other hand, chronic inflation has had a tendency to increase the percentage of the population seeking jobs, since one wage earner could no longer support the family in the style which growing affluence dictates. More college students had to find jobs, as tuition doubled and trebled.

In 1972 Congress ordered that mothers receiving welfare payments had to register for work. They were thus made, by Congressional fiat, part of the labor force, and automatically swelled the ranks of the unemployed, even though their real status had not changed at all.

Teen-agers and Women in the Labor Forces

But the impact of inflation and Congressional decisions on the growth of the labor force is minor compared with two basic factors: the vast influx of women workers into the labor force and the "baby boom" of the late 1940's and 1950's.

In 1947 the labor force included 16.7 million women 16 years and older; by 1976 the figure has risen to 38.5 million. Instead of 32 percent of the American women holding jobs or looking for work,

there are now almost 48 percent. Since 1947 the number of men in the labor force—employed and unemployed—increased by about one third, the number of women by more than 125 percent. If the number of women in the labor force had increased at the same rate as that of men, there would be today at least 12 million fewer workers, America would suffer from an acute labor shortage, rather than unemployment, and total production and the average standard of living would be much lower.

Sylvia Porter calls these figures "viciously sexist." Obviously, women have the same right to look for jobs as men. Moreover, almost 5 million of the 38.5 million working women are divorced or separated. Another 5 million work because their husbands earn less than $10,000 a year, which they regard as not enough to meet the modern concepts of an adequate standard of living. Cultural factors thus have a considerable bearing on the size of the labor force.

The other major impact on the employment market has been the postwar baby boom. In 1945, 2.9 million babies were born in the United States; in 1957, 4.3 million. Hence the large influx of teen-agers into the labor force since the late 1960's and the large increase in unemployed teen-agers. Add to this the often exaggerated expectations of school-drop-outs and high school and college graduates as to the type of job they are willing to accept, and the pay they should get despite their often woefully inadequate education and skills. According to a 1975 study of the federally funded National Assessment of Educational Progress, 13% of the 17 year old proved functionally illiterate; 10 percent had trouble reading a phone book. Among blacks, functional illiteracy ran as high as 40 percent, yet many of these functionally illiterates have since received their high school diplomas, and, if employed, have to be paid a minimum wage of $2.30* an hour—irrespective of their productivity.

Employment and Wage Levels

In 1969, the Department of Labor published a small book: "Youth Unemployment and Minimum Wages," in which the Department, very diplomatically, admitted that "the increases in the level and coverage of the federal minimum wage may have contributed to the employment problems of the teenagers." Since then the minimum wage has been increased from $1.60 to $2.30 and may shortly to be raised to a minimum of $2.50, or even $3 if the unions have their way.

And high wages are not only an obstacle to employment for high school drop-outs. There are many more college graduates than there are "college graduate" jobs, even though many jobs formerly handled adequately by high school graduates now require a college degree—with a correspondingly higher starting salary. The standard starting salary for a Harvard Law School graduate in a respectable Wall Street law firm was about $120 a month in 1929. Today a graduate with a BA in accounting is paid almost $1200; a 900 percent increase, while the cost of living rose by less than 250 percent. Forty years ago the untrained and inexperienced entrants into the labor force were probably underpaid; today many of them are certainly overpaid on basis of their productivity. Yet despite the sharp rise in minimum wages

*[Eds. Note]: The minimum wage as of 1981, stood at $3.35.

and starting salaries, the economy has been able to absorb 85 percent of the job-seeking teen-agers.

Labor theorists argue that the productivity of individual workers cannot be measured sufficiently exactly to ascertain whether a worker "earns" his pay or not. But the employer who pays the wages has a rough, if somewhat subjective, idea of what a worker is worth to him, and this idea guides his employment policies. If minimum wages are too high—or are regarded as too high by the prospective employer—marginal unskilled jobs gradually disappear. The Western Union boys of yesteryears are a perfect example.

If marginal workers are paid more than they produce, the difference can be made up in only three ways: by skilled workers receiving relatively less than they produce; by prices being pushed up; or by profits declining which means that the marginal jobs disappear.

As the late David McCord Wright used to tell his classes:

"We all (or nearly all) consent,
if wages rise by ten percent,
it puts the choice before the nation
of unemployment or inflation."

The percentage of unemployed—the figure which makes the headlines and dominates economic policies—depends upon the size of what is regarded as the labor force which, quite aside from long-range demographic and cultural factors, is a highly subjective concept.

Should teenagers who look for part-time work after school or for summer work to have additional spending money be regarded as part of the labor force? What about housewives who take a part-time job in a store between Thanksgiving and Christmas? Unemployment among the 16-19 year olds runs above 20 percent. They account for about one-fourth of the total number of unemployed, yet almost half of them are still attending school. According to a 1972 Bureau of Labor Statistics study, more than 40 percent of all the so-called unemployed were young people in the 16-24 age bracket who lived at home and drifted in and out of jobs. Some of them obviously needed work to help support the family. But how many? The statistics do not differentiate between the youth who needs spending money for a date or to fix his car, and the one whose dollars are badly needed to help support a large family. . . .

What is "Full Employment?"

There is also no agreement as to what constitutes "full employment." Beveridge and Wallace thought that there should always be at least as many job openings as there are potential job seekers. Nobody has ever taken this definition very seriously.

The Employment Act of 1946, which has formed the basis of the American full employment policy for thirty years, speaks of "maximum employment," but provides no concrete figures. The 1947 Economics Report of the President regarded a level of slightly over two million unemployed (about 3.9 percent) as "full employment." The 1951 Report mentioned the figure of 3.6 percent. In 1955 Arthur F. Burns, who was then Chairman of the Council of Economic Advisors,

indicated that 4 percent is "widely regarded as an approximate measure of the average amount of frictional and seasonal unemployment," but he objected to any definite figure being used to trigger action by the government.

Yet ten years later, after the tremendous influx of marginal workers, the Humphrey-Hawkins bill of 1976 proposed that "after the private sector has been fully utilized (to create jobs) the remaining unemployed above 3 percent adult unemployment" be put on government payrolls, where they would have to be supported either by those Americans who are productively employed, or with the help of the printing press. The Humphrey-Hawkins bill died unborn, but the Carter Administration sponsors less ambitious make-work schemes financed through deficit spending.

. . . Most of the spending increase in the Carter budgets will be channelled into social consumption, thus increasing overall demand and aggravating inflation, while the same amount of money invested by private enterprises in plant and equipment could create a million productive jobs for years to come. The system of which Kipling spoke which is based on "robbing selected Peter to pay for collective Paul," may be "humane" (in the short run); it tends to make for equality (by spreading poverty); and it is certainly politically expedient; provided one thinks in forms of the next election. But it makes for chronic inflation and unemployment, and in the long run destroys the economic strength of the nation.

● ● ●

POSTSCRIPT

SHOULD GOVERNMENT BE RESPONSIBLE FOR ACHIEVING AND MAINTAINING FULL EMPLOYMENT?

This issue is sharply drawn. Kirkland argues that employment serves the individual. Employment is also beneficial to the larger society for employment means production and more employment means a greater availability of goods and services. It also means more tax revenues for government. Full employment is also beneficial for it reduces inflation. Accepting that full employment is an appropriate objective, Kirkland goes on to argue that it is both a necessary and proper function of government. Necessary because today's economy is structured in such a way that there is little the individual can do about his or her unemployment status if it is caused by a lack of investment or unfair foreign competition. Government action is proper because in a democracy the state must be responsive to the needs of the people; if they need jobs, government must move to create those jobs.

Wiegand joins the debate at several different levels. At the most fundamental level he believes that the economy, if left to its own devices will grow and provide necessary jobs. This is the basic, free market, conservative creed. He also points out that government has taken certain actions, such as minimum wage legislation, which actually create unemployment. This is in addition to the indirect methods by which government contributes to unemployment; for example, through a reduction in the rate of capital formation. Wiegand even raises the question of accurately measuring the extent of "true" unemployment. The actual statistics reflect temporary as well as permanently out-of-work persons and even the rapid expansion of the number of women in the labor force. For all of these reasons and others Wiegand voices a loud "no" on this issue.

Readings on this issue might begin with the pieces of legislation mentioned in the introduction: the Employment Act of 1946 and the Full Employment and Balanced Growth Act of 1978. On the affirmative side, John Kenneth Galbraith's ECONOMICS AND THE PUBLIC PURPOSE (Houghton Mifflin, 1973) and Walter W. Heller's THE ECONOMY (Norton, 1976) offer complete and broad perspectives. On the negative side FREE TO CHOOSE (Harcourt Brace and Jovanovich) by Rose and Milton Friedman and THE ROAD TO SERFDOM (University of Chicago, 1953) by Friedrich A. Hayek present the conservative position on this as well as several other issues.

ISSUE 11

ARE FEDERAL BUDGET DEFICITS HARMFUL TO THE ECONOMY?

YES: Henry Hazlitt, from "What Spending and Deficits Do." THE IN-FLATION CRISIS AND HOW TO RESOLVE IT (Arlington House Publishers, 1978).

NO: Gus Tyler, from "The Dangerous Fallacies of a Balanced Budget Convention," *AFL-CIO American Federationist* (April, 1979).

ISSUE SUMMARY

YES: Author Hazlitt maintains that budget deficits can have a number of undesirable effects on the economy including inflation, a reduction in private productive investment, and the institution of higher taxes which impair production and employment.

NO: Union official Tyler believes that budget deficits can promote national goals like full employment, that budget deficits need not lead to inflation and economic collapse, and that a legal requirement to balance the budget would be nearly impossible to satisfy as a practical matter.

The Full Employment and Balanced Growth Act of 1978 lists a number of goals which the Federal government is to promote. Besides the familiar objectives of full employment, price stability, and increased real income, a balanced Federal budget is specifically mentioned. Ignoring other considerations, the Federal government is to collect taxes in an amount equal to its expenditures.

But other considerations can't be ignored and that is why there is a heated debate on this issue. Many argue that at any given time the balancing of the budget may be incompatible with other, more important goals. Attempting to balance the budget through expenditure reduction might mean the end of some social program. If tax increases are used instead, unemployment might increase. Still others counter that the fact of a budget deficit itself will have a number of negative effects on the economy.

The debate on this issue tends to divide neatly into a conservative versus liberal argument. The conservatives take the "yes" side. They believe that a balanced budget is consistent, not inconsistent with other economic goals. As

Hazlitt states, a balanced budget supports the attainment of price stability and increased production and employment. Even in those cases where there is conflict between the balanced budget goal and other goals, the balanced budget would be considered more important; it should be given a higher priority. This would be proper because of the many positive effects generated by a balanced budget.

Liberals normally take the negative side on this issue. Their position is based on the belief that a balanced budget may be incompatible with a number of other worthwhile objectives. And, in the same vein, a balanced budget is less important, not more important than these other goals. For example, if the budget is currently in deficit, efforts to balance the budget, according to the liberals, will increase unemployment. The harm of increased unemployment more than offsets any benefits associated with balancing the budget and, therefore, it is better to live with the budget deficit.

Recently the debate over the balanced budget has taken a new twist. In this new twist conservatives are not only concerned with balancing the budget but also with the level at which it is balanced. Consistent with their overall philosophy of minimizing the involvement of government in the economy, the conservative objective is to balance taxes and expenditures at a low level, usually expressed in terms of some percent of Gross National Product. To achieve their objectives, conservatives have alternatively pushed for a constitutional amendment to balance the budget or legislation that would limit government spending or tax revenues. Liberals rise in protest declaring that government expenditures must be large enough to complete necessary programs with taxes raised only to levels that would not harm other objectives such as low unemployment.

The thrust of the Hazlitt article is to identify the evils of an unbalanced budget as well as the evils of a budget that is balanced at too high a level. Tyler begins by arguing that inflation is not caused by budget deficits. He also demonstrates that in relative terms the national debt has become less important and that deficits can promote worthwhile goals. He then considers what would be necessary to achieve a balanced budget and concludes that from a practical perspective it would be difficult to achieve a balanced budget.

As a final point, it is interesting to note the position of the two major political parties on this issue during the 1980 presidential election as revealed by their platforms. The Democrats, consistent with their basic liberal philosophy, were categorically against a consitutional amendment mandating a balanced budget: "We oppose a Constitutional amendment requiring a balanced budget." Republicans, as conservatives, were more receptive to the consitutional amendment approach. They would initially try to obtain a balanced budget through the regular legislative process, but are willing to move to a constitutional amendment: ". . . if necessary, the Republican party will seek to adopt a Constitutional amendment to limit federal spending and balance the budget except in time of national emergency as determined by a two-thirds vote of Congress."

YES   Henry Hazlitt

WHAT SPENDING AND DEFICITS DO

The direct cause of price inflation is the issuance of an excessive amount of paper money. The most frequent cause of the issuance of too much paper money is a government budget deficit.

The majority of economists have long recognized this, but the majority of politicians have studiously ignored it. One result, in this age of inflation, is that economists have tended to put too much emphasis on the evils of deficits as such and too little emphasis on the evils of excessive government spending, whether the budget is balanced or not.

So it is desirable to begin with the question, What is the effect of government spending on the economy—even if it is wholly covered by tax revenues?

The economic effect of government spending depends on what the spending is for, compared with what the private spending it displaces would be for. To the extent that the government uses its tax-raised money to provide more urgent services for the community than the taxpayers themselves otherwise would or could have provided, the government spending is beneficial to the community. To the extent that the government provides policemen and judges to prevent or mitigate force, theft, and fraud, it protects and encourages production and welfare. The same applies, up to a certain point, to what the government pays out to provide armies and armament against foreign aggression. It applies also to the provision by city governments of sidewalks, streets, and sewers, and to the provision by states of roads, parkways, and bridges.

But government expenditure even on necessary types of service may easily become excessive. Sometimes it may be difficult to measure exactly where the point of excess begins. It is to be hoped, for example, that armies and armament may never need to be used, but it does not follow that providing them is mere waste. They are a form of insurance premium, and in this world of nuclear warfare and incendiary slogans it is not easy to say how

From, "What Spending and Deficits Do", THE INFLATION CRISIS AND HOW TO RESOLVE IT. Reprinted by permission of the publisher, Arlington House Publishers, Westport CT. 06880. Copyright © by Henry Hazlitt, 1978.

large a premium is enough. The exigencies of politicians seeking reelection, of course, may very quickly lead to unneeded roads and other public works.

Waste in government spending in other directions can soon become flagrant. The money spent on various forms of relief, now called "social welfare," is more responsible for the spending explosion in the U.S. government than any other type of outlay. In fiscal year 1927, when total expenditures of the federal government were $2.9 billion, a negligible percentage of that amount went for so-called welfare. In fiscal 1977, when total expenditures rose to $401.9 billion—139 times as much—welfare spending alone (education, social services, Medicaid, Medicare, Social Security, veterans benefits, etc.) came to $221 billion, or more than half the total. The net effect of this spending is to reduce production, because most of it taxes the productive to support the unproductive. . . .

Some forms of taxation have more harmful effects on production than others. Perhaps the worst is heavy taxation of corporate earnings. This discourages business and output; it reduces the employment that the politicians profess to be their primary concern; and it prevents the capital formation that is so necessary to increase real productivity, real income, real wages, real welfare. Almost as harmful to incentives and to capital formation is progressive personal income taxation. And the higher the level of any form of taxation, the greater the damage it does.

Let us consider government spending in more detail. The greater the amount of government spending, the more it depresses the economy. In so far as it is a substitute for private spending, it does nothing to "stimulate" the economy. It merely directs labor and capital into the production of less necessary goods or services at the expense of more necessary goods or services. It leads to malproduction. It tends to direct funds out of profitable capital investment and into immediate consumption. And most welfare spending, to repeat, tends to support the unproductive at the expense of the productive.

But more important, the higher the level of government spending, the higher the level of taxation. And the higher the level of taxation, the more it discourages, distorts, and disrupts production. It does this much more than proportionately. A one percent sales tax, personal income tax, or corporation tax would do very little to discourage production, but a 50 percent rate can be seriously disruptive. Just as each additional fixed increment of income will tend to have a diminishing marginal value to the receiver, so each additional *subtraction* from his income will mean a more than proportional deprivation and disincentive. The adjective *progressive* usually carries an approbatory connotation, but an income tax can appropriately be called progressive only in the sense that a disease can be called progressive. So far as its effect on incentives and production are concerned, such a tax is increasingly *retrogressive*, or *repressive*.

Though, broadly speaking, only a budget deficit tends to lead to inflation, the recognition of this truth has led to a serious underestimation of the harmfulness of an exorbitant level of total government spending. While a budget balanced at a level of $100 billion for both spending and tax revenues may be acceptable (at, say, 1978's level of national income and dollar purchasing power), a budget balanced at a level

209

above $400 billion may in the long run prove ruinous. In the same way, a deficit of $60 billion at a $400 billion level of spending is far more ominous than a deficit of the same size at a spending level of $200 billion.

An exorbitant spending level, in sum, can be as bad as or worse than a huge deficit. Everything depends on their relative size, and on their combined size compared with the national income.

How to Reduce a Deficit

Let us look first at the effect of a deficit. That effect will depend in large part on how the deficit is financed. Of course if, with a given level of spending, a deficit, of say, $50 billion is financed by added taxation, it ceases by definition to be a deficit. But it does not follow that this is the best course to take. Whenever possible—except, say, in the midst of a major war—a deficit should be eliminated by reducing expenditures rather than by increasing taxes, because of the harm heavier taxes would probably do in discouraging and disorganizing production.

It is necessary to emphasize this point, because every so often some erstwhile advocate of big spending suddenly turns "responsible," and solemnly tells conservatives that if they want to be equally responsible it is now their duty to balance the budget by raising taxes to cover the existing and planned expenditures. Such advice completely begs the question. It tacitly assumes that the existing or planned level of expenditures, and all its constituent items, are absolutely necessary and must be fully covered by increased taxes no matter what the cost in economic disruption.

We have had thirty-nine deficits in the forty-seven fiscal years since 1931. The annual spending total has gone up from $3.6 billion in 1931 to $401.9 billion—112 times as much—in 1977. Yet the argument that we must keep on balancing this multiplied spending by equally multiplied taxation continues to be regularly put forward. The only real solution is to start slashing the spending before it destroys the economy.

Given a budget deficit, however, there are two ways in which it can be paid for. One is for the government to pay for its deficit outlays by printing and distributing more money. This may be done either directly or by the government's asking the Federal Reserve or the private commercial banks to buy its securities and to pay for them either by creating deposit credits or with newly issued inconvertible Federal Reserve notes. This of course is simple, naked inflation.

Or the deficit may be paid for by the government's selling its bonds to the public and having them paid for out of real savings. This is not directly inflationary, but it merely leads to an evil of a different kind. The government borrowing competes with and "crowds out" private capital investment, and so retards economic growth.

Let us examine this a little more closely. There is at any given time a total amount of actual or potential savings available for investment. Government statistics regularly give estimates of these. The gross national product in 1974, for example, was calculated to be $1,499 billion. Gross private saving for the same year was $215.2 billion—14.4 percent of GNP—of which $74 billion consisted of personal saving and $141.2 billion of gross business saving. But the federal budget deficit in that year was $11.7 billion, and in 1975 $73.4 billion, seriously cutting down the amount that could go into the capital investment necessary to increase productivity, real wages, and real long-run consumer welfare.

The government statistics estimate the amount of gross private domestic investment in 1974 at $215 billion and in 1975 at $183.7 billion. But it is probable that the greater part of this represented mere replacement of deteriorated, worn-out, or obsolete plant, equipment, and housing, and that net new capital formation was much smaller.

Let us turn to the amount of new capital supplied through the security markets. In 1973, total new issues of securities in the United States came to $99 billion. Of these $32 billion consisted of private corporate stocks and bonds, $22.7 billion of state and local bonds and notes, $1.4 billion of bonds of foreign governments, and $42.9 billion of obligations of the U.S. government and its agencies. Thus of the combined total of $74.9 billion borrowed by the U.S. government and by private industry, the government got 57 percent and private industry only 43 percent.

Crowding Out

The crowding-out argument can be stated in a few elementary propositions: (1) Government borrowing competes with private borrowing. (2) Government borrowing finances government dificiencies. (3) What the government borrows is spent chiefly on consumption, but what private industry borrows chiefly finances capital investment. (4) It is the amount of new capital investment that is chiefly responsible for the improvement of economic conditions.

The possible total of borrowing is restricted by the amount of real savings available. Government borrowing crowds out private borrowing by driving up interest rates to levels at which private manufacturers who would otherwise have borrowed for capital investment are forced to drop out of the market.

Yet government spending and deficits keep on increasing year by year. Why? Chiefly because they serve the immediate interests of politicians seeking votes, but also because the public still for the most part accepts a set of sophistical rationalizations.

The whole so-called Keynesian doctrine may be summed up as the contention that deficit spending, financed by borrowing, creates employment, and that enough of it can guarantee "full" employment. The American people have even had foisted upon them the myth of a "full-employment budget." This is the contention that projected federal expenditures and revenues need not be, and ought not to be, those that would bring a real balance of the budget under actually existing conditions, but merely those that would balance the budget *if* there were "full employment."

To quote a more technical explanation (as it appears, for example, in the *Economic Report of the President*, January 1976): "Full employment surpluses or deficits are the differences between what receipts and expenditures are estimated to be if the economy were operating at the potential output level consistent with a 4 per cent unemployment." (p. 54).

A table in that report shows what the differences would have been for the years 1969 through 1975 between the actual budget and the so-called full-employment budget. For the calendar year 1975, for example, actual receipts were $283.5 billion and expenditures $356.9 billion, leaving an actual budget deficit of $73.4 billion. But in conditions of full employment, receipts from the same tax rate *might* have risen to $340.8 billion, and expenditures *might* have fallen to $348.3 billion, leaving a deficit not of $73.4 billion but only of $7.5 billion. Nothing to worry about.

Nothing to worry about, perhaps, in a dream world. But let us return to the world of reality. The implication of the full-employment budget philosophy (though it is seldom stated explicitly) is not only that in a time of high unemployment it would make conditions even worse to aim at a real balance of the budget, but that a full-employment budget can be counted on to *bring* full employment.

The proposition is preposterous. The argument for it assumes that the amount of employment or unemployment depends on the amount of added dollar "purchasing power" that the government decides to squirt into the economy. Actually the amount of unemployment is chiefly determined by entirely different factors, such as: the relations in various industries between selling prices and costs and between particular prices and particular wage-rates, the wage rates exacted by strong unions and strike threats, the level and duration of unemployment insurance and relief payments (making idleness more tolerable or attractive), and the existence and size of legal minimum-wage rates. But these and other important factors are persistently ignored by the full-employment budgeteers and by all the other advocates of deficit spending as the great panacea for unemployment.

It may be worthwhile, before we leave this subject, to point to one or two of the practical consequences of a consistent adherence to a full-employment budget policy. In the twenty-eight years from 1948 to 1975, there were only eight in

which unemployment fell below the government target-level of 4 percent. In all the other years the full-employment budgeteers would have prescribed an actual deficit. But they say nothing about achieving a surplus in full-employment years, much less about its desirable size. Presumably they would consider any surplus at all, any repayment of the government debt, as extremely dangerous at any time. So a prescription for full-employment budgeting might not produce very different results in practice from a prescription for perpetual deficit. Perhaps an even worse consequence is that as long as this prescription prevails, it can only act to divert attention from the real causes of unemployment and their real cure.

Perhaps a word needs to be said about the fear of a surplus that has developed in recent decades—ever since about 1930, in fact. This of course is only the reverse side of the myth that a deficit is needed to "stimulate" the economy by "creating purchasing power." The only way in which surplus could do even temporary harm would be by bringing about a sudden substantial reduction in the money supply. It could do this only if the bonds paid off were those held by the banking system against which demand deposits had been created. But in 1977, out of a gross public debt of $697.4 billion, $100.5 billion was held by commercial banks and $94.6 billion by Federal Reserve banks. This left $502.3 billion, or about 72 percent, in nonbanking hands. This could be retired, say, over fifty years, without shrinking the money supply in the least. And if the public debt were retired at a rate of $5 billion or $10 billion a year, private holders would have that much more to invest in private industry. . . .

In conclusion: Chronic excessive

government spending and chronic huge deficits are twin evils. The deficits lead more directly to inflation, and therefore, in recent years they have tended to receive a disproportionate amount of criticism from economists and editorial writers. But the total spending is the greater evil because it is the chief political cause of the deficits. If the spending were more moderate, the taxes to pay for it would not have to be so oppressive, so damaging to incentive, so destructive of employment and production. So the persistence and size of deficits, though serious, is a derivative problem: the primary evil is the exorbitant spending, the leviathan Welfare State. If spending were brought within reasonable bounds, taxes to pay for it would not have to be so burdensome and demoralizing, and politicians could be counted on to keep the budget balanced.

● ● ●

NO

Gus Tyler

THE DANGEROUS FALLACIES OF A BALANCED-BUDGET CONVENTION

. . . The mood of the country on reducing or holding down taxes is understandable. People who work for wages feel over-taxed—and they are. Those who live on "earned" income report virtually all of their earnings and pay on what they report because they don't have any loopholes. People who live on "unearned" income—stocks, bonds, properties—report about half their income and pay on only part of what they report because they enjoy many loopholes.

The problem is not that taxes are too high, but that they are too high for some because they are too low for others. A proper cure for this disorder would be tax reform that lifts some of the burden from America's middle class of wage and salaried people and imposes more of the burden on the rich who live on "unearned" income.

Fearing precisely such an eventuality, the wealthy have mounted a campaign to convince the nation that taxes in general are too high for everyone. This myth was the basis for Proposition 13 in California and is the basis for the present proposal to have a constitutional convention for a balanced budget.

Although the emotional urge for a balanced budget is the desire to keep taxes down, the constitutional amendment will not guarantee that taxes will be reduced or kept at present levels. Indeed, the mandated balance may actually increase taxes.

A budget can be balanced in one of two ways: either by reduced spending or by increased taxes. If, at some future time, the President and Congress are not allowed to borrow they will have to raise taxes to make ends meet. Hence, a balanced budget can mean higher as well as lower taxes.

Although some favor the idea on the mistaken notion that it will automatically hold down taxes, others favor it as a way to check inflation. The logic is embedded in the argument that government deficits lead, in one way or

From. "The Dangerous Fallacies of a Balanced Budget Convention", *AFL-CIO American Federationist,* the official magazine of the AFL-CIO, April, 1979. Reprinted by permission.

another, to more dollars chasing too few goods, and thereby forcing up prices.

For such monetary theorists, the expanded money supply is offered as the sole reason for inflation. They do not blame high interest rates; they do not blame monopolies and oligopolies; they do not blame government fixing of prices, as in the case of numerous agricultural products; they don't even blame high wages. They are single-minded: the culprit is the government that tries to pay for deficits by "printing money."

Their statistical evidence is that in years when the federal deficit is high, inflation runs high. Actually, this seemingly irrefutable proof is no proof at all, because a tracing of U.S. budget deficits shows they are more likely the result of wars and recession. Inflation may cause a deficit, but not vice versa. In a period of inflation, the government must pay more for many things. Hence, a neatly balanced budget, drawn at the beginning of the year, may well end up as a deficit at the end of a year when prices rise either because of crop failures, an act of OPEC, monopoly action or a jump in interest rates imposed by the Federal Reserve Board.

Most monetarists reveal their anti-government bias when they single out federal budget deficits as the sole or the primary source of an expanded money supply. There are many, many other factors at work expanding the money supply, traditionally defined as the total of all currency plus all demand deposits. Effective money supply is determined by at least two other factors: the amount of credit and the velocity with which money circulates. At present the "supply" of money generated by credit is staggering, with multibillions of dollars outstanding on any one day on credit cards alone—just to cite one small instance. Likewise,

the velocity with which money moves is decisive: one dollar spent 10 times in one day has the same impact as 10 dollars spent once. And neither the amount of credit outstanding nor the velocity with which money moves can be traced solely or mainly to government deficits.

In sum, although the monetarist theories about how deficits make for inflation are encased in seemingly sophisticated research and reason, the arguments are shockingly unsophisticated.

Equally fallacious is the argument that the national debt is growing at a dangerous rate and that, unless we stop this piling of debt on debt, the unbearable burden will break the government's back. William Simon, Secretary of the Treasury under President Ford, sounds the alarm: "Total federal debt has increased from $329.5 billion at the end of fiscal year 1966 to an estimated $633.9 billion at the end of fiscal year 1976—a rise of 92 percent in only 10 years' time." Simon says, "unless the lethal pattern is changed, this nation will be destroyed."

But why should the nation be wrecked by this debt? In 1966, when the Gross National Product (the sum of all goods and services produced here in one year) was $753 billion, the debt was 43.6 percent of the GNP. But in 1976, when the GNP was at $1,706 billion (rushing toward the $2 trillion mark) the debt had fallen to 37 percent of the GNP. In 10 years our debt shrunk as a portion of our total output.

This "shrinking" of the national debt is not some freakish occurrence peculiar to the years from 1966 to 1976. There has been a downward trend ever since the end of World War II: in 1946, the debt was 132.8 percent of GNP; by 1962, it was 55 percent; by 1965, 48 percent; by 1976, it was down to 37 percent; and by

ARE FEDERAL BUDGET DEFICITS HARMFUL?

1979, the debt is a mere 28.4 percent of GNP. Judged by ability to carry the burden, the debt is getting steadily lighter.

Debt—like weight—is only meaningful when measured against something. A 16-month-old infant would be crushed under a pack of 60 pounds; a 16-year-old lad would carry the load with ease. An America with a GNP of only $100 billion would stagger under a debt load of $100 billion; but an America with an output of $2 trillion can carry a $100 billion debt on its pinkie. A person with an income of $5,000 a year would find it hard to repay a debt of $100,000; but one with an income of $1 million a year would find it easy to borrow the money and easy to repay.

An irksome irony about the call for budget balancing is that those who cry loudest and longest about debt are the worst offenders: the states, the corporations and the individual consumers. They are all in debt and more deeply in debt than the government that, at the end of 1978, was only responsible for 19 percent of total indebtedness in America. From 1940 to 1976, the federal debt grew at a slower pace than all other kinds of debt. State and local, corporate and private consumer debt grew far more rapidly.

In 1940, the federal debt was $44.8 billion; by 1976, it stood at $515 billion—a twelvefold increase in 36 years. State and local debt for the same years rose from $16 billion to $236 billion—a fifteenfold increase.

Corporate debt rose (same years) from $75 billion to $1,414 billion—a nineteenfold increase. And, says Simon, "At the end of World War II, corporate liquidity—a measure of cash, cash equivalents, and assets that could readily be converted into cash—stood at just under 50 percent of total liabilities. By 1960, the ratio was down to almost 30 percent. And at the end of 1970 it was on the order of 19 percent."

The biggest sinners of all—if debt is considered a sin—are Richard Roe and Jane Doe. The debt incurred by consumers rose (same years) from $8 billion to $217 billion—a twenty-sevenfold increase.

The truth of the matter is that debt is a way of life not only in America but in every free enterprise (capitalist) country in the world. The reasons are pragmatically obvious and theoretically understandable.

Most homeowners in America would own no home if they had to pay in cash for the purchase. A mortgage is a loan that incurs a debt. Mortgage indebtedness rose (same years) 24 times over, which is about twice as fast as the federal debt.

It would be useless to put money in a bank, unless it is done purely for safekeeping. The bank could pay no interest—unless there were borrowers, ready to incur debt, who would pay interest to the bank so the bank could pay interest to the depositor.

No corporation of any size could operate without going deeply into debt—as they do. They float bonds and borrow directly and invent a variety of debt instruments to finance their undertakings. Debt is the lubricant for the business machine without which the gears would grind to a halt.

You add to the debt when you take out a small loan, when you buy something on the installment plan, when you make a purchase on a credit card, when you ask your local retail store to charge it, when you borrow against your insurance policy, when you work out a financing arrangement for your car. In one month of January 1979, installment indebtedness rose by more than $3.5 billion.

Viewed in an overall theoretical way, debt is the foundation of a "free enterprise," modern capitalist society. The capitalist lives by providing finance to corporations, to governments, and to individuals. He lives by renting out his money and charging for it. If no one borrowed—no government, no business, no person—the finance capitalist would be finished. Although this eventuality might indeed be ethically justified, for the moment our system still depends on capital to function—and capital, like that fabled lunch, does not come free: to get it you must incur debt.

There is a strong temptation to conclude that the states, corporations and private borrowers are hypocrites about budget balancing. But that would be unfair because they know not what they say. They are repeating a common cliche. An individual gathering debt is like a camel under a growing burden threatened by the straw that breaks the back. This fearsome image has caused fools and learned men to denounce deficit financing for many centuries.

For those who think that deficit financing began with President Franklin D. Roosevelt, Senator Edward S. Muskie (D-Maine) advises in a recent speech that the "distinction belongs to General Washington—first in war, first in peace, and first in federal deficit." Actually, Washington was following a pattern set on Dec. 15, 1692, in the British House of Commons, when the Committee on Ways and Means proposed to raise $1 million by way of a loan, at the rate of 10 percent up to year 1700 and 7 percent thereafter.

From that point on, the debt began to grow. "At every state in the growth," records Thomas Macauley in The History of England, "it has been seriously asserted by wise men that bankruptcy and ruin were at hand. Yet still the debt went on growing; and still bankruptcy was as remote as ever."

Several wars later, the debt multiplied several times over. The celebrated philosopher, David Hume, concluded that Britain had gone mad, the kingdom was in debt beyond its ability to raise money. "And yet," notes Macauley, "this great philosopher had only to open his eyes, and to see improvement all around him, cities increasing, cultivation extending, marts too small for the crowd of buyers and sellers. . . His prediction remains to posterity, a memorable instance of the weakness from which the strongest minds are not exempt."

After the war with the American colonies, the debt grew again. "Again England was given over," continues Macauley, "and again the strange patient persisted in becoming stronger and more blooming in spite of all the diagnostics and prognostics of state physicians. As she had been visibly more prosperous with a debt of $140 million, so she was visibly more prosperous with a debt of $240 million than with a debt of $140 million."

Concluded Macauley some 100 years ago in an analysis that is equally valid for today: "It can hardly be doubted that there must have been some great fallacy in the notions of those who uttered and of those who believed that long succession of confident predictions, so significantly falsified by a long succession of indisputable facts. . . . The prophets of evil were under a double delusion. They erroneously imagined that there was an exact analogy between the case of an individual who is in debt to another individual and the case of a society which is in debt to a part of itself; and this analogy led them into endless mistakes about the effect of the system of funding. They were under an error no less serious touching the resources of the country. They made no allowance for the effect produced by the incessant progress of every experimental science, and by the incessant effort of every man to get on in life. They saw that the debt grew; and they forget that other things grew as well as the debt."

For centuries nations had been using debt as a way to pay the way for governments. It was not until the first quarter of the present century, however, that government indebtedness was seen not simply as a way for the state to meet its bills but as a way to guide the total economy. This concept—the use of public debt to regulate economic growth—was the brain child of John Maynard Keynes and, unbeknownst to most Americans, became the theoretical base for the anti-recession policies of the New Deal and of every Administration that followed.

As a practical man, FDR had to resolve a practical, yet seemingly nonsensical puzzle: why wasn't the American economy running during the 1930s when all the factors for a viable economy was present—in super-abundance? There was plenty of capital, labor, raw material and entrepreneurial know-how. But they were all idle, rotting, festering. Why?

What was lacking in our market economy was the market which, in plain language, is buying power. Buying power was lacking because the big buyers—working people—were out of work. So long as they did not earn, the market would sag and sag and sag.

The private economy would not put these people to work because it could not. No business pays people to make things for which there is no market. So, to prime the pump, the government had to put people to work, so they would have buying power to put others to work.

The government could get the necessary funds to do so either by taxation or by borrowing. Taxation would not have yielded much in those depressed days; moreover, whatever taxation would yeild had to come out of consumers or investors, thereby undercutting the primary purpose of increasing employment. So, the government borrowed.

In a pragmatic way, the United States had backed into its own brand of Keynesian economics. When the private economy failed to generate the necessary market—buying power to sustain the economy, the government stepped in by deficit financing, by—as the monetarists would have it—expanding the money supply. And the formula worked.

Prior to 1929, the history of the American economy was a history of economic crises: they called them business cycles and they accepted those painful and convulsive ups and downs as the natural way of things. Since the New Deal, there have been recessions, but we have not had a single major depression in this country. Crises have been warded off with the weapon of deficit financing.

The big deficits of the Roosevelt period were not rolled up during the peacetime years but in wartime. In 1940, the deficit was only $5 billion. In the war years of 1943-45, the deficits ran between $47 and $50 billion a year. But whether it was to combat recession or to combat a foreign enemy, the money borrowed was used to serve national purpose and, in no case, did the deficit impoverish the people. . . .

What happens in the future—assuming a budget-balancing amendment is on the books—if we are hit by some new crisis:

another depression, another war, an internal insurrection, a massive earthquake from the Appalachians to the Rockies? Neither the President nor Congress could act swiftly because the funds would not be there and no new funds could be appropriated without going through the protracted process of once more amending the Constitution. . . .

A mandated balance of the budget assumes that the budget makers know, at the beginning of the year, what their income and their expenditures will be. But they have no way of knowing; they can only guess.

They do not know what their expenditures are for three simple reasons: First, they do not know what crises will arise. Second, they do not know what inflation will do to their costs in the course of the 12 months. Third, they do not know what they will have to pay out under a variety of government "entitlement" programs. Under the last, for instance, the government has an obligation under law to someone who is disabled, or is the head of a family under aid for dependent children, or is newly retired, or is eligible for a veteran benefit. Whoever meets certain criteria set down by law is "entitled" to certain government funds—and there just is no way that the government can know in advance just how big these payments will be.

The government knows even less about what its income will be. How much comes in depends on how much people earn, how corporate profits run, how sales stack up. Income through taxes is a mathematical function of the Gross National Product whose size nobody knows when the year begins or even when the year has passed its halfway mark. For 1980, the President forecasts a growth rate in the GNP of 3.2 percent; the

Congressional Budget Office sets it at a 3.9 percent; Wharton Econometrics sets it at a low 1.3 percent; and Chase Econometrics sets it at an optimistic 4.1 percent. The difference between the low and high estimate makes a difference of about $10 billion in taxes to the government.

Being less than omniscient then, Congress and the President would unwittingly and unwillingly find themselves in violation of the amendment. Who will prosecute, try and sentence them for their transgressions?

One way for the President and Congress to obey the law—more or less— would be to allow for a margin of error, like an arbitrary $10 billion. (Between September 1978 and January 1979, the estimated deficit rose by an unanticipated $5 billion.) By planning for a surplus of several billion, the lawmakers might be able to stay within the law. But to do so, they would either have to cut expenditures or raise taxes or do both.

The easiest way to cut federal taxes would be to stop federal aid to the states, which currently runs about $80 billion per year. If an Administration chose to cut grants to the states, you would hear a different tune from state politicians now so eagerly calling for a constitutional convention to balance the federal budget.

But this reduction in the federal budget would not necessarily mean a reduction in taxes for the taxpayer. Even if the government reduces taxes by virtue of the savings in grants to the states, and it is doubtful such a cut would be possible, the states would have to increase their taxes to make up for the funds they no longer get from the federal government. The end result would be higher taxes for the taxpayer.

The other alternative for the federal government would be to raise taxes to cover present and future costs. And it would have to raise taxes beyond a reasonable level because it would have to allow for that margin of safety so as to live within the mandate of the amendment. . . .

The Founding Fathers had three great purposes in composing the Constitution. They wanted a government that was strong, flexible and respectful of the rights of the individual.

Because they wanted a state that was strong they set up a central government to replace the feeble Articles of Confederation. Because they wanted a flexible government they wrote a brief declaration that distributed powers without prescribing what those powers should do in dealing with the special and specific problems of the changing times. To show their regard for the individual, they added the first 10 amendments—the Bill of Rights—to the Constitution as an integral part of the document at the time of original ratification. . . .

A balanced budget amendment would run contrary to this spirit of the Founding Fathers in all three respects. First, the amendment would narrow the scope of government, a purpose that is the underlying motive of most of the proponents. Second, the amendment would impose a staitjacket on government, turning fitting flexibility into brittle rigidity. Third, the amendment would deprive the individual citizen of a regular say over government in the most decisive area of legislation; namely the budget. . . .

● ● ●

POSTSCRIPT

ARE FEDERAL BUDGET DEFICITS HARMFUL TO THE ECONOMY?

Hazlitt's argument in favor of a balanced budget is straight forward: budget deficits lead to increases in the money supply and these, in turn, lead to inflation. He also argues that if a deficit exists, the appropriate procedure for the elimination of the deficit is to reduce expenditures and not to raise taxes. This follows because a budget balanced at too high a level also has negative effects on the economy. A tax discourages production and employment and the higher the tax the greater the discouragement. Taxes also distort production, increasing the output of "less necessary goods or services at the expense of more necessary goods and services." Hazlitt concludes with an attack on the concept of the "full employment budget." His position is that this concept is just an artifact to divert attention from the actual budget position of the government.

According to Tyler, the energy behind the push for a balanced budget, and a constitutional amendment is the belief that taxes are too high. He argues that this is generally not the case; taxes are too high for some because they are too low for others. He then dismisses the view that deficits cause inflation saying that the reverse is more likely to be true. As for the size of a national debt, as a percent of Gross National Product it has been decreasing over time; indeed, corporate debt, consumer debt, and even State and local government debt have all been increasing more rapidly than Federal debt. He also points out that historically, increasing debt has been associated with economic progress. There is also the question of being able to actually balance the budget if such a requirement were imposed. Tyler believes that as a practical matter such an objective would be almost impossible to achieve. Finally Tyler states that a balanced budget requirement would give persons less of a voice in government.

For a fuller discussion of the arguments for and against this issue see: "The Political Economy of Limitations on Federal Spending" by Andrew Brimmer in *Challenge* (March/April, 1980); "Restraining the Federal Budget: Alternative Policies and Strategies" by John Shannon and Bruce Wallin in *Intergovernmental Perspectives* (Spring, 1979); THE INFLATION CRISIS AND HOW TO RESOLVE IT by Henry Hazlitt (Arlington House, 1978); "Budget Cutting and Inflation" by Walter H. Heller in THE ECONOMY: OLD MYTHS AND NEW REALITIES (Norton, 1976).

ISSUE 12

IS ECONOMIC GROWTH DESIRABLE?

YES: Lester C. Thurow, from "The Implications of Zero Economic Growth."
Challenge (March/April, 1977).
NO: E.J. Mishan, from "Ills, Bads, and Disamenities: The Wages of Growth."
THE NO-GROWTH SOCIETY (Norton, 1973).

ISSUE SUMMARY

YES: Massachusetts Institute of Technology Professor Thurow argues
that economic growth is desirable because without it unemployment
would increase rapidly and inequalities between blacks and whites,
males and females, and young and old would be magnified substantially.
NO: British professor Mishan believes that continuous economic growth
is neither possible nor desirable. The size of the planet, pollution, and the
availability of resources set physical limits to growth and increased
output doesn't really improve the human condition.

Writing in 1798, Thomas Malthus projected a dismal future for mankind.
Because the food supply could only expand in an arithmetic ratio while
population tended to expand in a geometric ratio, periods of insufficient food
supply were to arise. If certain checks on population growth were not effective,
the result would be famine: " . . .gigantic, inevitable famine stalks in the rear,
and with one mighty blow, level the population with the food supply." This
ESSAY ON POPULATION was written to answer the more prevalent view of
the time, expressed by Goodwin, and others, that the condition of the human
race would continuously improve.

Although phrased in somewhat different terms, the same debate continues
today. An important book in the current controversy is *LIMITS TO GROWTH*
which reports on the analysis of the future conducted by a research group at
the Massachusetts Institute of Technology. This study, sponsored by a group
called the Club of Rome, takes into consideration population, industrialization, pollution, food production, and resource depletion in a complex,
dynamic computer model. The resulting forecast is as gloomy as the one
projected by Malthus: given present trends the limits to growth will be reached
within a century and "The most probable result will be a rather sudden and

uncontrollable decline in both population and industrial capacity." While this analysis did not create the no-growth philosophy, it did attract new believers and provided the whole no-growth movement with ammunition for the defense of their position.

In his attack on growth, Mishan makes reference to some of the same elements that are used in the LIMITS TO GROWTH analysis, especially in his discussion of the physical limits to the expansion of industrial activity. But while LIMITS TO GROWTH advocates a no-growth strategy as a means of avoiding global collapse, Mishan raises an additional consideration. He maintains that amassing ever increasing amounts of goods and services doesn't necessarily "add much to people's happiness"; indeed, it might even lead to a decrease in that happiness.

A full understanding and appreciation of the growth issue requires clarity on the definition of economic growth. One definition of economic growth stresses the behavior of total output. This is the definition employed by Thurow: zero economic growth means constant real Gross National Product. Another definition also concentrates on the availability of goods and services: real Gross National Product per capita or, as Mishan phrases it, real per capita income. In this instance growth occurs when production increases more rapidly than population. A third definition of economic growth involves a broader perspective than just the production of goods and services or the relationship between total output and population. This broader measure includes references to considerations such as health status, pollution, education, and even the amount of work effort expended in current productive activity.

Is the growth issue a conservative versus liberal debate? To some extent it is, with conservative, free market economists declaring that if basic and freely operating forces are moving the economy, then nothing should be done to restrict growth. Liberals, given their willingness to use government mechanisms to achieve an improved social order, typically support actions to limit pollution, to conserve scarce resources, and even to control population. However, it is important to note that many conservatives support these same goals. Thus, the distinction is really in terms of the means to achieve these ends; conservatives relying on the price mechanism and liberals relying on government controls. For example, conservation of scarce resources will occur automatically, according to conservatives, as depletion of available supplies drives up prices. Liberals have less faith in the efficiency of the price mechanism and, therefore, are more willing to use government action. Institutionalists-structuralists cannot really be identified as either for or against growth. Their position is that given current problems, new institutions must be developed to successfully achieve growth or to restrict growth. Radical reformists would argue that growth, at least in the way it occurs in capitalist economies, does more harm than good. Moreover, the negative aspects of capitalist growth cannot be remedied by cosmetic changes but only by a change in the ownership of the means of production.

YES

LESTER C. THUROW

THE IMPLICATIONS OF ZERO ECONOMIC GROWTH

No one questions that there are limits to economic growth. These can be seen either in actual economic histories or from the perspective of economic analysis. In the past thirty years the real per capita GNP has grown by only 1.8 percent per year in the United States. While our ability to manage aggregate demand has some impact on the per capita GNP in the short run, in the long run the limits to economic growth are set by the rate of increase of productivity. How fast is our ability to produce the same output with fewer hours of labor rising? How fast is our ability to economize on the use of nonrenewable resources increasing? How fast is our ability to produce goods and services without pollution improving? In each case there is a limit given by the rate of growth of productivity. As a consequence, the question is not one of limits—they already exist—but whether we should deliberately set limits to growth which are below those now set by the rate of growth of productivity.

The easiest way to do this is to analyze the consequences of zero economic growth (ZEG). We may not wish to impose limits this severe, but the consequences of any movement from where we are now toward ZEG will be qualitatively similar to the effects of ZEG itself. An analysis of the consequences that flow from ZEG can improve our ability to determine whether ZEG is desirable and what institutional changes would be necessary to make ZEG a feasible policy option. As I hope to demonstrate, the consequences of ZEG are so severe in the current institutional environment that any serious ZEG proposal must include substantial changes in the way in which the economy is operated.

What are the consequences of low or zero economic growth? To answer this question it is necessary to specify the institutional environment within which ZEG is to be accomplished. Are we talking about traditional primitive economies, advanced market economies, or planned communist economies? What economic policies coexist with ZEG? Do we transfer resources to those

From, "The Implications of Zero Economic Growth". *Challenge*. March/April. 1977. Copyright ©1977. Reprinted by permission of M.E. Sharpe, Inc., White Plains. N.Y. 10603.

who become unemployed or do we find some system of sharing the work that is available? Are we talking about an economy that is static with no growth in productivity or are we talking about a dynamic economy where total output is fixed but where components are rapidly rising and falling? Each of these questions and many more need to be answered if the consequences of low or zero economic growth are to be investigated. The consequences are not invariant with respect to the environment in which ZEG occurs.

Since the interest in zero economic growth springs from a desire to avoid depletion of nonrenewable natural resources and to reduce pollution, I shall assume that a ZEG economy is one in which technical progress occurs and where productivity continues to rise. Gains can be made in the efficiency with which natural resources are extracted and used and new processes can be designed to reduce pollution. Industries rise and fall within a fixed total. The problems with a completely static economy are so numerous and obvious that they hardly need analysis. To freeze the economy in its current state is something that does not appeal to either the opponents or proponents of ZEG.

Distribution of Economic Resources Under Current Institutions

Fortunately or unfortunately, post-World War II American economic history is full of periods of zero or negative economic growth—1949, 1954, 1957-58, 1960-61, 1969-70, 1974-75. Since history has provided us with repeated experiments in zero economic growth, we need merely analyze these recessions to see what would happen in the current institutional environment. Given an increase in productivity of about 3 percent per year and an increase in the labor force of 2 percent per year (the 1970 to 1975 rate of increase), unemployment will of necessity rise about 5 percentage points per year. With a dramatic slowdown in the rate of growth of the labor force in the 1980s, this number would drop into the 3.5 to 4 range, but ZEG still implies a rapidly rising unemployment rate.

Table 1

1975 Unemployment Rates

All workers	8.5%
Both sexes 16-19	19.9%
Men 20 and over	6.7%
Women 20 and over	8.0%
White	7.8%
Black	13.9%

Source: Council of Economic Advisers, Economic Report of the President, 1976; Government Printing Office, Washington, D.C., p. 199.

Since the structure of unemployment remains fairly constant, the pattern of unemployment can be seen by simply increasing the rates that now exist (see Table 1). In approximately two years the rates of unemployment listed in Table 1 would double. Over time the proportion of the unemployed who continued to be out of work for long periods of time (15 weeks or more) would gradually rise. As unemployment got higher and higher, the standards of employability would automatically rise and the number of "unemployables" would increase.

ZEG would also have an impact on the distribution of income. As our economic system now works, the inequality in the distribution of income would increase quite rapidly. There are many ways to

225

measure changes in the distribution of income, but one simple technique is to look at the gap between families who are at the 25th percentile of the population and those who are at the 75th percentile of the population. With ZEG this inter-quartile range rises by about 0.2 percent per year for whites and 2.3 percent per year for blacks. Since unemployment and reduced employment opportunities strike blacks harder than whites, inequality in black income distribution increases at a faster rate than that for whites. Moreover, black family incomes fall relative to those of whites by about 6.5 percent per year.

Since the models that generate these results are derived from analysis of short-run periods of ZEG I would not argue that you can multiply these numbers by one hundred to estimate what conditions would be like one hundred years from now, but they do indicate the direction and magnitudes of the initial changes that could be expected when the economy reached ZEG.

The male-female job problem would also be intensified in a society with zero economic growth. In 1975, female labor force participation rates were still 32 percentage points (78.5 versus 46.4) below that of males. For women to achieve parity with men, the labor force must grow by about 27 percent even if the population stops growing. In a ZEG world, there is no way to employ more women without more men becoming unemployed. Which men are to be thrown out of work? While there is ample evidence in rising participation rates that more and more women wish to work at paid jobs, male participation rates give no indication that men wish to be "liberated" from the world of paid work. There is a slight decline in male participation rates

due to earlier retirements and more extended periods of education, but the voluntary declines are not large enough to make room for women and are non-existent among males in the prime age group of 24 to 54.

The income split between old and young depends upon two quite different rationing mechanisms. Because of seniority provisions, older workers are less likely to be laid off in recessions. Once laid off, however, older workers find it difficult to find new employment. While the seniority pattern predominates, leading to a rising income gap between old and young, there is a group of older workers who are severely handicapped during periods of zero economic growth.

There is also a question of income opportunities for the young. These opportunities currently consist of two possibilities: (1) waiting for someone to retire or die; or (2) taking advantage of economic growth and the generation of new, as yet unfilled, opportunities. With zero economic growth, the first possibility is the only one. I do not pretend to be a psychologist who could testify as to what effect this reduction in opportunities would have on the psyches of the young, but there is no question that promotions are much less available in a ZEG world than in a world that permits economic growth.

Some new opportunities for young people would arise from the normal rise and fall of individual industries, but this exists now and thus would not be a source of new jobs for the young. With both an older population and the allocation of a larger fraction of total income to older workers, consumption patterns would be more rigid and opportunities for dramatic shifts in consumption would be more limited. This effect, coupled with the absence of new purchasing power, would probably lead to a much slower rise and fall of individual industries than now occurs.

If ZEG is not to imply a falling real standard of living, it must include the achievement of zero population growth (ZPG). If population growth continues at slightly less than one percent per year (the 1970 to 1975 rate), then the per capita GNP must fall by one percent per year. While the fertility rate has fallen to or below the level necessary to stabilize the population in the 21st century, the rate would have to fall from the long-term ZPG figure of 2.1 children per family to a short-run ZPG rate of 1.2 children per family if the population were to be stabilized at its current level. Unless this were done, ZEG could not be implemented until early in the 21st century without forcing real reductions in per capita standards of living.

While the negative aspects of ZEG are substantial, there is a positive side. With zero population growth, it is possible to reduce the investments that we now make in educating the young (there are fewer of them) and in equipping the young with the average amount of capital (private and social). In a short-run ZPG world—1.2 children per family—these savings would free enough funds to raise our real per capita living standards by about 11 percent. On the other hand, there would be some costs. If we shared work more than we do now, there would be extra on-the-job training costs. If everyone retired at 45, for example, you would need to train more people in any given period of time. On-the-job training costs are difficult to measure, but they would certainly eat up some substantial fraction of the resources which were freed

in formal education and physical investment.

Distribution of Producer's Welfare

If income were the only benefit flowing from work and work were really a negative good-generating disutility (meaning that earnings are a necessary bribe to get individuals to suffer the discomforts of work) the problems created by zero economic growth would be easily solved. Some system of transfer payments could be devised that would (1) sustain the incomes of those who became unemployed and (2) encourage those who do work to work less and share the work more. Given the hypothesis of disutility, everyone would, after all, like to quit his or her job if some alternative income support plan could be found.

The basic job rationing problem springs from the fact that jobs are more than a source of money incomes. There are a whole host of consumption benefits that flow from jobs that have little to do with money income. These nonpecuniary benefits include friends, status, feelings of accomplishment, fame, and power. Some jobs in our economy would be worth fighting over even if they generated no income. These benefits all come under the framework of producer's welfare. To whom is producer's welfare to be allocated? This question exists in every society, but a society with zero economic growth would make it more intense, since it would not be possible to generate new economic avenues to status, fame, fortune, and power. To achieve any of these goals someone else would have to be displaced.

This brings us to the question of whether a ZEG society would be more or less competitive. Unfortunately, this seems to be a question to which there is little chance of any firm economic answer. Imagine a world where a larger proportion of the citizens are elderly and have relatively fixed consumption patterns, where incomes do not rise, where most of us are customers of existing firms, and, given habit formation, we do not buy as many new things. With few opportunities for advancement, both the economy and interpersonal relationships might become much less competitive.

But it is also possible for the same factors to lead to a ruthlessly competitive environment where we are at each other's throats. Given a fixed pie, we fight over its division. Where some of our energies used to be devoted to enlarging the economic pie, all of our energies are now devoted to dividing the pie. If you look at other areas of life, zero-sum games are hardly marked by an absence of the competitive instinct. All sports are zero-sum games. In every game there is one winner and one loser. Yet sports are marked by an intense competitive spirit. In the current economy, I can win without forcing you to lose. It is not a zero-sum game. If it were, we might become more competitive, not less so.

Evading the Issue

Often the advocates of zero economic growth respond to the economic problems that have been outlined by arguing that such a system would not mean zero economic growth overall, but only in sectors that use nonrenewable economic resources or in sectors that pollute. Restraints would be placed on the growth of goods, but not of services. Therefore the job rationing problem could be avoided by expanding job opportunities in the service sector to offset those lost in the goods sector.

The service sector has certainly grown since World War II, but it is important to understand that government statistics on the service sector include everything that is not mining, manufacturing, or farming. The word "services" conjures up visions of human, person-to-person contacts, but these types of services have in fact been declining since World War II. Much of the service sector consists simply of those services that are necessary to produce, distribute, and use goods. Electrical power production, wholesale and retail trade, and repair services are simply ingredients necessary to service the "goods" economy. Without an increase in the supply of goods, these services will stop growing. The other main area of growth in the service sector has been education and health. Both of these activities are large in scale and involve substantial capital investments. Large quantities of goods are consumed in the process of producing educational or health services. If we look at other service industries such as utilities or transportation, the consumption of nonrenewable resources and the production of pollution are immediately evident.

The basic problem is a failure to make a distinction between the direct and indirect impacts of any economic activity. Universities may generate little direct pollution but if one looks at the products that they consume, there is much indirect pollution. Take education. What is the largest private consumer of electricity in the Boston area? The Massachusetts Institute of Technology. What is the second largest consumer of electricity? The affiliated hospitals of Harvard. Hospitals gobble up hard and soft goods at a prodigious rate. When indirect activities are considered, it is not at all obvious that we can have lots of health care and lots of education without pollution or without the use of nonrenewable resources.

Many of those who think that they live and work in a clean environment and that they conserve natural resources may find that when indirect demands are included, they are some of the world's great polluters and consumers of natural resources. The answer will only be known when input-output tables have been modified to allow for resource-using and pollution-producing columns. Only then will we be able to show the indirect as well as the direct effects of different types of economic activities. While there may prove to be a limited number of areas in which the economy could grow without using resources or generating pollution, these are apt to be very limited in number and most assuredly do not include most of what is officially classified as services.

As a result there is no way to evade the problems outlined in the previous sections. If ZEG is to be achieved without adverse effects, some radical changes must be made in the manner in which the economy works and in its institutions.

Influence of Other Countries

The attainment of zero economic growth implies an ability either to satiate or to control individual wants for more goods and services. From analysis of the process of want creation, we know that wants are to a great extent a matter of relative position. People who have the most goods and services are apt to be satisfied with their economic position regardless of the absolute amount of goods and services they have. People with the least goods and services are apt

to be dissatisfied with their economic position regardless of the absolute amount of goods and services that they have.

Today's underdeveloped countries are not underdeveloped relative to their past or relative to living standards in Europe and the United States 100 years ago. They are underdeveloped relative to the living standards currently enjoyed in Europe, Japan, and the United States. Having low relative standards of living, they object to the current performances of their economies and demand change. Let it be remembered that today's underdeveloped countries are those that have come closest to achieving the goal of ZEG. Let it also be remembered, however, that ZEG has not solved their social problems or made them content with their economic position.

Since human nature seems to be much the same everywhere, this lack of contentment should be taken seriously by anyone proposing a policy of zero economic growth in the United States while the rest of the world continues to grow. Such a policy would eventually turn the United States into an underdeveloped country and bring the same demands for economic changes that now exist in today's underdeveloped countries. While it is logically possible to imagine the construction of a culture that could sustain satiated wants in the face of noticeably higher standards of living in the rest of the world, there is no such culture now in existence. The demand for rising real standards of living is virtually universal. The only exceptions are the person or the society at the top of the economic heap.

When ZEG is spoken of in relation to other countries, a fallacious "impossibility" argument is often advanced. The argument starts with a question. How many tons of this or that nonrenewable natural resource would be needed if everyone in the world now had the consumption standards enjoyed by those in the United States? The answer is designed to be a mind-boggling number in comparison with the current supplies of such resources. Both the question and the answer assume that the rest of the world is going to achieve the consumption standards of the average American without at the same time achieving the productivity standards of the average American. This is, of course, algebraically impossible. The world can only consume what it can produce. When the rest of the world has consumption standards equal to those of the United States, it will be producing at the same rate and providing as much of an increment to the worldwide supplies of goods and services as it does to the demands for them.

As I mentioned at the beginning, productivity, here and abroad, sets a limit to growth, but as yet it has not set the limit at zero. The limit will be zero only when productivity ceases to grow anywhere.

Preventing an Increase in Inequality

Since zero economic growth implies rapidly rising inequalities both among and within groups under the current institutional arrangements, what changes in institutions would be necessary to prevent an increase of inequality in the distribution of income and wealth? The basic problem is one of rationing work and keeping standards of employability from rising to exclude most of those at the bottom of the distribution of work characteristics.

The work rationing system in turn depends upon the nature of the income transfer system. The basic problem with

transfer payment systems is that they can be easily used to establish minimum floors to consumption or to achieve complete equality, but they are very difficult to design so as to provide the same distribution of income as that which now exists. One can imagine lottery-like transfer payment systems where unequal incomes (transfer payments) were allocated to different families, but it is difficult to imagine that such systems could politically come into existence. Thus it is likely that transfer payment systems will continue to be used primarily to establish consumption floors and not to determine the distribution of income above some minimum level. This means that to some substantial extent, differences in family incomes are still going to be determined by work and earnings. As a result, the work rationing system is going to become the prime vehicle for assigning different positions to different families in the distribution of income. People are going to be rich or poor depending upon exactly how work is allocated.

Table 2

Hours of Work Per Week in 1975

Hours	% of those employed
1-4	1.0
5-14	4.8
15-29	11.7
30-34	7.0
35-39	7.3
40	42.3
41-48	10.2
49-59	8.5
60 and over	7.2

Source: U.S. Bureau of Labor Statistics, *Employment and Earnings,* Jan. 1976, p. 149.

The basic problems of a work rationing system are identical to those of any other rationing system. What is a fair distribution of work and how can the rules producing this distribution be enforced? As the data in Table 2 indicate, the U.S. work force is marked by a wide variance in the numbers of hours worked by different members of the labor force. Almost 6 percent of those employed work less than 15 hours per week. At the other extreme, slightly over 7 percent of those employed work over 60 hours per week. If one were simply to limit the total number of hours that anyone can work, only a small fraction of the work force would find themselves with lower earnings until the limit moved below 40 hours per week. This, however, would put the entire earnings burden of ZEG on those who now work the most. Their income would gradually fall relative to that of those who now work the least. Over time the distribution of earnings would gradually become more nearly equal as hours of work became more and more nearly equal. Absolute limits could also encourage a rapid increase in the number of secondary family workers, with a consequent need to reduce the maximum hours of work even more than was originally indicated.

Another option is to cut everyone's hours of work proportionally. This has the questionable advantage of preserving the current distribution of earnings, but proportional cutbacks are impossible to administer in anything other than very short-run periods of time. Given a very rapid turnover in the labor force, workers would quickly start exaggerating the number of hours of work they were seeking in order to be assigned the number of hours of work that they actually wanted. The history of actual work patterns would rapidly fade out of existence. As a result, proportional cutbacks are not an administratively workable option over any extended period of time.

As a consequence, an absolute across-the-board limit on hours of work would seem to be the only long-run option. To prevent the induced increase in part-time workers, the limit would have to be set in terms of hours of work per lifetime rather than per week or per year. This would prevent families from evading the rationing system by increasing their numbers of workers in the paid labor force. Teenagers would not work to supplement their parents' income because to do so would reduce their own adult earning capacity.

The economic costs of absolute limits on hours of work depend upon one's estimates of the relative importance of talent versus the willingness to sacrifice hours of time. As long as we are simply talking about hours of time, there is not economic loss (other than extra training costs) when one person's time is substituted for another's. To the extent that scarce talent is involved, however, society is deliberately cutting itself off from the consumption of a unique resource. The more special the talent, the greater the cost.

The major enforcement problem would occur in the area of paid hours versus actual hours. There would be a strong incentive from both employees and employers to devote substantial amounts of time to unpaid "preparation for work" and then to pay very high rates for a few hours of actual paid time. This would allow employees to avoid restrictions on hours of work and enable employers to avoid the training costs of having more employees. As a result, there is no doubt that there would be severe enforcement problems.

As mentioned, any absolute limit on hours of work will lead over time to a more nearly equal distribution of earnings than the one now in existence. ZEG and a more nearly equal distribution of earnings are to some extent complementary products. You cannot have the first without the second.

Since capital accumulation is allowed in the dynamic version of ZEG, inequality might increase in the entire distribution of income (earnings plus income from physical wealth) at the same time as equality increased in the distribution of earnings. If capital income rises relative to earned income, the inequality in distribution of income will grow. Those whose income now comes primarily from capital are at the top of the current income distribution and their share of total income would increase. The only way to prevent this would be to place limits on the total amount of capital accumulation that any family can undertake. The problems, however, would be similar to those of work rationing.

Weaknesses of ZEG

In the dynamic version of zero economic growth, where advances in productivity are permitted, ZEG automatically leads to less use of nonrenewable natural resources, but it does not automatically lead to less pollution. Pollution occurs because pollution is a privately costless but socially costly method of disposing of unwanted by-products. In essence, you dump your garbage on your neighbors since this is the cheapest form of garbage disposal. But since your neighbors are also doing the same thing, everyone ends up with garbage in his or her environment. Simply stopping economic growth does nothing to change this perverse incentive system. Our recessions illustrate the point. Pollution does not decrease when the U.S. economy stops growing. Pollution can only be prevented, in either a ZEG or a growth environment, by altering the relative costs of different forms of garbage disposal. Thus those interested in less pollution should focus on changing the incentive system rather than on ZEG. ZEG by itself simply will not lead to what they want.

While nonrenewable natural resources certainly present a limit to economic growth, the limit is not zero, but is given by the rate of increase in our efficiency in extracting and using nonrenewable natural resources. There is undoubtedly a finite number of tons of copper embedded in the earth, but the economic supply of copper is continually growing as we learn to use copper more efficiently and as we learn to extract copper economically from lower and lower grade ores. Thus ZEG implies an interest in setting a limit to growth below the limit set by the economic availability of nonrenewable natural resources. The reasons for wanting to do this are certainly not axiomatic, to say the least.

If ZEG were simply to be achieved in our current institutional environment, there would be rapid increases in inequality as more and more people were forced into unemployment and "unemployability." Inequality would increase on most of the major dimensions that now exist—family incomes, male-female, white-black, young-old, etc. The effects would be similar to those of a recession that gradually got worse and worse. Output would be fixed but increases in productivity would lead to the need for less and less labor, while more and more people were coming into the labor market as the result of population growth.

If rising inequalities were to be prevented, some form of work rationing would have to be instituted. To be administratively practicable, work rationing would have to take the form of an increasingly severe limit on lifetime work. This would lead to a more nearly equal distribution of earnings, but increasing capital incomes might lead to a more and more unequal distribution of total income. If this were to occur, controls on savings as well as work would be necessary to prevent rising inequalities.

A ZEG economy would necessitate a substantial increase in economic controls. The problem of work rationing is severe as long as work continues to be a major source of incomes. Individuals want to increase their own incomes by working more, but government must prevent them from doing so if ZEG is to be achieved. As a result, there is a direct clash between private incentives (the desire to raise one's own standard of living) and the social objective (ZEG). Whenever private incentives and social objectives clash, rationing systems are apt to be difficult to enforce. This conflict could be eliminated if there were some technique for eliminating individual wants for more goods and services. This technique is as yet, however, unknown.

● ● ●

NO

E.J. Mishan

ILLS, BADS, AND DISAMENITIES: THE WAGES OF GROWTH

Do People Have What They Want?

"I believe simply in giving people what they want." This expression of democratic largesse has come from a business tycoon and, I regret to say, from a well-known economist as well. The idea has, of course, a superficial appeal, so it is as well to point out at the start that people can have "what they want" only in a limited sense, before going on to consider the problems involved in the attempt to give them more of "what they want" in years to come.

If I want to be as strong as Hercules, as wise as Solomon, as talented as Michaelangelo, I shall want in vain. One need not be so innocently ambitious, however, to experience frustrations. A great many people ardently wish that they were taller, handsomer, and more gifted than nature ever intended them to become. And there may be moments in their lives when all the tea in China—assuming it could be sold at a reasonable price—would not compensate for their unfulfillment. Clearly, then, people get what they want, even in a liberal democracy, only in the narrow sense that policies are enacted by the party voted into power, and that the flow of market goods is adapted over time to the changing pattern of demand.

Confined as is the area of choice for society, it is yet further restricted for the individual. As far as government policies are concerned, he has to accept much that goes against the grain of his political convictions. As for the market, it may be that he wants all he buys, but he certainly does not buy all he wants. He has to accept as unalterable data, at least in the short run, the physical features of the environment in which he lives. The law permits him to go wherever he pleases, provided he does not trespass on private property, and to buy whatever he pleases, subject, however, to the constraints of his income, the time at his disposal, and the range of goods available at market prices. Again, he can choose any job he wants, provided he is qualified to hold it, and provided it is offered to him. . . .

We may conclude that, whatever the general level of consumption, a person

From, "Ills, Bads and Disamenities", THE NO GROWTH SOCIETY, edited by Mancur Olson and Hans H. Landsberg. Reprinted with the permission of the publisher, W.W. Norton & Co., Inc. Copyright ©1973 by the American Academy of Arts and Sciences.

obtains "what he wants"—or rather "what he chooses" (which is not the same thing)—only in a limited sense, and that his choices among the man-made goods on the market alter with changes in prices, taxes, advertising, and availabilities.

Having placed in a more sober light these much-touted privileges conferred by political democracy and the competitive private enterprise system on the citizen of a "free society," we may reconsider the urgency and perhaps question the wisdom of attempting to maintain the present pace of economic growth into the indefinite future. Two related questions are raised here. First, is sustained economic growth physically possible? Second, is it desirable for the West? . . .

Whether Continued Economic Growth Is Physically Possible

Alas, we have no methods as yet by which we can produce convincing answers to such questions. Indeed, it is entirely possible that we shall be unable, even in the future, to ascertain the physical limits to economic growth until we experience some manifest deterioration of living standards or incur some ecological catastrophe. The best we can do today is to infer tentatively, from highly simplified global models using controversial assumptions about future technological progress and about world reserves of materials, that growth at present rates, either of population or of industrial output, cannot continue for much more than a century.

Whether or not they believe these conclusions realistic, all the people debating this issue recognize that we inhabit all too tiny a planet. Most of them are alarmed at current population trends; the prospect of some fifteen billion human beings swarming over the planet in fifty or sixty years' time is not an inviting one. With the existing population of about four billion souls, we are already getting in each other's way and stepping on each other's toes. Assuming the mobility indices continue to rise—car ownership in Western Europe increasing at about 8 percent per annum, air travel at about 10 percent—the mounting frustrations of travelers and the resentments of indigenous populations may break out in civil disturbances.

Apart from population growth, though aggravated by it, there are the familiar problems of pollution, food supplies, and the depletion of natural resources. Although there have been some local improvements over the last quarter of a century—there is, for example, less sulphur dioxide (though much more carbon dioxide) in the air of London than there was twenty years ago, and some (possibly mutant) species of fish have recently been discovered in the murky waters of the Thames—nobody seriously challenges the fact that air and water pollution exist on a larger scale today than ever before in man's history. The global scale of pollution not only destroys flora and fauna but spoils the food we eat. Chemical pesticides enter our bloodstream either directly through our consumption of chemically sprayed plants or indirectly through our consumption of cattle that ingest them. The poisoning of rivers destroys fish in estuaries and renders the flesh of the survivors increasingly toxic to humans.

Turning to material resources, in particular fossil fuels and metals, a common estimate is that, if present consumption trends persist, we shall run out of oil by about the end of the century even allowing for the discovery of new reserves, and

235

of all but a few of today's "essential" metals within about fifty years. Indeed, at current rates of usage, all known reserves of silver, gold, copper, lead, platinum, tin, and zinc will have been used up within a couple of decades.

The conventional economic response to the threat of depleting resources is twofold: to quote history in illustration of the principle of resource substitution and to affirm faith in the future of technology and "the wit of man." Concerning the first, economists will point out that the shortage of a resource leads to a rise in its price which induces manufacturers to replace it by other materials that, though less suitable, are now less expensive. The less successful the search for suitable substitutes, however, the higher the resulting costs of the finished goods in question, and the smaller the amounts bought by consumers. . . .

Two Reasons for Skepticism about Technology

Over the future of technology a great question mark hangs, and for much the same reason. Two hundred years of scientific discovery and innovation have imbued us with a faith that man will eventually conquer. Thus, whenever some of the less happy consequences of modern technology and its products are brought to our attention—140,000 automobile deaths a year, the ecological disasters of DDT, the genetic effects of Thalidomide—or whenever account is taken of the increasing risks to which humanity is now exposed, the habitual response of technocrats is to transmute the risk into a "challenge" or to quote some historical piece of "doomsdayism." Yet if, as philosophers are agreed, there are no laws of historical development, the

proposition must be extended also to the development of science and technology. We cannot be sure of technological progress either. Man may, then, become engaged endlessly in some kinds of research that, in the nature of things, cannot come to fruition.

Apart from these real possibilities, there are at least two reasons for feeling less than sanguine about the future of technology. First, the unprecedented scale of the current exploitation of the earth's finite resources makes virtually a qualitative difference between the situation today and that of yesterday. For this reason alone, deriding yesterday's Jeremiahs affords little consolation. Time works vast changes, and the alarums of today should not go unheeded simply because those of yesterday were premature. The apprehensions of an octogenarian about his impending demise are not to be soothed by reminding him that he thought he was going to die when he was twenty. . . .

The second reason for feeling less than sanguine about the contribution of technology in maintaining the existing growth rates is that we are moving into an area of increasing uncertainty. In order of diminishing tractability we can list four types of global risk, none of which existed before the industrial revolution.

(1) Insofar as the chief effluents poured into the air, lakes, rivers, and coastal waters are known and their toxic effects understood, they can be effectively curbed in a number of ways, of which enforcing minimal standards of purity may well be the most economic. The success of this method depends upon the efficacy and frequency of monitoring, and on the severity of the penalties exacted for failing to comply. What economists do not sufficiently allow

for, however, are the limits to our present knowledge. There cannot be many effluents whose full range of toxic effects are known to us. Moreover, in consequence of rapid chemical innovation, new gases and fluids are being produced whose effects on the ambient environment and on our health may not be discernible for many years, and possibly only after substantial and irreversible damage has been done.

(2) To these risks that we run from pushing on in a state of semi-ignorance, we may add (a) those arising from the indiscriminate use of chemical pesticides such as DDT, from the gradual dissipation of the protective ozone mantle by the gases emitted in supersonic flight, and from the accumulating deposits of synthetic material that resist absorption into the ecological cycle, and (b) those arising out of the growing assortment of chemical compounds appearing each year on the market, about whose ultimate biological and genetical effects, taken singly or in combination, we know next to nothing. Nor can we reasonably expect to detect the dangers in time. . . .

(3) The third category of risk arises from our diminishing immunity to contagious diseases—a consequence, ironically, of the apparent success of modern medicine. Just as many insect pests have, over the last three decades, successfully adapted themselves to withstand, or even to thrive on, once powerful pesticides, so too, are micro-organisms, with their faster rate of reproduction, and therefore of mutation, becoming resistant to the action of penicillin, antibiotics, etc. . . .

(4) The fourth and the greatest immediate risk in the foreseeable future is that humanity will perish as a result of the great scientific discoveries of the last thirty years inasmuch as they have presented man with the means of illimitable thermonuclear destruction and biochemical warfare. . . .

The Desirability of Continued Economic Growth

Let us now turn to the second large question, whether further economic growth is socially desirable or, for that matter, whether the current pattern of overall expenditure is socially desirable. . . .

Assuming that per capita growth could be maintained indefinitely at the current rate, the question of its social desirability is still a bit vague and lends itself to a number of interpretations. We might, for example, be asking the question: Are we getting our money's worth from the rising tide of affluence, or is the overall pattern of expenditure socially desirable? The answer is surely no. Even the most conservative economist would agree that a little political initiative would rid us of a lot of unnecessary ill effects. Eighteenth-century believers in progress would be astounded at our technological capabilities, and they would be dismayed at what we have done with them. How could we justify the sheer ugliness and abandon of our cities; their endless clamor, litter, stench, tawdriness and desolation? Let us concede that we could have used our enormous wealth to create more sensible ways of living, and pass on to other possible interpretations of the question.

We might want to compare the quality or wholesomeness of life today with that of bygone ages. And growthmen are ever quick to make such comparisons. Yet the comparisons they make are unfair in several ways. First, they use what little history they know to select the bleaker

237

periods of the past: "the dark satanic mills" and other grim features of the earlier part of the industrial revolution being a much favored point of reference, or the ancient slave economies of the East, or the imaginary life of an early caveman: "nasty, brutish, and short."

Secondly, they accent those aspects of life which, just because of rising affluence and indiscriminate consumerism, absorb our attention—hygiene, longevity, youthfulness, mobility, instant entertainment, self-indulgence, effort-avoidance. Inadvertently, they omit to stress the features that were common to all pre-industrial ages, the (by our standards) inordinate number of holidays and holy days, the lack of clear distinction between work and living, and a vaster sense of time and space owing to slow travel, slow news, and few timepieces. Again, they tend to overlook the great myths that gave hope of life beyond the grave, a more settled way of life, a greater joy in nature, and easy access to the countryside—to clean air, to lakes, rivers, quiet fields, and woodlands.*

Thirdly, in comparing the quality of life at different periods of history, the notion of some average sort of life has to be abandoned. In all ages, including our

own, there are rich and poor, fortunate and unfortunate, and the proportions vary from place to place and from one age to another. A historian may be able to pick out certain periods over the last 5,000 years when for certain groups in particular parts of the world life appears to have been good and wholesome while for a fair proportion of the remainder, it was not burdensome.* Such comparisons are to some extent subjective and inconclusive, though there is more agreement among historians on some periods and places than on others. I doubt, however, whether many historians would agree to use GNP as a historical yardstick of well-being, and to conclude, on the basis of it, that life today is transparently happier than it has ever been before.

Finally, we might more reasonably be asking if life is becoming more enjoyable or if we are becoming better or more contented people in consequence of economic growth. Bearing in mind the facts of human nature, we could reflect on current economic and social developments in particular areas and endeavor to obtain clues about the extent to which the modes of living they give rise to accord with, or conflict with, men's biological and psychic needs. And by speculating about technological and economic developments over the foreseeable future, we can debate whether, on balance, we are likely to be better people, or more contented people, over the next few decades. This seems to me the more promising area of inquiry, and the one to which I suggest we direct our attention.

Obviously we cannot *prove* propositions about the decline in social welfare as

---

*In pre-industrial civilizations, according to Jacques Ellul, the time given to the use of techniques was short compared with the leisure time devoted to sleep, conversation, games, and meditation.

For primitive man and historical man, work as such was *not* a virtue. It was considered better not to consume than to work hard. Thus man worked as little as possible and was content with restricted consumption.

Today comfort means easy chairs, foam rubber mattresses, bathrooms, air-conditioning, washing machines, etc. Our chief concern is to avoid physical effort, and therefore we become more dependent upon the machine.

According to Giedion (quoted by Ellul) men of the Middle Ages were also concerned with comfort. But for them comfort represented a moral and aesthetic order. Space was the primary element. Men sought open spaces and large rooms. They did not care if the chairs were hard or the rooms ill-heated. What mattered was proportion and the materials used.

---

*For the recent history of England, I should be inclined to pick out the time of Chaucer, the Elizabethan age, the mid-eighteenth century, possibly the Edwardian age.

one can prove, for example, that a significant rise in the price of beef, *ceteris
paribus,* will cause a drop in the maximum amount of beef that people are
willing to buy. In debating social welfare,
subjective judgments are required—
judgments of fact, and possibly also
judgments of value.

Let us move now toward the hub of the
problem by asking an apparently naive
question: Why cannot a rise in GNP, or
rather in real per capita income, be
accepted as an index of an increase in
society's welfare? The theoretical economist's short answer is that the sufficient
conditions that would allow a translation
from GNP to social welfare are not met.

First, the identical population would
have to remain in being during a period
over which GNP rises. If the period
extends to two generations, and each
person in the second generation has
more goods than some corresponding
person in the first, the economist can only
report that fact. Since he eschews interpersonal comparisons, he is unable to
declare that persons in the second
generation experience more welfare than
those in the first. Secondly, and for the
same reason, the economist cannot state
that a person whose real income has
grown over time is better off unless it is
also known that his tastes and his capacity
for enjoyment have remained unchanged. . . .

In order to translate from increments of
GNP to increments of welfare there is
another condition that has to be met:
namely, that all changes in benefits and
"disbenefits" arising from economic activity be properly priced. People would
then be able to choose the amounts of
benefits they would pay for and the
amounts of the "disbenefits" they would
be paid to endure. But this crucial condi-

tion is not met in the dynamic economic
systems of the West for two reasons. One,
because the pattern of produced outputs
and the methods of production are continually being altered in response *not* to
the wants of the workers but, instead, to
changes in consumers' demand and in
technology. Two, because the operation
of many consumer goods and the processes by which they are produced
generate a range of injurious effects that
escape the pricing system and spill over
into the population at large. Some of
these spillover effects are evident to
everybody, being quite visible, audible, or
otherwise obtrusive. Some are directly
attributable to the output or use of particular goods. Others, however, are more
complex and intangible, and are virtually
impossible to attribute to any particular
good. . . .

Some Objections of Growthmen

Let me pause in passing to consider
some misunderstandings of the environmental issue. Of late, it has been asserted
that the new surge of concern about the
environment is no more than a cover
under which the middle classes are trying
to hang onto their privileges, that it has
nothing to offer to the working classes or
the poor. Strangely enough, the same
person may also be found arguing that in
order to make *desirable* environmental
improvements it is necessary to maintain
and, if possible, to increase the rate of
economic growth.*

*In this connection. Beckerman and Crosland are not
alone in objecting to my proposal to make inaccessible to
the automobile and airplane a number of beauty spots all
over the world on the grounds that the rich would be better
placed to enjoy them than the working man. But if the rich
did benefit more by the scheme (which need not be so), why
turn a blind eye to the other privileges enjoyed by the rich?
By definition. the rich form an economic elite. They already

IS ECONOMIC GROWTH DESIRABLE?

One can indeed think up environmental improvements that would benefit largely higher income groups, but for the most part these are undertaken by such groups at their own expense and initiative. Insofar as the improvements entail cleaner air, quiet, and purer water, there is no reason to suppose that the schemes proposed do not extend such benefits also to the poorer members of society. In fact it is plausible to believe that the poorer citizens benefit more than the richer ones who can always move with far less inconvenience than the poor from any district that is sinking in the scale of amenity. If, on the other hand, the revenues raised for environmental benefits happen to involve a greater proportional reduction of the income or purchasing power of the poor than of the rich there need be no difficulty in altering the tax structure in order to restore equity. This should present no financial difficulty inasmuch as the strict economic case for reducing pollution requires that aggregate benefits exceed costs—a condition that has to be met, incidentally, quite irrespective of the distribution of incomes.

As for the alleged need for more of this GNP stuff, as a condition for performing good works—removing the accumulated filth in the environment, reducing poverty in the cities, healing the sick, comforting the aged, educating the young—we find that the same arguments were used in the fifties; indeed, similar arguments have been used in justification of growing richer, individually or socially, as far back as Adam Smith. Since we can count on the poor always being among us—the relatively poor, that is*—we shall never lack for an excuse to push onward with GNP.

The obvious weakness of this line of defense is simply that we would not need to grow in order to do good works if we were just a little less reluctant than we happen to be to share what we have more equally with the less fortunate in the community. Had we stronger moral principles, or more patriotic virtue, neither of which, however, find much encouragement in the ethos of an affluent society, the bulk of the population would recognize at once that already it had enough to spare for good works. People would recognize that forever putting off the day of reckoning by claiming the need to grow richer is as transparent an instance of self-deception as that of the miser who claims the need to hoard more so as eventually to give more to charity. One need bear in mind the vast current expenditures on "demerit goods"—the "expendables," "regrettables," the "inimicals" and "near-garbage" that absorb so large a proportion of our resources—to recognize the moral implications of society's political choices.

And yet the case for spending more on environmental improvement would hold even if no such "demerit" goods were produced by the modern economy, and if our moral behavior as a community were already impeccable. As I have indicated above, the economic case for such improvements presumes, indeed re-

live in grander houses, in a better environment. They eat better food, wear better clothes, enjoy personal servants, own expensive jewelery and paintings, and they travel in style to the best places while others of their countrymen remain destitute in an environment made increasingly desolate by the products of enterprises in which the rich have shares. If one is against economic privileges there is far better sport to be found outside my modest scheme. These would-be growth men do not even have the goodness to admit that the problem of "tourist blight" is primarily a problem of numbers. Given the limited space on earth, it will arise *under any distribution of income* they care to imagine.

*It is a trifle mortifying for an Englishman to record that the "poverty-level" income in the United States today somewhat exceeds average earnings in Britain.

quires, an excess of social benefit over resource cost. The case for their introduction then depends no more on the rate of economic growth than it does upon the level of aggregate income or its distribution. Whatever the rate of economic growth—positive, zero, or negative—and whatever the aggregate level of income and its distribution, if there is an economic case for reducing pollution levels or enhancing the environment, the case is for doing so now.

Finally, insofar as ecologists and environmentalists reject sustained economic growth as a desirable social goal for the West, they are reminded by economists of the difficulties that arise when the economy does not grow. In each of the short-lived periods of stagnation of the American economy, for instance, there has been an appreciable rise in the number of unemployed, a decline in the share of labor income (except perhaps during the prolonged depression of the thirties), particular hardship among the poorest section of the populace, a frustration of people's expectations, and increased conflict among the working classes. But these recessional features are not pertinent to the issue. For they are peculiar to a growth-bound economy, one in which a period of no growth or decline in growth arises from market failure and inadequate monetary and fiscal policies, and necessarily entails unemployment, stagnation and, consequently, increased frustration. Those concerned primarily with the quality of life have never proposed to create unemployment in the growth economy as a means of slowing economic growth. Rather they seek to persuade the public to abandon the pursuit of economic growth in favor of a stable or steady-state economy within

which there is explicit consideration of the factors that enhance the quality of life. The actual means whereby a steady-state economy is to be brought into being—the rationing of raw materials, the controls on technology etc.,—and the level of affluence to be sought are important subjects of discussion. But in the existing state of social awareness, they are perhaps premature. Immediate concern must be with the revolution in thought and feeling that is necessary if men's aspirations toward the good life are ever to be realized. Thus the aim of the ecologist and environmentalist is not a no-growth economy per se. It is to win *acceptance* by the public at large of a no-growth economy. Once the ethics of a no-growth economy are accepted and the competitive striving for more, ever more, is a thing of the past, it will be that much easier to remove the wretched poverty that still lingers in Western countries, to redirect expenditure away from current extravagance and waste, and to bring about a more equal distribution of income. . . .

Other Intangible Spillovers

If it is acknowledged that, once subsistence levels are passed, the sources of men's more enduring satisfactions are to be found in mutual trust and affection, in giving love and accepting it, and, in any civilized society, are augmented by the sense of wonder inspired by the unfolding of nature, by the perception of beauty inspired by great art, and by the renewal of faith and hope inspired by the heroic and the good; if this much is acknowledged, it is just not possible to believe that sustained attempts to harness the greater part of man's energies and ingenuity to the task of amassing ever larger amounts of material possessions—

fashion goods, gimmickry, motorized implements, novelties, and tasteless inanities—can add much to people's happiness.

On the other hand, it is entirely plausible to believe that the competitive pressures of the technological society, the stifling specialization that makes material progress possible, and the insatiability and discontent that are the precondition of sustained economic expansion will come to grind ever harder against the grain of men's intuitive needs. Beyond a point in technological progress, and we are already beyond it, the innate capacity of ordinary people for open and warm-hearted enjoyment of each other begins to shrink. Sublimation translates into alienation, specialization into disintegration.

Apart from these unsalutary characteristics evolved so as to maintain the pace of economic growth in already wealthy countries, much of the technological innovation associated with economic growth is such as to diminish over time the opportunities for direct and informal communication among people. Human contacts decline with the spread of labor and time-saving machines. They decline with the growth of supermarkets, cafeterias, vending machines, private cars and airplanes, with the spread of transistor radios and television sets, with computerization in offices and patient-monitoring machines in hospitals, with closed circuit television instruction and teaching machines. Sanctioned by a restricted interpretation of economic efficiency, the main thrust of consumer innovation since the turn of the century appears to have been directed toward producing for us a push-button world in which our trendy whims are to be instantly gratified while our psychic needs are increasingly thwarted. The vision of such a world—a universe humming with recorded instructions and electronic devices that will herd the multitude along moving belts and through sliding doors, that will feed and tend and lull each one of us without so much as a human twinge—may inspire the technocrat and elate the growthman. But the unavoidable consequence is that the direct flow of sympathy and communication between people becomes ever thinner. And to that extent the quality of their lives becomes ever poorer.

A Concluding Remark

No one need trouble to declare that I have not *proved* that the pursuit of policies and the adoption of institutions that promote the existing economic expansion in the West will issue in a decline of social welfare, in an unhappier life, or in a less civilized one. I do not claim to prove things that can be neither proved nor disproved. What I have done is to attack the traditional presumption in favor of economic growth. In doing so I have sought to bring into the arena of debate some serious questions that cannot be readily resolved by scientific inquiry and, for that very reason, do not disturb the agenda of the Technocratic Enlightenment. In the process I have given utterance to a pessimism about the future that is evolving about us which others are beginning to share—a pessimism in which, however, is embedded a small seed of hope, one that can strike root only as that pessimism sinks deeper and spreads wider.

● ● ●

POSTSCRIPT

IS ECONOMIC GROWTH DESIRABLE?

In arguing the case for economic growth, Thurow is careful to establish precisely the context for his analysis. He is examining the consequences of constant, real, Gross National Product with an increasing population and an advancing technology. Under these conditions the unemployment rate must increase. Thurow examines the argument advanced by no-growth advocates that economic activity should focus increasingly on the provision of services rather than on the production of goods. He finds this position lacking because most service activities such as education and health require substantial capital investment. Thurow argues that pollution is not necessarily a consequence of growth but the result of "the relative costs of different forms of garbage disposal."

Mishan begins his case against economic growth by declaring that restrictions on what people can have are greater than is commonly supposed. This implies that people might adjust rather easily to a policy of no-growth. He then divides the growth question into two parts; considering first the physical possibility of continuous growth and then the desirability of continuous growth. Mishan accepts the existence of physical limits to growth. The size of the planet is, obviously, the ultimate limit and there are limits to the amount of pollution that can be absorbed, the quantity of food that can be produced, and the amount of available resources. Mishan believes that although technology has resolved problems in the past, it is unlikely to continue to do so in the future. As for the desirability of economic growth, Mishan is concerned with the relationship between the output of goods and services and the quality of life. An increase in output does produce benefits but it also produces "disbenefits"—increased pollution, depletion of resources, stifling specialization, competitive pressures, and distraction of man from more basic sources of satisfaction—which may actually lead to a reduction in the quality of life.

As for suggested readings, the interested student might begin with *LIMITS TO GROWTH,* Universe Books, 1972 by D.H. Meadows, D.L. Meadows, J. Randers, and W.W. Behrems, III. For a rebuttal to this argument see "Notes on 'Doomsday Models' " by R.M. Solow, *Proceedings of the National Academy of Sciences* (December, 1972). A collection of fine essays, including the complete Mishan article, expressing different points of views is presented in *THE NO-GROWTH SOCIETY* (Norton, 1973), edited by M. Olson and H.H. Landsberg. For a radical perspective see "The Irrationality of Capitalist Economic Growth," by T.E. Weisskopf in *THE CAPITALIST SYSTEM,* 2nd edition by R.C. Edwards, M. Reich, and T.E. Weisskopf (Prentice-Hall, 1978).

ISSUE 13

ARE NEW GOVERNMENT POLICIES NECESSARY TO AVOID ECONOMIC CATASTROPHE?

YES: David A. Stockman, from "How to Avoid an Economic Dunkirk," *Challenge* (March/April, 1981).

NO: Jimmy Carter, from 1981 ECONOMIC REPORT OF THE PRESIDENT.

ISSUE SUMMARY

YES: The Reagan administration's Director of the Office of Management and Budget, Stockman, argues that dramatic actions including the declaration of a national economic emergency are required to resolve the current economic crises.

NO: Former President Carter believes the economy recorded a number of successes during his administration and, although serious economic problems remain, he is confident that the basic economy is strong and will overcome the challenges it faces.

Political campaigns are built on disagreement. The challenger will normally work a dual strategy stressing the failures of the incumbant while confidently promoting new solutions. The incumbant also utilizes a dual strategy promoting his or her successes while strongly suggesting that the new policies offered by the challenger will fail or that they will create a whole new set of problems.

This was the case during the 1980 Presidential election campaign. Republican challenger Reagan pointed to a number of economic problems including high unemployment and high inflation rates (just as then challenger Carter had done during the 1976 Presidential election campaign), high interest rates, a deterioration in the international competitiveness of American firms, declining productivity, low rates of savings and investment, high tax rates, excessive governmental intrusion into private economic affairs, and a growing national debt. The policies Reagan proposed in order to solve these problems included cuts in taxes, deregulation, and efforts to curb government spending.

Democratic incumbant Carter underscored the positive: more persons were employed than anytime in the nation's history, incomes were growing, exports were expanding, investment was growing more rapidly than total output. As for his policies, they included deregulation and tax cuts with controls for spending.

In an overall sense the suggested alternative policies were similiar; they differed in specifics. While Reagan was recommending across-the-board tax cuts Carter was more in favor of tax cuts designed to stimulate investment. With respect to deregulation the difference was between a broad, vigorous approach for Reagan and a more specific, more cautious effort by Carter. Reagan wanted an attack on all areas of spending except defense; Carter also supported increases in defense spending, yet was more selective in his suggestions regarding how spending would be controlled. Clearly the Reagan campaign, as it addressed the economy, epitomized the conservative-free market approach while the Carter program promised only a minor retrenchment of the basic liberal program. Thus the choice before the American people, at least as it appeared on economic grounds, was between conservative and liberal philosophies. Although it is not obvious that economic issues were the primary force behind the Carter defeat and the Reagan victory, the election of Reagan and other Republicans ensured a swing to a more conservative economic program.

A leading spokesman for the Reagan administration and presumably a chief architect of its economic program is David Stockman. He was selected to fill a key economic position, Director of the Office of Management and Budget. In his effort to move the Reagan economic package forward he prepared his well known Dunkirk memo. It is that memo which forms the yes side of this issue. Less well known is the Carter assessment of the economy issued at about the same time. It is presented in the *1981 Economic Report of the President*, the last economic report prepared by Carter and his Council of Economic Advisors. In positioning itself on the no side of this issue, Carter's message stands in sharp contrast to the Stockman assessment.

But election does not automatically mean the passage of a new economic program. The process proceeds slowly with new legislation introduced into Congress, committee hearings, committee votes, House and Senate debates, House and Senate votes, and conference committee action if necessary. Only then does the legislation come before the President for his acceptance or rejection. It was unclear at the time of the election, at the time of his inauguration, and remains unclear now (late spring of 1981) exactly how much of the Reagan economic program would become reality. In short, the issue as viewed by the Stockman-Carter debate continues to occupy center stage in the Washington drama.

YES

David A. Stockman

HOW TO AVOID AN
ECONOMIC DUNKIRK

The momentum of short-run economic, financial, and budget forces is creating the conditions for an economic Dunkirk during the first 24 months of the Reagan administration. There are several major threats: (1) a second 1980-81 credit crunch; (2) a double-dip recession early in 1981; (3) a federal budget and credit hemorrhage; (4) commodity shocks and the final destruction of the Volcker monetary policy; and (5) a ticking regulatory time bomb.

A Second 1980-81 Credit Crunch

President Reagan inherited thoroughly disordered credit and capital markets, punishingly high interest rates, and a hair-trigger market psychology poised to respond strongly to early economic policy signals in either favorable or unfavorable ways.

The pre-eminent danger is that an initial economic policy package that includes the tax cuts but does not contain *decisive, credible elements* concerning outlay control, future budget authority reduction, and a believable plan for curtailing the federal government's massive direct and indirect credit absorption will generate pervasive expectations of a continuing "Reagan inflation." Such a development would almost ensure that high interest rates would hang over the economy well into the first year, deadening housing and durables markets and thwarting the industrial capital spending boom required to propel sustained economic growth. Thus, Thatcherization can only be avoided if the initial economic policy package simultaneously spurs the output side of the economy and also elicits a swift downward revision of inflationary expectations in the financial markets.

A Double-Dip Recession in Early 1981

Stagnant or declining real GNP growth in the first two quarters is a possibility in light of the conditions in the financial markets and gathering evidence from the output side of the economy. This would generate staggering political and policy challenges. These include a further worsening of an already dismal budget posture and a profusion of "quick fix" remedies for various "wounded" sectors of the economy. The latter would include intense pressure for formal or informal auto import restraints, activation of Brooke-Cranston or similar costly housing bailouts, maintenance of current excessive CETA employment levels, accelerated draw-down of various lending and grant aids, a further 13-week extension of federal unemployment benefits, and so on. Obviously, the intense political pressures for many of these quick fix aids will distract from the Reagan program on the economic fundamentals (supply-side tax cuts, regulatory reform, and firm long-term fiscal discipline) and threaten to lock in budget costs and policy initiatives that are out of step with the basic policy thrust.

There is a further danger: the federal budget has now become an automatic "coast-to-coast soup line" that dispenses remedial aid with almost reckless abandon, converting the traditional notion of automatic stabilizers into multitudinous outlay spasms throughout the budget. For instance, the estimates for fiscal year 1981 trade adjustment assistance have exploded from $400 million in the spring to $2.5 billion as of November 1980, and last summer's drought will cause Small Business Administration farm loan aid to surge by $1.1 billion above planned levels.

For these reasons, the first hard look at the unvarnished 1981 and 1982 budget posture by our own Office of Management and Budget people is likely to elicit coronary contractions among some, and produce an intense polarization between supply-side tax cutters and the more fiscally orthodox. An internecine struggle over deferral or temporary abandonment of the tax program could ensue. The result would be a severe demoralization and fractionalization of GOP ranks and an erosion of our capacity to govern successfully and revive the economy before November 1982.

Federal Budget and Credit Hemorrhage

As of late November, estimates placed fiscal 1981 outlays at nearly $650 billion. That represents a $20 billion outlay growth since the August estimates; a $36 billion growth since the First Budget resolution passed in June; an outlay level $73 billion above fiscal 1980; and a $157 billion growth since the books closed on fiscal 1979 just 13 months previously. For example, between June and November 1980, federal outlay estimates rose from $613 billion to $649 billion. Of the $36 billion growth in outlay estimates, fully $26 billion or 72 percent was due to automatic budget responses to the mechanisms listed above.

These illustrations drive home a fundamental point: achieving fiscal control over outlays and Treasury borrowing cannot be conducted as an accounting exercise or exclusively through legislated spending cuts in the orthodox sense. Only a comprehensive economic package that spurs output and employment growth and lowers inflation expectations and interest rates has any hope of stopping the present hemorrhage.

Commodity Shocks and the Final Destruction of Volcker Monetary Policy

The U.S. economy is likely to face two serious commodity price run-ups during the next 5 to 15 months. First, if the Iran-Iraq war is not soon terminated, today's excess worldwide crude and product inventories will soon be largely depleted. Under those conditions, heavy spot market buying, inventory accumulation, and eventually panic bidding on world markets will once again emerge. Indeed, unless the war combatants exhaust themselves at an early date and move quickly back into at least limited production, this outcome is almost certain. Under these circumstances, OPEC contract rates will rise toward spot market levels in the $40 to $50 per barrel range during the first and second quarters of 1981, with a consequent price shock to the U.S. economy. Even a $10 per barrel increase in average U.S. refiner acquisition cost would add $50 to $60 billion annually to aggregate national petroleum expenditures (assuming full decontrol).

The problem here is that demand for basic commodities is highly inelastic in the very short run; and this generates strong credit demands from both the business and household sectors to finance existing consumption levels without cutting back on other expenditures. If the Federal Reserve chooses to accommodate these commodity price-credit demand shocks, as it has in the past, then in the context of the massive federal credit demand and financial market disorders described above, only one result is certain: the already tattered

credibility of the post-October 1979 Volcker monetary policy will be destroyed. The Federal Reserve will subsequently succumb to enormous internal strife and external pressure, and the conditions for full-scale financial panic and unprecedented global monetary turbulence will be present.

Ticking Regulatory Time Bomb

Unless swift, comprehensive, and far-reaching regulatory policy corrections are undertaken immediately, an unprecedented, quantum scale-up of the much discussed "regulatory burden" will occur during the next 18 to 40 months. Without going into exhaustive detail, this is the basic dynamic. During the early and mid-1970s, Congress approved more than a dozen sweeping environmental, energy, and safety enabling authorities, which for all practical purposes are devoid of policy standards and criteria for cost-benefit, cost-effectiveness, and comparative-risk analysis. Subsequently, McGovernite no-growth activists assumed control of most of the relevant sub-Cabinet policy posts during the Carter administration. They have spent the past four years "tooling up" for implementation through a mind-boggling outpouring of rulemakings, interpretative guidelines, and major litigation—all heavily biased toward maximization of regulatory scope and burden. Thus, this decade-long process of regulatory evolution is just now reaching the stage at which it will sweep through the industrial economy with near gale force, preempting multi-billions in investment capital, driving up operating costs, and siphoning off management and technical personnel in an incredible morass of new controls and compliance procedures.

The Threat of Political Dissolution

This review of the multiple challenges and threats lying in ambush contains an inescapable warning: things could go very badly during the first year of the Reagan administration, resulting in incalculable erosion of GOP momentum, unity, and public confidence. If bold policies are not swiftly, deftly, and courageously implemented in the first six months, Washington will quickly become engulfed in political disorder commensurate with the surrounding economic disarray. A golden opportunity for permanent conservative policy revision and political realignment could be thoroughly dissipated before the Reagan administration is even up to speed.

The specific danger is this: if President Reagan does not lead a creatively orchestrated high-profile policy offensive based on revision of the fundamentals—supply-side tax cuts and regulatory relief, stern outlay control and federal fiscal retrenchment, and monetary reform and dollar stabilization—the thin Senate Republican majority and the *de facto* conservative majority in the House will fragment and succumb to parochial "fire-fighting as usual" in response to specific conditions of constituency distress.

To prevent early dissolution of the incipient Republican majority, only one remedy is available: an intial administration economic program that is so bold, sweeping, and sustained that it—

—totally dominates the Washington agenda during 1981;

—holds promise of propelling the economy into vigorous expansion and the financial markets into a bullish psychology;

—preempts the kinds of debilitating distractions outlined above.

The major components and tenor of such an orchestrated policy offensive are described below.

Emergency Economic Stabilization and Recovery Program

In order to dominate, shape, and control the Washington agenda, President Reagan should declare a national economic emergency soon after inauguration. He should tell the Congress and the nation that the economic, financial, budget, energy, and regulatory conditions he inherited are far worse than anyone had imagined. He should request that Congress organize quickly and clear the decks for exclusive action during the next 100 days on an Emergency Economic Stabilization and Recovery Program he would soon announce.

The following includes a brief itemization of the major components of the Stabilization and Recovery Program:

Supply-side tax components. There should be calendar year 1981 and 1982 installments of Kemp-Roth proposals, reduction of the top income tax rate on unearned income to 50 percent, further reduction in capital gains tax rates, and a substantial reform along 10-5-3 lines of corporate depreciation allowances.

Fiscal stabilization component. This would consist of two parts. First, the cash outlay savings measures for the remainder of fiscal 1981 would be aimed at holding outlays to the $635 billion range. A hiring freeze and a severe cutback in agency travel, equipment procurement, and outside contracting would be the major areas for savings.

The second part would be oriented toward entitlement revisions and budget authority reductions in fiscal 1982 and beyond. Some of this could be accomp-

249

lished through budget authority rescissions included in the remainder of the fiscal 1981 appropriations bill. This would have to be enacted before the expected December-March continuing resolution expires. Expiration of the continuing resolution would provide strong leverage. Another part could be accomplished through the revised fiscal 1982 budget and scaled-back requests for new budget authority. The remainder would require the legislative committees to address a carefully tailored package of initial entitlement revisions.

Expressed in functional program and spending areas the out-year authority reduction package should include the following items, with a view to reducing federal domestic program levels by $30 to $50 billion per annum in the fiscal 1982-83 period:

1. *Defer public sector capital investment.*

2. *Reduce expenditures for non-social security entitlements,* such as food stamps, cash assistance, Medicaid, disability, heating assistance, housing assistance, school lunches, and unemployment compensation, through a carefully tailored package to reduce eligibility, overlap, and abuse. The potential savings would be $10 to $20 billion;

3. *Cut back on low priority programs,* such as NASA, CETA, the Community Development Program, Economic Development Administration, urban parks, impact aid, Action, Department of Energy commercialization and information programs, arts and humanities, and the Consumer Cooperative Bank.

4. *Reform federal credit, lending, and guarantees.* As was indicated previously, concessional direct lending and loan guarantee activities by on-budget, off-budget, and government-sponsored enterprises are now running rampant, absorbing ever bigger shares of available credit market funds. Controlling Small Business Administration direct grant activities, for instance, will accomplish little if program activity is simply shifted to concessional loan authorities, with the resultant outlays laundered through the Federal Financing Bank.

Regulatory ventilation. This component also has two segments. The first and most urgent is a well-planned and orchestrated series of unilateral administrative actions to defer, revise, or rescind existing and pending regulations where clear legal authority exists.

Contingency energy package. The probable 1981 "oil shock" could entail serious political and economic disruption. Therefore, the preemptive step of dismantling controls before the crisis really hits is imperative. Incidentally, the combination of immediate decontrol and a $10 rise in the world price would increase windfall profits tax revenue by $20 to $25 billion during calendar 1981, thereby adding substantially to short-run budget posture improvement, if not to long-run energy production prospects.

If the crisis is severe enough, rapid statutory revision of the natural gas decontrol program and modification of the windfall tax might be considered as part of the 100-day agenda.

A Monetary Accord

The markets have now almost completely lost confidence in Volcker* and the new monetary policy. Only an extraordinary gesture can restore the credibility that will be required during the next two years. President Reagan should

*[Eds. note]: Paul Volcker was chairman of the Federal Reserve Board under the Carter administration.

meet with Volcker or the entire Federal Reserve Board at an early date and issue them a new informal "charter"—namely, to eschew all consideration of extraneous economic variables like short-term interest rates, housing market conditions, business cycle fluctuations, etc., and to concentrate instead on one exclusive task: bringing the growth of Federal Reserve credit and bank reserves to a prudent rate and stabilization of the international and domestic purchasing power of the dollar.

The President and Congress would jointly take responsibility for ameliorating credit and capital market conditions through implementation of the Stabilization and Recovery Program and would stoutly defend the Federal Reserve from all political attacks. Insulation of the Federal Reserve from extraneous economic and financial preoccupations, political pressures, recalibration of its monetary objective, and restoration of its tattered credibility is the critical linchpin in the whole program.

● ● ●

NO   Jimmy Carter

ECONOMIC REPORT OF
THE PRESIDENT

To the Congress of the United States:

Over the next few years our country faces several economic challenges that will test the will of our people and the capability of our government. We must find ways to bring down a stubborn inflation without choking off economic growth; we must channel a much larger share of our national ouput to investment and reverse a decade-long decline in productivity growth; and we must continue to reduce the Nation's dangerous vulnerability to disruptive changes in the world supply and price of oil.

In this *Economic Report* I set forth my views on how we can best meet those problems. . . . It is useful to start by recognizing that in many respects we approach these challenges from a position of strength, with a record of significant economic progress, and the knowledge that over the past 4 years our people and our government have successfully resolved a number of difficult and potentially divisive economic issues. While it would be folly to close our minds to the stubbornness of the problems we face, it would serve the Nation equally ill to underrate our strengths and our proven ability to handle difficult issues.

Strengths and Accomplishments

During the economic turmoil that characterized the decade of the 1970s, and especially during the past 4 years, the American economy succeeded in providing additional jobs for its people on a scale unsurpassed in our history. Employment grew by almost 25 percent over the decade, and by more than 11 percent in the past 4 years alone. Not only were jobs provided for a sharply rising population reaching working age, but job opportunities were opened up by the millions for new second earners, principally women. Neither Europe nor Japan came even close to the job performance of the American economy.

From, the *1981 Economic Report of the President*. Government Printing Office.

Along with employment, real per capita incomes grew during the past 4 years, despite the losses forced on the Nation by the huge increases in world oil prices and the effects of a slowing growth in productivity. As the year 1980 ended, per capita income, after taxes and adjusted for inflation, was some 8 percent higher than it was in 1976.

We have heard much about American industry losing its competitive edge in international markets and about the "deindustrialization" of America. In fact, during the 3 years prior to the onset of the 1980 recession—and the effects of that recession will be transient—the growth of industrial production in the United States was larger than it was in Germany, France, or the United Kingdom. The volume of American nonfarm exports rose by 35 percent between 1977 and the middle of 1980, and the share of U.S. exports among the total exports of the industrial countries rose by about 1¼ percentage points, reversing a declining trend that had been underway since the 1950s.

America's balance of payments is strong in large part because of its superior export performance. Despite a massive $40-billion annual drain of funds to pay for the oil-price increases of 1979 and 1980, our exports of goods and services now exceed our imports. Unlike the situation in most other oil-importing nations, our country's external balance is in surplus.

The dollar is also strong. After a period of weakness in its value abroad, we took decisive action 2 years ago to stabilize the dollar. Since then, in a world of sharply changing circumstances and disruptions of oil supply, the dollar has remained strong, and has risen in value compared to most major currencies.

While it is imperative that our country increase the share of its national output devoted to investment, the reason is not that investment has been weak in recent years. Between 1976 and 1980, real business investment grew almost 6 percent a year, substantially faster than GNP as a whole. Because of that rapid growth the share of business investment in GNP during the past 3 years exceeded that of any other 3-year period in the last three decades.

There are other areas where the Nation has made more progress than we sometimes realize. While we are properly concerned to limit the growth in Federal spending and voice our impatience with the waste and inefficiency that often exist in government programs, we should not forget the good that has been accomplished with these programs. Examples abound. In the early 1960s, for instance, infant mortality in the United States was scandalously high compared to other countries, and most of that high mortality was concentrated among the poor. Due in large part to programs like Medicaid, infant mortality has fallen sharply. More generally, we have dramatically improved access to medical care for the poor and the aged. Through Federal grants we have strengthened the mass transit systems of our major cities and helped our municipalities install critically needed waste treatment plants. We have helped millions of young people, who could not otherwise have afforded it, get a college education, and we have provided job training for workers who needed new skills.

Much attention is now focused on how to reduce the costs and ease the burden of Federal regulation to protect the environment, health, and safety. Concern about excessive regulatory costs is surely warranted, and my Administration has taken a number of specific steps to deal with the problem. In focusing attention on the burden of regulation, however, we should not lose sight of the substantial progress that has been made in enriching our lives, improving our health, and beautifying our country.

Tackling Difficult Issues

During the past 4 years the Nation has taken a series of important and in some cases painful steps to deal with its energy problems. Starting almost 2 years ago, we began to phase out controls on domestic oil and natural gas prices. We thus moved to end the dangerous practice of holding U.S. energy prices below the world market price, a practice which tended to subsidize wasteful consumption and perpetuate our excessive dependence on oil imports.

Working with the Congress we also put in place the other principal elements of a comprehensive program to increase energy production and conserve energy use. We levied a windfall profits tax to divert the inevitable windfalls from oil decontrol to pay for the National Energy Program initiatives and to reduce the impact of decontrol on the poor.

Partly as a result of these policies we have begun to see dramatic results in both the supply and conservation of energy. There are now 70 percent more drilling rigs in operation than when my Administration took office, and the number of oil and gas wells being drilled has reached a new record. By late 1980 the United States was importing almost 30 percent less oil than it did 2 years ago and our gasoline use had dropped by more than 10 percent over the same period. While some of the reduction in

energy use was due to the recession, most of it reflects real energy conservation.

What has happened in energy policy over the past 4 years augurs well for our country's future. Decontrolling domestic oil and gas was painful. It pushed up the prices each of us pay for driving and for heating our homes and added to our immediate inflation difficulties. But we showed that we were willing to take such painful steps when they were necessary in our Nation's longer-run interest. Because we are large-scale producers as well as consumers of energy, the energy problem was potentially a highly divisive issue in our country, involving the redistribution of hundreds of billions of dollars, pitting producer against consumer and one region of the Nation against another. But after prolonged and sometimes heated debate, we arrived at an approach that took account of the legitimate concerns of all groups and at the same time furthered the national interest. Dealing with the Nation's remaining economic problems will also require painful measures and the reconciliation of a number of different interests. Our handling of the energy problem should raise our confidence that we can be successful elsewhere.

We have also had major successes in other fields. After decades of inaction, the past 4 years have seen the elimination of price-propping and competition-deadening regulations in a number of American industries. In these 4 years we witnessed more progress in economic deregulation than at any other time in the century. In the face of great skepticism and initial opposition, the executive branch, the Congress, and some of the independent regulatory agencies have deregulated or drastically reduced regulation in the airline, trucking, and railroad industries, and in banking and other financial institutions. We have also made a promising start in the communications industry. The transportation, communications, and finance industries comprise a triad that links the various strands of our economy together. Better performance in these industries should have effects far beyond their own boundaries.

The gains from deregulation will be substantial. For example, productivity and efficiency will be directly increased as transportation load factors are improved and empty backhauls reduced. One survey of studies estimates that reform in the trucking industry alone will lead to $5 billion in annual cost reductions. Even more important will be the longer-run spur to innovation and the increased flexibility that comes from opening up these industries to the fresh winds of competition.

Population trends will be working to help the country deal with some of its economic problems in the 1980s, whereas in the late 1960s and 1970s these trends required some difficult adjustments. The generation of the postwar baby boom began entering the labor market in the 1960s and the influx of new workers continued during the 1970s. The percentage of the population aged 16 to 24 rose sharply. And as birth rates slowed, women entered the labor force in ever increasing numbers. On average, the labor force became less experienced, and average productivity per worker suffered. The increased proportion of women and young people in the labor force also contributed to an increase in the average unemployment rate because the transition from school or home to job takes time and because these new workers sometimes had periods of unemployment as they explored different career possibilities.

Because of the slowdown in birth rates in the past 15 years, the 1980s will see about half as fast a growth in the labor force as in the 1970s. The proportion of experienced workers will rise, contributing to an increase in productivity, while the proportion of young people will fall, leading to a drop in unemployment.

There are a number of reasons, therefore, to confront with hope the economic challenges that face us. We have a solid record of achievement. In the fields of energy and deregulation we have already laid the foundations on which the future can build. And there are some favorable trends underway that should help raise productivity and reduce unemployment in the years ahead.

Unresolved Problems

Despite much progress in recent years, we are faced with some serious problems. An inflation that was already bad became worse after the 1979 oil-price increase. Productivity growth, which had been declining sporadically for a decade, virtually ceased in the last several years. And although we have made substantial progress in adapting our economy to a world of higher oil prices, we remain dangerously vulnerable to serious supply disruptions originating abroad. . . .

Inflation

These realities dictate the broad tasks that economic policy must accomplish over the years ahead:
Our monetary and fiscal policies must apply steady anti-inflationary restraint to the economy. The restraint must be strong and persistent enough to convince

255

those who set wages and prices that the government means to stand by its guns in the anti-inflation fight. But it must not be so severe or so restrictive as to prohibit even moderate economic growth and recovery, and thus collapse under its own political unreality.

We must seek means to reduce inflation at a lower cost in lost output and employment. These include measures to increase investment, the reform of regulation, and incomes policies. An increase in investment raises productivity growth which, in turn, tends to slow the rise in business costs and prices. Demand restraint will then produce more reduction of inflation and less reduction in output. Measures to lower regulatory costs and increase competition and flexibility in our economy will also directly lower inflationary pressures and let us have more economic growth without sacrificing our inflation goals. An improved set of voluntary incomes policies can directly influence wages and prices in the direction of moderation, and thereby bring inflation down faster and at lower costs.

Finally, we must build upon the foundations already laid and hasten our progress toward energy conservation and increased domestic energy supplies. We must also work to improve our capability of weathering a severe disruption in foreign oil supplies, since even a highly successful energy program will still leave our economy vulnerable to such disruption over the coming decade. . . .

Budget and Tax Policies

The central feature of the tax policies I am proposing is their emphasis on increasing investment. By 1985, an unusually high 45 percent of the tax

reductions will be directed toward spurring investment. But even this will not itself be sufficient to raise investment to the levels our country will need in the decade ahead in order to improve its productivity growth and deal with its energy problems. Careful control of Federal spending, however, will create the leeway for additional investment-oriented tax reductions in later years, within the framework of the overall budgetary restraint required to fight inflation. I do not believe that we should now commit budgetary resources to large-scale personal tax cuts which will stimulate consumption far more than investment and thereby foreclose the possibility of meeting the Nation's critical investment requirements.

Monetary Policy

. . . Sustained restraint in monetary policy is a prerequisite to lowering inflation. The Federal Reserve exercises this restraint principally by keeping a strict limit on the growth of the Nation's money supply. In October 1979 the Federal Reserve modified its earlier policies and operating procedures to increase sharply the emphasis it gives to controlling the money supply. The Federal Reserve each year sets targets for monetary growth and seeks to hold the growth of the money supply within the targets. Increasingly the public in general and the financial community in particular have come to associate the credibility of the Federal Reserve and its determination to fight inflation with its success in keeping money growth continuously within the preannounced targets. It is very important, however, that public opinion not hold the Federal Reserve to such a rigid form of monetary targeting as to deprive it of the flexibility it needs to conduct a responsible monetary policy. . . .

Without reasoned and persistent monetary restraint, inflation cannot be licked. Perhaps more than in any other area of economic policy, however, achieving success in monetary policy depends on an informed public opinion.

Incomes Policies

. . . Broadly, we have concluded that an approach which provided a tax reduction to workers in firms whose average pay increase did not exceed some standard, set as part of a voluntary incomes policy, would be feasible and effective in helping to lower inflation. Two major conditions apply, however. *First,* such a policy must be a supplement to, not a substitute for, fiscal and monetary restraint. Without such restraint an incomes policy will produce only fleeting reductions in inflation or none at all. *Second,* a TIP program is likely to be desirable only on a temporary basis. After several years, such a program might cease to be effective and could induce significant distortions into wage relationships throughout the economy. But as an interim device to hasten the reduction in inflation and so shorten the period of reduced output and employment growth, a TIP program could serve the Nation well.

If the growth of Federal spending is restrained, periodic tax reductions will be both feasible and necessary in the years ahead as inflation and economic growth push taxpayers into higher brackets and raise average effective tax rates. Tax-based incomes policies are novel, and most people are unfamiliar with either the opportunities they present or the difficulties they pose. It is therefore highly unlikely that a TIP program could take effect in 1981. But it would be useful for the public in general, and the Congress in particular, to begin now to evaluate the pros and cons of TIP programs so that when the time comes for the next round of Federal tax cuts a TIP program will be seriously considered.

Energy

I am once again proposing that the Congress increase the Federal excise tax on gasoline by 10 cents per gallon as an additional incentive to cut petroleum consumption. The need for this tax is, if anything, even greater than it was 7 months ago when the Congress overturned my action to impose a gasoline conservative fee administratively. . . .

There is other important unfinished business to attend to in energy. The Congress failed to complete work on my proposed Energy Mobilization Board, but events since August of 1979 have only made the case for the Board's creation more persuasive. It is equally important that we move ahead with the production of substitutes for petroleum. The Synthetic Fuels Corporation is established and operating. Its mission—to encourage commercial-scale production of synthetic fuels through risk-sharing with American industry—is vital.

My program of phased decontrol of domestic crude oil, along with the revamping of natural gas pricing policy contained in the Natural Gas Policy Act, is paying rich dividends. Drilling and seismic exploration have reached near-record levels. The Natural Gas Policy Act should be reviewed, however, to ensure that progress toward decontrol of new natural gas is not jeopardized by the increasing gap between oil prices and their natural gas equivalent, since world oil prices are now about twice those assumed in the act. . . .

Increasing the Flexibility of Our Economy

. . . During the coming years, when many of our most important industries will be facing difficult adjustment pressures, we must avoid taking shortsighted actions which block rather than promote this adjustment. Federal policies should indeed cushion the blow when sharp external shocks force an industry, its workers, and the communities within which it is located to undergo massive change in a short period of time. The programs of economic development and trade assistance which exist to meet these needs should be humanely and effectively administered. But such aid must be aimed at facilitating adjustment to change, not preventing it. While we can and should demand that all nations abide by internationally agreed-upon rules of trade, we must avoid the temptation to use the discretion open to us to prop up weak industries.

Summing Up: The Need for Balance

In the years immediately ahead, our country will be wrestling with two central domestic issues. The first is economic in nature: How can we reduce inflation while maintaining the economic growth that keeps our people employed? The second is even broader: What is the proper role of government in our society as spender of tax revenues and regulator of industry?

I am confident we can successfully come to grips with both of these issues. We would make a costly mistake, however, if we approached these problems with the view that there is some single answer to the economic problem and a single criterion for determining the role of government. The resolution of both of these great issues demands a balancing of many approaches and many considerations. Indeed, the only helpful simple proposition is the one which states that any simple and quick answer is automatically the wrong one.

The approach I have set forth in this *Report* will successfully meet the economic challenge. But it relies on not one but a number of essential elements. To reduce inflation we must be prepared for a period of sustained budgetary and monetary restraint. But since we know that this also tends to depress the growth of output and employment, we must not conclude that the greater the restraint the better. We want a degree of restraint that takes into account society's interest in employment and production as well as its concern to lower inflation. We can improve our prospects significantly by introducing investment-oriented tax cuts that increase supply and productivity. But the supply response will not be so quick or so great as to constitute an answer in and of itself. And, in particular, it would be very dangerous to make budgetary policy in the belief that the supply response can be so large as to wipe out the need for fiscal prudence and budgetary restraint. We can improve our prospects still further by the use of voluntary incomes policies, strengthened when budgetary resources become available by tax incentives for wage moderation. But, again, incomes policies alone will not do the job. If we try to rely on them excessively, we will do more harm than good. Only with a balance among the various elements, and only with persistence in the realization that sure progress will come gradually, can we have both lower inflation and better growth.

Sorting out the proper role of government also requires us to strike a balance. At times Federal spending has grown too rapidly. But in recent years its growth did not result from the introduction of a host of new government programs by spendthrift politicians or a surge of profligacy by wasteful bureaucrats. It stemmed mainly from two sources: *first,* increased military spending to meet national security goals that are overwhelmingly supported by the American people; and *second,* the growth of long established and broadly accepted social security and social insurance programs that are directly or indirectly indexed against inflation or automatically responsive to an increase in unemployment.

There is some waste. There is some abuse. I have instituted a number of reforms to cut it back. I am sure my successors will continue this important effort. But waste and abuse are not the fundamental issues. The essence of the challenge that faces us is how to balance the various benefits that government programs confer on us against their costs in terms of higher taxes, higher deficits, and sometimes higher inflation.

It is my view that we must strike the balance so as to restrict for some time the overall growth of Federal spending to less than the growth of our economy, despite the faster increase of the military component of the budget. As a consequence, in my 1982 budget I have proposed a series of program reductions. I have suggested a delay in the effective date of new programs I believe important. I have recommended improvements in the index we use to adjust Federal programs for inflation.

I think we will do a better job in striking the right balance over the years ahead if we keep two principles in mind: The first is to recognize *reality.* The choices are in fact difficult, and we should not pretend that all we have to do is find wasteful programs with zero benefits. The second is to act with *compassion.* Some government programs provide special benefits for the poor and the disadvantaged; while these programs must not be immune from review and reform, they should not bear the brunt of the reductions.

The same general viewpoint is appropriate when we approach the problem of government as regulator, especially in protecting the environment, health, and safety. When we first awoke to the fact of generations of environmental neglect, we rushed to compensate for our mistake and paid too little attention to problems of cost and effectiveness. Sometimes the laws we passed and the deadlines we set took too little account of their economic impact. For 4 years my Administration has been engaged in a major program of finding ways to make regulations more cost-effective and to strike a reasonable balance between environmental concerns and economic costs. A strong foundation has been laid. Much remains to be done. But lasting progress will not come unless we realize that there is a balance to be struck. Those who believe that virtually all regulation is bad and that the best regulation is a dead regulation will come to grips with the real problem no more successfully than the enthusiasts who believe that concern with regulatory costs is synonymous with lack of concern for the environment.

I believe that the government has indeed overregulated and that regulatory reform must continue to be a major objective of the Federal Government, as it has been during my Administration. But

259

ARE NEW GOVERNMENT POLICIES NECESSARY?

I also believe that true reform involves finding better ways to identify and to give proper consideration to gains as well as costs.

My reading of the distant and the nearby past gives me confidence that the American people can meet the challenges ahead. There are no simple formulas. There will be no quick victories. But an understanding of the diverse concerns we have, a pragmatic willingness to bring to bear a varied array of weapons, and persistence in the effort will bring success.

January 17, 1981

• • •

POSTSCRIPT
ARE NEW GOVERNMENT POLICIES NECESSARY TO AVOID ECONOMIC CATASTROPHE?

Viewing the economy in November 1980, Stockman believed that a genuine economic crisis would confront the American economy during the first two years of the Reagan administration. This pessimistic forecast was based on five elements. First, Stockman felt that credit markets were in disarray making a credit crunch likely. Second, he foresaw a two quarter decline in Gross National Product in 1981. Third, he stressed the automatic growth in government outlays. Fourth was the threat of a new rise in oil prices and overreaction to these price increases by the Federal Reserve System. Fifth, there were the government regulations which were about to "sweep through the industrial economy with near gale force." To prevent the economic collapse and reverse the negative factors these would inflict, Stockman recommended that the President declare a national economic emergency so that Congress could devote itself exclusively to the consideration of a new economic package. This package included supply side tax cuts, efforts to bring Federal spending under control, relaxation of government regulation, and cooperative action with the Federal Reserve System to slow down the growth of Federal Reserve credit and bank reserves.

Carter begins by listing the strengths of the economy and its recent accomplishments. These include a rapid growth in employment, an increase in per capita income after adjustment for taxes and price level changes, growth in industrial production, rising exports, a strong dollar, and rising investment. Favorable patterns currently exist including more gas and oil exploration, energy conservation, greater competition, and favorable population trends. But problems remain—inflation, energy dependence, low productivity. Among the policies recommended by Carter are tax cuts to stimulate investment, monetary restraint, an incomes policy with tax reductions for workers in firms that exercise wage restraint, increased gasoline taxes, and assistance for workers whose jobs are lost because of "external shocks." But most of all Carter cautions against the view that all government spending and all government regulation is bad. What a society must seek is balance, a balance between alternative views as well as a balance between conflicting priorities.

Perhaps the best and most complete treatment of the Carter position is the 1981 ECONOMIC REPORT OF THE PRESIDENT (Washington, 1981). For a careful analysis of the choices involved in budget cutting see Rudolph G. Penner "Cutting the Budget: The Painful Choices" in *Challenge* (March/April 1981). For an analysis of the Reagan budget as it was announced in February, 1981 see "The Reagan Budget: A Sharp Break with the Past" by Sheldon Danziger and Robert Haneman also in *Challenge* (May/June 1981).

ISSUE 14

SHOULD THE UNITED STATES RAISE TARIFFS AND IMPOSE QUOTAS IN ORDER TO PROTECT DOMESTIC PRODUCTION AND EMPLOYMENT?

YES: George Meany, from COMMITTEE ON FINANCE, UNITED STATES SENATE HEARINGS ON THE TRADE REFORM ACT OF 1973.
NO: Council of Economic Advisors, from the 1978 ECONOMIC REPORT OF THE PRESIDENT.

ISSUE SUMMARY

YES: The late George Meany, speaking as the president of the AFL-CIO, argues that world conditions have changed dramatically, making old arguments over free trade obsolete. Because U.S. firms are exporting technology and because other countries are pursuing policies of self-interest, the government should take action to protect domestic production and employment.

NO: The Council of Economic Advisors maintains that tariffs and quotas would reduce the availability of goods and services, accelerate the rate of inflation, have no impact on domestic employment, and invite retaliation by other countries and should, therefore, not be enacted.

Writing in the early nineteenth century, classical economist, David Ricardo, developed the theory of comparative advantage. According to this theory, trade between two countries would benefit both countries even if one country could produce all commodities more efficiently than the other country. Today this theory is accepted by many economists. It has been and continues to be the essence of the argument for free trade and against protectionism.

Given this theoretical demonstration of the beneficial effects of free trade and its general acceptance over a long period of time, the question arises as to why this issue has been the subject of continuous and heated debate. The question has a number of answers but there seems to be a common theme: the theory of comparative advantage ignores an important real world consideration of one type or another. For example, some people argue that protective measures are necessary to maintain an industry that is vital to national defense. The theory of comparative advantage ignores the fact that nation states are belligerent and that a defense industry is essential. Others justify protectionism by invoking the so-called infant industry argument. In this argument, protection is afforded an industry in order to give it time to mature. After it has matured it can then compete without the benefit of protection. So, according to this argument, the theory of comparative advantage ignores the different ages of industries and different lengths of time necessary for the maturation process. Still another argument for protectionism is the more general argument presented by Meany; that is, the world pictured by the theory of comparative advantage is not the world as it exists today. The theory of comparative advantage cannot, according to Meany, apply in a world characterized by multinational or transnational corporations, where foreign subsidiaries are established in an effort to circumvent labor or tax legislation in the home country, where a number of foreign economies are government managed rather than reflecting free market conditions, and where technology represents a significant commodity in trade transactions.

At another level, the arguments against free trade follow from the fact that trade is a dynamic process. This means that at some point, a country, according to the theory, might be better off by producing one commodity and not another. As time passes and conditions change, the theory would suggest a reordering of production with firms and workers switching from the production of one good to the production of another. But this switching process is painful: some firms may go out of existence as new firms are created, some workers are unemployed even while new jobs are being created. Is it any wonder then, that the firms and workers made worse off by trade should demand protection from the government and raise the charge of unfair competition? While the Council of Economic Advisors recognizes the problems of the adjustment process it maintains that tariffs and quotas are not the appropriate government response.

YES

TRADE REFORM ACT OF 1973:
Statement of George Meany

MR. MEANY. Thank you very much, Mr. Chairman. The AFL-CIO welcomes the opportunity to appear before this committee to discuss the need for new trade legislation to meet America's problems in the rapidly changing world of the seventies.

Perhaps no period of history in this century, outside global war, has brought the avalanche of international changes which has occurred in this past year.

The situation as it relates to trade legislation is well put in the recent summary and analysis of the Trade Reform Act by the staff of this committee.

And I quote. "It's a totally new ball game which was not envisaged in the planning and conception of the Trade Reform Act."

The fact that it is now a totally new ball game has made the administration's so-called Trade Reform Act totally obsolete. Its provisions bear no connection with the events of the day. Indeed, it is worse than no bill at all.

We find it incredible, in the light of all that has happened and is still happening in the world, that administration officials could come before this committee and present the same, barren arguments as they did when it was first proposed last May.

We urge this committee to give the House-passed bill a quick burial, and turn its time and attention to the writing of new trade legislation which will be comprehensive, flexible, and realistic, and which will meet the complex needs demanded by today's world.

What America needs urgently is not just a revision of trade policies but an entire restructuring based on the recognition that the concept of free trade versus protectionism which dominated the thinking of the thirties and forties is badly out of phase with today.

America needs a positive policy that will put the well-being of the United States and its people above all else. What it doesn't need is a nonpolicy which, in the hands of this administration, puts the Nation and its people last.

Every other nation has built-in protection for their national self-interest. The

From, *Committee on Finance, United States Senate Hearings on the Trade Reform Act of 1973*, Government Printing Office, 1973.

recent events in the Middle East and Europe, Japan, Latin America, and the Soviet Union all reinforce this fact. Certainly it is not out of place for the United States to assert its self-interest.

The United States needs a policy that will assure American taxpayers, consumers, workers, and businessmen a fair and up-to-date set of laws so that the United States can conduct mutually fair and beneficial trade with other nations.

As a necessary condition to this, however, the United States needs a healthy and expanding economy, providing diverse jobs for Americans with a wide range of skills, an economy which will afford its people a decent and rising standard of living and provide a strong industrial base from which the United States can carry out the mutually beneficial trade we seek with the rest of the world.

Unfortunately, this Nation's economy of today falls far short of meeting this requirement.

The United States is clearly in a recession. At the same time, the American people are the victims of a rampant inflation which in part has been brought on by this administration's misapplication of present foreign trade and investment policies. The achievement of the $1.7 billion 1973 trade surplus, about which the administration is so boastful, came at the expense of the consumer. Much of the gain in the trade accounts was the result of heavy exports of farm goods and critical raw materials. And it was exports of these commodities which caused sharp domestic shortages and brought on the rapid acceleration of inflation.

What the United States has done is to put the nations of the world in competition with the American consumer for the food he buys. The New York Times, in a recent page 1 article, said, and I quote:

Agricultural and economics experts agreed in interviews over the last three weeks that a major reason for some of the sharp increases in food prices in recent years had been the sudden and vast expansion of agricultural exports from the United States.

And there is no sign of letup in this competition which is pushing food prices up so rapidly. The same article in the Times noted that:

In the fiscal year ending June 30, 1972, the total value of American agricultural exports was $8 billion. For the year ending this June 30, the Government is estimating total agricultural sales abroad of $20 billion, 2½ times as much.

The administration takes refuge of sorts in the fact that inflation in this Nation has been less severe than in many other nations of the world. But we have no such consolation. America's rate of inflation is now surpassing that of many other nations. The Wall Street Journal, on March 13, recently noted that there are 7 other countries in Western Europe, plus another 11 in other parts of the globe, where prices are rising at a more moderate rate than in the United States. A year ago, the Journal noted, the consumer price rise in the United States was 4.7 percent, well below the countries of Austria, Belgium, France, West Germany, the Netherlands, Norway, and Sweden. In the last 12 months, however, the Consumer Price Index in the United States has risen 9.4 percent. . . .

In addition to being inflationary, the trade surplus is a dangerous illusion.

SHOULD THE U.S. RAISE TARIFFS AND IMPOSE QUOTAS?

America still faces basic and painfully serious trade problems.

Imports continue to flood the U.S. market, wiping out jobs by the hundreds of thousands and sweeping away segments of industries. The 1973 total of manufactured imports was $44.8 billion—an increase of 18 percent over the previous year. These imports continue to curtail American production in electronics, shoes, apparel, steel, autos, and a wide range of industries. Two official devaluations of the U.S. dollar have made these imports more expensive for American consumers, thus adding to the inflationary pressures of the American pocketbook. In many cases, the consumer, because of the elimination of American production by the inundation of imports—for example, black and white TV sets, tape recorders, even baseball mitts—has no other choice than to buy these imports, whatever their price tag.

In spite of the dollar devaluations, there was no surplus of manufacturing exports over imports; these exports in 1973 totaled $44.7 billion. Furthermore, the exports of America are now increasingly the entire production process—jobs, technology, and capital. We are sending our businesses abroad as well as our products.

What's more disturbing is that the technology America is sending abroad is sophisticated technology, the job-generators of the future. Where U.S. exports were once plants which produced shoes, apparel and textiles, the United States is now sending abroad technology for electronics, computers, aircraft, aerospace equipment—areas in which we were once predominant in the world, thus giving up America's clear competitive lead. This transfer of technology can take place in many ways—by direct transfer, by licens-

ing, by patent agreement and other methods. But the sum total of it is an erosion of America's industrial base. . . .

While there is a small flow of technology to this country from abroad—oxygen furnaces and radial tires, for example—the overwhelming flow is the other way. If that flow were more balanced, we wouldn't be here raising these arguments.

The employment impact of these developments are difficult to determine. Unfortunately, the foreign trade experts show little interest and even less knowledge about measuring this impact. However, the Government not long ago made some rough calculations indicating the net loss of some 500,000 jobs and job opportunities in the period 1966 to 1969. The AFL-CIO, employing the same methods of calculation, has determined that the further deterioration in the U.S. position in the world trade through 1973 has brought the total loss to over 1 million jobs—and that's probably conservative.

We have attached to this testimony the resolution on foreign trade and investment passed by the AFL-CIO Executive Council at its meeting in February, which details our legislative recommendations.*

To highlight these recommendations, we believe that new legislation should regulate U.S. imports and exports as a means of establishing an orderly flow of international trade. Specific flexible legislative machinery is needed to control imports. This flexible mechanism should also be applied as a restraint on the excessive exports of farm goods, crucial raw materials and other products in short supply domestically. Exports, imports and U.S. production should be linked in relation to needs for supplies, production and job opportunities in the United States.

We should modernize trade provisions and other U.S. laws to regulate the operations of multinational corporations. Regulation of multinational firms, including banks, is necessary because these concerns are the major exporters and importers of U.S. farm products, crude materials, and manufactured products.

We should eliminate U.S. tax advantages and other subsidies for corporations investing abroad. Specifically, the tax laws should eliminate tax deferral of income earned abroad and foreign tax credits.

Clear provisions should be written into new legislation to regulate exports of capital and new technology.

The energy crisis has demonstrated that overdependency on foreign sources of any material can be costly and perhaps fatal. It has also demonstrated that nations, when faced with a choice, are quick to act in their own self-interest. And it has graphically demonstrated that multinational corporations hold corporate allegiance above national allegiance.

The energy crisis has also revealed the price America has paid for not curbing the activities of the multinational corporations. The United States might not be facing so severe an energy problem if it had not been made so profitable for the major oil companies to locate new refinery capacity abroad in recent years instead of in the United States.

The AFL-CIO has long been concerned over the devastating impact of the activities of U.S. multinational corporations on the economic health of the United States and its people.

In industry after industry, we have watched plant after plant close and jobs disappear—only to see the same plants and the same jobs appear overseas as the multinationals moved production facilities to Taiwan, Singapore, South Korea, Brazil, Spain, France, England, Germany, Mexico, Portugal, Tanzania, and a host of other countries.

Not only have we watched the jobs and production go abroad, but we have watched goods come back from the overseas plants of multinationals as imports, competing with domestically-produced goods and making further inroads into U.S. employment. Faced with such pressure, the domestic producer either sells out or, more likely, joins the crowd and relocates abroad.

These massive operations are taking a heavy toll among American families and American communities from coast to coast.

The shutdown of manufacturing operations here and their relocation abroad, where low-cost operations are more profitable, depress the whole American economy by the loss of domestic jobs, payrolls, domestic corporate revenues, local purchasing power, local taxes—and has a "ripple out" effect on the local service economy from the loss of an industrial base. Hard-hit communities face empty factories, slackened businesses, unemployed workers and heavy revenue losses.

The multinationals operate as supranational entities. Each makes decisions solely on its own interests. These are decisions which have major consequences for the America of today and of the future.

The multinationals are, or they would like to be, stateless in their operations, freed of any responsibilities except to themselves.

Robert Stevenson, when he was in charge of Ford Motor Co.'s international operations, expressed what they have in mind, and I quote: "It is our goal to be in every single country there is; Iron Curtain countries, Russia, China. We at Ford look at the world map without any boundaries. We don't consider ourselves basically an American company. We are a multinational company. And when we approach a government that doesn't like the United States, we always say 'who do you like? Britain? Germany? We carry a lot of flags. We export from every country.' "

Nor do the multinationals let national interest stand in the way when corporate interest is at stake. Just how the multinationals feel with respect to their role in relation to American interests was stated quite simply in a recent CBS television show in which William Martin, then president of Phillips Petroleum, was being interviewed. He was asked whether the corporation should be expected to serve the national interests of the United States by accepting less profit here than it could obtain abroad. "I don't think we should be expected to," Mr. Martin replied. And when asked whether a U.S. international corporation should be expected to hold the national interests of the United States above the interests of other countries where that corporation does business, he replied: "I think not. If we were expected to do that, we couldn't operate in those foreign countries. I think it's just that simple."

The Arab oil embargo put the multinational oil corporations in a position where, as Leonard Silk pointed out recently in the New York Times, and I quote: "They must obediently respond to the commands of such governments as Saudi Arabia and Kuwait, over which they have much less influence than over the Government of the United States, even if this means helping the Arab countries to levy economic warfare against the United States."

Mr. Silk points out that the multinational corporations "would like to be world citizens, but since there is no world government, no world community to which they are responsible, they must feign loyalty to every country where they do business, concealing the flag under which they really sail—the old Jolly Roger emblazoned with the motto, "short-run profit maximization.' "

What helps to make it so profitable for the multinational to locate and produce abroad is the U.S. tax code. Through loopholes available to these corporations, the U.S. taxpayer subsidizes their foreign operations.

The result is that American workers not only lose their jobs, the economy loses part of its industrial base and the Federal Government loses revenues and the American taxpayer picks up the tab for the whole bit. . . .

Every other nation on this Earth puts the self-interest of its own people first. We think that is sound policy for the United States of America.

Thank you, Mr. Chairman.

THE CHAIRMAN. Thank you for a very fine and thoughtful statement, Mr. Meany. I am going to yield my place to Senator Ribicoff, who is chairman of our Trade Subcommittee, for a quick interrogation.

SENATOR RIBICOFF. Thank you very much, Mr. Chairman.

I followed your testimony with great interest, Mr. Meany. You make many pertinent points. You make the point that although we have an overall trade surplus, we still had a billion-dollar trade deficit in manufactured goods. If this deficit in manufactured goods continues, what labor-intensive American industries do you see in danger?

MR. MEANY. Well, there are any number. The electronics industry is one that comes to mind, but we have any number of labor intensive industries that are going to be affected. It seems to be a tendency to toy with the idea of making this a service nation, and I do not think we could maintain our standard of life, let alone elevate it to any extent, as a service nation.

SENATOR RIBICOFF. Do you think that any nation can continue to be a great power if it does not have a great degree of self-sufficiency, in let us say, automobiles, chemicals, electronics, and steel, the basic industries that provide the sinew and muscle of a nation?

Do you think a great nation could exist without them?

MR. MEANY. Well, the history of our economy has been that we always had industries which were basic and key, for instance, steel, autos, construction. If we are going to lose our basic industries such as airplane construction, automobile and things like that, farm implements, I do not think we are any longer going to be the leading nation of the world.

Basically, you see, up to this minute we have the consumer purchasing power, and everybody, no matter where they manufacture, is looking to sell here. Now, if we lose our consumer purchasing power, we are certainly not going to be a great nation. So what is the basis of our consumer purchasing power? The basis of our consumer purchasing power is the consuming power of the great mass of the American people. The best customers of American industry are still the American people. No matter how much we put abroad, over 90 percent of the things we make must be sold here, and the basis for

the whole economy over the years has been the mass purchasing power of the great mass of the American people, right down to the lower levels.

SENATOR RIBICOFF. So the problem is not just a trade balance, but a trade balance in what? The necessity to preserve the economic health of American workers becomes very important to the entire future of our Nation.

Is that not correct?

MR. MEANY. Yes, I think so.

SENATOR RIBICOFF. Let me give you an example of what happened in Hartford, Conn., and I would like to get your reaction. For 60 years we had the Royal Typewriter Co. there. A few years ago the Royal Typewriter Co. was taken over by Litton Industries, a conglomerate, multi-national corporation. The average hourly wage of Royal in Hartford was $3.60 an hour. Litton acquired a typewriter company in Hull, England, where the average hourly wage was $1.20 an hour. 55 percent of what goes into making up a typewriter is labor cost. So, Litton moved Royal Typewriter to Hull, England, and about 2,000 people were out of jobs.

What do you consider to be the responsibility of a company to its employees and the community when they move an industry to a foreign country? What is their responsibility to the community and their employees?

MR. MEANY. Well, I think their responsibility certainly would be to the country of employment, but the point is, what does the Government do about this? What would another government do about this? What would other governments of the world do? They would develop a policy to protect their own people, and I think that the answer to this is in the tax structure and in the tariff structure. I think you have got to do

269

something to make it a little less profitable to these people.

You know, in the final analysis, if you carry this whole theory down to the idea that you go where the cheapest labor is, well, then, forget your American standard of life because the only way we are going to get down to these people is to reduce our standard of life. . . .

We had an academic expert over in the White House a few years ago. Thank God he is gone. But he had a very simple theory. He was discussing with a group of businessmen and labor people from New England the closing down of a shoe factory which put a town out of business, and he said very simply, well, if Yugoslavia and the Italians can make shoes cheaper than we can make them, we should stop making shoes, and we should turn around and make something that the Yugoslavs and Italians cannot make as cheap as we can make.

Now, you follow that sort of a philosophy to its natural conclusion, you forget your American standard of life. And you forget your American consumer purchasing power that made it possible to have these gigantic corporations. General Motors did not become a great corporation, Henry Ford did not develop a great corporation selling to those in the upper 20 percent. They became great corporations because they sold something that the people way down at the bottom of the economic ladder could buy.

SENATOR RIBICOFF. Let me ask you another question that the energy crisis highlights. Europe and Japan's oil bills are going to skyrocket because of the much higher cost of oil. Japan's increased costs this year will be some $8 billion. In order to get that kind of additional revenue, do you not see Japan and the European countries making a strong drive to increase their exports to the United States to earn dollars? What impact will that increased export drive have upon American industry and American jobs?

MR. MEANY. The drive is already there. You say a strong drive—

SENATOR RIBICOFF. A stronger drive.

MR. MEANY. They were making a strong drive before they had this problem. This may make them try a little harder. I do not know.

SENATOR RIBICOFF. I have many more questions, Mr. Chairman, but my time is up. . . .

. . . SENATOR HARTKE. Do you think that the trade bill which was passed by the House and which so many of these multinational corporations are giving their slick propaganda in support of. They have been propagandizing against the Hartke-Burke bill and criticizing it for having your blessing and your support.

Do you think that the President's trade bill which is before us now, is an unconscionable delegation of power to the President at a time when Congress is trying to get part of its power back?

MR. MEANY. Yes, I think so. Under the present circumstances, with the President's giveaway attitude toward the Soviet Union, I do not think we would want him to have that power.

SENATOR HARTKE. What about the harm such a bill would do to industries like the shoe industry? The president of U.S. Shoes said he would like to make shoes here, but he could not afford to do it. He could not afford to meet the competition of those slave labor wages in Brazil and other foreign countries where the majority of our shoes are produced.

MR. MEANY. Well, you know, if you look at the trade policies of other nations, you will find that they take a little different view.

If I were to come up with one very simple philosophy of our trade policy with other nations, it would be that every time they close the door on us, we should close the door on them. Every time they give us something in the way of an open door, let us give them an open door. In other words, give and take.

All of these multinational corporations go abroad to manufacture. As the fellow testified here a year ago, he said, I went to Taiwan, I brought American technology, I brought American machine tools, I brought American money, I brought American know-how. The only thing I did not bring American was labor, and I got 5 cents an hour labor over there. But, he said, I am selling back here in America. They do not sell any of this stuff in Taiwan. The consumer market is still here. We have the consumer market, and in the final analysis on trade, this is the strongest card that we have got in our deck, the consumer market.

And I say we should trade.

I want to remind you, Senator, we of the American trade union movement from the time of the Hull reciprocal trade pacts, were free traders. We were free traders right down the line, but we have got a different situation today. In those days we were for lower tariffs. We were dealing with backward European policies where they had the cartel system. But this is a different ballgame today entirely. This is American multinationals. This is American money. This is American technology. This is American know-how, and sitting back here is the American consumer, and I say that in trading with any of these other countries should be dictated by our own self-interests. That is the way they trade. That is the way they do busi-

ness. They shut the door. You could not go to any of these countries and come in there with some kinds of a trade deal that was going to take their jobs away.

Imagine going to the socialist Scandinavian countries, and you are going to take a few hundred jobs, a few thousand jobs away. They would not let you do it.

SENATOR HARTKE. Mr. Meany, in short what you are saying is we are exporting jobs. Ultimately we will destroy our consumer purchasing power if this policy of job exports continues. If we destroy our consumer purchasing power, we are no longer a viable marketplace and they will not need us anymore.

MR. MEANY. Yes, that is right.

Let me give you a sample of what other countries do.

France has quotas on many farm products, on tobacco and tobacco products. And on alcoholic beverages, you are not allowed to advertise bourbon. Now, you know bourbon is a pretty good old beverage, and you are not allowed to advertise that.

SENATOR HARTKE. Let me just point out that most of the bourbon is still bottled in southern Indiana rather than Kentucky. Please do not forget this fact!

MR. MEANY. Well, all right, but you cannot even advertise it in France. You cannot advertise it—

SENATOR HARTKE. You do not have to advertise bourbon. It advertises itself.

MR. MEANY. Well, some of the French might be better off if they drank good old Kentucky or Indiana bourbon.

SENATOR HARTKE. Right, I agree.

MR. MEANY. And a license is required to import some electronic components and textile goods. There are quotas abroad on motion pictures and television films from other countries. Japan has quotas on aircraft parts, on computers and parts for computers. Licenses are required for electric measuring instruments. Imports of coal are subject to quotas. There is an embargo on certain vaccines and serums in Japan. Screen time quotas are applied to motion picture imports. In other words, they only get a portion of screen time. The Japanese, through their devices, make it very difficult for American cars to get in their market.

In Canada, wheat, barley, and oats are state traded, which means that the Canadian Government effectively controls all sales through licensing.

Now, most nations of the world have state trading in their alcoholic beverages.

So, what I am saying in effect, "Sure, do business with the Soviets, do business with them. But do business on the basis of give and take. Do not let it be a one-way street."

SENATOR HARTKE. Be fair traders rather than free traders.

MR. MEANY. Fair trading.

SENATOR HARTKE. Because we have gone a long way, and I tell you there have been tremendous changes, not only since the Hull reciprocal pact, but there have been tremendous changes in the last 10 years, and tremendous changes in the last few months.

SENATOR HARTKE. Right.

MR. MEANY. And I think Congress should take a look at the whole ball of wax.

SENATOR HARTKE. The U.S. Congress should start representing the United States of America instead of representing all the foreign countries. This is what you really mean?

MR. MEANY. Well, I would not say that in the company of a group of distinguished Senators. . . .

SENATOR PACKWOOD. Let me ask you about something in your statment where you are questioning the loyalty of multinational corporations. Where do you think corporate loyalty belongs for a foreign company that operates in the United States?

MR. MEANY. A company that is based in the United States, its loyalty belongs here.

Where does the foreign company's loyalty belong that operates? Back home, that is where you will find it.

SENATOR PACKWOOD. When the Volvo plant opens in Virginia. That plant should be subjected to Swedish sovereignty and Swedish regulation and not, to that of the United States?

MR. MEANY. You think it will not be? You do not know the Swedes if you do not think it will be.

SENATOR PACKWOOD. I do not think the U.S. Government is going to tolerate it.

MR. MEANY. But the point is, let them pay their obligations to their own government, and as far as them operating here, we will try to do our bit for the workers and let our government—but the idea that they will not be loyal to their own government is ridiculous. Of course they will.

SENATOR PACKWOOD. But you are not suggesting, are you—

MR. MEANY. But what do you do with a U.S. corporation—

SENATOR PACKWOOD. You are not suggesting—

MR. MEANY [continuing]. That takes orders from the Arabs and will not supply our fleet in the Mediterranean? What do you think of that?

SENATOR PACKWOOD. What do you think if we have a Volvo plant down here and we get into a war and they are making tanks instead of whatever they might be making?

Who should they be subject to, Sweden

or the United States as to where they ship those tanks?

MR. MEANY. Not if we get into a war. If we get into a war we would certainly have emergency powers.

SENATOR PACKWOOD. How about the automobiles they make there?

Should they be able to ship them any place they want and not be subject to our rules?

MR. MEANY. We have had an open market, and you will find out that the automobile workers, like all other trade unions in this country, have been free traders, but I think you had better talk to Leonard Woodcock now. He might have some different ideas. I defer to this thinking on that. . . .

. . . I want to ask you your view as to how we can pass a trade bill, in what form we should pass a trade bill without undue trade restrictions, but at the same time, give some reasonable protection to the standard of living of the working people of our country?

MR. MEANY. Well, we think that we have supported a bill here and Senator Hartke introduced it but we are willing to concede that since that bill was introduced, there has been a major change in the whole world situation. We certainly have the same objective as you just stated, Senator, and whether it is a quota system or some other system, I think this Congress can find—and must find—a way so that we can trade with the rest of the world on some other basis than the complete one-way system we have now. I just cannot understand American industrialists. I can understand their short-term attitude toward quick profits, but I cannot understand their long-term philosophy. If they are going to lose their consumer market here—and I repeat again, and I will repeat this just as often as I can—that

the consumer market is the great mass of the American people. It is the American workers. You go through a little town in Germany outside of Bonn, you see a few television aerials. You will find out that here and there, there is a washing machine or a dishwasher or a refrigerator in these homes. But when you go out to one of our industrial cities, and in the residences there, there will not be a single home there that has not got all of these things. . . .

We have the highest standard of living for our workers, no question. And I just cannot see giving it away. I think we should trade with all of these countries, and I have no objection to trading with the Soviet Union, but let us get something, and if we cannot get something economic, let us get something political. We can go a long way if they would just say that they would live up to their commitment to the United Nations.

They made a commitment to the United Nations in writing. In fact, they had a ceremony, and old smiling Gromyko was there when he delivered the document that any person, any citizen has a right to move without restriction from any country, including his own, to any other country on Earth.

Now, this is something that they could help us with. They can help us settle this Middle East thing. God Almighty, do not tell me that the Arabs are pushing the Russians around. You know, I do not think Saudi Arabia is calling the shots for the Kremlin. In fact, when you look at the military situation, suppose in Iran or Iraq that the Russians wanted to take that oil. Well, it might take them 24 hours to move in, so they are the bosses there. They are the bosses in that area of the world.

This October war was started when they gave the signal, and it was so well coordinated that the minute the shooting started, they resupplied by planes. They knew their Arab friends. They knew their Arba friends well enough to know that the Israelis were going to knock out a lot of their equipment, so they had them resupplied. They were resupplying almost faster than they lost it. And what happened in those first few days? Where was détente in the first few days of that engagement over there?

Kissinger was begging for a meeting of the U.N. Security Council. They would not talk to him. They did not want to have anything to do with him because the Egyptians were doing quite well. The Israelis were getting it in the neck. But then when they turned around and they broke through and they cut across to the west bank of the Canal and split the Egyptian forces, boy, the Russians wanted a sudden meeting of the Security Council, and, boy, Henry obliged them right away, and he patted them on the back. There would have been no meeting of the Security Council if the Egyptian success had continued.

So this is détente, and détente is an absolute fraud. It is a fraud. The cold war—we talk about the cold war. The cold war was a Russian tactic. I showed you here why they dropped it. But the war is still on. But now the name of the war is détente, you see, that is the name of the war. It is détente and I do not think we can afford the luxury of self-delusion. We cannot deceive ourselves. We have got to go by the record. We have got to know who we are dealing with, and the idea that a dictatorial form of government is going to deal with us on the basis of human values and human rights, they have no concept of human rights. And Senator, here is a map.

You have heard of Solzhenitsyn's book, "THE GULAG ARCHIPELAGO." Well, here is a map published by the American Federation of Labor showing the central Gulag controlled system, and when do you think this map was printed? Twenty-five years ago. Twenty-five years ago, we printed this map and we documented all of the slave labor camps there, and the slave labor is still there.

So we have got our great big industrialists and our great big bankers embracing these guys, sending American capital over, mixing American capital and slave labor. Good God, have we no principle at all?

You know, in the days of Hitler, we heard a lot about Hitler's atrocities, but there was no validation of the gas chambers until the troops moved in, in the late days of the war. We heard a lot of rumors. We did not know about Dachau and a lot of these camps, but we heard a lot of rumors. But Franklin Roosevelt opted for human freedom before we got in the war. He did not appease Hitler. He came to the British rescue. He helped the British with Lend-Lease, so we opted for human freedom even before we got in the war.

I would like to see this administration take a similar principle on the question of human freedom and human decency and deal with the Soviet Union and deal with them on the basis of give and take.

Our policy should be: we've got something, what have you got? What have you got to give? We sell, what have you got to sell?

SENATOR BYRD. Thank you very much, I believe Mr. Meany, you agree with my favorite politician, insofar as Russia is concerned, when Al Smith said, let's look at the record.

MR. MEANY. That is right.

SENATOR BYRD. Thank you, Mr. Chairman.

THE CHAIRMAN. Senator Roth?

SENATOR ROTH. Mr. Meany, I would like to say that I appreciate the forthright statement, and frankly agree with much that you say. I sort of have the feeling that rather than adopt new trade legislation, maybe we ought to just appoint you our chief negotiator as I feel that too often we have been out-negotiated. . . .

Going back a moment to Russia and trading with her, I mentioned making you the chief negotiator. Are there any materials or things that we need from Russia that would be helpful to us?

I think you did say that on the proper basis you favor trade. Do you see a mutual basis of—

MR. MEANY. I do not know anything. I do not have all of the figures, but I do not know offhand of anything that they have that we need so bad that we have got to give them the Washington Monument.

SENATOR ROTH. Let me ask you this question.

We have seen the consequences of the recent oil embargo, and many of the American people feel that this country ought to be able in some way to counter-act such measures. It was said that the oil countries will be investing billions of dollars here in the future.

Would you see any merit to legislation to provide that in the event of future blackmail of that kind, this Government could take action against those assets to compensate for the adverse effect on our economy?

We did that during the war.

MR. MEANY. You mean assets that are overseas?

SENATOR ROTH. No; the assets of the Arab countries in this country.

MR. MEANY. Well, I think we are justified in protecting our people and protecting our interests. I think on the whole ques-

tion of energy, I think there should be a turnaround. I am quite sure that there is enough ingenuity in American management and American business to meet this problem, and I am for the Government encouraging—I think we ought to have more oil refineries here at home, but of course, we do have problems with the environmentalists and things like that, but we have got a lot of energy.

Now, I understand that there is going to be a slurry line built from Wyoming right into Arkansas, which is going to bring all of that coal down there. I think these things are all good, and I think our Government should encourage these things. We have always done that. . . .

SENATOR NELSON. Mr. Chairman, I had another appointment so I missed a great deal of the testimony, and I do not want to be repetitious.

On the question of competing with other countries, bargaining at arm's length, I certainly would agree with you, Mr. Meany. One, among many puzzling questions to me is, the production of automobiles in this country. General Motors Corporation is the world's largest industrial corporation.

The foreign automobile imports—most of which are small cars—are at a level of 16 percent of the total market. At least that was the figure a few months back. That number may have changed in the past few months. However 16 percent of the home market is foreign imports, if my memory is correct, as of some time last year. And almost 40 percent, of the market in California was foreign imports.

How can you account for the success of the foreign manufacturers in invading the American market?

Is it lack of productivity in the auto industry, lack of competitive capacity?

MR. MEANY. Lack of productivity? Oh,

SHOULD THE U.S. RAISE TARIFFS AND IMPOSE QUOTAS?

no. I think our automobile workers are as productive, if not more productive, than the workers in any other part of it.

SENATOR NELSON. I am talking about everything—all costs of production, all materials.

MR. MEANY. I am not an expert in the auto industry, but I assume that it was the attraction of the small cars. Now, you talk about percentage; you said 16 percent. I am sure the percentage of small cars, for instance in the State of California—and this may be due to the proximity of Japan—has been well over 16 percent for a good many years.

Now, the question of competition, I did not hear any complaints over the years from the auto workers, the American auto workers, but I do hear now that they are very, very much concerned, and I think they should be concerned.

Now, General Motors is a great corporation, but I think General Motors will meet this situation. I think they are very resourceful. And offhand, I think the answer is going to be smaller cars.

SENATOR NELSON. I was raising these questions in terms of competitive capacity or excessive profits or a desire to put into the marketplace an automobile that will give them four times as much profit per unit as a smaller one.

MR. MEANY. I cannot fill you in on that, Senator. I do not know.

SENATOR NELSON. In your statement, Mr. Meany, you make reference to excessive exports of farm goods, crucial raw materials, products in short supply. And then on page 6 you refer to the:

Energy crisis has demonstrated that over-dependency on foreign sources of any material can be costly and perhaps fatal. It was demonstrated that the nations, when faced with the choice,

were quick to act in their own self-interest.

How do you balance this whole trade thing out—the products that we do have in surplus, our proteins? We consume about 800 million bushels of wheat in this country, and we produce about 2,100,000,000 bushels, so we have a surplus in excess of our needs to export.

On the other hand, a much more serious crisis it seems to me is the coming metals crisis. So if we start to put some kind of a limitation on export of food products, are we in trouble with the countries that have the metals that we have to have?

In 1969, the United States had become more than 63 percent dependent on foreign sources for metals very important to our industry. Today U.S. dependence on foreign sources for some minerals is as high as 80 and 90 percent. Six of them are vital to the survival of the system.

What happens if we start putting restrictions on what we ship out, and they start putting quotas on what they will ship in?

MR. MEANY. I think this should be the subject of discussion across the table; and surely, if a country that needed our grains, as you say, would put on an embargo on ours, we would retaliate. But I would like to get away from this retaliation business. And surely, if we have got all of these grains to export, then—it seems that we have done quite a job of leaving ourselves short last year, but I understand we are going to be in great shape again this year—but if we have got all of this grain export, we have got a pretty good card at the bargaining table, have we not?

You are talking about confrontation and retaliation, and this is not the approach. I think the approach is if some country has got some raw material that we need and they need some of our grains, I think this gives it a pretty good basis to start talking.

SENATOR NELSON. Well, I do not know the answer to the question, but from reading your testimony, it looks to me like we would be suggesting that we need to put controls on what we would allow to be imported, controls on what we would allow to be exported.

MR. MEANY. That is possible; yes.

SENATOR NELSON. Then we do not have a world market situation? We do not let the world market determine what will be bought and sold, imported or exported from a country. We set up some kind of a control system.

Is that what you are suggesting?

MR. MEANY. I do not know. You say we do not have a world market control. I do not know. Is that good or bad?

SENATOR NELSON. I do not know either, but I would assume that your—

MR. MEANY. So that makes us even.

SENATOR NELSON. Well, I am assuming since you were suggesting that there need to be limitations on imports of some kind or another plus limits on exports, then you have to move to some control situation. I am wondering what the model design for that is, and how that would work.

MR. MEANY. This is what we are searching to find out. As I said earlier, Senator, this whole world situation has changed so rapidly, not just in the last few years, but even in the last few months. I think we have got to take a good look at it, and I think the basis should be give and take. And as I said before—I do not know whether you were here or not—but if some nation locks the door on us, we should lock the door on them. And this is

the way they do business. They do business in their self-interest.

And I think there can be world trade. I think there can be world trade with almost any nation; but at the same time, I do not think that you build up by making unilateral concessions to any nation. I think it is a little give and take.

SENATOR NELSON. But I do not understand how the system will work if we are going to change the whole policy and not have a world free market. Then what do we all do?

MR. MEANY. Well, do we have a world free market? In what commodity do we have a world free market?

Practically every other country on earth has controls of some kind. I do not think you are suggesting that we should live in that sort of a world market and have no control over our own policies.

SENATOR NELSON. I do not know how you define the word free, but there are many foods in a world market situation, with a few limitations here and there.

MR. MEANY. I do not know whether you were here or not, but I just went over some of these things. The French have quotas on many of their farm products— tobacco, alcoholic beverages. They even restrict advertising on good, old Kentucky bourbon, or Indiana bourbon as Vance Hartke said. And Japan has quotas; Canada—wheat, barley, and oats are controlled by the Government through what they call a State trading system.

So I am not saying that we should put controls on this, that, or the other thing; but I say we should put them where we need them and where it affects our economy, and that is what these other nations are doing. We should do the same thing. . . .

● ● ●

NO

TO MAINTAIN THE GROWTH OF WORLD TRADE

1978 Economic Report of the President Jimmy Carter

Over the past 25 years world trade has grown more rapidly than world output, playing a key role in economic expansion by widening available markets for raw materials, industrial products, and agricultural goods. During this period the volume of world trade showed a fivefold increase—an average growth of 6.6 percent a year. This growth was facilitated by a major movement to reduce tariffs and other trade restrictions under the auspices of the General Agreement on Tariffs and Trade (GATT). The Kennedy Round of tariff negotiations, which was completed in 1967, resulted in an average reduction of one-third in the tariffs set by industrial countries on industrial products. The growth of world trade was also supported by the reduction of trade barriers on a regional basis, such as the elimination of tariffs within the European Common Market. In 1970 agreement was also reached on a generalized system of preferences for industrial countries' imports from developing countries.

The growth of world trade has slowed since 1974; trade volume was estimated to have expanded only 4 percent in 1977. The slower growth of trade is mainly attributable to the general weakness in the world economy. However, there has been a disturbing reversal of the trend toward trade liberalization; this development has also contributed to the slowing growth of trade. The GATT Secretariat has estimated that new restrictive trade measures have been imposed on 3 to 5 percent of world trade since 1974.

The worldwide pressure for protection from imports was also evident in the United States. In 1977 the ITC investigated petitions for import relief by over 20 industries, covering imports of nearly $5 billion. The ITC recommended increased protection in the form of tariffs or quantitative restrictions on $3 billion of trade, including shoes, color television receivers, mushrooms, and above-ground swimming pools.

From, the *1978 Economic Report of the President*, Government Printing Office, 1978.

Steel trigger prices. Developments in the carbon steel industry presented the Administration with a particularly difficult trade policy problem. Steel industries throughout the world have been especially hard hit by the protracted weakness of economic activity in the industrial countries. Even under moderately optimistic assumptions about the growth of demand, excess steel-making capacity is likely to persist through 1980.

The cost of production of steel in the United States rose by 89 percent over the past 5 years, according to a study by the Council on Wage and Price Stability (CWPS). The increase in costs was to a significant extent the result of developments within the industry itself. In part, they were the reflection of broader economic forces. Steel wages have risen 27 percent faster than the average manufacturing wage from 1972 to 1977. Raw material and energy costs—particularly coal—have shown very sharp price increases, while pollution abatement costs have risen sharply and will be an increasingly important component of costs in the future. According to CWPS, however, costs have also risen rapidly abroad and the domestic cost of production is not significantly above that of efficient foreign producers plus transportation and tariffs.

Poor domestic sales, reflecting sluggish demand and an increase in the import share, led to a drop in steel production in 1977. This development and other factors led to a series of layoffs and plant closings in 1977. These were concentrated in older steel plants in Ohio, Pennsylvania, and New York. This pattern was dictated by the desire of domestic firms to consolidate their operations in their most efficient installations. The timing and allocation of the layoffs were also affected by provisions in the new labor contract that will increase the cost of layoffs after 1977. The cost of meeting environmental standards at older facilities also played an important role. Thus, the layoffs reflected efforts by the industry to reduce costs over the long term, as well as to respond to the immediate problem of weak demand and import competition. Although several factors contributed to the layoffs, public attention focused on the problem of imports.

The industry filed a series of dumping cases in 1977, some of which led to findings that foreign steel was being sold in the United States below full costs of production. In light of evidence that significant volumes of foreign steel may have been dumped, the Administration developed a program designed to respond to the problems of the steel industry. The centerpiece of the program is a system of trigger prices for steel imports, based on the cost of production in the most efficient foreign country—currently Japan. If imported steel is sold in the United States below the trigger price for that product, an antidumping investigation will be initiated immediately by the Department of the Treasury. The industry maintains the right to file petitions under the regular procedure. Nevertheless, it is hoped that the system will eliminate the necessity for anti-dumping actions.

The trigger price concept has significant advantages over alternative measures. Although in a static and certain world of perfect competition a trigger price, a quota, and a tariff that gave the same protection would have the same effects on prices, their effects differ in practice. A tariff that assured the same protection would have directly increased steel prices by more than the trigger prices will. A quota would have resulted ultimately in an even larger rise in the price of imported steel and reduced competition in steel markets; it would also have undermined incentives for domestic producers to control costs and prices. Under the trigger price system, domestic producers will continue to face foreign competition at prices that reflect the costs of efficient foreign producers. If domestic steel prices are set to meet this competition, domestic producers should be able to regain the market share they lost in 1977.

Progress in Multilateral Trade Negotiations

The Administration has been working with foreign governments to reverse the worldwide slip toward more restrictions on imports and restore the trend toward trade liberalization. These efforts are centered in the round of multilateral trade negotiations now being held in Geneva. After being stalled for some time, the negotiations made significant progress in 1977 with agreement among the major participants on key procedures that will guide the negotiations during 1978. A working hypothesis was developed calling for an average reduction of tariffs on industrial products of about 40 percent. Procedures were established for participants to exchange requests for the reduction of agricultural tariffs and of specific industrial and agricultural non-tariff barriers to trade. Draft texts aimed at improving international trading rules were prepared for use as the basis for further negotiation. In January 1978 countries are exchanging specific offers for reductions of tariff and nontariff barriers. This exchange marks the beginning of the final phase of the negotiations.

The trade negotiations are being con-ducted under difficult conditions in the world economy. These same conditions make it essential that agreement on significant liberalization be reached, however, so that further steps toward protection can be averted, the dynamism of world trade can be restored, and the potential contribution of trade expansion to overall economic growth can be realized.

The Benefits of an Open Trading System

Despite rising domestic pressures for protection from imports at home and abroad, the Administration remains committed to a policy of open markets for both U.S. exports and imports. The case for open markets and against import restrictions is strong. In an open trading system a country will export those goods it can produce at relatively lower cost than other countries and import goods that other countries can produce at lower cost. Countries thereby realize gains from trade that make possible higher levels of consumption and investment. Import restrictions reduce these gains. Through an open trading system the United States can obtain larger quantities of goods for consumption and investment than it could by restricting imports and diverting resources from export industries to import-competing industries.

In addition to reducing the gains from trade, the imposition of import restrictions has an immediate inflationary impact. Consumers pay higher import prices and usually higher prices for domestic substitutes as well. Competition from imports not only helps to keep prices down but fosters efficiency and responsiveness among domestic producers. For example, production of attractively priced American small cars has obviously been hastened by the availability of small, low-priced, fuel-efficient imports.

Import restrictions do not increase employment, even if potential retaliation against exports is ignored. As a result of decreased imports and higher domestic prices, there may be an increase in domestic output and employment in the industry that is granted protection from imports. But the higher prices associated with reduced import competition reduce real consumer incomes and hence tend to reduce real consumption and output. In the absence of changes in overall economic policy, the net effect of these opposing tendencies in the protected industry and in the rest of the economy is usually a *reduction* of real output and employment. Only in the rare instances when import protection results in very small price increases and very large import reductions will protective measures increase employment.

Responses to import restrictions will make the net employment reduction larger. Unilateral imposition of new tariffs or quotas invites retaliation through higher barriers for our exports. Indeed GATT rules allow tariffs to be raised on imports from a country that imposes unilateral trade restrictions. Induced upward exchange rate adjustment also decreases the demand for exports. Thus, in most cases, import protection has the effect of shifting employment from dynamic export industries to contracting import-competing industries, while reducing aggregate employment.

Recent restrictions have primarily taken the form of quotas, import licensing requirements, and other nontariff barriers to trade. Quantitative restrictions are more damaging than equivalent tariffs to an open system of world trade. During recessions they provide less protection from imports at a time when business and labor are in a weaker position; during expansions they do not permit imports to play their role as safety valves, limiting sharp price increases when supplies are tight.

Dealing with Trade Problems

Although the advantages of an open trading system are widely understood, two conditions give rise to demands for protection. First, as markets evolve, countries lose comparative advantage in some products and gain comparative advantage in others. For example, as developing countries have entered markets for products that rely primarily on well-established technologies, the more advanced industrial countries have found their comparative advantage shifting to products using more skilled labor and more sophisticated technology. However, firms in industries that have lost markets to new competitors have capital in place, and their workers have specialized skills that make shifting to new industries costly for them. Their demands for protection from imports are often more effectively voiced than the demands of consumers for lower prices, even though the gains to consumers from an open trading system outweigh the costs to domestic firms and workers.

Second, excess capacity and high unemployment increase domestic sensitivity to competition from imports. Under these conditions, displaced labor and capital are less likely to be absorbed in industries where the United States has a comparative advantage. Moreover, imports that might have been considered a welcome supplement to limited domestic production in some industries during periods of high employment are blamed for domestic unemployment during periods of low utilization. Economic slack abroad also adds to trade tensions because it provides an incentive for some foreign producers to increase exports by cutting prices in the U.S. market. Selling abroad at less than home market prices constitutes grounds for assessing countervailing duties under GATT rules if the domestic industry is injured.

Adjustment assistance. The Federal trade adjustment assistance programs are designed to facilitate the adjustment of workers, firms, and communities injured by import competition. They provide readjustment allowances, training, and relocation payments for workers displaced by import competition. Technical and financial assistance is provided to affected firms, and public works money is allocated to trade-impacted communities. The Administration reviewed these programs in 1977 and is implementing a number of administrative improvements. A major effort has been undertaken to speed up and improve the delivery of assistance, and efforts have also been made to tailor assistance to the needs of particular industries.

Import relief. Problems created by rapid growth of imports in several industries were so acute that the Administration established temporary import restrictions. These restrictions were intended to provide an opportunity for the affected domestic industries to stabilize, to permit firms to take measures to restore competitive positions, and to allow for more orderly adjustment. In two major cases—footwear and color television receivers—where the International Trade Commission had found that increased imports were a substantial cause of serious injury to the domestic industry, the Administration decided to provide temporary import relief. Temporary orderly marketing agreements (OMAs), which are negotiated quotas, were established with major exporting countries. These OMAs will halt the rapid rise of imports and give domestic producers an opportunity to adjust to import competition over the longer term.

• • •

POSTSCRIPT

SHOULD THE UNITED STATES RAISE TARIFFS AND IMPOSE QUOTAS IN ORDER TO PROTECT DOMESTIC PRODUCTION AND EMPLOYMENT?

Meany begins his discussion by forcefully declaring that world conditions have changed so drastically that the old free trade-protection arguments are obsolete. He does not call for a revision of trade policies but rather he calls for a more basic restructuring in which the self interest of the United States becomes the primary consideration. In terms of changes in world conditions Meany identifies several: other countries have made their own self interest the primary consideration in their trade policies; the U.S. is experiencing both rapid inflation and significant unemployment; American firms are exporting technology which gives other countries the ability to compete with domestic industries; the tax code makes it advantageous for companies to move their production facilities abroad. As a consequence the government should revise its tax code, be willing to impose tariffs and quotas on imported goods, and be willing to take action to limit the export of materials in short supply domestically.

In its discussion, the Council of Economic Advisors begins by making the case for free trade. The case rests on four basic points. First, as suggested by the theory of comparative advantage, free trade will increase the quantity of goods and services available for consumption and investment. Second, when import restrictions are imposed, the prices of imports increase and so do the prices of corresponding domestic products. In short, import restrictions tend to be inflationary. Third, even without retaliation, there will be no increase in domestic employment if tariffs and quotas are imposed. Simply put, the higher prices consumers face for protected goods reduces purchases of other goods leaving overall employment unchanged. Fourth, a move to restrict imports will likely result in retaliation by other countries, reducing employment in domestic export industries. In dealing with foreign trade problems, rather than resorting to tariffs and quotas, the government should provide improved adjustment assistance and other more flexible and industry specific assistance programs.

For additional reading on this issue, the following are useful: the complete COMMITTEE ON FINANCE, UNITED STATES SENATE HEARINGS ON THE TRADE REFORM ACT OF 1973 (Government Printing Office, 1974); "Imports and Jobs—The Observed and the Unobserved" by Clifton B. Luttrell in *Federal Reserve Bank of St. Louis Review* (June, 1978); "The U.S. Auto Industry Under Seige" in the *National Journal* (March 15, 1980). For an excellent interpretation of the conservative free market case for free trade see the section on international trade in FREE TO CHOOSE by Milton and Rose Friedman (Harcourt, Brace and Jovanovich, 1979).

ISSUE 15

DO MULTINATIONALS BENEFIT LESS DEVELOPED COUNTRIES?

YES: Ken W. Sayers, from BEYOND THE NEW MYTHOLOGY: THE MULTINATIONAL CORPORATION IN THE MID-SEVENTIES," (Cyanamid).

NO: Ronald Muller, from "More Multinationals: Poverty is the Product," *Foreign Policy* (Winter, 1973-74).

ISSUE SUMMARY

YES: Ken Sayers, a business economist working for a large multinational maintains that MNCs are not only a positive factor in the economies of developing countries but they are a critical factor if these countries are to develop.

NO: Academic economist Muller asserts that MNCs are not only a negative factor in the economies of developing countries, but their presence insures that the rich will get richer and the poor poorer.

At any moment, nearly one-half of the world's population experiences some degree of malnutrition. Some persons, generally the very young and the very old, literally starve to death. Other persons endure a life which is marked with constant hunger pangs. Still others are physically, emotionally or intellectually stunted because of the lack of an adequate diet. These are the residents of "less developed countries" (LDCs).

The inhabitants of these countries cannot be ignored. They account for sixty (60) percent of the world's population, yet they receive only twelve (12) percent of the world's income. Compared to North America and other "developed countries," the residents of LDCs are undereducated, face a truncated life expectancy, and are deprived of the tools of production which increase productivity and reduce physical effort. In short, they are the "poor of the poor." Their world is so removed from that of the developed world, that we can barely comprehend the type of life they are forced to lead. Indeed, few of us are willing to comprehend this reality: It is simply too emotionally disturbing.

Why do countries like Bangladesh, Mali or Ethopia have a per capita income which is less than fifty American dollars a year while we in North America have an income per head which is greater than $10,000 per year? In part, these income differentials can be explained by differences in natural resources, climates, customs, and cultures. Certainly the ninety million Bangalis who reside in a country equal in size to the state of Wisconsin, which once a year experiences floods that cover sixty percent of its land area, are at a disadvantage compared to most Western countries. So are the Malis and the Ethiopians. They cannot hope to match our natural resources, or the advantages of our temperate climate, and at the same time, their customs and cultures often place obstacles in the path of economic development.

However, economic development, or more precisely the lack of economic development goes beyond the questions of resources, climate and cultures. In order to initiate economic development many things must come together at one time. First, incomes must be above subsistence levels so that part of these incomes can be directed to capital formation. If this cannot be achieved domestically, the country must depend upon external funds. Second, technology and a trained labor force must be available. If the transition from the farm to industry is to be made, new methods of production must be introduced and utilized. Third, transportation systems, communication systems, energy delivery systems and a host of other publically provided "support" systems must be available to the fledgling industrial sector. A modern industrial state is unthinkable without this basic social overhead capital. Fourth, domestic and export markets must be developed; there is little value to production if that production cannot be sold or exchanged. Lastly, a corporate bureaucracy must come into existance. Books must be kept. Tariffs must be calculated and paid. Production schedules must be established and maintained. Some workers must be hired and other fired. Inventories must be controlled. Shipments of finished goods must be dispatched on time. The list of everyday middle management duties and decisions goes on and on. Without these much maligned bureaucrats most industrial systems would come to a grinding halt.

How does a country acquire capital, technology, a trained workforce, support systems, markets for their finished goods and an efficient bureaucracy? One source is the multinational corporation. Sayer argues that MNCs in their search for profits will make all these things available to the LDC. In the process, the MNC will send the LDC on its way to economic development. Muller replies that all the MNC will do is to raise domestic expectations while the vast majority of the population and resources in the host country are systematically exploited.

YES Ken W. Sayers

BEYOND THE NEW MYTHOLOGY: THE MULTINATIONAL CORPORATION IN THE MID-SEVENTIES

During the past few years, U.S. multinational corporations have been examined and investigated by economists, labor unions, Congress, federal agencies, foreign governments, various regional economic and political organizations and the United Nations. As a result, there has been an explosion in print of studies, reports, articles and books on this topic, and most of them have been highly negative and undiscerning.

One of the more extreme examples of the genre is GLOBAL REACH by Richard Barnet and Ronald Muller, although other works, such as Peggy Musgrave's study on corporate foreign investment, also misrepresent the MNC.

Our disagreement at Cyanamid with analysts such as Barnet, Muller and Musgrave is basic and very nearly total. Since those of us in multinational business have been in the bull's-eye of criticism for so long and because we believe the public needs balanced and alternative information from which to form its opinions, we believe that companies like Cyanamid must present their own views on the controversy. . . .

Image and Reality

"Words," wrote the Norwegian scholar Sommerfelt, "have become something more than actions: they become the means by which society not only acts on the surrounding world, but also conceives the world." Similarly, the concept of the "multinational corporation" has been so hammered and misshaped by language over the years that it bears little resemblance to reality.

The Barnet-Muller book exemplifies this process. By repeated use of terms such as "global corporation," the authors imply an omnipotent business enterprise with the ability to subvert most of the nations on earth. This logic suggests a world dominated by relatively few businessmen who together manage the affairs of humanity through the instruments of corporate power: capital, technology and marketing. In short, Barnet, Muller and others construct organizational stereotypes that are no more reflective of reality than are the ethnic or religious stereotypes that have misled so many generations throughout history.

Definitions

In the first place, the very term "multinational corporation" has varying definitions. . . .

Perhaps the most appropriate definition is one taking in several criteria. For example, *Industry Week* has suggested that an MNC is frequently defined as one with at least 20 percent of sales outside its home country, manufacturing or research facilities in more than two countries, and a significant number of foreign nationals in its management structure. By this definition, the journal reported, at least 30 of the top 50 U.S. companies and 26 of the largest companies elsewhere in the world can be classified as multinational. . . .

Corporation and Government

This notion of supranationality bears some examination because it underpins many of the assumptions surrounding the MNC issue.

Essentially, many critics maintain that MNCs have more power than most sovereign governments to influence society; that, indeed, MNC managers "are seeking to put into practice a theory of human organization that will profoundly alter the nation-state system around which society has been organized for more than 400 years. What they are demanding, in essence, is the right to transcend the nation-state and, in the process, to transform it."

Governments, some authors claim, are at a disadvantage in their dealings with the MNCs because the corporations plan centrally and act globally while nation-states do not. This reasoning completely dismisses the massive power of government to regulate commerce and the economy, and conduct foreign relations. Within these two rather broad theaters of activity, governments influence and control a variety of international transactions, including business.

The sovereign authority of government rests in its body of laws which separately and collectively govern the affairs of citizens and companies under its jurisdiction. A country's legal system provides it with the means to impose extreme solutions to its problems: politico-military action vis-a-vis other countries; fines, nationalization or expropriation vis-a-vis corporations; and fines, imprisonment and death vis-a-vis individuals. As Rodney Gott, Chairman of AMF Incorporated, has pointed out, the only power possessed by an MNC is the ability to refrain from new or further investment. Compared to this, the power of national authority is overwhelming.

Nor is size or GNP a determinant of a national government's ability to exercise its sovereignty. Each country is endowed with the means to set the conditions under which subsidiaries are established and operated. And, as will be discussed, governments are exercising greater influence along these lines.

In fact, it can be argued that because MNCs are subject to all of the laws and regulations of the countries in which they operate, the companies are more compliant with local requirements than are purely domestic firms because of their relatively vulnerable position as foreign enterprises.

MNC Nationality

MNC nationality is the source of another misunderstanding running through many studies. Commonly, multinationals are thought to be solely an American phenomenon, and as such they are often characterized as appendages of U.S. governmental policy.

Fully a century before the formation of the United States, English and Dutch traders were already active in multinational business. While there are many U.S. firms engaged in international operations, about two-thirds of the foreign affiliates of the world's MNCs are owned by non-U.S. companies. . . .

Economics and the MNC

Because the multinational corporation is primarily an economic mechanism, it is natural that much of the commentary about it falls in the realm of finance and capital. Messrs. Barnet and Muller, for example, write that the rise of the MNC represents the "globalization of oligopoly capitalism," and that the corporations' interests require dampened competition and "world profit maximization."

To buttress this indictment many authors assemble data to portray an outward flood of production and capital abroad, with detrimental effects on both the host countries and the domestic economy. This overall theorem embraces a number of allegations of various economic abuses by multinationals, which are woven together to fashion a web of injurious behavior. Each of these allegations is best understood by isolating it

from the rhetoric filling the literature and discussing it separately.

Foreign Direct Investment

One of the principal impressions one gets from reading works like GLOBAL REACH and the Musgrave study is that the investment by U.S. corporations in overseas operations is somehow inimical to the well-being of Americans and the citizens of the developing countries. Barnet, Muller and Musgrave continually refer to the trend toward additional overseas production and the greater use of finance capital in foreign countries. . . .

We at Cyanamid, of course, see foreign investment differently and we reject the notion that this activity is either malevolent or harmful.

Foreign Investment and the U.S.

The purpose of corporate investment overseas was summed up succinctly in a 1973 study performed by the U.S. Tariff Commission. According to its report to the Senate Finance Committee, capital moved abroad because of the market growth potential in developed countries or the threat of being denied access to foreign markets through exports.

Another view of foreign investment is provided by a recent study by The Conference Board. In a survey covering 65 foreign investments made by 56 U.S. corporations in the 1967-1971 period, the study identified the reasons why specific products are made overseas by American firms. Two major causes stood out: the first was the opportunity to manufacture products not generally exported from the United States to the country of investment; the second was protectionist restraints by foreign governments on imports or an inability to compete effectively with local companies.

U.S. corporations do not enter foreign markets through a single massive step or out of an elaborate plan to "globalize oligopoly capitalism." Rather, the transition of a purely domestic company into an MNC is evolutionary and a response to competitive pressures.

Typically, a firm takes the initial step of becoming multinational when it identifies a market for a product it makes and sells in the United States, and exports that product for sale by local agents or distributors. If the introduction is successful, the company will first expand its exports and then, as local and third country competition develops, it will establish local production and marketing facilities to better serve the distant market. . . .

This touches on the first point we wish to make in this regard: *foreign direct investment by U.S. multinationals is beneficial to the United States.*

One measurement of this benefit is the flow of capital into and out of the country as a result of investment. The 1976 International Economic Report of the President indicated that receipts from U.S. direct investment abroad were $8.9 billion in 1975, against an outflow of $5.3 billion. Thus, the U.S. was a net gainer from foreign direct investment income by $3.6 billion in one year (see Figure 1).

There are other data to indicate the stimulative effect of MNCs on the American economy. In 1974 Business International Corporation undertook a study of 133 U.S. corporations with varying degrees of foreign investment activity. These companies were found to increase U.S. exports almost twice as fast as those of all U.S. manufacturers in the 1960-1972 period. Additionally, companies

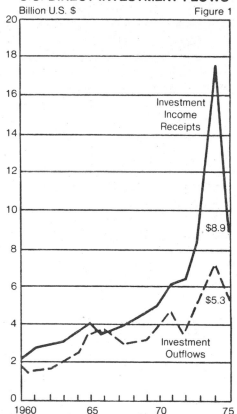

U.S. DIRECT INVESTMENT FLOWS*

Billion U.S. $ Figure 1

*Source: International Economic Report of the President, March 1976, p. 65.

with a higher proportion of foreign investment over the whole period increased their exports at a more rapid rate than companies with less foreign investment. The surplus of exports over imports of the companies studied rose from about $2.7 billion in 1960 to $6.3 billion in 1972 at the same time the U.S. trade balance was falling from a $5.6 billion surplus to a $5.8 billion deficit.

The Business International study also drew the significant conclusion that foreign investment stimulates investment at home, a fact missed by the Musgrave paper. While all U.S. manufacturers increased their spending on domestic plant and equipment in 1972 by 108 percent over 1960, the participating companies increased theirs by 141 percent. . . .

Another way to understand both the magnitude and effect of foreign investment is to consider what would happen in its absence. In testimony before the Senate Subcommittee on International Trade, the late Dr. N.R. Danielian, President of the International Economic Policy Association, estimated that "if all U.S. investments abroad were suddenly eliminated, the United States would be worse off by nearly $17 billion in its international receipts, two-thirds in exports and one-third in investment income, not including the $1.5 billion income from royalties and fees."

Foreign Investment and the Developing Countries

As we mentioned earlier, the nature and scope of multinational operations varies from industry to industry and locale to locale to the extent that many conclusions drawn about these activities are necessarily general. This is particularly true in studies of the impact of MNC investment in the less developed countries (LDCs).

Historically, the involvement of American companies in the developing world was a function of the abundant raw materials located there. Thus, in the early part of this century mining, smelting and petroleum firms constituted the bulk of U.S. enterprises in the LDCs. Later, however, manufacturing subsidiaries began to appear in greater numbers until they now occupy a significant role in U.S. business activity in the LDCs. . . .

Some ideas of the size and origin of this financial commitment to the developing countries is derived from a United Nations report on the role of MNCs in world development. Based on 1967 data, this report indicates that there was $33.1 billion in overseas direct investment in the LDCs by the industrialized countries. About half of this amount came from the United States alone, with Britain contributing the second largest share, 20 percent.

All parties in the MNC debate agree that these capital flows have caused economic changes in the recipient countries; the dispute centers on the nature of those effects. We at Cyanamid are convinced that private investment in the LDCs has produced positive overall results for both host and guest.

This conviction has a logical basis: national governments tend to implement policies which benefit, not harm, the state. Therefore, as Vernon says, "though developing countries follow different policies, most try to limit the operations of foreign investors to those which they believe will improve the production performance of the country or enlarge its export markets. The assumption is that some part of the production, therefore, would not have taken place or would only have taken place at a higher cost. . . .

But more to the point, Professor Vernon also concluded that "beginning in the early 1960's, as exports of manufactured goods began to grow in the developing countries, it became apparent that foreign-owned subsidiaries were contributing to these exports in very much the same way." Hence, the subsidiaries of multinational companies help to boost LDC exports. . . .

Once a firm has been established in a developing country and it produces a product that is destined for local consumption and export abroad, then that enterprise is contributing to the host country in two ways: import limitation or substitution and export generation. Either or both activities should serve to strengthen the host's balance of payments performance. It should be acknowledged, however, that from the standpoint of some of the LDCs, older subsidiaries perform less well in this regard than do newer firms. This is partly because affiliates of more recent vintage are responsible for the largest capital inputs to the LDCs whereas older subsidiaries produce a greater percentage of earnings, some of which are repatriated back to the home country.

Host governments also benefit by the revenues they receive through corporate taxation. Despite the impression created by Barnet, Muller and others, U.S. multinational companies are subject to all of the taxes imposed by the countries in which they operate. Naturally, the tax rate fluctuates from country to country depending on the needs of each government. Just as many U.S. communities set tax policies designed to encourage companies to establish businesses there, a number of LDCs have framed tax regulations to attract new investment by foreign companies. This in itself is recognition of the favorable role played by multinational enterprises in the local economy.

Two other major by-products of MNC investment in the LDCs are important: technology transfer and employment. These are discussed separately later. But perhaps the most significant contribution of all is not the individual elements constituting an MNC's presence—such as its physical plant and financial inputs—but rather the total development capability which the MNC implants in the host country.

Joseph S. Nye, Jr. described this concept in *Foreign Affairs:* "The contribution of the multinational corporation is not so much the movement of capital as the organization of capital, management, technology and access to rich country markets into an economic package which is greater than the sum of its parts.". . .

Profits

It should not be necessary to explain here that commercial enterprises in a free market economy are in business to make a profit. But some observers, such as Barnet and Muller, take the profit motive and convert it into an evil design by MNCs to exploit customers and governments throughout the world. Reduced to its basic elements, this argument is that American-based companies have a higher rate of profit from operations abroad than from domestic operations, and that the interests of MNCs is "world profit maximization," a goal supposedly in conflict with the interests of the host countries.

Once again, the reality is far more complex than the stereotype contained in books like GLOBAL REACH. For example, Barnet and Muller tells us that a 1972 Business International survey showed that 122 of the leading U.S. MNCs had a higher rate of profit abroad in 1971 than in the United States. But the authors fail to mention that when Business International took another look in the following year, the findings were reversed. In 1972 the overseas profitability of 162 firms was lower than profitability inside the United States. U.S. profits as a percentage of net worth climbed to 14 percent while foreign profitability fell slightly to 11.9 percent. A year later the results had reversed again. In fact, the Business International survey has shown U.S. earnings to be higher than foreign profits in about half of the years since 1967 (see Figure 2).

WORLDWIDE PROFITABILITY COMPARISONS, 1968-1975*

Figure 2

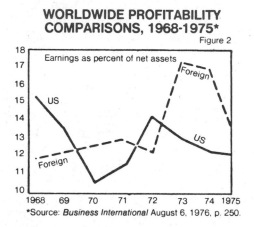

*Source: *Business International* August 6, 1976, p. 250.

This modulating pattern is echoed in a 1973 report by the U.S. Tariff Commission to the Senate Finance Committee:

> The popular view of overseas affiliates as considerably more profitable—exorbitantly so, some think—than their parents is contradicted by the evidence . . .Even in 1970, the recession year at home and the boom year abroad, average profitability in manufacturing for the affiliates was virtually identical to the parents' experience. In 1966, when the business cycle phases were roughly the reverse as between the United States and Europe, the profitability of the parent firms at home was clearly higher than that of their foreign branches and subsidiaries. . . .

Taxes

In GLOBAL REACH, Barnet and Muller repeat the refrain of many critics that MNCs avoid taxation by the very existence of their plants and other facilities in foreign countries. For example, they charge that the companies are able to keep a greater share of dollars earned abroad than dollars earned in the United States through the use of the tax deferral on foreign earnings and the foreign tax credit. . .

In terms of total magnitude, American corporations pay out several billions of dollars each year to the U.S. Treasury and host governments. In data obtained by the Senate Finance Committee, American companies paid more than $5 billion in taxes on income from foreign sources in 1968. According to a study performed by the Joint Committee on Internal Revenue Taxation two years later, the tax bill for U.S. firms had risen to $6.2 billion.

Moreover, according to similar data developed by the U.S. Tariff Commission, the affiliates of U.S. multinationals paid $11 billion in foreign income taxes in 1970 and had a profitability of 6.1 percent as the ratio of aftertax income to sales. In analyzing the difficulties in tax load comparisons, the Tariff Commission study states: "Nonetheless, these data tend to show that, quite aside from any incentives that may be accorded to the affiliates by host countries at the outset, the average foreign tax rates applicable to the earnings of manufacturing affiliates tend to be somewhat higher than the average paid by parents in the United States. . . .

Tax Credit

In general, income tax systems are designed to achieve equity while producing revenue. Numerous tax treaties have been negotiated among nations to prevent double taxation on an international basis. In recognition of these principles, the United States grants U.S. corporate taxpayers a credit against the U.S. income tax imposed on foreign earnings based on the taxes they and their overseas subsidiaries have paid to other governments on that income.

While Barnet, Muller and Musgrave disapprove of the tax credit, they should keep in mind that revocation of the provision would negate the long-standing U.S. tax policy of neutrality between foreign and domestic income. It would, in effect, constitute a flagrant imposition of double taxation in contravention of the basic principle of equitable taxation of income.

Beyond that, the tax credit is in harmony with the tax policies of other developed countries. Industrialized nations recognize the economic necessity and benefit of permitting their domestic corporations to operate overseas without bearing a higher tax burden than their local competitors. . . .

Tax Deferral

Barnet, Muller, Musgrave and others also criticize the U.S. income tax system, which does not impose a tax on unremitted earnings of foreign subsidiaries until they are repatriated to the United States as dividends to the parent company. This concept of taxing income only when received by the taxpayer is internationally accepted by all countries.

For example, a 1972 study by the National Foreign Trade Council's Tax Committee found that no foreign country taxes its companies on the undistributed earnings of foreign subsidiaries. It also discovered that more than 25 countries do not tax the earnings of foreign subsidiaries at home, whether or not the earnings are distributed.

In recent years there have been suggestions to alter the existing policy by either taxing the U.S. parent company on the income of its foreign subsidiaries on a current basis, regardless of the distribution of such earnings, or by setting a minimum percentage of overall foreign subsidiary earnings which would be subject to current U.S. taxation. Cyanamid disagrees with measures of this type. . . .

[By] taxing retained earnings abroad, the United States would probably force dividend payments as a practical result. Yet, the revenue benefit to the United States may be minimal due to the imposition of foreign withholding taxes on such distribution. . . .

[Also], we have to consider the effect of such a policy change on the host nations. In 1973 testimony before the House Committee on Ways and Means, Professor Robert B. Stobaugh of Harvard offered this analysis:

> The reaction of foreign governments is that any attempt by the U.S. to tax the undistributed earnings of companies incorporated within their countries would represent an infringement of their sovereignty, and those governments would probably make selective increases in their taxes in order to obtain for themselves most of the increased tax revenue which the U.S. would hope to gain. Increased tax payments would reduce U.S. parent company dividends to shareholders and would give a cost advantage to foreign-owned competitors, causing U.S. MNCs to incur a loss of market share, a reduced rate of growth, and a decline in profits. . . .

Labor and the MNC

The relationship between labor and management can be a source of tension and occasional friction in any business.

293

Such tension is often magnified within the framework of international business where the scale of management and labor is global and where specific local conditions can vary widely. In addition, as the emphasis shifts from the national to the international scene, many unique aspects of management-labor relations come into play and these then become fertile ground for commentary by MNC critics. . . .

Labor in the U.S.

The expansion of U.S. manufacturing operations in foreign markets during the past decade and a half has led, almost inevitably, to the claims that, first, American companies have built foreign plants to take advantage of cheap labor outside the United States, and second, overseas plants of American companies represent the loss of American jobs. Both claims are incorrect.

A recent study of foreign investment by The Conference Board, for instance, found that only nine percent of the companies surveyed were motivated by low-cost labor in making their overseas investments. In fact, the study indicated that foreign investment occurs not because of labor considerations but because exporting is unfeasible or uncompetitive, and, moreover, that it often provides supplementary employment in the United States.

The U.S. Tariff Commission came to a similar conclusion. "There are many refinements, variations, and subtleties that can be added in describing this market-oriented motivation, yet they all relate to the essential characteristic—that capital moves because of opportunities or threats appearing in foreign mar-

kets . . . Cost considerations take second place." . . .

The 1974 survey by the Emergency Committee for American Trade found that the rate of increase in domestic employment of multinational companies from 1960 to 1970 was 3.3 percent a year, more than twice as much as the 1.4 percent rate of the average U.S. manufacturing firm. Moreover, the data from the 74 companies covered in the ECAT survey reveals that during the 1960s these enterprises increased the number of their domestic employees by nearly 900,000—to about 3.4 million—at the very time they were increasing their overseas operations.

Similarly, 128 respondents to a Business International survey on the effects of corporate foreign investment in the 1960-1972 period indicated that they had increased their combined U.S. work force from 1.9 million to 2.9 million, an expansion of nearly 50 percent.

Some of this expansion is tied to exports by U.S. multinationals. The Bureau of Labor Statistics has estimated that each million dollars of exports supports about 49 domestic jobs. According to a study of 20 companies conducted by the International Economic Policy Association, one-third of the exports of the firms examined went to subsidiaries and affiliates, and this activity alone accounted for 19,294 jobs in the United States. In addition, the surveyed group employs in excess of 65,000 people in export-related positions, two-thirds of whom work in direct labor, engineering and finance. . . .

In its review of this whole question, the U.S. Department of Commerce concluded that elimination of overseas affiliates owned by Americans would not result in increased U.S. employment.

Indeed, the study found that the output of the absent U.S. subsidiaries would be replaced by foreign production. "A reasonable interpretation of available evidence leads to the conclusion that U.S. foreign direct investment is not contrary to the interests of U.S. workers but may, in fact, be a positive factor in stimulating U.S. employment and economic activity."

Clearly, therefore, the increase in overseas manufacturing and investment in the last 15 years has not led to the loss of U.S. jobs but rather to an expansion in domestic employment. This is not that each of the new positions at home was created as a direct result of foreign operations. The total number of Americans whose livelihoods are dependent on U.S. business abroad has been estimated variously at more than one-half million. Andrew F. Brimmer, a former member of the Board of Governors of the Federal Reserve System, has said: "Studies I have made suggest that the foreign trade sector of the United States economy may be generating more than 750,000 jobs, even after allowing for the number of jobs that might be displaced by competitive imports."

Thus, the better than average performance of U.S. multinational companies in creating employment at home—jobs which could not exist in the absence of foreign investment—indicates that American workers have benefited and prospered from international business.

Labor Overseas

When dealing with the overseas aspect of the labor question most critics such as Barnet and Muller assume that corporations establish production facilities abroad to exploit the low cost of labor

resident outside the United States. However, the authors go further by claiming that multinationals destroy employment opportunities in the developing countries through the use of capital-intensive technology.

A 1975 survey by the Pharmaceutical Manufacturers Association, representing 131 drug firms including Cyanamid, gives a different picture entirely. The survey, covering corporations responsible for $6.6 billion in U.S. prescription drug sales and $3.9 billion in overseas sales, found that 110,900 foreign workers were employed. The long-term ratio of foreign to total employment has changed little in the last 10 years, rising from 41 percent in 1973 to 42 percent in 1974.

Therefore, there was virtually no displacement of U.S. workers by foreign employees. The survey found that 12,100 workers in the United States—or about eight percent of the total—were engaged in jobs related to international operations. Since foreign employment represented 42 percent of the total employees and foreign sales constituted only 38 percent of global sales, overseas operations are shown to be somewhat more labor-intensive than those in the United States.

Further evidence of the MNCs' ability to generate employment is available in data compiled by the Department of Commerce. According to its special survey, 41 U.S. multinational chemical companies created 50,000 new jobs overseas in the 1966-1970 period. It should be pointed out, furthermore, that these foreign jobs did not lead to competition with American workers. Commerce Department data indicate that less than one percent of the chemical industry's overseas production was re-exported back into the United States.

Business International has also quantified the contribution of U.S. multinational companies to overseas employment. Its survey of 115 firms covering the 1960-1972 period showed a total of 458,048 workers employed outside the United States at the beginning of 1960; by the end of 1972 this total had grown to 1.4 million jobs—for a gain of more than 200 percent. . . .

Marketing and the MNC

In examining the role played by marketing in multinational corporations, observers such as Barnet and Muller allege that the companies, first, try to create a "world customer," and second, carry out "ideological marketing."

For example, these authors conclude that in order to service what they term a "global shopping center," corporate managers must "retail old needs to new customers . . . and create new needs for old customers," and that they exploit the developing countries by using marketing to shape the tastes and values of workers, suppliers, government officials and customers. The writers thus depart the purely commercial plane by introducing the notion of the "consumption ideology."

Many of the companies that are discolored by this broad-brush attack are among the world's leading developers of applied technology. These firms spend billions of dollars annually to carry out sophisticated research programs, discover solutions to our most intractable problems and develop products to improve the quality of life across the globe. . . .

The technology created by a business enterprise usually evolves into a product or service which is offered for sale. The box or bottle containing the product becomes the vehicle to carry the company's technology from the laboratory to the consumer. Yet the consumer, who is ill-equipped to trace the development of thousands of products from initial research through testing to production, has no systematic method for discovering the availability of a product he needs. It is only through marketing, then, that a corporation can inform a customer that it can satisfy his specific requirement.

The medical products field illustrates this point. A new product which is unknown to the physician is worth absolutely nothing in terms of saving human lives or alleviating suffering, no matter how good it may be therapeutically. Marketing plays a key and essential role in bridging the gap from discovery to practical medical use which benefits the patient.

A new product may take up to ten years to develop and may cost $10 million or more in research, clinical evaluation and in capital cost for new production facilities. At that point this new product is unknown, except to clinical investigators, and within the originating firm.

Unfortunately, not every physician learns about a new product in short order. An authoritative market study conducted over a period of years reveals that, on average, only 30 percent of doctors are aware of a new product after two months of intensive marketing efforts. Another month of marketing only increases this figure by three percent. Thus, after three months, most doctors still are not aware of the new product and its use, and its assistance is denied to people who may need it.

Rather than create needs, as Barnet and Muller charge, Cyanamid and companies like it are hard pressed to meet both new and continuing needs. Rather than exploit the people of the developing countries, Cyanamid and other multinationals save thousands and thousands of lives outside the United States by making products available to wipe out hunger, eliminate disease and raise public health standards. . . .

Doubtless Messrs. Barnet and Muller are motivated by a sincere concern that overseas customers may become frivolous customers, that they will engage in an orgy of spending that disrupts the orderly patterns of economic development. We at Cyanamid are also concerned that scarce economic resources are sometimes poorly applied—by governments and consumers alike—in both developed and developing societies. Yet a free market economy is predicated on individual choice and not on an imposed system of selection established by authorities, academic or otherwise.

The duty of the corporation within the framework of free enterprise is to identify the specific needs of its customers around the world, structure its research and development efforts to meet a variety of current and evolving requirements, and tailor its products to satisfy customer demand—not only today but tomorrow as well. And marketing is the means by which American businessmen accomplish these objectives.

Technology and the MNC

A fourth broad subject covered by the critics of multinational corporations concerns the economics of technology and its use by MNCs.

Many writers hinge their arguments on the assumption that multinationals are oligopolies and that, as such, they must control exclusive technology. Some authors decry the imbalance between the high proportion of research and development (R&D) centered in the United States and the lesser percentage conducted by U.S. companies in the poorer nations. Barnet and Muller, for instance, say that this imbalance and control leads to "technological dependence on foreign corporations [which] enormously enhances the power [such] corporations can wield—power which, as everywhere, is abused when it is not checked." The patent system is frequently cited as the instrument by which MNCs "control" their technology.

We are also told that the technology actually transferred by the multinational to its foreign subsidiaries is often obsolete and overpriced, and that the impact of the MNCs' technology is harmful to the developing countries of the world, primarily because it produces insufficient new employment.

But there are other critics, many of whom speak for labor unions, who do not favor the export of technology by U.S. companies. They believe this transfers our international competitive strength to other countries—as though the United States had a monopoly on technology and could not benefit from either its sale or purchase.

In Cyanamid's view the idea that technology is the exclusive preserve of U.S. multinational corporations is false. Although the immedite postwar era marked a period of American ascendancy in science, more recent U.S. scientific discoveries account for a smaller portion of the world total. The following indices illustrate this point.

According   to   the   Manufacturing

Chemists Association, only three of the top 10 chemical research organizations in the world belong to U.S. companies; the other seven are foreign-owned. Moreover, the $1.7 billion spent by the U.S. chemical industry in R&D annually represents only 40 percent of the total expended in the entire free world for research and development of new chemicals and related products. Finally, the Association reported that 11 of the 19 great chemical innovations of the past 30 years were based on foreign discoveries or developments.

Thus, we agree with the U.S. Department of Commerce statement that "caution should be exercised so as not to place too much emphasis upon the United States as a generator of technology—it is the leading innovator, but the United States has also benefited from the work done in foreign countries."

Yet it is true that much of the research and development performed by U.S. multinational companies is conducted in the United States. This concentration exists because the parent company cannot fragment and disperse its research activities without undue expense, duplication of effort and wasted motion. However, this does not exclude American R&D facilities from foreign countries; U.S. firms can and do locate technological units in many overseas locations. . . .

The pricing of the transferred technology is another process misunderstood by many critics. Foreign affiliates pay a price that is determined by a wide range of economic and political factors, often beginning with price controls imposed by the local government at every step of the distribution. In Cyanamid's experience, this has been especially true with medical product technology.

In this regard, the parent company must also consider differences in registration requirements, taxes and tariffs, competitive and market conditions, wages, distribution costs and many other factors. The Pharmaceutical Manufacturers Association also points out that many governments of developing countries review all technology transfer agreements for royalties and management fees, and are empowered to alter or disapprove these contracts according to national policy.

Moreover, the U.S. government has taken the position that "there is no convenient formula by which the fair price of technology can be determined. While the marginal cost of disseminating technological information may be low, the actual cost of transferring technology in an effectively utilizable form to another country may be very high. In addition, it must be recognized that private innovation will not take place if the innovators are not paid sufficiently to compensate them for the risks inherent in innovation, and to provide them with a reasonable return."

While some of our critics are correct in pointing out the capital-intensive nature of technology, they are incorrect when they imply that technology must be labor-intensive in order to satisfy the needs of the LDCs. Surely technology offers the host country benefits beyond those keyed to generating large numbers of jobs. The importation of technology, first of all, upgrades local skills, improves host country scientific and manufacturing know-how, stimulates industrialization and broadens the base of R&D within the recipient nation. And, more importantly, the new technology is utilized to enhance the quality of life for society.

Thus, the global community would do well to encourage rather than restrict or manipulate the flow of technology from the industrialized societies to the developing countries. In the words of the State Department, this can be accomplished by "providing an environment which facilitates the process of innovation. This includes support for higher education and research institutes, security for foreign investment, and protection of industrial and intellectual property rights." In recognizing the benefits offered by technology, both the developing world and the United States, we at Cyanamid fully concur in this recommendation.

The Developing Countries and the MNC

One of the most significant geopolitical developments of the current decade has been the increasing ability of the less developed countries (LDCs) to influence international events. No longer content to serve merely as sources of raw materials for the industrialized countries, the LCDs are now trying to frame a "new economic order" in which they will join in an equitable partnership with the developed nations. Robert S. McNamara, President of the World Bank, foresaw this trend years ago when he wrote: "The outlook for the Seventies is that the fault line along which shocks to world stability travel will shift from an East-West axis to a North-South axis, and the shocks themselves will be significantly less military and substantially more political, social and economic in character.

The 1973 oil embargo by the OPEC states and the 1974 special session of the UN General Assembly on economics and development are but two examples of the growing militancy and influence of the LDCs. It is no accident, therefore, that much of the recent wave of MNC criticism deals with the relationship between the developing world and multinational companies.

Generally, books such as GLOBAL REACH present the view that MNCs exploit the poorer nations through their manipulation of foreign investment and financing, employment of lowcost labor, application of sophisticated marketing techniques and control over technology. Earlier, we analyzed these subjects in detail and revealed the weaknesses in many of the arguments that are in vogue today.

Perhaps the worst case of unfair criticism we have seen is the charge by Barnet and Muller in GLOBAL REACH that MNCs have "compounded the world hunger problem." They describe three ways in which so-called global corporations aggravate hunger on the planet. "First, they have contributed to the concentration of income and the elimination of jobs. Second, through its increasing control of arable land in poor countries, agribusiness is complicating the problem of food distribution. . . . Finally, the companies' control of ideology through advertising has helped change dietary habits in unfortunate ways.". . .

Basically, the primary cause of food scarcity in the LDCs is not the existence of multinational companies but decreases in foreign exchange reserves (prompted by the OPEC escalation in oil prices), and shortages in energy, fertilizers, pesticides and other agricultural outputs. Obviously, the multinational company is often the source of these badly-needed inputs. . . .

We must also mention that American business contributes more than just products to help solve the hunger problem in the LDCs. Roger E. Anderson, the chairman of the Continental Illinois Corporation, has said that:

299

The multinational agricultural corporation could be an effective vehicle for infusing capital into the now labor-intensive farming systems of developing nations, for transmitting programs leading to the development of technical and farm management skills, and for marshalling local incentives to explore additional food sources and improve present sources through more effective production practices. There are, of course, multinational corporations doing these things now, especially in the field of food growing and processing, commercial fishing and fish meal, production, farm machinery, pharmaceuticals and others . . .

However, the long-term solution to the problem of hunger in the LDCs requires more than just greater agricultural inputs from the MNCs. [Former] Secretary of State Henry Kissinger, for one, looks toward a comprehensive approach. "The global economy must achieve a balance between food production and population growth, and must restore its capability to meet food emergencies. . . The global economy requires a trade, monetary and investment system that sustains industrial civilization and stimulates its growth." In other words, multinationals can only perform their special function within the framework of a stable international economic system geared to a free market which provides adequate financial incentives to private companies. . . .

In a 1975 address to the UN General Assembly, [then] Secretary Kissinger discussed the problems associated with the MNC presence in the Third World. Multinational companies, he said, "have been powerful instruments of modernization both in the industrialized nations—where they conduct most of their operations—and in the developing countries, where there is often no substitute for their ability to marshal capital, management skills, technology and initiative. Thus, the controversy over their role and conduct is itself an obstacle to economic development." . . .

Conclusions

The last quarter of the 20th century is a complex period for the international community. Our most staggering problems—population growth, finite natural resources, a fragile ecological system, widespread hunger, pestilence, nuclear proliferation and intergovernmental rivalry—will have to be solved before the next millennium if mankind is to survive.

Many of these problems are often translated into economic terms. And because the multinational corporation is a highly visible force in the global economy, it has received considerable attention and critical analysis. Unfortunately, much of this attention originates in an illiberal cynicism and flows from the false premise that the relatively affluent nations and their MNCs are the cause of such economic problems as poverty and unemployment. Such a premise has resulted in the call for a so-called "new international economic order," i.e., a redistribution of wealth from the industrialized countries to the developing nations.

However, Cyanamid's experience indicates that the removal of whatever inequities presently exist in the world lies not in the redistribution of wealth but in its creation in the first place. And this is the primary function of the multinational corporation.

In many ways the MNC acts as a sophisticated pipeline supplying new wealth.

On one end there are clusters of laboratories, drawing boards, test sites and creative people whose imagination and courage leads to new technology. On the other end there are individual customers and the larger community of which they are a part. The MNC thus develops and delivers products and services to match a range of current and emerging requirements throughout the world. Obviously, this is a vital process out of which comes progress and prosperity. And obviously, too, there are considerable rewards and satisfactions for the collective society.

Thus, we have seen that the MNC is a commercial enterprise conducting business across national frontiers. Many studies we have examined find that both the distribution and magnitude of this multinational business have benefited the populations of rich and poor lands alike.

Secondly, we have shown that the MNC disperses the fruits of innovative technology among nations. Life-saving drugs and pesticides, for example, can help the citizens of Bangladesh and Chad as well as the people of the United States and Japan.

Thirdly, we have demonstrated that the multinational company is an efficient mechanism for the expansion of employment and capital. Hundreds of thousands of men and women in the Americas, Europe, Africa and Asia work in jobs created by these corporations. Thousands of local entrepreneurs in all parts of the world have established businesses which are sustained by international trade. This is the essence of the creation of wealth.

Fourthly, multinational companies are an instrument for international stability and cooperation. Commerce—one of the most ancient of human activities—has brought man into contact with his near and distant neighbors for centuries. These contacts have created a universal link for understanding and agreement. They often transcend political, religious and other differences and are a positive basis for the exchange of ideas between nations.

In sum, we at Cyanamid believe that the multinational corporation is one of the better tools available for enhancing life on this planet. While our immediate efforts are commercially directed toward meeting the needs of our diverse customers, we are also aware that the cumulative effect of our activities engenders prosperity and improves the human condition. As long as we are permitted to maintain this enterprise within an open and free economy, we will continue to meet our commitment and responsibility to society.

There is much to be done on behalf of a great many people: new products to be discovered, solutions to be devised and services to be delivered. All we are seeking, therefore, is the opportunity to get on with our work.

● ● ●

NO

Ronald Muller

POVERTY IS THE PRODUCT

Countries are called "less-developed" for specific reasons. Less-developed means a lack of adequately-trained government civil servants to examine and investigate whether or not commercial and business laws are being enforced, let alone complied with by multinational corporations (MNC's) or locally-owned companies. But this lack of expertise has even a deeper meaning because it indicates that the laws themselves are usually quite old, designed for times past, and too-long unrevised.

A basic part of being less-developed is having institutions which are either lacking or misfunctioning relative to similar institutions in industrialized societies. For those of us accustomed to life in the advanced nations, it is essential to understand this aspect of underdevelopment. The "bargaining power" of the MNC's is far greater in less-developed countries (LDC's) than in rich countries, because of this absence or weakness of institutional mechanisms to control the behavior of their subsidiaries. Stated in Galbraithian terms, Third World countries are characterized by an absence of the "countervailing" power of government and organized labor for setting limits on the power of the modern corporation.

Another aspect of underdevelopment further intensifies this power—the economic structure of these societies. There are two key characteristics of this structure which are important here: first, the need for and the sources of *technology*; and second, the need for and the sources of *investment financing*.

The Structure of Technology

Most Third World nations have already set in motion a process of industrialization highly similar to that found in more-developed countries (MDC's). This industrialization is not only similar in terms of the output of industry, but also in terms of the technology and human skills needed for its implementation. In other words, the voluntary or involuntary institutionalization of MDC's consumption values as the goal of economic growth has, in turn, brought about the need for a technology which can satisfy this pattern of consumption. . . .

Clearly, LDC's are virtually entirely dependent upon foreign sources for their technology. . .

Also, the foreign versus local control of technology does not indicate the actual concentration of control in the hands of a very few foreign corporations. Looking at the foreign countries involved we find that, for example, in the United States, of the 500 largest industrial corporations, the top 30 own 40.7 percent of the patents in their respective industries. The mirror-image of this concentration of technology-control in the advanced nations is found to even a greater extent in the underdeveloped areas. For instance, in Colombia, in the pharmaceutical, synthetic fiber, and chemical industries, 10 percent of all patent-holders own 60 percent of all patents, and these 10 percent are all foreign MNC's.

Such concentrated control of technology is one of the most effective means of establishing oligopoly power over the market place, restricting the development of local competition, and permitting an astounding rate of profits, the bulk of which leave the country. Once such a *process* is under way, it becomes cumulative and self-perpetuating. . . . In the end, as is the case today in Latin America, domestic firms are either absorbed by the MNC's or must resort to the "licensing" of their technology, and with such licensing comes a number of significant restrictions.

The Structure of Finance

A similar set of vicious circles is also at play in the financial patterns of these countries. Of first importance is the expense of the technology being used. It is well known that in almost all LDC's there is a scarcity of local savings available for productive investments. This scarcity is not only due to the LDC's low level of income, but also to the fact that savings leave the country. Foreign firms repatriate a significant part of their profits and indigenous wealth-holders also channel a part of their savings out to MDC's (the latter is the so-called phenomenon of "capital flight"). Adding to this is the increasing debt-repayments to bilateral (e.g., AID) and multilateral (e.g., World Bank) aid agencies on loans granted in the 1960's. Together, the magnitude of these outflows have led a number of writers to comment that in aggregate terms the poor countries of the world are now ironically helping to finance the rich countries, i.e., the financial outflows from LDC's far exceed the inflows.

There is thus a twofold dilemma in the financial structure of LDC's. On the one hand there is a growing gap between the supply of *available* local savings and the demand for investment funds to alleviate the growing poverty *and* the growing awareness of it by the people of these countries, via increased literacy, improved communications, and the ensuing demonstration effects. On the other hand, the particular technology which the industrialization process necessitates is not only expensive, but must be paid for in foreign, not local, exchange. . . .

The upshot of this twofold dilemma (inadequate amounts of local savings and foreign exchange), from the viewpoint of domestic enterprises, is a rather perverse

303

form of noncompetitive financing patterns in most LDC's. Contrary to the generally accepted notion, MNC's do not bring their own finance capital from abroad, but rather derive the overwhelming majority of their financing from local, host country sources. The subsidiaries of MNC's in LDC's borrow from local financial institutions with the credit-rating and financial resource back-up of the entire global network of their parent MNC. This is in contrast to the credit-rating and financial resource back-up of the smaller typical local business enterprise when it attempts to obtain finance capital. The vicious circle begins to close. The local financial institution, faced with limited loan capital relative to demand, and (like any other business) interested in risk-minimization, will inevitably be biased towards the subsidiaries of MNC's. . . .

Employment: Impacts and Causes

It is well known that unemployment and underemployment in LDC's is very high and increasing sharply. It is now probably over 30 percent of the active labor force. Is there any hope for at least a partial diminution of the problem in the near future? If the past is any indication, the answer is no.

An underlying cause of the unemployment crisis is the particular industrialization process used to bring about economic growth. The technology transferred to the Third World by the MNC's has been designed for the advanced industrialized nations where there is a relative abundance of capital and a relative scarcity of labor. Thus, the MNC drug companies use a technology in which only 3.4 percent of total costs are due to labor. There is, of course, an obvious contradiction in bringing such technology

to Third World countries where there is an abundance of labor and an acute scarcity of capital. . . .

It is this process of ever more intensive substitution of capital for labor in the technology transferred by the MNC's, which is one of the prime causes of the startling degree of unemployment in the Third World—a situation which Africa and Asia only recently have begun to face, but which has been gnawing at Latin America since the 1920's, given its earlier entry into "modern" industrialization. . . .

With over 99 percent of the industrial technology of most of the Third World coming from the industrialized nations and controlled largely by MNC's, our conclusion is that the MNC's are eliminating more jobs than they are creating.

Income Distribution: Impacts and Causes

Unemployment is only one dimension of poverty; the other is income distribution.

In focusing on the relationship between MNC's technology and income distribution in LDC's the first question is the extent to which capital versus labor is used to produce output. We have seen that capital is replacing labor at a growing rate, so that the second and more important question is who receives the income generated by capital resources? Most LDC economies are based on the legal institutions of capitalism, meaning that the owners of capital resources receive the income generated by those resources. Where there are only a very small number of owners (and thus a very large number of non-owners) of capital, and where the technology used generates a larger proportion of income from capital than labor resources, then, by definition, income distribution will be highly unequal. In addition, where there is a relatively rapid change in technology biased towards laborsaving techniques, and where capitalist legal institutions are not modified via, for example, more progressive tax rates, to keep pace with this change, then, again by definition, income distribution will become even more unequal over time. This is the second dimension of the growing poverty in LDC's. Just how unequal is the distribution of national income in LDC's, and how has it been changing over time? The answer is very unequal and more unequal over time.

Irma Adelman and Cynthia Taft Morris, in a worldwide study of income distribution in Third World countries undergoing the industrialization process we have been describing, noted that from subsistence levels throughout the industrial "take-off," until an average per capita income level of about $800, there is a profound change in income distribution. During this "take-off," the richest 5 percent of LDC populations experience a "striking" increase in incomes compared to the poorest 40 percent of the population. While their countries are achieving what economists call rapid economic growth, as indicated by increases in output and the misleading term average per capita income, many people's actual intake of food, clothing, and shelter is declining! Latin-American countries, in the midst of industrialization, provide a dramatic verification of this finding. In the 1960's, for example, Chile's average per capita income was approximately $600, but the richest 10 percent were receiving 40 percent of the national income, or an actual per capita income of some $2,400—thus giving a family income

higher than the majority of Western European families.[1] In Mexico and Brazil, the situation is worse, and it is notable that these two countries have been by far the most favored investment targets of the MNC's in Latin America. . . .

Financial Contribution of Domestic Firms

A traditional argument in favor of MNC expansion in the Third World has been that they bring much needed finance capital. The key assumption here is, of course, that the MNC's in fact do utilize foreign savings to finance their LDC operations. This assumption, incidentally, is also made by Marxist scholars who have held that MNC's expand from their home countries because of an excess of surplus finance capital. Upon investigation, however, the assumption proves to be incorrect.

Only 17 percent of the total finance capital used by MNC's in their gross investments came from nonlocal savings. In the last three years of the 1957-65 period, the figure dropped to 9 percent. Of more importance is the use of local savings in manufacturing, the most rapidly expanding of the three sectors. Here the figure of 78 percent of total financing being derived locally has been constant since 1960. Individual country studies covering the latest years of 1965-1970 also have shown no change.

Although the MNC subsidiary's future profit represents a net gain in income for itself, it will be largely *externalized* out of the LDC, and therefore not for the

[1]Morris and Adelman, "An Anatomy of Income Distribution Patterns in Developing Nations: A Summary of Findings," Economic Staff Paper No. 116, International Bank for Reconstruction and Development (IBRD), September 1971. Osvaldo Sunkel, IDB/U.N. Seminar, Santiago, 1970, p. 36.

consumption or investment benefit of the local citizenry. This is borne out by the fact that, from 1960 to 1968, MNC's repatriated an average of 79 percent of their net profits, not to mention their additional remissions of royalties, interest, and other fees. In manufacturing, repatriated profits were somewhat lower but increasing, going from 42 percent of net profits in 1960-1964 to 52 percent in 1965-1968. In the manufacturing sector, for each dollar of net profit earned by an MNC subsidiary, 52 cents will leave the country even though 78 percent of the investment funds used to generate that dollar of profit came from local sources. If we look at all sectors in which MNC's operate in Latin America, the inflow-outflow accounting gets even worse. Each dollar of net profit is based on an investment that was 83 percent financed from local savings; yet only 21 percent of the profit remains in the local economy.

Do the MNC's make a financial contribution to LDC's: i.e., do they make a net addition to the supply of available local savings over time? The answer is no. Although we cannot make an exact quantitative estimate of this loss, from the magnitudes of the above indicators it is clear that there is a net decrease in the amount of local savings being utilized for the benefit of either indigenous consumers or investors in local LDC's.

The Buying-Out of Domestic Firms

We now turn to the specific uses to which MNC's put finance capital. It is commonly held that when an MNC invests in an LDC, even if it uses largely local savings, it at least channels that investment into the creation of *new* production facilities; facilities which otherwise could have been absent from the local economy, i.e., a net addition to the productive assets of the LDC.

Again, reference to the facts shows this notion to be more myth than reality.

This conclusion can be demonstrated by the data now available on the 187 largest U.S. MNC's, which account for some 70 percent of all U.S. foreign investment in Latin America. From 1958 to 1967 these firms established 1,309 subsidiaries. Of this number there are 173 cases for which no information was available on method of entry. For the 717 known new manufacturing subsidiaries, 46 percent or 331 did not establish new production but rather purchased existing domestic firms. . . .

The implications are clear. In the manufacturing sector, currently the most important to the future development of Latin America, 78 percent of MNC's foreign investments are financed in actuality from local savings. With this finance capital, an estimated 46 percent is used to buy out existing locally controlled firms, whose profits would otherwise have been retained domestically and would thus have contributed to either local consumption and/or savings. But from the date of the acquisition and henceforth, some 52 percent of those profits will leave the country, resulting in a net decrease in the LDC's savings which would have been otherwise available *and* a net increase in their already acute shortage of foreign exchange. Given these results, it is impossible to see how the MNC's financial impact on Third World countries could possibly assist in the alleviation of their underdevelopment. . . .

It has been claimed that the MNC's can make a significant contribution to raising the foreign exchange earnings of Third World countries through their ability to export (particularly manufactured goods). On the surface this argument would appear correct given the competitive advantages of the technology and worldwide marketing systems of the MNC's compared to local firms. There are a number of considerations, however, which this argument overlooks. First, if MNC's have subsidiaries manufacturing similar products in many countries, as most of them do, would these subsidiaries want to compete with each other through exports? Second, even where the parents have complementary production between subsidiaries so that intersubsidiary exports and imports are desirable, what are the prices on such exports and imports, since as nonmarket transactions they are not subject to competitive pressures? Third, what are the tax and other financial criteria which would make these prices different from those received or paid by local firms dealing with independent buyers and sellers on the international market? Fourth, what does the available empirical evidence tell us concerning the initial argument and the considerations we have introduced? Fifth, besides the exporting by MNC subsidiaries, what impact does the licensing of their technology to local firms have on the latter's ability to export?

The MNC's and Exports: Restrictions

We shall start with the last question first. In detailed investigations of the licensing agreements between local firms in LDC's and the MNC's, it has been found that in most cases there are total prohibitions on using this technology in the production of exports. . . .

The impact of these "restrictive business practices" on the export capacity of domestic firms and their LDC economies

is profound. For at a time when the political leaders of the MDC's are encouraging Third World countries to export more, their own MNC's are making it virtually impossible for them to enter the one export market which in the long run is viable—namely, manufactured exports.

We turn now to the question of the export performance of the MNC subsidiaries themselves. It does not necessarily follow that the MNC's will export from LDC locations even though they may have the technology and marketing prerequisites. In the Andean Group, 79 percent of the MNC subsidiaries were prohibited by their parents to engage in exporting, and these findings are not unique to these countries. In fact, studies for Latin America have found that manufacturing MNC's on the average export less than 10 percent of their total sales, while in Europe, U.S. firms average about 25 percent. There are exceptions, however. Some MNC subsidiaries do export significant *volumes* depending on the industry and country in which they are located.

Performance and Pricing

We have already alluded to the fact that U.S. MNC's account for some 40 percent of Latin America's manufactured exports, and they have achieved this level of export participation within the span of the past 20 years. Yet the figure is a deceptive one if it is intended to imply that MNC's are therefore making a significant positive impact on the balance of payments of Third World countries. First, manufactured exports constitute only 16.6 percent of the region's total exports, and well over half of these exports come from only 3 of the 21 countries: Argentina, Brazil, and Mexico. The above-cited detailed

DO MULTINATIONALS BENEFIT L.D.C.s?

econometric analysis has determined that, relative to local firms, MNC subsidiaries performed significantly better only in these three countries and only in terms of export sales to other Latin-American countries. In contrast, for exports to the rest of the world, where one would expect the technological and marketing superiority of the MNC's to be most crucial, their export performance was not significantly different from domestic enterprises. For the remaining countries of the region, the MNC's were outperformed on exports to the rest of the world by firms which had substantial domestic participation, while on exports to other Latin-American countries, the MNC's performed no differently than their domestic counterparts.

The price put on an export or import between MNC subsidiaries of the same parent is termed a "transfer price." Frequently, transfer prices deviate sharply from the market price of these goods. For example, if a subsidiary exporting in country X is faced with higher corporate tax rates than the importing subsidiary of the same parent in country M, then the parent will pay less *total* taxes for both subsidiaries and earn more *total* net profits by directing the exporting subsidiary to undervalue its exports. Another variant of this pricing technique, even more profitable, is to direct the underpriced exports first to a tax-free port (so-called tax havens) and then re-export the goods at their normal market value (or perhaps now overvalue) to the subsidiary of final destination. There is an obvious impact on the economy of the LDC in which such exports originate: the LDC governments, seriously short of needed tax revenues, are now deprived of that much more, so that an MNC can "maximize" their global profits.

In looking at the export pricing of MNC's in Latin America, the above cited study, [UNCTAD, Restrictive Business Practices, Santiago, January 7, 1972], found that 75 percent of the these firms sold exports only to other subsidiaries of the same parent and, on the average, *underpriced their exports by some 40-50 percent* relative to the prices being received by local firms.

We should also mention an additional "restrictive clause" in the transfer of technology contracts negotiated between MNC parents and their subsidiaries and licensees. This is the so-called "tie-in clause," which requires the subsidiary or the licensee to purchase intermediate parts and capital goods from the same parent MNC which supplied the basic technology. This practice is common operational behavior for MNC's in the Third World. For example, in the Andean Group study, 67 percent of the investigated contracts had tie-in clauses. The results were no different in other countries such as India or Pakistan.

The irony is that these types of clauses are in basic violation of the antitrust laws of the home countries of the MNC's which practice them in LDC's. In the United States, tie-in clauses are prohibited by Section 1 of the Sherman Act and Section 3 of the Clayton Act. Whether or not these laws are applicable to the MNC's in their overseas operations is still a moot question, but the fact that underdeveloped legal institutions of LDC's do not yet deal with these restrictions strongly underlines the differences in the oligopoly power of MNC's in advanced industrialized *versus* Third World countries.

The Triangular Trade

In [a] Colombian investigation, it was

found that a large proportion of the overpriced imports involved a "triangular trade." That is, they were shipped from a U.S.- or European-based parent or subsidiary of the parent to a holding company in Panama. In Panama, a tax haven, the prices of these articles were raised to their stated overpriced levels and then re-exported on to Colombia. Thus, the MNC's involved avoided tax payments on their true profits in *both* the country of export origin and in Colombia.

Panama serves still another function. MNC subsidiaries in Panama often hold the registration for many of the parent companies' other foreign investments in Latin America. In Peru, for example, Panama is the second largest foreign country in which foreign investments are registered. This procedure permits the channelling of royalty and fee payments to Panama, thereby giving the MNC's a substantial flexibility as to where they ultimately report their income. The income from royalties and fees alone is large and, in fact, most often considerably greater than reported profits received from subsidiaries. In the Andean Group for MNC subsidiaries, royalties paid to the parent are fixed at anywhere from 10 to 15 percent of gross or net sales, depending on the particular company. Since a considerable part of the final sale price is based on imported intermediate parts, which are overvalues, the MNC's multiply their unearned profits, first via the import overpricing and second through that component of royalties derived from an inflated sales due to the overpricing. The earnings thus generated are impressive both relative to the MNC's reported profits and to the foreign exchange shortages of these countries. Thus in Chile the outflow of royalties is three times greater than profit remittances.

Reported vs. Actual Rates of Return

Taken together, overpricing of imports plus reported profits, royalties, and fees gives the total dollar value of profits generated by a subsidiary in a given year. This total dollar value of "effective profits" can then be divided into the subsidiary's declared net worth of its investments (including reinvested earnings). The resulting answer is what we call the "annual rate of return on investment." Vaitsos and his group performed this exercise for 100 percent parent-owned MNC drug subsidiaries in Colombia. The results showed an annual rate of investment return by wholly-owned MNC drug subsidiaries in Colombia in 1968 ranging from a low of 38.1 percent to an astonishing high of 962.1 percent. The average of declared returns to Colombia tax authorities was 6.7 percent, while the average effective rate of return was 136.3 percent.

As high as these rates of return are, they undoubtedly *understate* the actual sums earned by these MNC's. First, if any of these firms exported, the above calculations do not include the probability of export underpricing, which as shown earlier is quite high. Second, and more important, these returns are based on the net worth of investment as declared by the subsidiaries. As pointed out previously, all evidence to date indicates there is substantial overvaluation of declared investment of approximately 30 to 50 percent. One Colombian economist, Dario Abad, has commented on the fact that between 1960 and 1968 the average *reported* rate of return for MNC's in all manufacturing sectors of the country was 6.4 percent. He found it "difficult to accept" that these MNC's would continue to enter Colombia at this rate of reported profitability while national firms were showing higher returns and the interest rate in financial markets was running between 16 and 20 percent.

Conclusions

My over-all conclusion concerning the impact of MNC's on Third World countries is clear. With respect to the 1950-1970 period investigated, I have found more myth than reality in the claims made about the three most important contributions of MNC's. My analysis of the technology contribution revealed instead a basic cause of further unemployment and a further concentration of already extremely unequal income distribution, while noting the excessive prices being charged by the MNC's in transferring this technology. Upon examination, the financial contribution turns out to be a financial drain, thereby decreasing both current consumption and available local savings and thus future consumption for the vast majority of LDC inhabitants. In contrast to a balance-of-payments contribution, the data showed no superior export performance by MNC's relative to local firms unless it was accompanied by export underpricing. Concomitantly, exports were further limited via restrictions placed on their technology by the MNC's. While potential inflows were minimized, the balance-of-payments outflows were accentuated through import overpricing and inflated royalty payments.

Such an impact can only contribute to the further impoverishment of the poorest 60 to 80 percent of Third World populations. Summing up the specific consequences thus far analyzed, however, leads to an overall consequence which should be given at least brief mention. In the Third World, the MNC's are involved in a structural process which cannot be ignored. I have already referred to the fact that this process permits an ever greater control over the technology and finances of the majority of LDC's, resulting in what Celso Furtado, among others, has shown to be an ever growing external dependence of the poor nations on the few rich nations of the world. Besides the transfer-in of inappropriate technology and the transfer-out of financial resources, this process includes one further destabilizing force.

The MNC's are also involved in the transfer of a consumption ideology, the goals of which only, at best, 30 percent, and more realistically 20 percent of LDC populations, can hope to achieve in the foreseeable future. Still, these consumption goals do not go unheeded by the greater majority in these countries. There is a rather blatant contradiction at work here. The new structure of consumption is in serious imbalance with the inadequate consumption capacity generated by the very production structure which the MNC's have largely helped to create, and which negates any possibility of attaining the new consumption goals by any except a small minority. Perhaps here we can find a major cause for the profound and growing frustration in many underdeveloped countries. When many share the same frustration, the problem goes beyond the realm of economics and becomes social and political. . . .

● ● ●

POSTSCRIPT

DO MULTINATIONALS BENEFIT LESS DEVELOPED COUNTRIES?

Sayers' essay reflects the position of the classical economist. Leave the market alone and it will generate benefits for not only the businessman but also for all members of society. Sayers argues that the activities of MNCs benefit the parent countries, such as the U.S., and also the host LDCs. That is, the U.S. experiences an increase in its exports, a reduction in its imports, the creation of new jobs for U.S. workers, and improved technology. On the part of the LDCs, they experience a considerable increase in new jobs, a rise in per capita income, the injection of new technology, a marked increase in their capital stock, the development of their own domestic markets and export markets, and of course the creation of a corporate bureaucracy.

Muller responds with a radical economist's critique of the classical economist's position. He maintains that the LDCs are left worse off due to the presence of MNCs. In particular, he is concerned that the inappropriate technology which is employed actually reduces employment opportunities, that income is redistributed from the poor to the relatively affluent, that expropriated profits leave the LDCs with a net decrease in savings and a net increase in their already acute shortage of foreign exchange, and that the MNCs transfer a consumption ideology which only a small fraction of the LDC's population can ever expect to achieve. In sum, for Muller, MNCs increase expectations while they further impoverish 60 to 80 percent of the poorest persons in LDCs.

Many books and articles have been written in defense and in criticism of the activities of MNCs. One of the most notable supporters of multinationals is Raymond Vernon. His books, THE ECONOMIC AND POLITICAL CONSEQUENCES OF MULTINATIONAL ENTERPRISE: AN ANTHOLOGY (Harvard Business School, 1972) and STORM OVER THE MULTINATIONALS: THE REAL ISSUES (Harvard University Press, 1977) are standard works in the area. However, Vernon's work does not go unchallenged. Ronald Muller/Richard Barnet's, GLOBAL REACH: THE POWER OF THE MULTINATIONAL CORPORATIONS (Simon and Schuster, 1975) has received much attention by both academic economists and those who are directly involved with the problems of LDCs. A new wave of critical work is also beginning to appear in print. Some of the most interesting work has been completed by Richard Newfarmer and is presented in his TRANSNATIONAL CONGLOMERATES AND THE ECONOMICS OF DEPENDENT DEVELOPMENT (Jai Press, 1979).

CONTRIBUTORS
TO THIS VOLUME

EDITORS

THOMAS R. SWARTZ was born in Philadelphia in 1937. He received his B.A. from LaSalle College in 1960, his M.A. degree from Ohio University in 1962, and his Ph.D. from Indiana University in 1965. He is currently a Professor of Economics at the University of Notre Dame and Director of the Notre Dame Center for Economic Education. He writes in the areas of Urban Studies and Economic Education. He often co-authors with Frank J. Bonello. Recently they co-edited ALTERNATIVE DIRECTIONS IN ECONOMIC POLICY (Notre Dame Press, 1978).

FRANK J. BONELLO was born in Detroit in 1939. He received his B.S. from the University of Detroit in 1961, his M.A. degree from the University of Detroit in 1963 and his Ph.D. from Michigan State University in 1968. He is currently Associate Professor of Economics at the University of Notre Dame. He writes in the areas of monetary economics and economic education. This represents the fourth book which he has either authored or edited.

AUTHORS

WILLIAM ABERNATHY is a Professor of Business Administration at the Harvard Business School. He is a leading authority on the automobile industry.

ROBERT ALMEDER is a Professor of Philosophy at Georgia State University. He is a highly regarded philosopher who has published widely.

GAR ALPEROVITZ is Co-Director of the National Center for Economic Alternatives and has a Ph.D. from the London School of Economics.

JOHN M. BLAIR served for thirteen years as the Chief Economist of the Senate Subcommittee on Antitrust and Monopoly. Shortly before his death in 1976, he published a comprehensive book on the oil oligopoly entitled THE CONTROL OF OIL and drafted the article contained in this book.

BARRY BLUESTONE teaches at Boston College and focuses his work on public policy and regional labor markets. He also serves as the director of the Social Welfare Research Institute.

ROBERT H. BORK is Alexander M. Bickel, Professor of Public Law at the Yale Law School. He has also served as Acting Attorney General and Resident Scholar at the American Enterprise Institute.

JIMMY CARTER, former governor of Georgia, was elected the 39th president of the United States in 1976 and lost in a bid for reelection in 1980.

STEPHEN CHAPMAN served as the Associate Editor of the *New Republic* and is currently a columnist with the Chicago Tribune.

JEFF FAUX is co-director of the National Center for Economic Alternatives and previously was Director of Economic Development for the U.S. Office of Economic Opportunity.

PETER J. FERRARA is a 1980 graduate of the Harvard Law School and is currently an associate in the New York City law firm of Cravath, Swaine, and Moore.

MILTON FRIEDMAN is probably the best known spokesperson for conservative economics. A long time Paul Snowden Russell Distinguished Service Professor at the University of Chicago, he is widely read professionally and by a lay audience. He is also one of the few Americans to win the Nobel Prize for Economics.

MARK GREEN is an author and attorney who is actively engaged in citizen and political action groups. He is currently the Director of the Public Citizen's Congress Watch and he served as President of the Board of Directors for Big Business Day—1980.

BENNETT HARRISON is currently a Professor of Economics and Urban Studies at Massachusetts Institute of Technology. He has also taught at the University of Maryland and the University of Pennsylvania.

ROBERT H. HAYES is a Professor of Business Administration at the Harvard Business School. An author and journalist, he has served as the Chairman of the International Senior Managers Program.

HENRY HAZLITT is editor of *Freeman* and has been a financial and economic reporter for a number of publications including *Newsweek* and the *New York Times*.

JOHN W. KENDRICK serves as Professor of Economics at George Washington University and as Chief Economist with the U.S. Department of Commerce.

DONALD W. KIEFER is an economist for the Library of Congress Congressional Research Service and a former director of the Indiana Commission on State Tax and Financing Policy.

LANE KIRKLAND is President of the American Federation of Labor - Congress of Industrial Organization (AFL-CIO).

JOHN M. KUHLMAN is the Middlebush Professor of Economics at the University of Missouri - Columbia. He is a noted authority on antitrust.

The late GEORGE MEANY was President of the American Federation of Labor - Congress of Industrial Organizations (AFL-CIO).

RICHARD B. MC KENZIE is a Professor of Economics at Clemson University. He is a noted journalist and author who is known for his many contributions to the area of public choice.

E.J. MISHAN is Professor of Economics at the London School of Economics and has written extensively in the areas of welfare economics and growth theory.

RONALD MULLER teaches Economics at the American University in Washington, D.C. He has served as a consultant to the Undersecretary of Commerce and to the U.N. Center for Transnational Corporations.

ALBERT REES is President of the Alfred P. Sloan Foundation and Professor of Economics at Princeton University and has served as a Director of the Council on Wage and Price Stability.

KEN W. SAYERS has authored and edited several books. After serving as Communications Manager for the American Cyanamid Company he accepted a position as Program Administrator with the International Business Machines Corp.

LARRY SMEDLEY holds a Ph.D. degree from American University and currently is Assistant Director of the Department of Social Security for the AFL-CIO.

DAVID STOCKMAN served as a Congressman from Michigan and presently is the Director of the Office of Management and Budget in the Reagan administration.

LESTER C. THUROW is currently Professor of Economics at the Massachusetts Institute of Technology and has been a member of the Council of Economic Advisors.

GUS TYLER has held a number of union positions and has written extensively including the authorship of nine books. He is presently the Assistant President of the International Ladies Garment Workers Union.

NORMAN WAITZMAN is currently a graduate student of Economics at the American University in Washington, D.C.

JUDE WANNISKI is a former editor of the *Wall Street Journal.*

MURRAY L. WEIDENBAUM writes widely in the area of government regulation. He has served as the Director of the Center for the Study of American Business at Washington University, the assistant Secretary for Economic Policy of the U.S. Treasury, and most recently he has been appointed to the Council of Economic Advisors by President Reagan.

G.S. WIEGAND is Professor Emeritus of Economics at Southern Illinois University and is a trustee of the American Institute for Economic Research.

INDEX

Aaron, Henry, 135
Aaronovitch, Sam, 35
ABC News-Harris poll, on social security reform, 121
Abernathy, William J., on management as cause of productivity decline, 36-48
Accounting for Slower Economic Growth: The United States in the 1970s (Denison), 57
Accounting for the United States Economic Growth (Denison), 57
Adams, J.G.U., 88, 89
Adams, Walter, 73
Adelman, Irma, 305
AFL-CIO: 186; definition of political platforms, 188, 189; on protectionism in industry, 264-277; on sex discrimination in Social Security, 133; on tax burden of Social Security, 128; on wage and price controls, 170
aggregate demand: and inflation, 182, 183; and unemployment, 197
Allied Chemical Corporation, and chemical dumping in James River, 90, 91
Almeder, Robert, on moral responsibility of businesses, 18-28, 35
allocation system of gasoline: 150-151; and priority users, 151
Alperovitz, Gar, on wage and price controls helping inflation, 168-178
Aluminum Company Case, as example of antitrust violation, 59
American Petroleum Institute (API), cost of compliance by, 94
Amish communities, resource allocation in, 19
Anderson, Jack, on oil industry, 146
Anderson, John, and general revenue funding of social security, 121
antitrusters, 8
antitrust laws, 54, 58; and issue of market conduct, 59

antitrust policy: books on, 73; and conglomerates, 59; effect on economic freedom, 58-65, 73; vs. efficiency and competition, 61; in Europe and Asia, 60; at local and state levels, 71; misunderstanding of, 62-64; vacillation in, 59
automobile industry: and Ford Motor Company suit involving Pinto, 27, 92; government regulation on, 78, 80

baby boom, impact on labor force, 119, 202
baby bust, impact on labor force, 119
backward integration, and American industry, 45-46
balanced budget: and deficit financing, 210-212; and effects of deficit spending, 208-212; difficulty achieving, 219, 220; through full employment, 190, 191; and Republican philosophy, 155; and taxation, 209, 210; ways to achieve, 214
Barnet, Richard, 286, 287, 288, 291, 292, 295, 296, 297, 299, 311
barter economy, vs. money economy and Laffer Curve, 156
Bates Manufacturing Company, as example of closing of profitable plant, 100, 101
beryllium, cost to control fumes in production of, 93-94
Bethlehem Steel Case, antitrust ruling in, 59
Beveridge, Sir William, 197, 199, 204
Big Business: cost of errors in, 68; ethics of, reflected in society, 66-67; availability of market information from, 68-69, 93; difficulty discerning ownership and control of, 66-67; rise of, 65; see also, combines; conglomerates; multinational corporations
Big Oil, see oil industry
Blair, John M., on energy conspiracy among seven major oil companies and government, 136-143

316

Bluestone, Barry, on plant closings as exploitation by corporations 96-107

Bork, Robert H., on antitrust policy vs. competition, 58-65, 73

Bosworth, Barry, 170

Bowman, Ward, 62

Brown Shoe case, antitrust ruling in, 59

budget: see, balanced budget; federal budget

Burns, Arthur F., 77, 204

Business International Corporation, 289, 291, 294

business mobility: books on, 117; legislation restricting, 106-110, 115-116; from North to South, 111-116; pros and cons of, 96-117; effect on regional incomes, 113-114; see also, plant relocations and closings

Business Roundtable, 86

buying power: effect of multinational corporations on, 271; importance of to healthy economy, 218; and trade deficit, 269

Can Capitalism Survive? (Rogge), 35

Capital and Communities: The Causes and Consequences of Private Disinvestment (Bluestone and Harrison), 117

capital gains tax, reduction or indexation of, 53

capitalism: 12; according to Keynes, 1

Capitalism and Freedom (Friedman), 34

capital mobility, as essential to free-market economy, 98-107

Carter, Jimmy: 53, 120, 154, 169-171, 183, 244, 245; economic report to Congress, 252-260; and free trade, 278-282

Carter administration: budget and tax proposals of, 256, 257; economic policy of, 255, 256; energy platform for 1980, 257, 258; energy problems during, 254; and government's role, 258; monetary policy of, 248; problems caused by, 247-251; regulatory policy of, 248; strengths and accomplishments of, 252-255

"cash-cow," 101, 117

cash management, American businesses' preoccupation with, 43-44

Cellar-Kefauver Antitrust Act, 59

CETA, 247, 250

ceteris paribus, 85

Chapman, Stephen, on energy conspiracy among seven major oil companies, 136-137, 144-153

chemical dumping as example of murder for money, 24; in James River by Allied Chemical Corporation, 90; in Tennessee River by Olin Corporation, 89

Chicago School Economist, 6

Chrysler, government assistance to, 55

classical economist: 6; books criticizing, 35

Clayton Antitrust Act of 1914, 58

Coal Mine Health and Safety Act of 1969, 80

Cohen, Wilbur J., 122

Colonial Press, failure of due to parent corporation, 103-105

combines: 58; see also, Big Business, conglomerates, multinational corporations

commodity shocks, and effect on budget, 248

communism, 12

comparative advantage theory: 262-263; criticism of, 263; and protectionism, 281

competition, and monopolies, 70, 72, 73

compliance, see government regulation

Comprehensive Employment and Training Act, 54

conglomerates: appropriation of subsidiaries' profits by, 101, 117; and "cash-cows," 101, 117; closings of profitable plants by, 96-117; nonproductive costs imposed on subsidiaries by, 103-105, 117; see also, Big Business; combines; multinational corporations

Congress: impact of antitrust public opinion on, 61; Carter's economic report to, 252-260; role in encouraging productivity growth, 55-56

Connally, John, 176

conservative economist: 6; and balanced budgets, 206, 207; and economic growth, 223; and full employment, 187; on government regulation, 14-15; on multinationals, 15-16; on productivity decline, 37; on social security reform, 120, 121; on tax reductions, 155; on wage and price controls, 14

Constitution of Liberty (von Hayek), 83

Consumer Price Index (CPI): 170, 171; inaccuracy as measure of inflation, 179, 180; and wage and price controls, 183

Consumer Product Safety Commission (CPSC), 78

consumer sovereignty, 5

Cook, Fred J., on oil industry, 146

Coolidge, Calvin, 160

Corporate Democracy Act of 1980, 108, 110

corporate executive: primary responsibility to owner, 29-35; time spent on government regulations, 78

General Motors Corporation: and foreign competition, 275, 276; marketing of defective product by, 20

general revenue funding, of social security, 119-122, 128-130

General Theory of Employment, Interest and Money, The (Keynes), 8, 199

Germany: oil imports, 38; productivity growth of, 38, 177; use of Laffer Curve philosophy, 160, 161

"global corporation," 286

Global Reach: The Power of the Multinational Corporations (Muller and Barnet), 286, 288, 291, 292, 299, 311

Gorkom, J.W., 135

Gott, Rodney, 287

government assistance: to declining industries, 55, 70; to oil companies regarding production rates, 139-140

government regulation: of automobile industry, 78, 80; impact on business, 76-83; effect on capital formation, 81; conservatives on, 14; of corporate responsibility, 35; and cost-benefit analysis, 15, 76, 79-83, 95; effects on employment, 80; free market economists on, 5, 6, 35, 74-75; as factor in gasoline shortage, 148, 149; on health, environment and safety, 78, 84-95; liberal economists on, 7-8, 15, 75; literature on, 95; of oil industry, 143; overstatement of cost of, 93-94; and price increases on products, 80; and productivity growth, 54-57, 80; public demand for, 70, 93; radical reformists on, 15

government spending: 209; and full employment, 187; *see also*, deficit spending

Green, Mark, on costs of government regulation, 74, 75, 84-95

Hall, Gus, 153

Harding, Warren G., 159, 160

Harrison, Bennett, on plant closings as exploitation by corporations, 96-107

Hayes, Robert H., on management as cause of productivity decline, 36-48

Hazlitt, Henry, and positive effect on economy of balanced budget, 208-212

health and safety regulation: 78; cost-benefit analysis of, 84-95; public demand for, 93

health care industry: growth of, 90-91; and services, 174

Heller, Walter W., 199, 200

Herkimer plant, as example of closing of profitable plant, 100, 101, 104

hidden tax, due to government regulations, 80, 81

History of the Standard Oil Company (Tarbell), 141

Hofstadter, Richard, 60, 145

Hoover, Herbert, 160

Howard, Sherman, 35

H.R. 8333, 154, 163

Hull reciprocal trade pacts, 271, 272

Humphrey-Hawkins Act, and full employment, 187, 195, 204

hurdle rate, of parent corporation for subsidiary company, 99, 100

imports: and benefits of open trading system, 280, 281; dollar devaluation and inflation, 266; and restrictions on, 281, 282

income distribution: impact of multinational corporations on third world, 304-305; and Zero Economic Growth, 225, 226, 227

Industrial Market Structure and Economic Performance (Scherer), 73

industrial societies, resource allocation in, 19

infant mortality, 253

inflation: 37, 265; and Carter's economic policy to reduce, 255, 256, 257; controls vs monetary policy, 182, 183; and deficit spending, 209, 210; effects of energy and food on, 172, 173, 174, 175; and full employment, 189, 192, 193, 194, 197, 199; and indexes as inaccurate measure of, 179, 180; and money supply, 215; "necessities," 171, 172, 173; and functions of prices, 180, 181; responsibility of government to control, 192, 193, 194; and special sectoral problems, 172-176; effect of tax reductions on, 154; and effects of wage and price controls on, 168-184

innovative vs. imitative product design, 44-45

In Pursuit of Price Stability (Weber) 185

institutional economics: 9; on multinationals, 16; on wage and price controls, 14

insurance industry, growth of, 91

International Telephone and Telegraph Corporation (ITT), and Chilean government, 20

Interstate Commerce Commission Act, 71-72

Interstate Oil and Gas Compact Commission, 139

invisible hand, 11, 21

Japan: productivity of, 177; and trigger prices in steel industry, 279

job rationing, problem of with Zero Economic Growth, 227, 228, 230, 231
Johnson, Lyndon B., 169, 170
Joint Economic Committee, 49

Kahn, Alfred, 172
Kaplan, Robert S., 135
Kaufman, Burton, 153
Kaufmann, Henry, 170
Kemp, Jack, and Kemp/Roth tax cut bill, 154, 163, 164, 166, 167
Kemp/Roth tax cut bill: 154, 155, 249; description of tax cuts in, 163
Kendrick, John W., on causes of productivity decline in America, 36-37, 49-57
Kennedy, John, 169
Keynes, John Maynard, 1, 2, 8, 186, 197, 199, 211
Kiefer, Donald N., and effect of tax reductions on production and employment, 163-167
Kirkland, Lane, on government responsibility for full employment, 187-194
Knight, Frank H., 35
Kuhlman, John M., on need for tighter antitrust policy, 58-59, 65-73

labor costs, and productivity growth, 49
labor force: changes in composition of, 37; decline in growth of, 51; and defining problems concerning, 201, 202; dependency ratio in, 51, 119, 125, 129; in sixties vs. eighties, 51; effect of teen-agers and women in, 202-204; after World War II, 119; youth and elderly in, 52
labor market, and multinational corporations, 294, 295, 296
Laffer, Arthur, and Laffer Curve, 156-162, 163, 165
Laffer Curve: 154, 155; arguments against, 164-166; chart, 157; description of, 156-158; historical uses of, 159, 160, 162; and prohibitive range for government, 158, 164, 165; and supply-side economics, 163, 164; for tax rates and tax revenues, 158, 159
Leebeler, Wesley, 73
Lekachman, Robert, 170
Lend-Lease, 274
less-developed countries (LDC's): buy-outs of domestic firms by multinationals, 306-307; economic development initiatives in, 285; financial structure of, 303-304; and foreign investment, 290, 291; income distribution and employment in, 304-305;

impact of multinationals on, 290, 291, 299, 300, 302-310; technological structure of, 302-303; see also, Third World
liberal economist: 6; on balanced budgets, 207; beliefs of, 7-8; on economic growth, 223; on full employment, 187; on government's role, 7-8, 15, 75; on multinationals, 16; on productivity decline, 37; on social security reform, 120-121; on supply-side economics, 123; on tax reduction, 155; on wage and price controls, 14, 169
Love Canal, 90, 91

Macauley, Thomas, 217
MacLaury, Bruce K., 170
macroeconomics, 7, 14
Madison, James, 159
malnutrition, 284
management: and backward integration, 45-46; cash, 43-44; corporate portfolio, 48, 57; European and Japanese compared to American, 39-48; filling top positions in, 42-43; value of hands-on expertise to, 43-44, 57; innovation and competition in American, 45, 47-48; labor and government pressures on European, 41; and process development, 46-47; as cause of productivity decline in America, 36-48; pseudo-professionalism in, 42-43; time frames in, 39-42; after World War II compared to today, 39
"management by the numbers," 46, 47
mandatory retirement requirements, eliminating, 52
market analysis, for product development, 44
market-driven strategy, effect on innovation, 44-45
market information, availability of in Big Business, 68-69
"Market Power and Competitive Superiority in Concentrated Industries," (Leebeler), 73
market structures, 4
Marx, Karl, 11
McKenzie, Richard B., on plant closings as a necessity for economic efficiency, 96-97, 108-117
Meany, George, and need for protectionism, 262-277
Mellon, Andrew, and use of Laffer Curve philosophy, 159, 160
mergers: American preoccupation with, 43-

44; benefits of as questionable, 40; conglomerate, 59, 71; requirements of advanced notification for, 62; vertical and horizontal, 59, 62, 71

Mexico, 175

microeconomics, 1, 14

mild inflation, 200

minorities, discrimination of social security system against, 126

Mishan, Ezra: 88; on ills of economic growth, 234-242

Modern Corporation and Private Property, The (Berle and Means), 66

monetarist, 6

monetary policy: in Carter's 1980 platform, 256, 257; and commodity shocks, 248; vs. controls and inflation, 182, 183

monetary restraint, 257

money economy, vs. barter economy and Laffer Curve, 156

money supply: determination of effective, 215; and inflation, 215

moral responsibility: argument against in corporate behavior, 29-35; argument for in corporate behavior, 18-28, 35; vs. legal responsibility, 23-24; vs. profit making, 18-34; as socialism, 19, 29, 31, 34; by trade unions vs. business leaders, 32

Morris, Cynthia Taft, 305

Muller, Ronald: 286-288; 291, 292, 295-297, 299, 311; on multinationals, 302-310

multinational corporations: buy-outs of domestic firms in less developed countries, 306-307; conservative vs. institutionalist view of, 15-16; defense of, 288-298; definitions of, 287; effect on economy of United States, 267; export restrictions in less developed countries, 307; foreign governments controlled by, 287, 288; and foreign investment, 288-290; use of foreign savings in Third World operations, 305-306; and international hunger problem, 299, 300; use of labor market in United States, 293-296; impact on less developed countries, 290, 299, 300; loyalty to United States, 268, 272; and marketing role, 296; power and negative effects of, 267, 268; pricing and performance in less developed countries, 307-309; effect on purchasing power in United States, 271; reported vs. actual rates of return, 309-310; tax avoidance of, 292; tax credits for, 292; tax deferrals,

293; and use of technology, 297, 298; impact on Third World countries, 302-310; and triangular trade, 308-309; and U.S. tax code, 268

murder for money, examples of corporate rationale of, 23-26

Musgrave, Peggy, 286, 289, 293

Nader, Ralph, 61; on responsibilities of corporate America to general interest, 108

National Employment Priorities Act, 109, 110

Natural Gas Policy Act, 257

Newfarmer, Richard, 311

Nixon, Richard M., 162, 168, 169, 175, 176

North: effect of legislation restricting business mobility on, 115-116; decline in manufacturing jobs in, 114-115; effect of plant relocations on, 111-116; population shifts in, 111-112; vs. wage-attraction of South, 115

Nye, Joseph S., 291

Occupational Safety and Health Administration (OSHA), 75, 78

October War, 273

Odell, Peter R., 153

Oil and World Power: Background to the Oil Crisis (Odell), 153

Oil Cartel Case: A Documentary Study of Antitrust Activity in the Cold War Era, The (Kaufman), 153

oil: and conspiracy theory explaining gasoline shortage, 146-148; conspiracy to prevent appearance of "distressed," 136-143; decontrolling of, 254; and energy problem in Carter administration, 254; government allocation system during shortage of, 150-151; and mandatory import quota system, 140; OPEC price hike, 137; production rate as contrived, 139; cause of shortage, 148-150; spot market purchases of, 148-150

oil industry: conspiracy theory involving, 136-143, 146-148; divestiture of, 144; restriction of production by, 136, 138-144; popular resentment of, 145-146; and factors contributing to shortages, 148-150

"oil shock," 250

Okun, Arthur, 171, 176

Olin Corporation, and chemical dumping in Tennessee River, 89

orderly market agreements (OMA), 282

Organization of Petroleum Exporting

Countries (OPEC), 145, 172, 173, 174, 175, 176, 248; conspiracy with seven major oil companies, 137-143; oil production growth rate, 139; price hike of oil, 136-137; support of seven sisters, 141-144

output per man-hour worked, 36

pay-as-you-go system, social security as, 124-125

payroll tax, vs. general revenue funding of social security, 119-122, 128-130

Peltzman, Sam, 73

pesticides, 235

Petroleum Industry Competition bill, 62

Pinto, and indictment of Ford Motor Company, 27, 92

plant relocations: of Bates Manufacturing Company, 100, 101; of Chicopee Manufacturing Company, 100, 101; and closings as exploitive, 108-117; impact on community, 97; legislation on, 106-110; effect of legislation restricting, 115-116; as necessary, 96-107; North to South, 111-116; of profitable plants, 99; effect of on regional incomes, 113-114; by Uniroyal, 100, 101

political campaigns, of 1980, 244, 245

Political Economy of Capitalism (Aaronvitch), 35

political platforms, definition of according to AFL-CIO, 188, 189

pollution: and economic growth, 235, 236; cost of prevention, 91; of rivers by chemical dumping, 24, 89, 90, 91; and Zero Economic Growth, 232

population, changes in growth rates by region, 111-112

Posner, Richard, 62

post-Keynesians, 10

presidential campaign of 1980, and Carter economic report to Congress, 252-260

price fixing, 59

prices, functions of and effects of controls on, 180, 181

price-to-earnings ratio, 99

private pensions: defects of, 130-131; vs. social security, 124-125

process development, American vs. European management on, 46-47

production, factors of, 19

productivity: and Carter administration, 225, 256; effect of deficit spending on, 209, 210; and Laffer Curve, 156, 157, 158;

effect of tax reductions on, 154-167; and Zero Economic Growth, 225-233

Productivity Dilemma: Roadblock to Innovation in the Automobile Industry, The (Abernathy), 57

productivity growth: abroad, 50; and antitrust laws, 54; books on, 57; cost of measures needed to increase, 51; and economic growth, 49-57; in Europe and Japan vs. United States, 38; government assistance, 54-55; decline in United States due to government intervention, 36-37, 49-57; as a priority in government policy, 56; effect of government regulation on, 54-57, 80; and labor force, 51-52; decline in United States due to management failures, 36-48; roles of private and public sectors in, 50-51; regulatory agencies, 54; and savings and investment, 52-53

profit margins, lower European, 41

Profit or People? The New Social Role of Money (Robertson), 35

profits: as corporate executives primary responsibility, 29-34, 35; criticism of corporate pursuit of, 21-28, 35; vs. moral responsibility of businesses, 18-35; and murder for money, 23-26

prohibitive range for government and Laffer Curve, 158, 159, 164, 165

Proposition 13, 214

protectionism: conditions which demand, 281, 282; vs. free trade, 262-283; benefits of open trading system vs., 280, 281

pseudo-professional, manager, 42-43

purchasing power, see buying power

Radical Political Economy: Capitalism and Socialism from a Marxist Humanist Perspective (Howard), 35

radical reformist economist: 1, 9; beliefs of, 10-13; on government regulation, 15; on multinationals, 16; and socialism, 12; on wage and price controls, 14

rate of investment (ROI), 41, 48

Reagan administration, and social security reform, 120, 121

Reagan, Ronald: 154, 244, 245; need for Emergency Economic Stabilization and Recovery Program, 249-250; need to restore Republican Party, 249

real income per capita, and productivity growth, 49, 51

recession: 265; double-dip, 247